D1605898

PRESTIGE, MANIPULATION, AND COERCION

PRESTIGE, MANIPULATION, AND COERCION

Elite Power Struggles in the Soviet Union and China after Stalin and Mao

JOSEPH TORIGIAN

Yale

UNIVERSITY PRESS

New Haven and London

Published with assistance from the foundation established in memory
of James Wesley Cooper of the Class of 1865, Yale College.

Yale University Press books may be purchased in quantity for
educational, business, or promotional use. For information, please
e-mail sales.press@yale.edu (U.S. office) or sales@yaleup.co.uk
(U.K. office).

Set in Janson Text type by Newgen North America, Austin, Texas.
Printed in the United States of America.

Library of Congress Control Number: 2021945449
ISBN 978-0-300-25423-5 (hardcover : alk. paper)

A catalogue record for this book is available from the British Library.

This paper meets the requirements of ANSI/NISO Z39.48-1992
(Permanence of Paper).

10 9 8 7 6 5 4 3 2

For my Mom and Dad

Contents

Acknowledgments

This is a book about elite politics in the Soviet Union and China after the deaths of Iosif Stalin and Mao Zedong. For a topic like this one, the world files its information miscellaneously. Scholars cannot simply go to one single set of archives, collect the relevant material, and write up what they find. Instead, the research is more about luck and the people who help you find more evidence and teach you how to interpret it. Simply put, this book is the result of funding that gave me the "deep time" to discover and digest new sources and the people who guided me.

I am deeply grateful to my dissertation committee of Richard Samuels, Kathleen Thelen, Taylor Fravel, and Barry Posen. During my time at Massachusetts Institute of Technology, I also benefited from conversations about my work with Roger Petersen, Suzanne Berger, Francis Gavin, Fotini Christia, and Stephen Van Evera. Thank you to my colleagues who read segments of the dissertation or listened to me present: Mark Bell, Chris Clary, James Conran, Fiona Cunningham, Jeremy Ferwerda, Toby Harris, Chad Hazlett, Sameer Lalwani, Austin Long, Kacie Miura, Rachel Odell, Andrew Radin, Josh Shifrinson, Peter Swartz, David Weinberg, and Alec Worsnop. The Center for International Studies at MIT and an MIT

International Science and Technology Initiatives China Seed Funds Program supported two trips to China.

The Institute for Security and Conflict Studies at George Washington University was a very welcoming home for a year. Comments from Stephen Biddle, Alexander Downes, Charles Glaser, Harris Mylonas, Janne Nolan, Elizabeth Saunders, and Jane Vaynman were very important at an early stage of the project.

The Center for International Security and Cooperation at Stanford provided funding for two years to work on this book. My advisers David Holloway, Tom Fingar, Amir Weiner, and Andrew Walder all had a major impact on how the project developed. Thank you also to Jennifer Erickson, Kate Cronin-Furman, Lynn Eden, Ashley Fabrizio, Edward Geist, Morgan Kaplan, Chris Lawrence, Andreas Lutsch, Anna Péczeli, Terrence Peterson, Farzan Sabet, Scott Sagan, Nina Silove, Rochelle Terman, Gil-li Vardi, Anna Weichselbraun, Amy Zegart, and Katarzyna Zysk.

Thank you to the Princeton-Harvard (now Columbia-Harvard) China and the World Program for a year at Princeton. The project has played a crucial role developing a new generation of China scholars. Thank you to Tom Christensen, Iain Johnston, Maria Adele Carrai, Andrew Chubb, and Yeling Tan for this opportunity.

The School of International Service at American University has provided a wonderful intellectual home for me. I am deeply grateful to so many colleagues for their support: Boaz Atzili, Claire Brunel, Chuck Call, Susanna Campbell, Lauren Carruth, Christine Chin, Elizabeth Cohn, Ken Conca, Audrey Kurth Cronin, Keith Darden, Michelle Egan, Daniel Esser, Anthony Fontes, Carole Gallaher, James Goldgeier, Louis Goodman, Hrach Gregorian, Austin Hart, Patrick Jackson, Miles Kahler, Ji-Young Lee, Nanette Levinson, Garret Martin, Malini Ranganathan, Joshua Rovner, Mike Schroeder, Judy Shapiro, Susan Shepler, Sarah Snyder, Megan Stewart, Matthew Taylor, Sharon Weiner, Nina Yamanis, Yang Zhang, and Quansheng Zhao. A Dean of Academic Affairs International Travel Award allowed for a final two-month trip to China for interviews and collecting material.

Thank you to the librarians and archivists who made this research possible: Jing Zhong and Yan He at the GW Asia Library; Svetlana

Savranskaya at the National Security Archive; Hugh Truslow at the Harvard Fung Library; Xiao-he Ma at the Harvard Yenching Library; Harold Leich at the Library of Congress; Richard Siao and Hong Cheng at UCLA; Haihui Zhang and Xiuying Zou at the University of Pittsburgh; Zhaohui Xue at Stanford; and all the archivists at Russian State Archive of Contemporary History (RGANI), Russian State Archive of Sociopolitical History (RGASPI), Archive of the Foreign Policy of the Russian Federation (AVP RF), and Russian State Military Archive (RGVA). Nancy Hearst at the Harvard Fung Library deserves a very special mention for her advice and help over the years. She graciously helped ensure the accuracy of my notes. Thank you to Joshua Seufert at Princeton University for keeping me updated on so many wonderful new sources and for working so hard to make the Princeton collection one of the best in the world.

This book would not have been possible without the Wilson Center's Cold War International History Project. Christian Ostermann and Chuck Kraus have provided an extraordinary service to the academic community. Sergey Radchenko shared crucial documents from the Hubei Provincial Archives that allowed the revisionist history in this book to happen.

Every conversation I have with Chung Yen-lin feels like "a single word is worth a thousand pieces of gold," yet there is always something else to discuss. Thanks for being a *zhiji*. A very, very special thank you must be extended to Warren Sun and Frederick Teiwes. They saved me from some real howlers in the China chapters and shared some crucial documents. They set the bar for the study of elite politics in China and are my models. Enormous thanks.

To a significant extent, this book is a work of translation. If not for the help and research of numerous Chinese and Russian scholars, this research project would be impossible. Thank you in particular to Iuliia Abramova, Iurii Aksiutin, Chen Donglin, Cheng Xiaonong, Han Gang, Hao Jian, Ho Pin, Hu Ping, Oleg Khlevniuk, Li Danhui, Li Haiwen, Li Nanyang, Li Shengping, Lin Yunhui, Lu Lilin, Niu Jun, Mikhail Prozumenshchikov, Shen Zhihua, Wang Haiguang, Wu Si, Xiao Donglian, Xu Qingquan, Xu Youyu, Yang Jisheng, Zhang Boshu, and many others. All mistakes in this book remain my own.

The person who has spent the second most amount of time contributing to this book is my dear friend Anna Pan. I have probably learned most of the Russian I know from her, even though I still often cannot seem to get the soft sign to come out correctly.

This book benefited from the numerous opportunities to present its findings to different audiences: the Princeton-Humboldt "Comparing Dictatorships in Transition" Conference; the Tianwen Lianhe Society Cultural Revolution Museum Preparatory Committee; the Association for Asian Studies; the Association for Slavic, East European, and Eurasian Studies; the International Studies Association; the East China Normal University History Department; and Hoover Institution Workshop on Authoritarian Regimes.

The US Department of State funded Russian language acquisition as part of the Critical Language Scholarship Program in Ufa as well as eight months on an IREX fellowship to work in the Russian archives. Thank you to Carol Sorrenti for making sure everything ran smoothly. Thank you also to the Higher School of Economics in Moscow for sponsoring me. Katherine Zubovich, Rhiannon Dowling, Bathsheba Demuth, and Courtney Doucette took me under their wing and taught me how to use the archives.

Special thanks for suggestions, comments, and other help over the years to Jude Blanchette, Chris Buckley, Sam Casper, Lizi Chen, Frank Dikötter, Steven El Aile, Paul Gregory, Mark Kramer, Alexander Lanoszka, Wendy Leutert, Simon Miles, Norman Naimark, Marc Opper, Adam Segal, Robert Service, Katie Stallard, Chun Han Wong, and Sophia Yan. Thank you to Rebecca Johnston and Erik Fliegauf for help with the herculean task of proofreading. Michael Gordin, one of the reviewers of the manuscript, provided especially useful comments. Thank you also to the two anonymous reviewers for their very careful read and suggestions. Thank you to Jaya Chatterjee at Yale University Press for support throughout the process.

As I try to come up with the right way to express gratitude to my parents, Kathryn and Ronald Torigian, I find myself at a loss for words and a sinking suspicion that any words would not do them justice anyway. They have devoted their lives to me, so the least I can do is dedicate this book to them. Thank you.

Necessarily, all work on elite politics in closed regimes can only be considered the most recent draft. The late Roderick Mac-Farquhar, whose class convinced me to spend my life doing this kind of research, once told me that a Chinese scholar scolded him for not including information on a particular meeting. "Of course I didn't write about it," MacFarquhar retorted to him. "I didn't know about it." So, thanks to all the future grad students and other scholars who move forward whatever I have been able to achieve here.

Abbreviations

AVP RF	Archive of the Foreign Policy of the Russian Federation (Arkhiv vneshnei politiki Rossiiskoi Federatsii)
CC	Central Committee
CCP	Chinese Communist Party
CIA	Central Intelligence Agency
CMC	Central Military Commission
CPSU	Communist Party of the Soviet Union
GDR	German Democratic Republic
GPD	General Political Department
KGB	Committee of State Security (Komitet gosudarstvennoi bezopasnosti)
KMT	Kuomintang
MR	Military Region
MVD	Ministry of Internal Affairs (Ministerstvo vnutrennikh del)
NEP	New Economic Policy
NKVD	People's Commissariat for Internal Affairs (Narodnyi komissariat vnutrennikh del)
NPC	National People's Congress
PLA	People's Liberation Army

PRC   People's Republic of China
PRC FMA   People's Republic of China Foreign Ministry
             Archive
PSC   Politburo Standing Committee
RGANI   Russian State Archive of Contemporary History
             (Rossiiskii gosudarstvennyi arkhiv noveishei istorii)
RGASPI   Russian State Archive of Sociopolitical History
             (Rossiiskii gosudarstvennyi arkhiv sotsial'no-
             politicheskoi istorii)
RGVA   Russian State Military Archive (Rossiiskii
             gosudarstvennyi voennyi arkhiv)

CHAPTER ONE

Theory

Introduction

At the festivities celebrating the founding of the People's Liberation Army (PLA) on August 1, 1977, when a giant portrait of Deng Xiaoping in front of a waving military flag appeared on the stage backdrop, the entire crowd stood up to applaud wildly. The problem, however, was that Deng had returned to work only less than a month earlier, and Chairman Hua Guofeng, Mao Zedong's chosen successor, was still the leader of the country. The party center released a notification labeling the event a serious political incident. Yet staff officers mocked the notification, and even the military's General Political Department (GPD) was not serious about promulgating it.

The son of General Zhang Aiping writes of the incident, "This was the first time that the voice of the center seemed so weak and powerless. For generals who led troops, the mind-set was 'Mao Zedong is gone, Zhou Enlai is gone, Commander Zhu [De] is gone. It's just you guys, but you still issue orders right and left. Who do you think you are?' Deng Xiaoping, this secretary of the forward committee in the Huaihai and Dujiang campaigns, in the eyes of the generals of the PLA, after the deaths of [Marshals] Peng Dehuai and Lin Biao, was the undisputed commander in chief of the military."[1]

Twenty years earlier, the Soviet military had a rather different attitude about its own former revolutionaries. When senior leaders Viacheslav Molotov and Lazar' Kaganovich, along with their younger allies on the Presidium,[2] attempted to remove Nikita Khrushchev, Minister of Defense Georgii Zhukov refused to acknowledge the Presidium's decision. Instead, Zhukov demanded the summoning of a full Central Committee (CC) plenum, and he used military planes to bring the members of that body to Moscow.

At the meeting, Zhukov accused Molotov and Kaganovich of giving permission to execute 38,679 individuals during Stalin's Great Terror. Zhukov quoted at length from Marshal Iona Iakir's last letter to Stalin, in which he begged for his life, as well as from Stalin's response on the document: "A scoundrel and a prostitute." Molotov wrote, "a completely accurate definition." Kaganovich added, "The scum, bastard, and whore deserves one punishment—death." The hall exploded into shouts of "Butchers!" For Zhukov, the crimes of the old men in the party were damning—in his words, if the people had only known about how "their fingers dripped with the blood of innocents," then they would have been met not with applause but with stones.[3]

These two anecdotes are enormously revealing of politics at the elite level in China and the Soviet Union after the deaths of Mao Zedong and Stalin—a politics of personal prestige, historical antagonisms, backhanded political maneuvering, and a substantial role for specialists in violence. In other words, disentangling the post-cult-of-personality power struggles in history's two greatest Marxist states requires decidedly non-Marxist explanations. Using a wide selection of newly uncovered documents, memoirs, and secondary sources, this book shows how two of the most important successions in twentieth-century world history were not so much victories of "reformers" over "conservatives" or "radicals," as previous accounts have argued, but a settling of scores.

This revisionist historical narrative sits uncomfortably with popular theories within the discipline of political science. As Paul Pierson notes, "power doesn't really fit in the leading frameworks" of the discipline.[4] Many scholars of authoritarian regimes emphasize systems of exchange based on patronage or policy interests within a single defined group of decision-makers. Institutions are in vogue;

coercion is not.[5] For example, scholars such as Bruce Bueno de Mesquita and Alastair Smith argue that "it is the successful, reliable implementation of political promises to those who count that provides the basis for any incumbent's advantage."[6]

This book, however, demonstrates that even immediately after the deaths of exceptionally dominant leaders, when the lessons of strongman rule are at their most robust, and even in the most "institutionalized" Leninist authoritarian systems, rules are simply not potent enough to allow for a politics of deliberation and exchange. Despite consensus historiographical views to the contrary, and to the dismay of many top figures at the time, neither Khrushchev nor Deng had any interest in sharing power.[7] The legacies of Stalin and Mao were not overcome, and collective leadership remained out of reach. As the late pro-reform party elder Li Rui put it, "Deng Xiaoping was half a Mao Zedong."[8]

This book goes beyond simply arguing that institutions were less important than previously thought—it also delineates the full implications of weak institutions. First, weak institutions are unable to provide a serious platform for policy deliberation or to convey "rational-legal" authority to leaders. Therefore, interpersonal forms of authority, such as personal ties and prestige, as well as the use of incriminating personal information, prove to be of greater importance in power struggles than economic interests or policy positions. Second, no clear, defined rule book exists, and politics instead are marked by a messy mix of ambiguous formal and informal rules. Hence, victory is not the result of politicking within a single defined group of individuals but of manipulation of multiple layers of potential decision-making bodies. Third, low institutionalization means that the key groups that enforce decisions, most importantly the military or the political police, do not simply execute orders as if those orders are presented to them on a card spit out of a little box. Since the legitimacy of competing orders in the absence of a deliberative process is unclear, enforcement is politicized. Even in cases when the military or police are not used in a coup, power struggles often manifest themselves primarily in the form of control over those organizations.

Certainly, institutions are not entirely irrelevant in Leninist regimes. Competitors do not shoot at each other during Politburo meetings. Violence is not the only coin of the realm. Instead, we see what is best understood as a "knife fight with weird rules." This book not only provides a different answer for why certain leaders, and not others, are able to win power struggles in Leninist one-party regimes but also explains the extent to which institutions, although weak, still matter.

In this introductory chapter, I provide two dueling explanatory models: the *economic model*, which assumes robust institutionalization, and the *authority model*, which suggests otherwise. Next, I explain why plotters avoid unnecessarily violating rules, losers accept defeat, and violence is never used in the total absence of political legitimacy. The following section addresses why it is appropriate to simultaneously study the power struggles immediately after the deaths of Stalin and Mao and what they teach us about politics in Russia, China, and authoritarian regimes more broadly. I conclude with a brief discussion of methodology and a preview of the individual cases and how they relate to my theory.

The Theory

This book combines the analytical tools of political science and the rigor of deep historical investigation not only to provide a new account of key historical moments in Russian and Chinese history but also to determine what these events tell us about the nature of politics more broadly. To better situate and contextualize the available evidence, I test two competing sets of each of three hypotheses. These three pairs of alternative hypotheses answer three separate questions: the primary reason someone decides to support a competitor; the environment in which a competitor canvasses for support; and how the outcome of a decision is enforced.

The first set of the three hypotheses is drawn from the current dominant approaches to authoritarian regimes, and these hypotheses are grouped together because of their common intellectual affinity with one of Weber's two conceptions of power: as a "constellation of interests." According to this model, authority is a form of exchange that operates according to market principles. As J. M. Barbalet explains, "Possession of goods . . . confers influence over others who nevertheless remain formally free and are motivated by the pursuit of their own interests."[9] I call this first set of hypotheses the economic model because the idea of politics being used to "aggregate individual preferences into a collective choice in as fair and efficient a way as possible" meshes well with ideas from the discipline of economics.[10]

The first hypothesis in the economic model, which answers why individuals support one competitor over another, is rooted in the research of political scientists who posit the overriding importance of material and economic benefits in authoritarian regimes.[11] Bueno de Mesquita and Smith, for example, argue that "paying supporters . . . is the essence of ruling."[12] Daron Acemoglu and James A. Robinson similarly provide an approach to researching dictatorships that is "'economic-based' in the sense that [they] stress individual economic incentives as determining political attitudes."[13] *Hypothesis 1a: The leader who provides the best patronage model or popular policy platform wins the power struggle.*

The second hypothesis, which envisions the competitors' political environment, draws on selectorate theory, according to which a formally defined group of individuals (the selectorate) has a say in who leads them.[14] Within this defined group, the victor will be the one whose platform best meets the demand of a "median voter" or achieves the most popular support according to the average of an ideal goal for voters.[15] Bueno de Mesquita and Smith write that "in today's China (as in the old Soviet Union), [the real selectorate, or 'the group that *actually* chooses the leader'] consists of all voting members of the Communist Party."[16] Robert V. Daniels characterizes Leninist systems as a "circular flow of power" in which leaders promote allies in exchange for political support.[17] *Hypothesis 2a: A defined group is enfranchised to choose their leader, and a "median voter" makes the final decision.*

The third hypothesis, which addresses the role of enforcement, is based on scholarship that minimizes the role of the power ministries, such as the military and the political police. Samuel Huntington limits this argument to Leninist states: "Political systems such as those of the United States and the Soviet Union . . . have almost impeccable systems of civilian control."[18] Bueno de Mesquita and Smith, however, minimize differences in enforcement democracies

and all kinds of nondemocracies, writing, "Governments do not differ in kind. They differ along the dimensions of their selectorates
and winning coalitions." By making this argument, they assume that
the power ministries do not play different roles across regime types.[19]
*Hypothesis 3a: The power ministries (military or secret police) do not play
an independent or unique role: enforcement of decisions is automatic.*

The economic model has led to rather counterintuitive suggestions for dictators, such as the usefulness of a dictator's improving his political prospects by "subjecting himself to oversight in a
court where his mistreatment of any past supporters could cause
his own downfall" or casting his population into penury.[20] But are
the assumptions behind such a model credible? Each of the three
hypotheses of the model is based on an assumption of a high level of
institutionalization.[21]

Institutionalization in this book entails two definitional com-
ponents. First, rules are clear and unambiguous, and second, rules
are maintained by an objective third-party arbiter that enforces decisions. These characteristics are drawn from the definition of institutions provided by Wolfgang Streeck and Kathleen Thelen: "In
sum, the institutions in which we are interested here are formalized
rules that may be enforced by calling upon a third party. . . . With an
institution we are dealing only if and to the extent that third parties
predictably and reliably come to the support of actors whose institutionalized, and therefore *legitimate*, normative expectations have
been disappointed."[22] In this book, "institutionalization" refers *only* to
these two characteristics. Other scholars have used this term to refer
to the incorporation of other social forces in the ruling elite or high
levels of indoctrination, skill, and bureaucratic strength in an organization.[23] These topics are important but are not addressed here.

Having theorized the implications of a regime with strong institutions, we can now turn to the question of what we should expect
to see if institutions are weak: the second set of the three hypotheses that I call the authority model. This model is rooted in Weber's
second conceptualization of power, which he contrasts with the
"constellation of interests" approach described earlier. According to
the authority model, "The manifested will (command) of the ruler
or rulers is meant to influence the conduct of one or more others
(the ruled)."[24]

In contrast to the economic model, in the authority model actors are not "freely-contracting individuals."[25] In other words, we have moved away from the market to the realm of politics, where winners impose their will on losers.[26] Terry Moe writes that "politics is fundamentally about the exercise of public authority and the struggle to gain control over it."[27] Pierson similarly concludes that "politics involves struggles over the authority to establish, enforce, and change rules governing social action in a particular territory. In short, much of politics is based on authority rather than exchange."[28]

The first hypothesis in the authority model posits that low institutionalization discounts the significance of policy differences while raising the importance of personal prestige. In a weakly institutionalized system, elites have no guarantee that they will have an opportunity to present their opinions or that expressing an opinion will not cause them to be punished later. Leaders have an incentive to quash real debate because the lack of robust institutions means such a debate will be hard to control. Without the free exchange of information, elites have trouble understanding how others feel, and they have a strong incentive to mischaracterize the positions of their opponents.

In this kind of political environment, policy differences do not distinguish competitors. Moreover, because the leadership selection process is vague or unfair, the degree of "rational-legal" authority that procedure can impute is limited.[29] The result is that the true coin of the realm is personal reputation and prestige. Because this form of authority is so decisive in such systems, the use of compromising material and character assassination is extremely important. *Hypothesis 1b: Sociological ties and prestige are more important than the dispensation of patronage or real policy differences.*

With regard to the next hypothesis, if rules are ambiguous or simply not respected, then a "selectorate" will not be able to operate in the way described earlier. Within a group of elites that might have a say in the outcome of a power struggle, there are a number of different party and state bureaucratic organs that have complicated and ambiguous relationships. These relationships are ambiguous because they are shaped by a mix of unclear formal and informal rules whose coexistence further muddles the legitimacy of both.[30] In other words, this book does not test formal institutions against informal institutions, but rather it argues that elites interact in a complex environment that allows for multiple interpretations of the rules. In many cases, a leader wins a power struggle *even though* his interpretation of the institutional environment is obviously more tendentious and illegitimate than that of his competitors.

Because of this lack of institutional clarity, the term "selectorate" is not appropriate for the elite as a whole. The particular body that makes the final decision cannot be assumed. This has a crucial implication: *which* body within the party or state apparatus makes a decision is decisive, as leaders are not politicking within a single defined selectorate. Therefore, power struggles are not so much about seeking support within a single, amorphous group as determining which part of the group gets to choose. *Hypothesis 2b: Which bureaucratic organ makes a final decision is more important than a search for a "median voter" in the elite as a whole: institutional manipulation explains more than open vote-seeking.*

Finally, a crucial element of institutionalization is the presence of an impartial organization that enforces the rules objectively. If the rules are ambiguous, then the legitimacy of any particular decision is suspect. In other words, what distinguishes nondemocracies from democracies is not only the size of the selectorate but also the absence of nonarbitrary enforcement.[31] Amos Perlmutter and William M. LeoGrande allow for the possibility that "the party-in-uniform [the military] retains the ability to use its military command to settle inner-party conflicts by force of arms, and the coercive potential of the party-in-uniform is often enough to resolve inner-party conflicts."[32] Brian D. Taylor similarly emphasizes that inner-party conflicts can drag the military into elite power struggles.[33] *Hypothesis 3b: Power ministries have leeway when choosing to obey certain decisions about leadership selection and not others.*

In summary, according to the economic model, leaders win power struggles by providing the most attractive patronage or policy platform; the struggle takes place within a single defined group; and the power ministries do not play a special role. In the authority model, prestige and nonmaterialistic relationships override material interests; the struggle revolves more around how the ultimate decision is made as opposed to politicking within a single "selectorate"; and the power ministries are not excluded from the political process.

"Low" Institutionalization, Not "Absent" Institutionalization

The ambiguity of rules and the lack of an external enforcer define Leninist regimes. The similarities with the international system, where laws are equivocal and no world government is present to enforce them, are therefore unmistakable.[34] Because of these common structural features, both Leninist regimes and the international system are marked by constant struggles for dominance. The "bloodiness" of politics is omnipresent. Competitors seek security because losers are eliminated.

However, states do have a common interest in maintaining the system and avoiding constant unrestricted warfare. Even if laws are ambiguous and unenforceable, they do exist.[35] States recognize that at least pretending to appear legitimate can facilitate the achievement of their goals.[36] Obvious violations damage perceptions of fairness and reputation.[37] The more obvious the breaking of a rule or a norm, the more likely that action will inspire a negative reaction. Therefore, even in systems with low levels of institutionalization, important boundaries and limitations can persist. In Leninist regimes, we see the following three characteristics of institutionalization.

First, although Leninist regimes are shaped by a complicated interaction of formal and informal rules, those rules do at least serve as a frame of reference. They are useful to the extent that, to use the words of the political philosopher John Dunn, they soften the "intrinsic humiliations" of being ruled and set "some hazy limits to the harms that [rulers] will voluntarily choose to do us collectively."[38] In other words, even in the context of truly Machiavellian political machinations, institutions allow leaders to at least clothe themselves in a fig leaf of respectability and prevent them from simply shooting one another at meetings. This has several crucial implications. If the winner is only able to win by clearly violating even ambiguous rules, this will cost them popularity, although perhaps not ultimate victory. Although competitors will not adhere to the rules so closely as to risk losing a power struggle, they will not needlessly go beyond what is necessary. That explains why victors go through so many somersaults to make their victory look legal and why elites in Leninist states are not assassinated. Both sides try to cast the opponent as a violator of the rules, and competitors suffer if their behavior is seen as putting the stability of the entire system at risk.

Second, such regimes are institutionalized to the extent that even the most antagonistic competitors almost always refuse to exit the party and oppose it from the outside. This attitude is rooted in a deep-seated belief among such groups that the party is a manifestation of historical will.[39] The common goal not to let the regime collapse helps explain why such regimes last longer.[40] One Soviet leader remarked, "There could be no life for him . . . outside the ranks of the Party, and he would be ready to believe that black was white, and white was black, if the Party required it. In order to become one with this great Party he would fuse himself with it, abandon his own personality, so that there was no particle left inside him which was not at one with the Party, did not belong to it."[41] Even Mao remarked on this quality of communist parties in 1971: "China is also strange, China's party has never split, fifty years have already passed and it never split."[42] When a loser is outmaneuvered, they will not challenge a decision if doing so will threaten the stability of the system as a whole.

Third, naked force without even the semblance of political legitimacy does not occur. Norms of civilian supremacy can influence behavior.[43] In Leninist regimes, the party qua party enjoys supreme legitimacy. Communist states are extremely sensitive to the danger of "Bonapartism": the use of military force from within to destroy the revolution. This attitude contributes to some skepticism not only toward powerful military figures among civilians but also toward members of the military elite.[44] Therefore, we do not see purely military figures or the political police overthrowing a unified civilian leadership.

Case Selection

Of all the elite power struggles ever fought, what is the benefit of looking specifically at the ones that occurred after the deaths of Stalin and Mao? Stalin and Mao were unique leaders who led two of the most ambitious political projects in history. What can these moments in time tell us about Russian and Chinese politics in particular and the study of politics more generally?

First, the transitions away from Stalin and Mao were two of the most important events in the twentieth century. The choices of their successors had fundamental implications not only for the individuals who lived in these two great communist states but also for people around the world. The past several years have seen an explosion of newly available material relevant for the study of Soviet and Chinese history. Getting the story of what happened right, even in only these cases, is important, especially in contemporary China, where a debate has emerged about whether Xi Jinping has departed from Deng's path and, if so, what that means.

Second, the periods investigated in this book regularly catch the attention of political scientists, both generalists and area-studies scholars, who use them to develop their respective theories. The historiography of the Khrushchev and Deng eras, therefore, has significant theoretical implications. Bueno de Mesquita and Smith, for example, apply their selectorate theory directly to China and the Soviet Union.[45] Jessica L. P. Weeks, in her influential work on foreign policy in authoritarian regimes, portrays Stalin and Mao as "personalist" dictators and Khrushchev and Deng as "elite-constrained" dictators.[46] China in the Deng era is almost universally depicted as a textbook example of collective leadership in an institutionalized setting.[47] This book, however, stresses that collective leadership failed to coalesce after Stalin and Mao.

Third, with regard to generalizability, if the Soviet Union or China ever truly experienced a time when it was possible to establish resilient institutions, it was after Stalin and Mao. The lessons and dangers of strongman rule were obvious, and open political warfare threatened regime collapse. Most individuals in the elite did indeed expect that collective leadership would prevail, and some competitors even believed that sharing power would contribute to their political standing. One of the great puzzles that this book answers is why more consensus-oriented figures such as Georgii Malenkov or Hua Guofeng were defeated by individuals such as Khrushchev and Deng, who refused to share their authority. If collective leadership failed even at these particular moments, then its likelihood in other countries and times is also low.

Fourth, this book is explicitly about succession politics in communist states, a time when, some scholars believe, policy contestation with power-political implications for the competitors is at its most intense. Valerie Bunce writes, "The communist 'selectorate,' to borrow Grey Hodnett's term, is quite capable of measuring the policy performance of fellow elites; thus, considerable pressures can be exerted on communist leaders to earn and maintain their positions through policy initiatives. Because the mandate is conditional, succession in the Soviet Union and other communist countries is often a referendum on public policy; whether a new leader follows a successful or unsuccessful predecessor, he must prove himself in the policy sphere and meet or better the expectations of his superiors who control his advancement."[48] As this book demonstrates, however, policy differences explain neither the origin nor outcome of elite contestation, even after the tenures of leaders who left behind a powerful desire to change.

Fifth, Leninist regimes in particular are seen as highly institutionalized authoritarian states.[49] What does it mean if even in two of the most famous Leninist regimes institutionalization remained low? If this book effectively proves the greater usefulness of the authority model for even these states, then we can safely predict that it will be even more relevant in other cases. To the extent that the caveats presented in the previous section are accurate, then, relatively speaking, Leninist regimes should be placed somewhat higher on the "institutionalization" scale. In comparison with other authoritarian regimes, struggles in Leninist regimes will in general be marked by (somewhat) less brutality, will be less likely to split during a crisis; and military strongmen will find it more difficult to seize total control.

Methodology

I use a wide variety of previously unavailable material to reconstruct the most important power struggles immediately following the deaths of Stalin and Mao. Evidence is categorized according to whether it validates or weakens the two sets of competing hypotheses introduced earlier. To connect theory and empirics, each chapter asks a series of clear, answerable questions related to the competing hypotheses. All of the chapters answer the following questions in precisely the same order.

Hypothesis 1a versus Hypothesis 1b: Did the winner have a leadership style that was unambiguously more prone to consensus, collective leadership, and co-optation than that of the losers (Political Style)? Were policy differences real, or were alleged differences manipulated and overblown for the purposes of political struggle (Policy)? To what extent did the outcome revolve around personal prestige, historical antagonisms, and the threat of compromising personal material (Historical Legacies and Compromising Material)?

Hypothesis 2a versus Hypothesis 2b: Was there serious deliberation about the strengths and weaknesses of a competitor, or did the winners conduct discussions in an unfair, conspiratorial spirit and present the decision as a fait accompli (The Deliberations)? Were the winners determined by a power struggle within a single, defined group, or which group was empowered to determine the winners (The Decision-Making Body)? To what extent did the winners violate even ambiguous rules (Legitimacy of Behavior)?

Hypothesis 3a versus Hypothesis 3b: Did leaders consider the power ministries to be irrelevant to struggles within the party, or did they consider control over the coercive organs to be essential (Views of Power Ministries)? When members of the power ministries expressed an opinion on the power struggle, was the effect equivalent to their voting power in the political bodies on which they had a seat, or did their positions threaten the potential use of force and, therefore, have an outsized effect (Threat of Coercion)?

This type of approach is not common in political science, and some of the recent theoretical work on authoritarian regimes has even stated explicitly that the secretive nature of such states means that qualitative research is insufficiently "systematic."[50] Victor Shih writes that the "collection of systematic data on elite networks" will "permit a much more nuanced understanding of elite factions than previous generations of scholarship on elite politics, which depended on elite interviews, close reading of memoirs, and analysis of selected official publications."[51]

Given these doubts, the benefits of the methodology used in this book should be addressed. First, as we better understand what types of statistical analysis are persuasive, we also recognize that these analyses are applicable only in restrictive situations, such as natural experiments.[52] Important reviews of the quantitative literature on key issues reveal a troubling lack of conclusions.[53] Second, a wide variety of new findings now call into question the usefulness of homogenizing assumptions that define game-theoretic accounts.[54] The best modelers in this school are those who accept the impossibility of universalistic explanations.[55] Although these powerful quantitative approaches will continue to provide crucial insights, the growing realization that they are imperfect tools based on foundational assumptions that are different from qualitative approaches speak to the need for keeping the tent of political science large.

Giovanni Capoccia and Daniel Ziblatt suggest the use of "episode analysis" as a way to avoid the pitfalls of ahistorical approaches. Their basic insight is that it is important to systematically analyze the moments in which institutions are "created or substantially shaped." This method adopts "an explicitly historical approach to causality" that "identifies the key political actors fighting over institutional change, highlights the terms of the debate and the full range of options that they perceived, reconstructs the extent of political and social support behind these options, and analyzes, as much as possible with the eyes of the contemporaries, the political interactions that led to the institutional outcome." This allows an assessment of "how structural factors often seen as driving long-term trajectories of democratic development actually influence the politics of democratic reform in key episodes." Therefore, by focusing on political interactions, episode analysis works as a critical filtration device for understanding if and how antecedent conditions actually shape outcomes.[56] Thelen similarly points to the importance of doing "the empirical work to make sure that the actors to whom we attribute certain strategic behaviors are in fact 'players' in the first place."[57]

Although Capoccia and Ziblatt do not state this explicitly, "episode analysis" has strong elements of scientific realism: a philosophy of science that prizes concepts and mechanisms over cross-case variation. The "real" in "scientific realism" is the belief that "causation is a relation between mechanism and outcome rather than premise and conclusion as in the deductive-nomological model."[58] Cases are not "manifestations of one or another theoretically derived instance[s] in a typology" but a combination of different structural elements.[59]

This approach, therefore, differs from both a statistical analysis that measures an average causal effect and a logic-based analysis that identifies necessary and sufficient conditions through the use of Mill's methods of fuzzy sets.[60] Scientific realists instead use the historical record to deeply investigate individual moments, construct a narrative of what happened, and then conceptualize the factors that had a gravitational pull on that event—a technique known as "retroduction."[61] In other words, they are not interested in a precise constellation of variables that leads to a particular outcome or even a causal chain of *a* to *b* to *c*, but rather they are interested in determining what factors were pushing and pulling on events as they transpired. This approach has the added benefit of identifying elements that are of crucial importance in shaping an event but do not have a determinative effect. For example, the "old comrades" in the Soviet Union in June 1957 were defeated despite their legitimacy as major revolutionary figures, but to say that this legitimacy did not matter would be a gross exaggeration.

The Cases

After Stalin and Mao died, their successors found themselves facing similar legacies. In both countries, the top leadership believed that without fundamental changes the regimes were at risk of collapse. As Xiao Donglian, one of China's premier historians on the reform era, puts it, "Facing the situation at the time, no matter who was in power, they would need to find a new development path for China."[62] That realization imposed a strong degree of cohesion among the leadership about necessary policy innovations. The brutal suffering most experienced at the hands of the late strongmen meant that a significant contingent believed collective leadership would be better than allowing another dominant leader to emerge. Even those individuals who believed that an authoritative leader was necessary for stability hoped that such a figure would allow for at least some discussion of key issues. At the same time, however, the extremely bloody nature of the Stalin and Mao eras left behind not only a legacy of historical antagonisms but also an abundant amount of potentially compromising material about how certain individuals acted in those difficult circumstances.

Crucially, in both systems, leaders drew on relations forged in moments of intense political violence, and the size of an individual's perceived contributions to the regime was equated with that person's authority.[63] In China, the point in time at which an individual entered the Communist Party and how their exploits were evaluated during the wars against the Kuomintang (KMT) and the Japanese were crucial not only to someone's self-worth but also to their placement in the elite. In the Soviet Union, some civilian leaders could draw on the Russian Revolution to buttress their legitimacy, while military leaders could point to the war with Germany as their own source of prestige.

These findings, therefore, have much in common with political science theory that emphasizes the historical legacies of violence in consolidating political regimes. Lucan A. Way and Steven Levitsky, for example, show that "cohesion is greater in parties that are bound by salient ethnic or ideological ties or a shared history of violent struggle, such as revolutionary or liberation movements."[64] Dan Slater provides an example in his description of "protection pacts," which are the result of "a wide range of transgressive, collective mass actions."[65] With regard to authority within insurgencies, Elisabeth Wood demonstrates the importance of emotional and moral motives for insurgent collective action; and Jeremy Weinstein shows how social endowments, such as shared beliefs, expectations, and norms, as opposed to economic patronage, contribute to better command and control.[66] Both Deng and Zhukov wielded what is perhaps best called "martial prestige"—respect derived from their contributions on the battlefield.

Yet the fallout in the Soviet Union and China after Stalin and Mao suggests that legacies of violence may have positive implications for regime resiliency but not necessarily for cohesion among the ruling elite. In both the Soviet Union and China, the deaths of the old leaders opened up an opportunity for historical antagonisms to resolve in the favor of one group or another (in the Soviet and Chinese cases) or for old, traditional hierarchies to reassert themselves (in the Chinese case).

In chapter 2, the first of the two chapters on the Soviet Union in this book, I investigate the defeat of Lavrentii Beria in 1953, only several months after the death of Stalin. First, I show that Beria had no real policy differences with his opponents, and in fact most of his policy initiatives were intended to increase his popularity. Second, I show that isolating Beria in such a way was necessary for a smooth victory. The arrest prevented him from making his case to the CC as a whole, as was his right as a member of the Presidium. Third, I show that the military's behavior was not apolitical; it played a clearly illegal, coercive role by arresting Beria during a meeting of the Presidium.

Chapter 3 analyzes Nikita Khrushchev's struggle with the so-called anti-party group—an incident during which a majority of the Presidium attempted to remove Khrushchev from power. Policy differences between Khrushchev and his opponents were minimal, and to the extent such differences could be determined, Khrushchev's policies were not necessarily more popular. In any case, the power of the anti-party group was clearly more rooted in its prestige as revolutionary leaders. That prestige was challenged by Zhukov, who emphasized its culpability in the destruction of other revolutionary figures during the Great Terror. The outcome of the struggle was determined by an emergency session of the CC, which allowed Khrushchev to overcome his minority position in the Presidium. Zhukov, who controlled the military, refused to submit to the majority on the Presidium who opposed Khrushchev.

Chapter 4, the first chapter on China in this volume, tells the story of the fall of the Gang of Four. Although the Gang did not consist of pushovers, they combined aggressive tactics with a desire to coexist with other members of the leadership. Despite their policy inclinations that were different from those of other party leaders, those differences were not fundamental, and the Gang did not have their own coherent policy platform. The Gang's most serious problems were personal, especially with regard to "historical" problems—a lack of major accomplishments before 1949 and association with the worst excesses of the Cultural Revolution from 1966 to 1976. The Gang were unexpectedly arrested instead of being openly confronted at either a Politburo or CC meeting, the second option being too risky given the number of Gang supporters in the CC. The palace guards played a decisive role in the arrest of the Gang, and the military played a role as a crucial backup force.

Chapter 5 describes Deng Xiaoping's defeat of Mao's initial successor, Hua Guofeng, from 1977 to 1981 and shows further evidence for the authority model. The economic model predicts that the figure with more democratic sensibilities would have won because of his ability to co-opt threats, but Deng was the less-consensus-oriented figure. Deng had limited policy differences with Hua, who deserves greater credit for beginning the reform process than previously appreciated. Historical legacies proved to be more important than policy differences. Deng's strength was rooted in his role as a revolutionary-era figure, while Hua suffered from "historical" problems from his career during the Cultural Revolution. Hua's most important setback took place at a full CC work meeting, an event with no precedence in the People's Republic of China (PRC), which to that point had been dominated by the top leadership. Deng only allowed an interpretation of the rules that benefited him and sometimes even engaged in conspiratorial behavior. Finally, Deng believed political power revolved around the question of military control. His move against Hua started over a struggle regarding who had the greater say over the armed forces, and Deng used his unique relationship with the PLA to weaken Hua's political position. Deng's decision to purge Hua entirely from the leadership, rather than let him remain as a sign of stability, was partly because of his fear that young leftist forces within the military would rally to Hua's banner.

CHAPTER TWO

The Defeat of Beria

Introduction: Stalin's Belated Victory

In October 1952, the most powerful men and women in the Soviet Union sat dumbfounded as Iosif Stalin gave a speech to the first CC plenum after the Nineteenth Party Congress. He viciously attacked his old comrades who had served with him for decades and proposed the creation of a new leadership body of young men who had played no role in the October Revolution.[1] Viacheslav Molotov, previously seen by the party as Stalin's deputy, was portrayed as being unprincipled and suffering from a number of serious political problems. Another old leader, Anastas Mikoian, had allegedly committed major mistakes during the war: "His lack of responsibility dearly cost our state and people."[2]

A new twenty-five-person "Presidium" would now replace what had been a much smaller Politburo. How Stalin had compiled the list of people who would make up the new group was a mystery to other members of the leadership. He also named an elite "Bureau" of nine members, mostly men younger than the old revolutionaries but older than those newly named to the Presidium: Georgii Malenkov, Lavrentii Beria, Nikita Khrushchev, Maksim Saburov, Mikhail Pervukhin, and Nikolai Bulganin. Iosif Stalin, Lazar' Kaganovich, and Kliment Voroshilov (who was apparently only included by mistake) were the only members from the old guard. Molotov and Mikoian were conspicuously absent.[3] Historians agree that Stalin intended to liquidate the older leaders and promote a new generation.[4]

If that was in fact Stalin's plan, he did not have time to complete it. As he lay on his deathbed on March 5, 1953, the CC, Council of Ministers (the Soviet government), and Presidium of the Supreme Soviet (the Soviet legislature) held a joint session. After introductory remarks about Stalin's condition by the head of Soviet public health, Malenkov said, "It is clear to all that the country cannot stand even one hour of interruption in the leadership." He emphasized that the situation demanded "the greatest cohesion." Then Beria told the audience that the Bureau nominated Malenkov as premier. After Beria finished, Malenkov named Beria, Molotov, Bulganin, and Kaganovich as his first vice chairmen, Molotov as foreign minister, Voroshilov as chairman of the Presidium of the Supreme Soviet, and Mikoian as head of the newly combined ministry managing external and internal trade. Despite lacking the necessary approval of a full Party Congress, Malenkov had disbanded Stalin's Bureau and established a new Presidium.[5] Even before Stalin took his last breath, the old men of the party had returned to participate in the top leadership, the middle generation had seized dominance, and the younger cohort had been cast into political oblivion.[6]

Khrushchev was removed from his position as head of the Moscow party committee and ordered to "concentrate" on CC work. In this position, Khrushchev's authority was rather unremarkable. According to one Russian expert of this time, "By 1953 from the perspective of formal leadership Khrushchev had the most unfavorable odds."[7] Another historian concurred, "The authority of Khrushchev in the party at the time was not comparable with the high authority of Malenkov, Beria, Molotov."[8] Khrushchev was not even made first secretary until September.[9] William Taubman, the author of Khrushchev's definitive biography, writes, "Virtually no one in the USSR or abroad imagined that Khrushchev had a chance of besting them all."[10]

Yet middle-aged Khrushchev, who lacked both the formal and informal authority of other leaders, became the first dominant leader after Stalin's death. This curious progression of elite politics after Stalin is all the stranger given that in China "old-person" politics dominated the political environment for many years after Mao.

This chapter explains the purge of Lavrentii Beria, who remains a controversial and disputed figure in Soviet historiography. Some popular historians portray him as nothing short of a superman.[11] Others stick to the more conventional narrative of him as a murderous, sex-crazed maniac. This intense interest has had some unfortunate consequences: in 2010, a forged document claiming to be Beria's private diaries was published.[12] Extreme claims and dubious sources make the study of the man exceptionally challenging.

What exactly was the nature of Beria's power? Why was he arrested and executed soon after Stalin's death? And what does that teach us about the nature of politics? Political scientists have yet to provide theoretically useful answers to these questions.[13] Like elsewhere in this book, I test the competing hypotheses as described in chapter 1. The economic model fails on all counts. First, focusing on the material benefits of one policy over another, or even policy platforms in general, would explain nothing and in fact be misleading. Beria sought out close relationships with other members of the elite, deliberately selected reformist policies that he believed would gain him support, and rarely had meaningful differences with his colleagues on policy. What proves to be of much more importance were legitimacy issues tied to party seniority, historical antagonisms, and the threatening role of compromising material that would allow Beria to make incendiary charges against his colleagues.

Second, Beria's arrest entailed a blatant series of violations of party rules. The move against him was preceded by a conspiracy within the top leadership in a process so secretive that even today we are not entirely sure who first proposed Beria's arrest. We have tentative evidence that even on the Presidium a significant number of individuals either were unsure about the propriety of arresting Beria or were presented with false evidence of his alleged crimes. Beria was not allowed to present his case to the CC—an outrageous trick that was not even employed during the 1930s.

Third, the power ministries played a crucial role. One of the most important reasons behind the move against Beria was fear of his control over the political police. The arrest of Beria was only made possible because high-ranking military officers agreed to seize him illegally during a meeting in the Kremlin. As the case against him was prepared, he was placed in a military bunker to prevent him from communicating with his forces in the Ministry of Internal Affairs (MVD).

Hypothesis 1a versus 1b

Political Style

According to Hypothesis 1a, we should expect to see consensus-driven leaders achieve victory. This personality type would be more conducive to aggregating support. However, evidence shows that Beria was indeed friendly with other members of the leadership. He offered them perks, provided them with what he thought they wanted, and solicited their opinions. Beria also sought to build up his position by introducing popular policies. Counterintuitively, however, the popularity of those policies actually *hurt* him because others in the elite feared they would make him too powerful. That outcome is the exact opposite of what Hypothesis 1a predicts.

Beria actively sought the approval of his colleagues. Molotov claimed that Beria hinted to him that he had assassinated Stalin, saying, "Apparently [Beria] wanted to evoke my sympathy. He said, 'I did him in!'—as if this had benefited me. Of course he wanted to ingratiate himself with me."[14] The day after Stalin's funeral, Beria released Molotov's wife, who had been sent to prison by Stalin.[15] Molotov later remarked, "With the departure of Stalin the country was orphaned. He did not leave a successor: in the last years of his life he was suspicious and trusted no one. And we were confused—who would we follow? Beria pushed Malenkov to power. And pleased Khrushchev—suggested he focus on the apparatus of the CC. I got the Ministry of Foreign Affairs. I did not oppose this."[16]

Beria reached out to others as well. On May 6, 1953, he wrote a memorandum to the Presidium rehabilitating Kaganovich's brother Mikhail, who had committed suicide after being accused of participation in a "rightist-Trotskyite" organization.[17] According to Khrushchev, Beria promoted Voroshilov to the chairmanship of the Presidium of the Supreme Soviet so as to "make Voroshilov into someone whom he could rely on when he started his next round of butchery."[18]

Malenkov, Beria, and Khrushchev were especially close. Together they were put in charge of managing Stalin's documents as the leader lay on his death bed.[19] Mikoian in his memoirs describes how Beria would often meet with Malenkov, Molotov, and Khrushchev before Presidium meetings and decide how to present issues to the rest of the leadership. Beria would walk with Khrushchev and Malenkov in the Kremlin "conversing excitedly. . . . They were together after work as well."[20] Molotov saw Beria, Khrushchev, and Malenkov as a "trinity" who together were trying to dominate the political arena and enjoyed close relations, if not friendship.[21] Khrushchev writes in his memoirs that Beria tried to buy support by suggesting that the government build dachas for the elite.[22] He even admitted at the CC plenum after Beria's arrest that he had enjoyed the best relations with the fallen leader in the time period after Stalin's death, saying, "If I did not call him for a day, then he would call and ask, 'Why don't you call.' I would say there was no time, there was work. [Beria]: 'But still call.' I, comrades, started to think: Why is there such love shown to me? What's the matter?"[23]

In a letter to Malenkov after the arrest, Beria described his relationship with others on the Presidium as being exceptionally friendly. The letter suggests he was shocked by his arrest. Regarding Molotov, he wrote, "We all highly rated [you,] considered you a true disciple of Lenin and a true colleague of Stalin, the second most important figure after Comrade Stalin"; to Khrushchev, "We were always great friends[.] I was always proud of the fact that you are a terrific Bolshevik and a terrific comrade and I repeatedly told you this"; to Malenkov, "Dear Georgii[,] I ask you to understand me, that you know me better than others."[24]

Beria cultivated popularity by ending the worst abuses of the Stalin era. On March 13, eight days after the death of Stalin, Beria ordered the creation of special investigative groups to reevaluate the infamous Doctors' Plot as well as the arrests of former members of the Ministry of State Security, officers in the General Artillery Department, and Georgian party officials.[25] On April 4, he distributed a document that criticized the use of torture in the past and explicitly forbid its use in the future.[26] On May 13, he proposed an end to restrictions on where Soviet citizens could live within their own country.[27] He suggested greater restrictions on the extrajudicial Special Council, which had been responsible for many of the worst abuses of the Stalin era.[28] According to the Soviet poet Konstantin Simonov, Beria even chose to show the CC documents delineating Stalin's role in the Doctors' Plot in a way that showed his paranoia and brutality—a first step toward "de-Stalinization."[29] The historian Mark Kramer writes, "Reports transmitted by local and regional officials to the central authorities in Moscow indicated that Soviet citizens heartily welcomed the political reforms."[30]

These reforming steps, however, had negative side effects for Beria. Other members of the leadership believed that Beria was improving his own prestige at the expense of the party. Kaganovich told the CC, "It was impossible [for Beria] to speak before the people in the name of the MVD. He needed to speak in the name of the party, and for this he needed to break away some individuals, turn some individuals into his agents and act."[31] Beria's attempts at reform were a mark against him in Kaganovich's eyes: "This person is a careerist, an adventurist, who wants, by discrediting Stalin, to undermine that base upon which we sit and clear a path for himself."[32] Dmitrii Shepilov, the former CC secretary and Soviet foreign minister purged by Khrushchev, writes in his memoirs, "Beria, the man who for years on end was one of those mainly responsible for the reign of arbitrary will and lawlessness in the country, decided to don the mantle of a champion of legality, individual freedom, and democracy."[33] Later in court, Marshal Kirill Moskalenko asked Beria whether he would admit that all of his activities after the death of Stalin were directed toward seizing power. Beria responded, "I categorically deny this. . . . I will say that I did not stand out by any special humility—this is a fact. I certainly did stick my nose into other areas of work that had no relation to me, this is also true. . . . That I tried to popularize myself—that happened. With regard to my Bonapartist contortions, that is not true."[34]

Policy

Robert Service wrote in 1981 that the need to overcome Stalin's disastrous legacy led to a common position among the elite that serious changes were needed.[35] The new historiography, based on new documents, confirms, in the words of Kramer, that "the precariousness of the new political arrangements and the intensity of the power struggle in Moscow were attributable mainly to personal ambitions rather than fundamental policy differences. . . . What does seem clear is that Beria's positions on specific issues—domestic or foreign—had little, if anything, to do with the effort to eliminate him."[36] Beria wrote to Malenkov in a letter after his arrest, "The MVD introduced to the CC and government *by your suggestion and with regard to certain questions by the suggestion of N. S. Khrushchev* a series of deserved political and practical suggestions, such as: rehabilitation of the doctors, rehabilitation of those arrested in relation to the so-called Mingrelian national center in Georgia and the return of those incorrectly exiled from Georgia, the amnesty, the liquidation of the passport regime, the correction of distortions in the party line in the nationality policies and the punitive measures in the Lithuanian SSR, [w]estern Ukraine, and western Belorussia."[37]

A common belief about the fall of Beria is that he was removed because he supported an unpopular, radically liberal solution to the growing crisis in the German Democratic Republic (GDR). In a letter from jail, Beria did admit to "unacceptable rudeness and insolence" toward Khrushchev and Bulganin during the discussion of Germany.[38] Numerous memoir accounts claim that a major fight took place on May 27 on this issue.[39]

However, the idea that Beria differed fundamentally from his colleagues, especially Molotov, on the question of Germany has come under attack by historians such as Mark Kramer and Aleksei Filitov.[40] Filitov writes, "New archival documents have qualitatively weakened the argument of a special radical position on the Germany question on the part of the head of the MVD at the time, as well as a total rejection of this position from other members of the post-Stalin leadership of the USSR."[41] At first, the Ministry of Foreign Affairs under Molotov was in fact *less* conservative than many on the Presidium, although ultimately the leadership came around to Molotov's position. Beria's positions were hardly all "liberal." In any case, according to the declassified documents, the positions of Molotov and Beria were quite close. Memoir accounts of Beria's supposed radical position at the May 27 meeting differ fundamentally

on even basic questions; and those accounts were almost certainly
colored by the later fall of Beria. Filitov concludes that Molotov's
criticisms of Beria at the July plenum were a "180-degree turn" from
the foreign minister's own earlier position. The charges against
Beria were made at least in part to find a scapegoat for the riots in
that country, not out of real policy differences.[42]

Although Beria had reason to dissemble, he also denied that his
position was fundamentally different from that of his compatriots.
During an interrogation on July 11, after his arrest, Beria stated emphatically that he was not an opponent of constructing socialism
in East Germany: "My position on the German question was the
same as that of the Presidium of the CC." He said he did not reject the construction of socialism but was in favor of "an extremely
careful approach"—a sign that perhaps his opponents were using
a disagreement on tactics as a political wedge to make it seem like
differences were bigger than they really were.[43]

Historical Legacies and Compromising Material

Having shown that Beria sought friendly relations with others in
the elite, was associated with generally popular policies, and did not
strongly differ from others in the leadership on those policies, we
have discounted the value of Hypothesis 1a. We can now turn to
Hypothesis 1b: the importance of sociological factors. In this section, I show that the more important drivers of the struggle were
questions of party seniority, historical antagonisms, Beria's prestige
as the miracle worker behind the atomic program, the danger of information being used as a weapon, and the threat of compromising
information.

The old guard believed that Beria was not respecting proper
norms of party seniority. This factor is evident in Kaganovich's
speech at a January 1955 CC plenum in which he stated that Malenkov and Beria did not associate with the others as Stalin was dying,
instead keeping to themselves on the second floor of Stalin's dacha:

> We, old members of the Presidium, are older than they are
> by many years in terms not of age but of work in the party,
> [of work] in the Politburo with Stalin. After all, we walked by

Lenin's side—they [Malenkov and Beria] could have come up [to us] and said what they were doing there, what they were discussing, what decisions they were making, what they were preparing. Nothing of the sort happened. They would stop by to take a look and go upstairs. There was Voroshilov, me, Khrushchev, Bulganin, Molotov, Mikoian, others— nothing of the sort happened. We do not exist for them.[44]

Also at the plenum, another CC member, Viacheslav Malyshev, spoke of Beria's disdainful attitude toward old revolutionaries such as Shvernik, Andreevich, and Voroshilov, saying, "We are not accustomed [to see] such an attitude to old leading comrades." He spoke of the curiosity of the old revolutionaries not holding prominent positions: "We see how in recent times tried-and-true comrades whom the entire country, the entire people, know—Comrades Molotov, Voroshilov, Mikoian—were forced out from the leadership of our party and country. This is a fact. This was very offensive to us. We have known Comrade Molotov since we were Komsomol age. . . . It is clear that Comrade Stalin did not speak with his own words. Beria provided him with this material."[45]

Historical grudges also played an important role. Kramer points out that Molotov, Bulganin, Saburov, and Pervukhin all believed Beria had used compromising material against them in the past.[46] Antagonism against Beria was especially prominent in the military. Marshal Zhukov writes, "They knew that I had an old animosity toward Beria, bordering on enmity. Even while Stalin was alive, we had clashes on more than one occasion. It is enough to say that Abakumov and Beria wanted to arrest me at some point in the past. . . . By the way, Stalin one day told me directly that they wanted to arrest me. Beria whispered to Stalin, but the latter said, 'I do not believe it. A brave colonel, patriot, and traitor. I don't believe it. End this dirty stunt.' Believe me that after this I gladly undertook his arrest."[47]

Beria's triumphs with the nuclear weapons program also made him formidable. According to Pavel Sudoplatov, a top operative in the MVD in charge of secret operations outside the country, the most important reason Beria was removed was because of his increasing prestige as a result of the victories he had achieved with the atomic program. This work "raised him in the eyes of all members of the Politburo and members of the Central Committee who knew about this work."[48]

Beria's most important noneconomic form of authority, however, was his control over information. This took two forms. First, the MVD could serve as an independent information channel for Beria that he could use to monitor and control party structures. Second, Beria had access to historical documents that could be used as weapons against his opponents.

The leadership's concern over Beria's use of the MVD in the first way is most apparent in the debate over policies in the republics.[49] Beria supported policies that increased the representation of non-Russians, and he was criticized for this after his purge. However, the evidence tells a different story: no real policy differences existed among the leadership on the question of cadre policy per se. The real concern was over Beria's use of the MVD as a source of private information.

On May 8, 1953, Beria wrote in a note to the Presidium that the MVD, during an investigation, had learned that the struggle in Lithuania against the nationalist underground was not proceeding in a satisfactory way: 270,000 Lithuanians—10 percent of the population—had been arrested, killed, or exiled between 1944 and 1952. Beria blamed the failure to defeat the insurrection on the lack of Lithuanians in the Lithuanian MVD and then drew attention to the absence of ethnic Lithuanians in the party leadership of the republic.[50] On May 16, he submitted a similar memorandum on Ukraine, in which he criticized tax policy, noted that up to 500,000 Ukrainians had been arrested, killed, or exiled, and pointed to the lack of ethnic Ukrainians in leadership positions in western Ukraine.[51] On June 8, Beria submitted a proposal to the Presidium in which he suggested the removal of the Belorussian party chief, Patolichev, in favor of an ethnic Belarusian.[52]

Beria's moves were not problematic because of opposition to promoting national cadres. The Presidium supported Beria's memoranda on Ukraine and Lithuania by telling those republics to study them.[53] Most strikingly, in June 1953, Khrushchev himself wrote a memorandum about Latvia that touched on the same themes as Beria's memos on Ukraine, Belorussia, and Lithuania and may even have used some of Beria's material.[54] Following the purge of Beria, the Soviet Union still continued its move toward allowing greater representation of local cadres in the leading political positions of their constituent republics. The more critical threat was that Beria was using the MVD as his own information source. Geoffrey Swain puts the issue succinctly: "It was not what Beria was trying to do, but how he was doing it that Khrushchev objected to."[55]

Beria himself admitted that his behavior was politically problematic. In a letter to Malenkov written on July 1, Beria wrote that the reform proposals he had made as head of the MVD were "in accordance with the existing directives of the CC and government." He did, however, admit that it was inappropriate to distribute decisions of the CC alongside the MVD memoranda, as this made it seem like the MVD was running the CCs in Ukraine, Lithuania, and Belorussia.[56] Beria did not deny that he had asked the MVD to collect information on a number of non-Russian cadres. He claimed to have done so with "the best intentions—to present the material to the Presidium of the CC CPSU [Communist Party of the Soviet Union]."[57]

Even more important than allowing Beria to shape policy in the satellite republics were the MVD's archives and eavesdropping capabilities. Fear of Beria's use of compromising materials was one of the most decisive reasons for others in the leadership to unite against him. By the summer of 1953, Beria had proposed the arrest of former secretary of the CC and minister of state security S. D. Ignat'ev (Malenkov's protégé) and had arrested M. D. Riumin, former head of the investigative unit for particularly important cases and a man who could make accusations against Malenkov and Khrushchev.[58] According to the rough notes of Malenkov's speech to the Presidium meeting where Beria was arrested, Malenkov emphasized better control over the system of eavesdropping ("comrades are unsure of who is listening to whom").[59] In Khrushchev's speech to the CC after Beria's removal, he claimed that Beria wanted to control the political police "so that through his intelligence gathering [he] could spy on the members of the Politburo, eavesdrop, monitor, create cases, intrigue, and this will lead to bad consequences for the party."[60] Bulganin told the CC that the Presidium had confiscated from Beria recordings of Khrushchev, Malenkov, Molotov,

Bulganin, and Voroshilov.[61] At the June 1957 CC plenum, Malenkov and Khrushchev agreed that they would not speak at Malenkov's home because they were afraid of eavesdropping, although they acknowledged that it later turned out that no eavesdropping was taking place.[62]

At the same plenum, Malenkov was accused of serving Beria until ultimately joining the conspiracy because the latter had compromising material on him. The head of the MVD at the time read to the plenum a letter written to the Presidium by Malenkov's secretary. According to this letter, Malenkov failed to "tell the plenum of the CC CPSU about the reasons and character of his long (from 1937 to 1953), close, and business-like relationship with Beria"— Beria's possession of compromising material on him.[63]

Malenkov was not the only leader whose behavior was shaped by the threat of compromising material. As former leader of Ukraine, Khrushchev probably saw Beria's criticisms of policies in the republic as a challenge to his legacy. The former MVD official Sudoplatov told the historian Dmitrii Volkogonov in personal correspondence that Khrushchev wanted to remove Beria because the latter knew that Khrushchev had organized mass repressions in Ukraine from 1938 to 1949, and "it was extremely imperative to get rid of unnecessary witnesses."[64] One of the men tried along with Beria said after being arrested, "So, for example, with regard to the issue of excesses in western Ukraine, Beria in a draft memorandum and draft resolution to the Presidium of the CC CPSU showed that mass repressions and other operations were triggered by the situation [there], and verbally commented in an ironic tone that at that time N. S. Khrushchev worked in Ukraine."[65]

Significantly, Beria denied during his interrogations that he had ordered the MVD to eavesdrop on party and state leaders.[66] Sudoplatov's memoirs provide an example of a time Beria indignantly ignored an offer of compromising information on Malenkov. A Georgian playwright named Georgii Mdivani had given the chief of Beria's secretariat a memo claiming that Malenkov's speech to the Nineteenth Party Congress plagiarized a czarist minister. Although Beria disregarded the document, the memo "found its way from Beria's secretariat to Malenkov's office, and the damage was done." Sudoplatov also claims that "all the members of [Beria's] secretariat who knew about the memo . . . were promptly arrested and imprisoned." Therefore, we have reason to believe that Beria's accomplices might have truly thought that Beria had compromising material, but whether he was actively seeking it out or planned to use it may never be known.[67] In any case, the possibility that Beria *might* use such material was enough of a reason to move against him.

Hypothesis 2a versus 2b

The Deliberations

The move against Beria was an intrigue reminiscent of old-style palace coups. The evidence demonstrates that the most important discussions took place in a conspiratorial fashion that prevented preferences from being structurally aggregated. Beria's arrest was presented as a fait accompli to the CC—even some members of the Presidium might not have expected Beria would be arrested. As Shepilov concludes in his memoirs, "It really was undemocratic and unconstitutional."[68]

According to Khrushchev's memoirs, when he sought out Voroshilov's support for the conspiracy, Khrushchev ended up not revealing his plans because the conversation began with Voroshilov loudly praising Beria. When Khrushchev approached Kaganovich, the latter first asked who else opposed Beria. When Khrushchev said that Malenkov, Bulganin, Molotov, and Saburov were already in agreement, thus forming a majority of the Presidium, Kaganovich agreed to support Khrushchev. The implication here is not only that Kaganovich was going along with the majority but also that Khrushchev had the ability to shape Kaganovich's response by mischaracterizing the positions of others.[69]

In Kaganovich's own memoirs, he denies that he asked whether there was a majority in favor of ousting Beria. He told an interviewer that when Khrushchev summoned him, he was told that Beria was engaged in intrigue and wanted to overthrow the leadership and take power. Although Kaganovich denies asking about the position of others on the Presidium, he claims to have suggested that Beria only be weakened but not removed.[70] Mikoian also had reservations. Ivan Serov, who would later go on to lead the Committee of

State Security (KGB), writes in his memoirs that in a drunken confrontation in a bathroom during a visit to China in 1954, Bulganin
grabbed Mikoian by the collar and screamed, "You did not want to
arrest Beria immediately too. You wanted an investigation."[71]

No official transcript has been found of the Presidium meeting at which Beria was arrested, and we are, therefore, unable to
state with certainty what specific accusations Beria faced or what
positions the others took. Both Molotov and Khrushchev claimed
that Mikoian spoke against removing Beria.[72] The evidence suggests that some top leaders did not expect that the military officers
would arrive.[73] According to Kaganovich, Mikoian was surprised by
the arrest.[74] Mikoian claimed to have only agreed to Khrushchev's
proposal to make Beria head of the oil industry, as Beria "might still
be useful."[75] Curiously, according to the rough draft of Malenkov's
speech to the Presidium, he did not propose arresting Beria but only
removing him from his position as deputy premier and putting him
in charge of the oil industry.[76]

Most interesting is the evidence that this meeting did not
even bother to go through the motions of appropriate party procedure. Instead, the doubters were presented with a fait accompli.
Khrushchev claimed that there was not even a formal vote. According to his memoirs, he had proposed that the Presidium suggest to
the next plenum of the CC that Beria be removed from all his posts.
But Malenkov, apparently rattled, instead pressed a secret button
that summoned the military officers in the next room to arrest Beria.
Malenkov only said, "I propose as chairman of the Council of Ministers of the USSR that you detain Beria."[77] Khrushchev gave an
adviser a different version: Malenkov was too nervous even to make
an opening statement, so Khrushchev proposed that Beria be removed from the Presidium, CC, and the party and be turned over
to a military court. Then he was the first to raise his hand to vote in
favor of his own proposal, followed by everyone else. Khrushchev,
not Malenkov, ordered Moskalenko to make the arrest, saying,
"Take this snake, traitor to his motherland, and take him where he
belongs."[78]

Dmitrii Sukhanov, Malenkov's former assistant, goes so far as to
claim that Malenkov was essentially the only member of the Pre-

sidium who opposed Beria. Malenkov allegedly invited Khrushchev and Bulganin to his office, where without even saying hello, he told them he knew about a supposed Beria-led conspiracy and their participation in it. They were warned that their lives would be spared if Bulganin smuggled military officers into the Kremlin in his car. At the actual meeting on June 26, Pervukhin and Saburov supported arresting Beria; Molotov, Voroshilov, and Kaganovich were opposed; and Khrushchev, Bulganin, and Mikoian were noncommittal. While Molotov was speaking, Malenkov summoned Zhukov and the other officers. When Malenkov again suggested arresting Beria, suddenly everyone was in favor. Before removing Beria, Zhukov suggested to Malenkov that he arrest the other members of the Presidium who had cooperated with Beria. Sukhanov even argued that Khrushchev and Bulganin had tried to warn Beria by writing the word "alarm" on a piece of paper and placing it in Beria's office; if Beria had gone there before the meeting, in Sukhanov's mind, he would have saved himself.[79]

Accounts from members of the military also suggest that not everyone had made up their minds about Beria before the arrest. Zhukov told an acquaintance of Khrushchev's adviser that when he seized Beria, "it seemed to [him] that not all members of the Presidium knew about the arrest and that they suspected that [he] was executing a military coup."[80] Moskalenko writes that "other than members of the Presidium Bulganin, Malenkov, Molotov, and Khrushchev, apparently, no one knew or expected the arrest of Beria."[81] According to another military officer involved in the operation, "When we entered, several members of the Presidium jumped from their seats; apparently they did not know the details of the arrest. Zhukov immediately calmed them down: 'Relax, comrades! Sit down.'" Then, Malenkov proposed that the question of Beria be discussed once again.[82]

The Decision-Making Body

According to the party's own rules, if the Presidium was split, then the CC should have been able to referee a decision. However, once again, we do not see a serious discussion of Beria's strengths and weaknesses. The CC's membership was stunned. At the CC plenum, one speaker said, "We, workers in the regions, before the Plenum of the Central Committee knew very little, and it was difficult to guess to at least some extent about the treachery of this man."[83] Another admitted that he had only learned of the arrest the day before the plenum.[84]

Khrushchev struggled to explain why Beria had been removed in the way he was. He admitted that people were confused why he and Malenkov had turned on Beria, given that they were often seen walking hand in hand with each other. Yet he argued, "With a treacherous man it was necessary to behave in this way. If we had said that he was a bastard when we had realized that, then I am sure that he would have finished us. Don't delude yourself, he is capable of this. I already told several comrades, and they told me that I am exaggerating. . . . We were not dealing with a member of the party that should be struggled against by party means. We were instead dealing with a conspirator, with a provocateur, and, therefore, it was impossible to expose ourselves."[85] Mikoian admitted, "It was hard for me to agree to the arrest of a member of the CC Presidium. But in the process of discussion, the totally adventurous nature of Beria became apparent, and there was clearly a conspiratorial threat. This led to the total isolation of Beria and the unanimous decision on his arrest."[86]

Khrushchev was using the nature of the threat that Beria represented to justify special measures. Yet those measures also prevented Beria from defending himself. Moreover, they beg another question: If Beria needed to be isolated from the political police out of a fear he would use force to protect himself, why was he not allowed to address the CC after he was stripped of his position as leader of the MVD? The obvious answer is that Beria could have pointed to the weaknesses in the charges against him, as well as made powerful accusations against his opponents. As the Soviet historian Vladimir Naumov writes, "[The conspirators] sought to physically liquidate as quickly as possible Beria, who knew too much about his former comrades. They wanted to avoid a detailed and thorough investigation of his crimes in order to hide their own participation in them. Therefore, the leaders of the Presidium of the CC did not even think of observing the law."[87]

Legitimacy of Behavior

Brian D. Taylor suggests that "the handful of officers involved in the arrest had every reason to see the order as a legitimate one handed down by the party and the government."[88] But was that indeed the case? Although many questions about the purge of Beria remain, the evidence shows beyond a reasonable doubt that the plotters were relying on extremely tendentious interpretations of party rules. The plotters explicitly decided that it would be impossible to use purely "party methods" to defeat Beria. According to Khrushchev's memoirs, when he proposed to Molotov that Beria simply be relieved of his positions, Molotov disagreed, saying, "Beria is very dangerous, and I think we need to take more extreme measures." Khrushchev then suggested that Beria be detained for investigation.[89] Because of Beria's control over the political police, simply voting to remove him was not an option. Khrushchev writes, "As soon as we brought up this question, Beria could order his guards to arrest us."[90] Khrushchev and the other plotters, therefore, requested that military officers hide in the waiting room of Malenkov's office and wait for a signal to come and arrest Beria.[91]

Beria's opponents acted illegitimately in several ways. First, Beria easily could have accused the plotters of factionalism. At the January 1955 CC plenum, Malenkov spoke of the importance of party solidarity as the primary reason for why he did not move against Beria immediately after Stalin's death. Khrushchev started his speech to the CC plenum after Beria's arrest by claiming that "the striving for unity . . . was very cleverly used by adventurist Beria."[92] These comments reveal that members of the leadership understood that their actions could be seen as violations of the party's code against factionalism. In Lenin's famous anti-faction resolution passed at the Tenth Party Congress, point 4 stipulates that matters should only be discussed at party meetings, not in "groups" forming around a "platform."[93] Moreover, the party constitution's section 3-A described maintaining the unity of the party as the primary obligation of each party member. Beria's arrest also arguably violated the recently passed resolution that demanded "the greatest solidarity of the leadership."[94]

Second, the Presidium did not have the right to make personnel decisions. That power lay in the hands of the CC. According to point 34 of the party constitution, "The Central Committee of the Communist Party of the Soviet Union organizes, for the leadership of the work of the CC between plenums, a Presidium." Certainly, a majority of the Presidium could have suggested to the CC that Beria be removed from the leadership. Yet technically this should not have been a rubber-stamp process. Instead, the differing positions should have been explained to the CC, which would then serve as an adjudicator.

Third, Beria should not have been refused access to the CC plenum that passed a resolution supporting the Presidium after his arrest. Point 12 of the party constitution stipulated that an individual could only be removed from the CC when two-thirds of the body supported such a decision, while point 3-G allowed every party member the right "to demand personal participation in all situations when a decision is made about his activities or behavior." Therefore, according to the party's own rules, Beria could not have been removed from the CC unless he was present at the deliberations. Without access to the CC, Beria was prevented from defending himself, especially against the charge that he was plotting a conspiracy. This lack of access was crucial. Even Molotov later admitted, "And here Khrushchev added fear, declared that Beria was preparing a coup. Foolishness, but we believed it. . . . We did not have time to figure things out, whether Beria was guilty. He was dangerous. And we could not take a risk."[95]

Finally, the investigation proceedings after Beria's arrest were politicized. No external judicial arbiter made an unbiased decision. The top procurator who would have tried the case was replaced by the more pliable Roman Rudenko immediately after Beria's arrest. On June 29, 1953, Rudenko was ordered by the Presidium to "proceed immediately, based on the directions of the session of the Presidium of the CC, to identify and investigate the facts of hostile anti-state, anti-party activities of Beria through his entourage."[96] Once the political decision was made, the procuracy's only task was to provide a conviction. This was despite Beria's desperate pleas in a letter to the Presidium on July 2: "Dear comrades, I strongly implore you to name the most responsible and strict commission for the strict investigation of my affair led by C[omrade] Molotov or C[omrade] Voroshilov. Do you really think a member of the Presidium of the

CC does not deserve that his affair is carefully sorted out, accusations be presented, explanations be demanded, witnesses be questioned[?] From all points of view, this is good for the matter and the CC."[97]

Yet Beria's wishes were denied. Khrushchev himself flatly admits in his memoirs, "We had no confidence in the ability of the State Procurator to investigate Beria's case objectively, so we sacked him and replaced him with Comrade Rudenko."[98] A special eight-man court was created. Only two of the members had any relationship with the justice system, and two others had a purely military background, including the head of the court, Marshal Konev. According to his widow, Konev was opposed to his nomination to lead the court that condemned Beria: "He so did not want this! He said, 'I am a military man. Leave me in peace. I am not a judge and do not know legal subtleties.'" He received numerous threatening letters at home (which, according to Konev's widow, cost him ten years of his life).[99] The other military member was Moskalenko. Even the author of a biography that is generally positive about Rudenko acknowledges that this was outrageous: "Apparently, this was a whim of Khrushchev or some other of the top party bosses. . . . That the same person [Moskalenko] would arrest, investigate, judge, and execute the sentence—this did not occur even during the 'rapid-fire justice' of the Stalin era!"[100]

Hypothesis 3a versus 3b

Views of Power Ministries

Due to the absence of robust political institutionalization, evidence strongly points to fear among members of the leadership that Beria could simply arrest them. After he was removed, the leadership moved together to weaken the power of the political police. Signs that Beria was arrogating control over the military were probably a significant reason why the plotters decided that they could no longer wait to move.

Khrushchev later told an adviser that when he went to speak to Malenkov about removing Beria, he said, "Special divisions are being brought to Moscow for some reason," implying that the troops might be used by Beria for a coup.[101] We have absolutely no real, reliable evidence that Beria was planning a coup.[102] But even if he was not, the fact that some plotters played up this fear means they believed that such a charge was politically powerful and a credible threat. No one felt safe.[103]

One of the reasons the conspirators moved against Beria was signs that he intended to expand his influence over the military. Bulganin told the CC plenum that on the eve of the arrest, it became clear that Beria was collecting "material of a military nature." This material was collected allegedly for "special reasons related to rocket weapons [*reaktivnym vooruzheniem*]," but Bulganin asked rhetorically why it was collected without the knowledge of either the CC or the minister of defense (him).[104]

Beria made threatening remarks about Bulganin that troubled members of the elite. Mikoian writes that when Khrushchev told him that Beria had threatened to remove Bulganin from his position as minister of defense, "this, of course, left an extremely negative impression on me." On the morning of the move against Beria, when Khrushchev in an attempt to enlist Mikoian asked him to stop by, "as evidence [Khrushchev] raised the fact of the intolerable conversation with Bulganin after the dispute over the GDR. Here Beria threatened a member of the Presidium of the CC, apparently taking into consideration his influence. This truly was an extremely serious fact."[105] In other words, for Mikoian, a key swing voter, Beria's attitude toward the minister of defense was hugely important.

The plotters were apparently also concerned about Beria's control over the nuclear program. One former nuclear specialist, Vasilii Makhnev, claimed that Beria had in fact taken a series of decisions, including the KB-11 design bureau, production of heavy water, and tests of the R-5 rocket, without the knowledge of the CC or government.[106] The Soviet nuclear physicist Andrei Sakharov writes in his memoirs, "Malenkov had been kept in the dark about our work on thermonuclear weapons before Beria's arrest, since all information on the subject was tightly held within Beria's immediate entourage," a fact that shocked Sakharov.[107] At the July plenum, Malenkov accused Beria of single-handedly ordering preparation for the first test explosion of a hydrogen bomb.[108] After Beria's arrest, Makhnev argued, "It is necessary to more closely include military men (leaders of the Ministry of Defense, commanders of the services) in atomic affairs. . . . Beria in every way tried to prevent proximity to this weapon, and we were powerless to do anything."[109] According to David Holloway, "There had been some anxiety that Beria might use the atomic bomb—or threaten its use—in a *coup d'etat*."[110]

Threat of Coercion

Hypothesis 3a suggests that the military would not have played a politicized role in the enforcement of a political decision on Beria's removal. However, the evidence shows that the military's assistance in the arrest of Beria was entirely inappropriate from a legal point of view and, moreover, that it was necessary for Beria's defeat.

We have strong evidence that the military high command was reluctant to execute this mission. Malenkov later told Moskalenko that they had earlier asked another marshal to execute the mission, but he had refused. In his memoirs, Moskalenko is clearly concerned about justifying the legitimacy of his behavior, suggesting that he was aware of how problematic it was for a military officer to arrest a sitting member of the Presidium in the middle of a session. Moskalenko emphasizes a lack of personal antagonism by claiming not to know Beria personally and justifying his decision to accept the order to arrest Beria as "an assignment of our party, our CC, its Presidium." Moskalenko also claims that he had refused to be awarded Hero of the Soviet Union for his role in Beria's arrest.[111] According to Volkogonov, the participating officers did likewise, so as "not to shame them with an award for such work."[112]

Most interesting is Moskalenko's refusal to interrogate Beria alone with Serov and Kruglov, two *chekists* (political police): he demanded that two other high-ranking military officers participate as well. Moskalenko went to the Bolshoi Theater and said to the Presidium, "'I am a soldier and a communist. You told me that Beria is an enemy of the party and the people. Therefore, all of us, including myself, treat him like an enemy. But we are not treating him badly.' . . . I had a clean conscience before the party, before the people and its Armed Forces both during Stalin's life and after."[113] The phraseology hints that Moskalenko was concerned about the propriety of the proceedings against Beria, especially when they seemed to be taking an even more sinister turn.

Despite the legal murkiness of the act, the military's role was decisive. Beria was hidden in the lounge of the chairman of the Council of Ministers with Moskalenko and four other high-ranking military officers. Beria clearly tried to give a signal to the guards. Around midnight, thirty armed military officers came to replace the Kremlin guards surrounding the building where Beria was held. He was then put in the middle seat of a military vehicle and brought to a Moscow garrison. Later he was brought to a bunker deep underground in the staff office of the Moscow Military Region (MR).[114]

The military took many other steps to incapacitate the political police and ensure a guaranteed outcome. The commander of the Moscow MR, Pavel Artem'ev, a former commander of the People's Commissariat for Internal Affairs (NKVD), was a supporter of Beria. Zhukov suggested that a major military exercise be organized in Kalinin that required Artem'ev's presence and nominated Moskalenko as temporary commander of the MR.[115] Moskalenko stationed the Kantemir and Taman tank divisions in the capital; naval frontier guards took control of the Kremlin; bodyguards of the top leadership were replaced; and the MVD buildings were surrounded.[116]

At the June 1957 CC plenum, Malenkov acknowledged the military's key role: "It was not that simple, not that easy to unmask Beria. At the time we relied on military comrades in this matter at the most necessary moment. Comrade Moskalenko provided us a decisive service in this matter. We approached him at the difficult moment with Comrade Khrushchev. We were without power or means in this regard."[117] Molotov also later admitted,

> So, finally, it is the year 1953. C[omrade] Khrushchev and I agreed before a meeting of the Presidium where the issue of Beria was discussed how to approach this issue so that there would be no disagreements and so that he would be arrested at the meeting of the Presidium, and we agreed beforehand, took certain measures, certain individuals wavered with regard to this issue, but already outside the doors there stood a military group, and when the decision was made, [the group] came in and arrested Beria at a meeting of the Presidium. These things happen when the interests of the party demand informal measures.[118]

How Did Institutions Matter?

Beria's fall was hardly a case of robust institutionalization in force. But institutions were not entirely absent. First, the plotters went to great pains to persuade the CC that they had behaved appropriately. Second, the political police did not rally to save their leader, although the reluctance to fight a civil war with the armed forces, which had already seized Beria, was probably more important. Third, the initiative was not in Zhukov's hands: the military was invited to participate in politics. Although Beria's arrest was clearly illegal, the positions of figures such as Khrushchev, Malenkov, and Molotov provided crucial political cover. Fourth, almost all of the plotters were most concerned about the position of Malenkov, who was formally in charge. Finally, at first Beria was only "detained," not "arrested." Khrushchev writes in his memoirs that during a conversation with Molotov, he said, "'detain' rather than 'arrest' because there were still no criminal charges against Beria": "As far as Beria's provocational behavior was concerned, we had only our intuition to go on, and you can't arrest a man on intuition." However, the very fact that Khrushchev admitted that Beria was "detained" based on "intuition" suggests the flimsiness of the charges against Beria and the weakness of party institutions.[119]

Implications

The fall of Beria was followed by a series of powerful steps intended to weaken the political police as an independent political force. Eavesdropping on Marshals Budennyi, Zhukov, and Timoshenko immediately ended.[120] All compromising material on Zhukov was destroyed.[121] On June 2, the MVD was ordered to cut 8,704 personnel. A military officer, Lieutenant General S. N. Perevertkin, was made one of the MVD's vice ministers, and a commissar was appointed head of military counterintelligence.[122]

The political police had been under such intense criticism that at a meeting of the Presidium on February 8, 1954, Kaganovich remarked that after the July plenum (when Beria was purged), the MVD was "behaving passively" and suggested writing a "motivating document." At that same meeting, the leadership established a

Committee of State Security, as opposed to a Ministry of State Security. As Kaganovich put it, a "Committee" was a department of the party and thus entailed even greater control. He emphasized that the chekists must report to party organs. Malenkov agreed: "The matter must be dealt with in such a way that there is no abuse. . . . [Matters] must be brought into the hands of the party." No longer would "eyes be watching friends and not enemies."[123]

What were the historical implications of Beria's removal? As Rudolf Pikhoia concludes, "He was, without a doubt, the most informed person in the leadership of the time, and his information was diverse, precise, and independent from other offices."[124] One major Russian historian of the political police notes, "Beria's desire for power . . . is mentioned by many memoirists. But Beria's 'lack of ideological content [*bezydeinost'*]' was pretty much what perhaps everyone who dealt with him agreed upon."[125]

Thinking about the possible extent of Beria's reformist inclinations is even more tantalizing given how differently he would have ruled compared to Khrushchev had he emerged triumphant. As will be shown in chapter 3, Khrushchev often executed poorly planned reforms. Yet Beria was a superb organizer, which is proved by his work on the nuclear bomb.[126] He sought support through popular changes. He could have potentially used the political police as a power structure parallel to the party.

This chapter provides clues about why such a method of rule proved to be unsustainable. Most importantly, the evidence shows that Beria's greatest strength was also his greatest weakness: it was precisely his leadership of the political police that terrified his comrades and turned them against him. In a system where party rules could not be used as a defense, Beria's control over *kompromat* (potentially compromising material) and his own armed forces proved too mortally dangerous for his colleagues to tolerate. Yet to overcome Beria's authority, the plotters resorted to the illegal use of force and the manipulation and violation of the party's own rules. Although the political police had been weakened as a political force, at the apex of Soviet power the problem of weak institutions had yet to be solved. Having failed to use the opportunity to achieve this institutionalization, the KGB was given the opportunity once more to play a decisive role in elite politics in 1964 when Khrushchev himself was removed from the leadership.

Whether the Soviet Union could have more successfully managed Stalin's legacy with an effective leader allied with a new cohort of non-Russian leaders in the regions, reformers, and the chekists will remain a mystery. What is clear, however, is why that historical path was closed: having suffered Stalin's repressions, the party elite had reason to oppose a powerful political police. The support of the armed forces, which had seen their ranks decimated by that organization over the decades, gave them the opportunity to achieve their objective. Chapter 3 will explore why another potential source of authority, the old revolutionaries, also failed to assert their dominance over the CPSU.

CHAPTER THREE

The Anti-Party Group

Introduction: The Passing of a Generation

On October 7, 1957, Charles Bohlen, who had recently concluded his ambassadorship to the Soviet Union, wrote a letter to Frank Wisner, a close personal friend who worked at the Central Intelligence Agency (CIA). In the letter, Bohlen provided his understanding of the recent attempt to remove Nikita Khrushchev as leader of the Soviet Union. Bohlen concluded that the outcome proved that "collective leadership was indeed a reality and not a fiction." The old Russia hand saw no evidence that "would indicate that police or other armed force was used or threatened to bring about the final result." As Bohlen explains in his memoirs, "I expressed doubts that events could be explained as a personal power struggle, pure and simple, between Khrushchev and Malenkov.... My explanation was that, at a certain point, policy disputes in the Kremlin, as in all governments, end in a power struggle among the disputants if the differences are critical." In other words, Bohlen used the economic model to explain the nature of the so-called anti-party-group incident of 1957. He was almost completely wrong.[1]

This chapter reveals that the time period from 1955 to 1957 is most interesting not because of a struggle over the future of the Soviet Union but because of its lessons about how Khrushchev

44

overcame the power of the old men of the party.[2] That victory is especially stunning given the persistence of the old revolutionaries in China after Mao's death.

In June 1957, a majority of the Presidium, known as the anti-party group, tried to remove Khrushchev from his position as first secretary of the CPSU. His opponents were formidable, including two of Stalin's most famous former right-hand men (Viacheslav Molotov and Lazar' Kaganovich), the former premier and initial successor to Stalin (Georgii Malenkov), the reigning premier (Nikolai Bulganin), and the head of state (Kliment Voroshilov). As Mikoian puts it in his memoirs, Khrushchev "hung by a thread."[3]

How was Khrushchev able to emerge triumphant? According to the economic model, Khrushchev would have won because he promised more popular policies or more material benefits, only had to politick among one group of elites, and did not rely on the power ministries to play a special role. If the authority model explains his victory, we would observe the elevation of prestige and interpersonal ties over policy, the manipulation of ambiguous party rules, and the military and political police enjoying some leeway to decide which orders to obey.

I provide the following evidence with regard to the first set of hypotheses. Khrushchev did not co-opt colleagues, as the economic model predicts, but instead antagonized his colleagues on the Presidium and violated the principles of collective leadership. The primary issue was whether other members of the Presidium would have any right to express their own opinions as opposed to any real fundamental struggles about policy. In fact, policy differences explain very little about the leadership struggle. On foreign policy, contrary to popular belief, Molotov was not a dogmatic hardliner opposed by a more open-minded Khrushchev.[4] On the issues of industrial reform and Stalin, the Presidium was in fact shaped more by consensus than difference. Significantly, to the extent that the leaders disagreed, Khrushchev was not necessarily the more popular individual. Finally, a key reason for the group's defeat was the deployment of kompromat and the use of Marshal Georgii Zhukov's authority as a legendary military leader.

With regard to the second set, Khrushchev won not by politicking within a single defined group but by manipulating multiple decision-making bodies. He and Zhukov stalled for time while the CC rallied and ultimately overturned the will of the majority of the Presidium—an event without historical precedence. Although both Khrushchev and his opponents operated within an ambiguous system of formal and informal rules, and they all violated the spirit of them, Khrushchev more egregiously went beyond previously established practice to achieve his victory.

Finally, I demonstrate that Zhukov's role as a military leader was important not only because of his popularity but in an operational sense as well. Zhukov's refusal to support the anti-party group frightened Khrushchev's opponents, who were clearly afraid that the military would arrest them. Moreover, Khrushchev's tight grip on the KGB was a major reason for the move against him in the first place.

Hypothesis 1a versus 1b

Political Style

Hypothesis 1a predicts that a leader would slip from power if they failed to co-opt challengers and adopt their policies. However, in this first section, I show that the prime reason for the crisis was Khrushchev's increasingly dictatorial tendencies, not policy differences. As Mao Zedong put it, the anti-party group "was just opposed to Khrushchev."[5]

For a brief time after the defeat of Beria, Stalin's successors did attempt to achieve a truly consensual model of leadership. In 1954, a Soviet delegation to China was asked to identify their top leader. Their answer was "collective leadership." The Soviet ambassador to China said he simply did not know who the leader was. The leadership was so collective at the time that the Chinese at first thought that Bulganin might be the top man because of his physical stature, his mannerisms, and the fact that he often spoke first at public meetings.[6]

Khrushchev sparked the crisis by attacking other members of the Presidium and violating the principles of collective leadership. His first target was Malenkov, who was removed from the premiership in 1955. In that position, Malenkov had been formidable: the chairmanship of the Council of Ministers was seen as the most important position in the country, as Lenin and Stalin had both held this title.[7] Malenkov clearly figured higher in the hierarchy than Khrushchev after Stalin's death.

Malenkov was defeated despite attempting what the economic model predicts: by acting as a conciliatory figure. The historian Elena Zubkova contrasts Malenkov as a "man of compromise" to the "impulsive and brusque Khrushchev."[8] Dmitrii Shepilov writes, "As chairman of the CC Presidium and the Council of Ministers, Malenkov did his best to run things in a fully democratic fashion. . . . In his own demeanor there was not a trace of pretentiousness. He did not try to stand out; his whole matter seemed to say, 'I have no edge over the rest of you. Let us reason together.'"[9] Andrei Sakharov recalls Malenkov handling meetings "smoothly, never once interrupting the speakers."[10] Malenkov told Mikoian, "Act freely in the development of trade, I will always support you."[11] Andrei Gromyko believed that Malenkov was the most capable individual in Stalin's circle.[12] Khrushchev's son thought that his father disliked how easily Malenkov agreed with people and obeyed their wishes.[13]

Malenkov carefully avoided signaling that he was trying to establish a new personality cult. After Stalin's funeral, he complained to two CC secretaries that *Pravda* had published his speech more prominently than those by Beria and Molotov. Malenkov also complained about a forged picture that placed him sitting between Stalin and Mao.[14] Malenkov explained, "We believe it is necessary to end the politics of the cult of personality!"[15] When Malenkov was described as the successor at the CC plenum after Beria's defeat, he stated that they were all successors to Stalin, not him alone.[16]

Malenkov was removed from the premiership in 1955 largely because his greater popularity was seen as a threat to his competitors in the Presidium. Among Malenkov's alleged crimes was his attempt to achieve "cheap popularity" in a speech to the fifth session of the Supreme Soviet in August 1953.[17] During this speech, Malenkov declared that the party would guarantee food and consumer goods for the population, force the development of light industry, and cut agricultural taxes. The speech was broadly admired, and peasants started calling overfull glasses of moonshine "malenkovskii."[18] At a private Presidium session on January 22, Saburov accused Malenkov of "succumbing to parliamentary popularity."[19] In a report to Belgrade, the Yugoslav ambassador wrote that Malenkov's "main weapon" was his popularity among the peasant masses.[20] Molotov later reminisced in a private conversation that Malenkov was at first selected as Stalin's successor because he was democratic and trusted by Stalin: "He was selected precisely because he was worthless. He was not capable of acting independently; he always had to rely on someone. We counted on this. He could take any post." Molotov regretted the fall of Malenkov: "I, of course, should not have rushed to criticize Malenkov. Beria was already gone. He already felt unsure anyhow. Khrushchev cleverly used this and in January 1955 suggested he be removed. I must admit, I helped him in this. Khrushchev tricked me."[21]

Although some policy differences existed between Khrushchev and Malenkov, as William Tompson points out, the "disagreements between them, though real, were limited."[22] Zubkova writes, "The cause of their conflict lies not in conceptual disagreements (of which there were none, even on the question of developing the Virgin Lands) but in personal competition, which Khrushchev initiated."[23] Although Khrushchev played up contradictions between the party and government to improve his position against Malenkov, Khrushchev was still "not shy of castigating party organisations for bureaucratic errors or rebuking party officials for personal mistakes," which undermined the ability to derive political capital from this differentiation.[24] To undermine Malenkov's popularity, his detractors resorted, unsurprisingly, to historical matters, in this case Malenkov's relationship with Beria.[25] Khrushchev probably conspired outside Moscow to determine Malenkov's fate before the showdown at the Presidium.[26]

Kaganovich later stated that Khrushchev behaved within the norms of collective leadership until mid-1955, after which he began to emphasize his own role.[27] Even Khrushchev's ally Ivan Serov writes in his memoirs about Khrushchev's increasingly domineering style in 1955: "However, at the meetings of the Presidium sometimes there were hot words particularly between Khrushchev and Molotov, Voroshilov, Kaganovich about a series of issues of an even nonprincipled nature. Khrushchev wants to solve one question or another faster and in his own way, and the others say, 'Don't hurry, let's deliberate, weigh [the issue] and then make a decision.' Some leading comrades, members of the Presidium, would more often appear at factories to speak publicly. This is good. But for some reason this displeased some people, especially Khrushchev."[28] A decision was even made that leaders had to get permission from the Presidium before giving speeches. Serov continues,

> I don't know about other people, but I do not like the relationships among the members of the [Presidium], especially Khrushchev's quarrelsome tone. With regard to all major issues discussed in the [Presidium], he expressed his own opinion, wants it to be solved in that way. And with regard to a series of issues V. M. Molotov opposes this, and I think, with good reason. Khrushchev gets angry and sometimes makes offensive remarks such as "Viacheslav, you truly do not understand agriculture." . . . I understand that Khrushchev wants to do everything faster, so that the people live better, as he says everywhere, but unfortunately this is not always successful in life; it is necessary to wait and test things in practice![29]

After Malenkov, Khrushchev's next target was Molotov—a somewhat surprising choice because Molotov originally sought a working relationship with Khrushchev. Molotov was one of the two Presidium members (along with Voroshilov) who had wanted Khrushchev, not Bulganin, to replace Malenkov as chairman of the Council of Ministers.[30] In other words, he wanted Khrushchev to assume the positions of *both* first secretary and prime minister—a clear sign he felt a cooperative relationship was possible.

Nonetheless, Khrushchev chose not to pursue cooperation. Instead, he engineered a plenum of the CC in June 1955 to criticize and politically weaken Molotov. Molotov later admitted that by the Twentieth Party Congress in February 1956, he had already been sidelined.[31] At a Presidium meeting on May 26, 1956, Khrushchev accused Molotov of being "an aristocrat who is used to bossing people around and not working" and suggested he be removed from his position as minister of foreign affairs.[32] Two days later, at another Presidium meeting, Molotov denied any wrongdoing: "I sincerely and honestly execute the decisions of the CC." Mikoian, Bulganin, Kaganovich, Shepilov, and Voroshilov argued that he should keep his post at least for a little longer. Yet Khrushchev carried the day.[33] By the end of 1955, Khrushchev had also humiliated Kaganovich by secretly developing a railways plan that he knew Kaganovich would oppose, even though transportation was Kaganovich's bailiwick.[34]

Despite Khrushchev's aggression, at first other members of the Presidium tried to work with him. At the June 1957 CC plenum, Brezhnev admitted that for a time after the Twentieth Party Congress, members of the anti-party group would shout, "That's correct, terrific!" even before Khrushchev finished expressing himself. Kaganovich approached Khrushchev and said, "I want to be friends with you, Nikita Sergeevich. And Molotov [does too]. We will support you in everything."[35]

Yet Khrushchev's continued striving for dominance changed their minds. Pervukhin told a colleague that Khrushchev reached decisions completely independently and made inappropriate remarks, paralyzing the government.[36] At the same plenum, Malenkov argued that the prime danger was not what person held the position of first secretary but the concentration of too much power in their hands, saying, "We had a tragic experience [of this] in the history of our party."[37] One of the anti-party group's goals was for Presidium members to take turns chairing meetings, instead of having the first secretary do so.[38]

The move against Khrushchev in June 1957 was defensive. On May 19, 1957, Khrushchev told a meeting of intellectuals, including many individuals who were not even members of the party, "To my great regret, Molotov's points of view did not always coincide with mine, and I regret this very much. Later they may condemn me for drinking a lot, but I do not want to invoke that I drank and, therefore, am saying this. I am fully conscious and take full responsibility for every word said by me." Khrushchev stated that the party would ultimately decide who was right and wrong.[39] Kaganovich remarks in his memoirs that "the attack of Khrushchev on Molotov, a member of the CC Presidium, among nonparty intelligentsia was quite an exceptional case and [implied] far-reaching goals. . . . If before this he could count on a majority in the Presidium of the CC, then after his attack on a member of the Presidium it can be said directly that a majority of members of the Presidium adopted more critical positions toward Khrushchev and his method of leadership."[40] Even Khrushchev's ally Mikoian identified the meeting with the intellectuals as a critical moment, and he criticized Khrushchev publicly for this act at the June 1957 CC plenum.[41] The exact date of the plot against Khrushchev was timed to prevent a joint trip to Leningrad, where the anti-party group was afraid Khrushchev would once again behave as he did in front of the writers.[42]

As Brezhnev's rough notes of the Presidium meeting before the CC plenum reveal, Khrushchev's detractors were primarily concerned about the collapse of collective leadership, not any particular policy issue. The record does note that Molotov mentioned that Khrushchev's foreign policy was not "Leninist," and Khrushchev defended himself against accusations that foreign policy had become "weaker." Kaganovich complained that Khrushchev wanted to move resources away from industrialization. But the concerns of Molotov and Kaganovich were first and foremost about Khrushchev's habit of rushing to decisions without careful deliberation, not so much the content of the policies. Crucially, they did not portray Khrushchev as representing a different party "line."

At the June 1957 CC plenum, Khrushchev's opponents characterized their position as a *rejection* of Stalin's cult of personality. Malenkov stated, "We are required to learn lessons from this tragic experience and not to allow it under any circumstances."[43] He complained about a decision to remove a tax on *kolkhozy* without a CC decision—even though there was widespread agreement. He asked why Khrushchev would reveal disagreements within the Presidium to the intellectuals, stating emphatically, "We have a cult." Molotov complained that Khrushchev was "not uniting us but splitting us apart."[44]

Significantly, even Khrushchev's key supporter Zhukov was concerned about his increasingly dictatorial tendencies. According to Shepilov, during the Presidium deliberations on whether to remove Khrushchev, Zhukov wrote a note to Bulganin that read, "I propose that we bring the discussion to an end. Issue a stern reprimand to Khrushchev for violating the principle of collective leadership, and leave everything as is for the time being, and look again at the situation later."[45] Zhukov admitted at the June 1957 CC plenum that during the Presidium meetings he had proposed that instead of a first secretary there be a secretary of general issues: a compromise that would have saved Khrushchev but limited his power.[46]

After Khrushchev defeated the leadership challenge, Serov and Zhukov agreed that "Khrushchev had a habit of commanding, and his main tragedy [is]: he loves to say 'I.'" Serov told Zhukov, "You are now a member of the Presidium, so influence [him] there." Zhukov grinned and said, "I will try."[47] At the October plenum in 1957 at which Zhukov was purged, the Presidium member Nikolai Ignatov stated, "Before the June plenum, at one stage you [Zhukov] were in favor of a different leadership in the party. You even suggested powerful measures such that the first secretary would not only be removed but that Com[rade] Khrushchev would be punished with a severe reprimand and a warning."[48]

The evidence presented in this section shows that Khrushchev's striving for dominance caused the move against him. Therefore, Khrushchev's victory despite his habit of attacking, not co-opting, potential allies casts doubt on the economic model. As Serov put it after the move against Khrushchev, "Generally speaking, for those of us close to the backstage affairs of the CC and Council of Ministers, all of this looked like a fight over first roles, a game of pride for some of them."[49]

Policy

Khrushchev's disregard for collective leadership instigated the move against him. But to what extent did real policy differences also motivate antagonism? The historian Nikolai Mitrokhin argues that Khrushchev formed a "clan" that "had a certain common view of how to solve tasks facing their sphere of activity" and that this faction allowed Khrushchev to defeat his opponents in 1957.[50] Yet, as early as 1988, Robert Service understood, despite limited sources, that the story of competing policy platforms was not fully persuasive: "Although the regime's collapse was not an immediate likelihood in 1953, the urgent need for reconstruction was recognized by most of the most influential members of the Soviet Presidium." Although Service suggests that "the precise position of Molotov and Kaganovich over the entire range of proposals for reform has not yet been investigated," he reasons, "Molotov and Kaganovich in any event evidently resisted innovation in general more than did other Presidium members. They were undoubtedly the greatest obstacles to de-Stalinization on most issues."[51] However, a closer look suggests that even Service's measured analysis overstates policy differences.

Molotov, in particular, deserves special attention—Khrushchev described him as the "ideological mastermind" of the anti-party group.[52] But did Molotov really have such significant differences of opinion with Khrushchev? The evidence in fact indicates that Molotov's practical differences with Khrushchev on the issues of foreign policy, economic reform, and even Stalin were extremely limited. Moreover, to the extent that differences existed, Khrushchev's positions were not necessarily more popular. Most of the individuals who moved against Khrushchev in 1957 aligned more with his policy preferences.

Molotov is often associated with conservative, hardline foreign-policy positions.[53] However, new evidence strongly contradicts this earlier viewpoint.[54] At the Geneva Conference in 1954, the former British foreign secretary Anthony Eden observed that Molotov "was genuinely anxious that the Conference should succeed."[55] Under Molotov's leadership, the Soviet Foreign Ministry drafted a document in January 1956 that acclaimed the steps taken by the socialist camp to ease international tensions, including improving relationships with Yugoslavia, Austria, Finland, and West Germany. The document stated that easing international tensions was "appropriate for the cause of building socialism and communism in our countries" and called for "attention to the task of improving relations of the socialist camp with certain capitalist powers."[56] In April 1956, speaking to the Chinese ambassador, Molotov said, "Every single one of our policies in politics, economics, culture, and society is intended to relax the tense international situation." He also praised the effects that unilateral cuts in military spending in the USSR were having on international affairs. Molotov even admitted that "currently, at the present moment there is no fatal inevitability of war" and the "main foreign policy task of the Soviet Union" was to delay war.[57]

In January 1956, Molotov supported the introduction of "peaceful coexistence" into the party platform at the Twentieth Party

Congress.[58] Khrushchev told the US ambassador in 1960 that "even with Molotov there had not been basic disagreement over his policies, particularly coexistence," but said, "Molotov carried the burden of his age and background in his thinking."[59]

On the specific foreign policy issues of Austria, Germany, and Yugoslavia, the economic model is extremely weak—Molotov's positions were displayed as the *opposite* of what he truly believed, and sometimes his caricatured position was the more popular. Using newly available documents, Geoffrey Roberts and Aleksei Filitov demonstrate that it is incorrect to see Khrushchev as the supporter of détente and Molotov as its opponent.[60] In fact, "it could be said that Khrushchev was in favor of a 'small détente,' while Molotov—a 'large one.'"[61]

Although Molotov was criticized for opposing a treaty with Austria, the documents show that as early as the summer of 1953 he was taking steps toward easing tensions between Moscow and Vienna.[62] Filitov notes that "the anti-Molotov dossier (and the historians who have cited it) left unmentioned that the foreign minister's cautionary (to put it mildly) approach to the Austrian settlement in 1953 and 1954 was the common position of the 'collective leadership' shared, among others, by Khrushchev as well. . . . In general, there is no evidence of a basic conflict or dissent in the Soviet ruling body in regard to the Austrian question during most of the first two years after Stalin's death."[63] The reason for the ultimate signing of the treaty had less to do with domestic Soviet politics than with changes in Austrian politics, but Molotov was blamed for the delay. When several years later Khrushchev told the visiting Richard Nixon that the US vice president was behaving as Molotov behaved during negotiations with Austria, Molotov wrote a letter to the CC in which he stated, "I believed and believe now that the treaty with Austria was concluded correctly and in a timely fashion. . . . At the time, I was opposed not to concluding the treaty with Austria but to rushing the matter."[64]

Molotov was accused at the June 1957 CC plenum by Foreign Minister Andrei Gromyko of opposing the decision to improve relations with West Germany. Molotov denied the accusations, claiming to have supported the decision.[65] And indeed, the evidence suggests that Molotov was anything but a hardliner on Germany.

Molotov was the first to develop "a far-reaching compromise solution of the German question after Stalin's death" and sought a non-confrontational relationship with NATO. Filitov concludes that in 1955, when Soviet policy became more hardline, the "real 'hawk' was Khrushchev. . . . As for Molotov, he seems to have doubted the prospects of this reorientation and continued to cherish some hopes for the 'grand détente.'"[66] Bizarrely, just like with the triumph of the treaty with Austria, improved relations with West Germany, which Molotov had strongly supported, became a weapon against him. According to Filitov, "In the situation of the growing struggle for power and influence in the Soviet party-state leadership the undeniable success of Soviet diplomacy in the achievement of normalization of relations between the USSR and FRG on conditions beneficial to the Soviet side paradoxically became a means for attack against the head [of Soviet diplomacy]—Molotov. This occurred at the 1957 June plenum of the CC CPSU. The history of the July 1955 plenum in connection with the evaluation of the genesis of the State Treaty with Austria happened again."[67]

In July 1955, Molotov was also severely criticized over foreign policy toward Yugoslavia at an important plenum meeting.[68] In 1962, in a series of speeches defending his behavior before June 1957, the issue of Yugoslavia was the one area where Molotov admitted to having a different point of view from the majority of the Presidium (possibly because Soviet-Yugoslav relations would deteriorate again later).[69]

Yet the differences between Molotov and the others on Yugoslavia were not necessarily fundamental. The transcript of the July 1955 plenum shows Molotov explaining, "we all want to improve relations between the Soviet Union and Yugoslavia," but disagreeing with the position of others in the leadership that previous poor relations should be blamed on Beria or that the foundation of the relationship should be based on the principles of Marxism-Leninism. Molotov believed improvement in relations could still happen based on other principles.[70] During his last speech at the plenum, Molotov denied having fundamentally different positions on any issue. He stated emphatically, "There was an attempt from certain comrades to present the matter in such a way that Molotov opposes this question, and others as well. It is true, comrades, that in practical work, with regard to individual issues we would oppose and make suggestions and some of them were incorrect, but I declared and declare: I have no special opinions on the decisions taken."[71]

Moreover, one historian of Soviet-Yugoslav relations points out that "it would be inappropriate to exclude the possibility that the goal of Khrushchev's activities was not normalizing relations with the Yugoslav leadership, but raising his own authority in the Soviet leadership."[72] Kaganovich writes in his memoirs that the Presidium did not support Molotov on the question of Yugoslavia but that "Khrushchev essentially went somewhat further and made it about the party line, thus violating the directives of the CC."[73] Therefore, although Molotov certainly had his own inclinations on Yugoslavia, the more important dynamic was Khrushchev's deliberate transformation of those differences from normal discussions among a collective leadership into a major debate.

If foreign policy was not particularly salient, what about political reform? Between March 1953 and February 1956, Khrushchev replaced forty-five of eighty-four first secretaries of republic-level and oblast'-level party committees directly under the purview of the CC.[74] Khrushchev took steps to gain the confidence of these leaders by expanding the authority of regional party committees over budgets and personnel.[75] These steps did contribute to Khrushchev's popularity within the CC, which does support the economic model. According to the editors of a collection of documents on Khrushchev's policies toward the regions, "It was precisely because of the support of regional secretaries who made up a significant part of the CC CPSU that Khrushchev was able to defeat the so-called 'anti-party group.'"[76] Molotov himself later said, "Khrushchev is no idiot—he was able to forge his own CC [*sumel skolotit' svoi TsK*]."[77] But how overwhelming was Khrushchev's popularity in the CC? A closer look at individual policy issues raises doubts.

We have reason to believe that industrial reform, which has been described as a key factor explaining support for Khrushchev in the CC, was not as much of a winning policy as later portrayed. Between December 1956 and early 1957, Khrushchev repeatedly pressed for increasingly ambitious industrial reforms.[78] Presidium members such as Pervukhin, Molotov, Voroshilov, and Saburov were skeptical and believed Khrushchev was unfairly going beyond the decisions made by the full CC on the matter.[79]

Crucially, members of the Presidium were not the only ones with doubts. Nuritdin Mukhitdinov, head of the Uzbek Party Committee, and Aleksandr Zasiad'ko, minister of the coal industry in Uzbekistan, both complained that the economic districts should not be based on territorial divisions. Aleksei Kosygin argued that the problem was not organization but poor planning, and the minister of heavy metallurgy cautioned that decentralization would damage national security.[80]

Another CC plenum was held in February 1957 that came closer to Khrushchev's prescriptions. Khrushchev had written another memorandum about the specifics of the reforms. At a Presidium meeting on March 22, the leadership expressed general support for that document.[81] However, on March 24, Molotov wrote a memorandum to the CC in which he described Khrushchev's proposals in stark terms: "The presented draft is clearly not finished; it suffers from one-sidedness and without significant changes can bring serious difficulties to the system of managing Soviet industry. The draft one-sidedly reflects the decision of the February CC plenum with regard to decentralization of the management of industry, bringing this decentralization to an intolerable extreme."[82]

Molotov's act is one of the few cases in the history of communist regimes when an individual deliberately revealed a different view from that of the top leader to the broader party membership (although Molotov did characterize his difference as tactical, not fundamental). Khrushchev swiftly submitted a memorandum to the Presidium on March 26 in response in which he complained that Molotov did not express his concerns at a Presidium meeting and instead revealed his concerns to the entire CC in his letter. Khrushchev wrote, "Therefore, Comrade Molotov's memorandum was caused not by business-like considerations but by some other kind. . . . I cannot agree with this form of presenting comments that Comrade Molotov selected."[83] At a Presidium meeting the next day, Bulganin, Pervukhin, and Malenkov complained that Molotov's memo threatened party unity.[84]

Why would Molotov take such a dramatic step? One possibility is that he believed Khrushchev's disregard for collective leadership and deliberate planning had gone too far. Even after *another* plenum that came closer to what Khrushchev wanted, Molotov was still arguing that Khrushchev was not proceeding according to the directives of the CC.

However, Molotov's decision also suggests that he did not believe his position would be entirely unwelcome in the CC. Why might this be the case? First, a significant number of CC members were leaders in Moscow, not the regions. The CC member Aleksei Kirichenko in his speech at the June 1957 plenum acknowledged that Molotov had reason to believe that a significant portion of the CC would have supported him over industrial reform: "They thought that in the membership of the CC there are many ministers, vice ministers, and CC candidate members [that] are being sent to the regional economic councils [*sovnarkhozy*]. They thought that these comrades were in agreement with the reorganization but not with their exit from Moscow."[85]

Second, the quick nature of the reforms led to concerns no matter whom they were intended to benefit.[86] Leningrad party activists, for example, bombarded the Presidium candidate member Frol Kozlov with demands for details, and enterprise directors and economists also raised concerns. Even Khrushchev supporters thought the reform plans were rushed.[87] Mikoian himself admitted at the June 1957 CC plenum that "some people believe that even if it is a correct measure, it was poorly executed."[88]

Third, the differences between Molotov and Khrushchev were not fundamental. At the Presidium meeting on March 27, 1957, Molotov claimed that he was operating within a broad consensus on the issue. He stated that Khrushchev misrepresented him and that he did not, in fact, disagree with the decisions of the February plenum. At the June 1957 CC plenum, when Molotov was accused of opposing the *sovnarkhozy*, he denied it: "I had corrections [*imel popravki*]."[89] Nataliya Kibita notes, "Ironically enough, the branch committees that Molotov talked about started appearing immediately after the regional economic councils took over production and construction."[90] Another historian argues that "the decentralizing effects were not as substantial as it might have seemed. The sovnarkhozy were still strictly subordinate to the Council of Ministers, and Gosplan's profile was raised sharply as it took over many of the planning duties formerly held by the ministries. This meant that planning was still largely centralized."[91]

Scholars have also often identified the contest between Khrushchev and Molotov as a battle over Stalin's legacy. Derek Watson's important biography of Molotov, for example, describes him as an "unrepentant Stalinist."[92] In this narrative, the defeat of the old guard was the result of a policy process in which the reformist Khrushchev emerged victorious. Polly Jones, a scholar who has worked extensively in the Russian archives, has concluded that "the collective leadership remained deeply divided over whether and why to proceed further with de-Stalinization."[93] In a recent biography of Khrushchev, Geoffrey Swain still describes Khrushchev as an individual "determined to confront Stalinism" in the form of his competitors on the Presidium.[94] As will be demonstrated shortly, some members of the leadership believed that a complete debunking of Stalin would be inappropriate. This idea of significant, meaningful political cleavages over one particular issue has clear similarities to the arguments in Hypothesis 1a.

However, the available evidence shows that this characterization should not be overstated. Rolling mass purges of the Stalin era had already ended, and everyone was united on the need to make sure they would never occur again.[95] As for other aspects of "Stalinism," as Miriam Dobson argues in her book on the Gulag and legal reforms, the Khrushchev era was not marked by a clear differentiation on the issue of Stalin: "Few—including political leaders—maintained an unambivalent attitude toward Stalinism, itself a complex and ill-defined entity: people might be enthusiastic about some changes but resentful of others."[96] The issue of de-Stalinization should be divided into several separate issues: rehabilitations, the evaluation of Stalin as a historical figure, and responsibility for crimes committed during his reign. On each of these issues, in contrast to Hypothesis 1a, we see either limited policy differences between Khrushchev and his opponents or, in some cases, his opponents actually being associated with a *more* popular policy.

Regarding the rehabilitation of figures who suffered during the Stalin era, the situation was hardly a showdown between "Stalinists" and "reformers." Molotov was not opposed to rehabilitations. Even before Khrushchev's "Secret Speech" to the Twentieth Party

Congress denouncing Stalin, the Presidium made a decision to create special committees to make decisions on individual cases for rehabilitation. Molotov said that the measures needed to be worked out (*vyrabotat' mery*) but also that the idea itself was basically correct (*pravil'no vneseno predlozhenie*).[97] In fact, Molotov was in charge of the high-level committee managing particularly sensitive rehabilitations.[98] In one case, he forwarded a letter to Khrushchev from a former editor of *Izvestiia* on a particular rehabilitation, implying that the matter should be discussed by the CC.[99]

If "Stalinists" were opposed to rehabilitations, it is difficult to explain the nearly one hundred special committees created for such a purpose and the 170,000 individuals whose cases were reviewed.[100] Members of the leadership were unified on crucial issues. They did not fight over the rehabilitation of such major figures as Chubar', Rudzutak, Kosior, Postyshev, Kaminskii, Gamarnik, or Eikhe, nor did they fight over giving the relatives of those who had died in the camps false information about the conditions and date of death so as to hide the true extent of the repressions. They also agreed on not rehabilitating Trotskyites, Socialist Revolutionaries, Mensheviks, or members of other parties.[101]

At the June 1957 plenum, Molotov noted that with regard to the work of the commission on rehabilitations, "it is necessary to keep in mind that the results of this work were signed by all members of this commission unanimously."[102] Serov notes in his memoirs that "the Molotov Commission established facts of lawlessness" and that even Molotov and Bulganin wanted to investigate the "Leningrad Affair"—a notorious incident that ended with the execution of the top Leningrad leadership by Stalin.[103] Khrushchev only accused Molotov of blocking the research of material related to Bukharin, Rykov, Zinov'ev, and Tomskii.[104] However, Khrushchev himself told Ol'ga Shatunovskaia, who was actively engaged in rehabilitation issues, that Bukharin and the others could not be rehabilitated for at least another fifteen years; otherwise it would discredit the party.[105] Khrushchev was off by a significant amount of time, as none of these men were rehabilitated until perestroika.[106]

Even if Molotov had been more skeptical about rehabilitations than Khrushchev, that position was not necessarily unpopular, as not everyone was certain the rehabilitation process should proceed too far. Serov was certainly skeptical of the rehabilitations.[107] Some party members feared that the Old Bolsheviks would steal their jobs.[108] As Stephen Cohen concludes, "Some officials were supportive, but many were not. They viewed former zeks 'with suspicion,' rehabilitation as 'something rotten,' and did not trust people with an 'unclean past.'"[109] Most striking, after the defeat of the anti-party group, the process of rehabilitation slowed down rather than sped up. After Molotov was removed from the committee on rehabilitation, that committee did not work for a long period of time and made no decisions.[110]

The debate over how to treat Stalin as a historical figure is also not nearly as clear-cut as traditionally portrayed. The move away from Stalin's cult began immediately after his death. As early as April 1953, Malenkov wanted to hold a special plenum to condemn "the propagation of the cult of personality" as foreign to Marxism and the principle of collective leadership.[111] Immediately after the purge of Beria, Molotov in a meeting with Italian communists "made it plain that the Presidium did not in fact regard Stalin in a totally favourable light. . . . Molotov also adduced evidence about Stalin's megalomania. . . . Molotov's picture gives us Stalin in his alleged dotage after the Second World War. . . . If only Stalin had hearkened to and worked alongside his other leading advisers, Molotov implies, then so much of the political and economic travail of the postwar epoch could have been avoided."[112] At the July 1953 plenum that accepted the defeat of Beria, Molotov indirectly criticized Stalin: "Beria found certain human weaknesses in I. V. Stalin, but who does not have them?"[113] No Stalin Prizes were ever again awarded. By November 1955, the Presidium was already discussing the creation of a Lenin Prize, and an edition of the *Great Soviet Encyclopedia* completed in July 1955 had nixed the entry for Stalin Prizes.[114]

Everyone agreed on the need for an admission of Stalin's mistakes. This step was needed for two reasons: to provide at least some justification for the ongoing rehabilitations and to prevent the issue from being forced on members of the leadership at a later date in a way they could not control.[115] A deluge of requests for clemency from arrested people led to the creation of an investigatory commission headed by Petr Pospelov. The original idea was to hold a special plenum of the CC to listen to Pospelov's report. In other words, the Presidium *as a whole* recognized that the question of the repressions had to be addressed.[116] At a Presidium meeting on November 5, 1955, that discussed how to commemorate the anniversary of Stalin's birth on December 21, Kaganovich and Voroshilov advocated holding assemblies at factories. However, when Bulganin and Mikoian resisted that proposal, Kaganovich emphasized that he supported the decision of the CC against the cult of personality: "There is no difference between you and me, Comrade Khrushchev. . . . I do not intend to battle against you."[117]

A Presidium meeting on February 1, 1956, began with a discussion of how during the Stalin era a former chekist named B. V. Rodos had been ordered to extract confessions from prominent party members. Molotov did not deny any mistakes but insisted that Stalin still be recognized as a great leader: "It is impossible not to say in the report that Stalin was a great heir to Lenin's cause. I insist on this as well." He admitted that the truth must be told, but he was also resolute that, under the leadership of Stalin, socialism was triumphant. Voroshilov also accepted that the "party must know the truth," but historical context must be emphasized so as not to "throw the baby out with the bathwater." Khrushchev agreed that the Terror would not be discussed at the upcoming Congress.[118]

At a meeting on February 9, everyone supported telling the Party Congress the "truth" about Stalin. The only difference was that some believed these truths included Stalin's triumphs as well. Kaganovich and Voroshilov thought Khrushchev should give a report on Stalin but agreed with Molotov that it was necessary to proceed carefully. Bulganin explained what many must have been thinking: "If we do not speak at this Congress, they will say that we were cowards." Shepilov concurred: "We must tell the party; otherwise they will not forgive us." Khrushchev ended the meeting by stating explicitly, "There are no disputes over whether the Congress should be told. The debate was only over shades of meaning." Therefore, although Molotov, Kaganovich, and Voroshilov did not want Stalin to be entirely debunked, they still recognized the need to give some explanation of the Terror.[119] Even Kaganovich and Molotov spoke out against the cult of personality at the Twentieth Party Congress. Molotov stated that the CC "strongly spoke out against the cult of personality that is foreign to Marxism-Leninism, which played in a certain period such a negative role." As the plenum applauded, Molotov expressed certainty that "this Congress will completely approve this principled position."[120]

At the June 1957 CC plenum, Kaganovich said, "I believe it was correct that we revealed and exposed this matter [regarding Khrushchev's Secret Speech]."[121] Even Molotov remarked that "along with successes certain deficiencies in Stalin grew more powerful, the very dangerous and damaging ones, of which we speak now all in unity."[122] He stated, "We, comrades, remember that at the Twentieth Party Congress we completely legally, correctly, strongly, bravely revealed those mistakes and perversions of revolutionary legality that were committed in the period of Stalin's leadership."[123]

Despite this general agreement, Molotov certainly believed that Khrushchev was using de-Stalinization as a weapon. According to a document in Molotov's personal files, he believed that the issue was not so much Stalin per se but the way Khrushchev was using the issue:

> The political intent of this "anti-Stalin" campaign that would often get to the point of outright libel against the party was not so simple. The matter is not a certain person's mistakes or some personal negative characteristics. No one interfered with and can interfere with correcting and removing mistakes in a way that observes the interests of the party and does not do a service to the imperialists and all their echoers [*podgoloskam*] to help them increase persecution of our party and Soviet state enhanced by the damaging speech Khrushchev gave to the Twentieth Party Congress. Khrushchev's political goal and that of his more vehement supporters was primarily to blacken the party leadership of the 1930s.[124]

In other words, Molotov was claiming that he did not oppose the *policy* of de-Stalinization; instead, he opposed the use of de-Stalinization as a *weapon*. Later, when he was faced with expulsion from the party in 1962, Molotov emphasized in speeches that the killings had indeed gone too far; that he had played a role in reversing the mistakes even in the 1930s; that he never praised Stalin as a genius, as Khrushchev, Mikoian, Kalinin, and others did; that even his wife had suffered at the hands of Stalin; that Stalin would probably have killed him if the Soviet leader lived longer; and that Khrushchev also would have known about the killings. He also repeatedly affirmed, "I not only did not differ from the CC in the evaluation of the events of Stalin's cult of personality but participated in the adoption and working out of those decisions in complete agreement with other members of the CC."[125] That same year, and for the same purpose, Kaganovich said, "I believe that I actively participated in the exposure of the personality cult, and not only me but the whole bureau, the whole Presidium."[126]

If Khrushchev's intent was to damage the political position of Stalin's former henchmen such as Molotov and Kaganovich, then his plan clearly failed: neither rehabilitations nor the evaluation of Stalin were at first a clear winning strategy. Khrushchev became even less popular as the full implications of the Secret Speech for social stability became apparent, and over time he moved toward a more balanced appraisal of Stalin.

Mukhitdinov writes that although in Uzbekistan everyone was generally in support of rehabilitating those innocent individuals who suffered during the repressions, "with regard to Stalin himself, his personal responsibility for the committed lawlessness and serious mistakes at the beginning of the war, in several other areas, our position somewhat differed."[127] The majority of workers at the journal *Kommunist* reacted to Khrushchev's criticisms of Stalin negatively, as Stalin was associated with too many achievements and the entirety of ideological life.[128] The Yugoslav ambassador writes in his memoirs that "in various circles Soviet citizens prefer the Chinese statement [which had a more positive evaluation of Stalin] to Khrushchev's speech. They say that the Chinese are objective, tactful, balanced, truthful, and wise—which cannot be said about Khrushchev."[129] Aleksandr Iakovlev, who would later be a top adviser to Gorbachev, believed that "the overwhelming majority of the bureaucracy of the CC apparat reacted to Khrushchev's report negatively."[130]

According to a Ministry of Defense report on discussions of Khrushchev's speech in the Moscow MR, officers made comments such as, "Why did they publish this?" "After this report you don't know whom to trust," and "I will not be surprised if tomorrow a different document is published by the CC CPSU that takes a completely different position than the report 'On the Cult of Personality and Its Consequences.'"[131] One military officer, named V. M. Malkin, remarks in his private diary about a Chinese delegation's respect at Lenin and Stalin's mausoleum in January 1957, "What is this: the Chinese have corrected us? It very much looks like that. I am in complete agreement with the Chinese."[132]

Members of the top leadership acknowledged to foreigners that Khrushchev was losing popularity to his competitors. Bulganin told the Yugoslav ambassador that protesters in Moscow and Georgia wanted Molotov to become head of the government, which the ambassador interpreted as a subtle hint to a dispute within the leadership. According to the Yugoslav ambassador, "To judge by a 'poll' we have taken, the people here still prefer people like Molotov and Malenkov."[133] Khrushchev also told a delegation of Italian communists that the Georgians shouted, "Down with Khrushchev, Mikoian, and Bulganin" and "Form a government by Molotov."[134]

By the time of the June 1957 CC plenum, Khrushchev had spent a great deal of effort making it seem as if he had no differences on Stalin with other members of the leadership. As early as April 1956, the CC distributed a letter to the party that restricted discussion of the Secret Speech. A crucial June 29 CC document took an official position on Stalin that was much more positive than in Khrushchev's speech. The document pointed to the "objective concrete historical conditions" in which Stalin's actions took place and explained why other members of the Politburo were not able to stop the repressions, thus absolving them of any responsibility: "Why did these people not openly oppose Stalin and remove him from the leadership? In those conditions this was impossible. Without a doubt [*bezuslovno*]." If they had spoken out against Stalin, they "would not have received support among the people." Moreover, his worst crimes were allegedly not discovered until after the defeat of Beria.[135]

Meanwhile, Khrushchev was changing his own tone. On May 1, he gave a speech at a reception in which he said no differences on Stalin existed within the leadership. Khrushchev said to Voroshilov, "Stalin was a man of genius, but his tyranny covered his genius. He ignored the party, ignored the Central Committee. Isn't that the case?" Voroshilov agreed. Khrushchev noted that Stalin had turned against members of the leadership who might have been seen as the most inveterate "Stalinists." Khrushchev said, "Stalin did not trust Bukharin, Kaganovich, Molotov, and Mikoian, these true Bolsheviks. . . . I often disagree with Molotov, but I respect him; I believe he is a pure, outstanding communist."[136]

On December 19, the Presidium approved the draft of a letter to be sent in the name of the CC to all party organizations on ending attacks by anti-Soviet and enemy elements. The letter took an extremely hard line and ended hopes that the Secret Speech signified the start of a new era.[137] At the Presidium meeting that decided to release the document, Khrushchev even stated that "regarding those freed from jails and exile—some of them are not deserving."[138] On New Year's Eve, Khrushchev gave a speech at a reception in which he said, "Stalinism is Marxism," and expressed "pride" that "we are all Stalinists."[139]

Khrushchev also backed down from a planned CC plenum on ideological issues that would have affirmed a negative appraisal of Stalin at the Congress. On April 5, the Presidium decided to hold the plenum on June 4 and that Shepilov would give the main speech. On May 18, the date shifted to June 7. On May 19, Zhukov submitted a draft speech for this plenum. He was emphatic: "some comrades" who did not believe that it was appropriate to further investigate the problem of the cult were wrong. Zhukov lambasted Stalin for his assault on the military leadership in 1937–39, lack of preparation for the Nazi attack, poor understanding of military principles, and suspicious attitude during and after the war toward members of the military who had been taken prisoner. Significantly, Stalin was not Zhukov's only target. The marshal attacked both Stalin *and* Molotov for ignoring the warnings about the Nazis' intentions: "Did Stalin and Chairman of the Council of People's Commissars V. M. Molotov know about the concentration of Hitler's troops on our borders?—Yes they knew." Zhukov even included in his speech a document he had submitted to Molotov on April 11, 1941, about German border violations, which Zhukov said was ignored. On May 23, Shepilov submitted his own speech, which acknowledged that Stalin was a "great proletarian revolutionary" and primarily addressed Stalin's mistakes, including the repressions, from an ideological point of view. On May 25, the Presidium again shifted the date, to June 6. On June 1, the plenum was moved to fall. On August 31, the date was delayed to December, and, instead of Shepilov, Khrushchev was given the role of main presenter. Two Khrushchev draft speeches, dated December 1956 and January 1957 and prepared by Pospelov, drew on the more measured Shepilov text, but ultimately Khrushchev's speech was not finalized because the plenum on ideological issues was never held and the plenum held in December ignored Stalin.[140]

In January 1957, Khrushchev gave a speech at the Chinese embassy in which he described Stalin as a man who devoted his whole life to the victory of the working class and socialism. Khrushchev said, "Recently in the West they have been accusing us of being 'Stalinists,' 'Stalin followers.' In response to this, on multiple occasions we declared that in our understanding 'Stalinist,' like Stalin himself, is inseparable from the great title of communist." Khrushchev went on to express a hope that every communist could struggle (*borot'sia*) like Stalin.[141] The Yugoslav ambassador noted that the crowd was surprised to hear this and that his comments "evoked a storm of applause." He believed that Khrushchev did this to save his own skin: "The extent to which he then felt he was going to lose his position in the Presidium can be judged from the way he made himself out in public to be a greater Stalinist than Molotov and Malenkov."[142]

Khrushchev publicly continued to play the pro-Stalin card. He referenced his speech at the Chinese embassy explicitly at the February CC plenum, the last before the anti-party-group incident, to emphasize the nonexistence of any policy splits in the leadership:

[The Yugoslavs] also divide us into Stalinists and non-Stalinists. We answered. They write that Khrushchev in his speech at the reception at the Chinese embassy made a step backward from the decisions of the Twentieth Party Congress. I spoke of Stalin there. I think that it should have been said in the sense I said it and it was said this way. . . . But at the same time we do not deny what we created with Stalin and the results of what was contributed by our party, our people, what resulted in having such a wonderful country that the Soviet Union is.[143]

Khrushchev went so far in this direction that at a meeting of the party *aktiv* in the Ministry of Defense and Moscow garrison following the June 1957 plenum, Marshal Moskalenko stated, "Kaganovich, Malenkov, and Molotov accused Khrushchev of spitting on Stalin, that he spoke only of his deficiencies. We all loved Stalin, and while Khrushchev did speak poorly of him on multiple times, he also emphasized his contributions to the people and the party."[144] To say that Khrushchev defeated "Stalinists," therefore, fails to acknowledge the extent to which Khrushchev had backtracked from his Secret Speech to the Twentieth Party Congress.

Significantly, the anti-party group came together despite a lack of similar policy positions. Bulganin pointed out that he had always suffered troubled relations with Molotov, Kaganovich, and Malenkov. Pervukhin remarked that he had no differences of principle with either foreign-policy or domestic-policy issues. Voroshilov emphasized, "Neither I nor the majority of the so-called faction had any differences with the line of the party with regard to foreign or domestic issues; we were always united. Why attribute that which is not true?" Even Molotov affirmed, "Suslov spoke incorrectly that I have a different understanding of the policies of our party." Molotov tried to explain to the party that "there is no political platform, and without a political platform . . . there is no faction." Molotov was clearly frustrated: "It is not true; I was not opposed to the Virgin Lands. Com[rade] Khrushchev framed me for so many incorrect things." Molotov repeatedly emphasized, "I affirm that in this case [Yugoslavia] as well as in a series of other occasions things were attributed to me that I did not say." Mikoian tried to square this circle by arguing that removing Khrushchev from the leadership had to affect policy. However, even he could go only so far, lamely arguing that "it is obvious there is a group working behind the back of the CC, and it has *elements* of a platform; there is no platform yet, but all the elements of a platform are there."[145]

Historical Legacies and Compromising Material

A crucial reason for why the anti-party group felt capable of opposing Khrushchev's behavior was its members' personal prestige. The threat that this prestige posed for Khrushchev supports Hypothesis 1b. The evidence demonstrates that Khrushchev was concerned about his enemies' status as legendary revolutionary leaders and their alleged understanding of Marxism, not their political positions. Khrushchev tried to undermine Molotov in three ways: by dismantling his right to judge what was "Leninist," by portraying him as old and out of touch, and, most importantly, by relying heavily on Zhukov's prestige as a World War II hero and the skillful use of compromising material.

Molotov himself understood authority not in terms of policy popularity: "It goes without saying that leaders are not born, that authority and the influence of leaders on the masses are not acquired and do not appear immediately—they are produced in the course of a prolonged period of time, they are produced as the result of the gradual *internal persuasion* of people that a certain individual figure 'understands events deeper and sees them deeper than others,' that he conducts policies that answer their common interests."[146] As Sheila Fitzpatrick writes, letters to *Pravda* and the CC reveal that people were "uneasy at this summary dismissal of Old Bolsheviks with many services to their country": "I was particularly interested to see what a strong following Molotov had in 1953–1954, particularly but not solely, among party members, making his acceptance of collective leadership and failure to bid for the top job all the more striking. Equally striking is Khrushchev's *lack* of popularity."[147]

Molotov had the greatest prestige of any high-ranking Soviet leader. Khrushchev said, "We, the people of the prewar era, had previously regarded Molotov as the future leader of the country," before Stalin turned on Molotov after World War II.[148] In 1952, Mikoian told Stalin that he thought Molotov should be the successor.[149] After his removal, Shepilov once told an interviewer, "Among the people it was like this: if not Stalin, then who? Of course, Molotov."[150] Gromyko also believed that Molotov was the most qualified individual to lead the Soviet Union after Stalin's death, even telling his daughter, "I think that if instead of Khrushchev it was Molotov, the development of the country might have proceeded in a more balanced way."[151]

Other members of the leadership were given an opening by Stalin's decision not to include Molotov in the Presidium Bureau formed in 1952. Molotov later complained that because of this action, his "authority and influence were undermined."[152] Yet Molotov remained a serious force. Even while opposing Molotov's attempt to remove Khrushchev from power in 1957, Mukhitdinov, then a candidate member of the Presidium, stated, "Viacheslav Mikhailovich, we all respect you, you have great achievements, high authority. . . . You are the oldest member of the party, you were a member of the Politburo while Lenin was alive, you worked with him; since that time [you have been] at the highest level of the party and government. . . . Even as a schoolchild, with happiness I carried your portrait at demonstrations. I was proud to do so in front of the other boys."[153] The editor in chief of *Izvestiia* told John F. Kennedy in 1962, "Mr. Khrushchev was of the opinion that if a plebiscite had been taken in 1957, Molotov would have obtained 95 percent of the votes and he only 5 percent."[154]

Molotov, Kaganovich, and Voroshilov all had significant prestige as old revolutionary figures. As one party member asked at a lower-level meeting following the failure of the anti-party group, "Who can believe that Old Bolsheviks who have been in the government for forty years have become enemies of the people, enemies of the party that they had created together with Lenin? Who will believe that Molotov, Kaganovich, Malenkov, Bulganin, Shepilov, Pervukhin, Saburov, Voroshilov—all of them were wrong, but Khrushchev was right with regard to everything, along with Furtseva?"[155] Leaflets declared, "Comrades, it is unbelievable that such experienced, forged Bolsheviks as Malenkov, Molotov, Kaganovich, and Shepilov, who even worked with Lenin, could really organize an anti-party group."[156] The archival file containing records on local party meetings after the plenum is full of questions about why Khrushchev was trustworthy but Molotov was not: "How could Molotov oppose Leninism if he himself created the party with Lenin?"[157] Some party members even accused Khrushchev of creating his own cult of personality.[158]

Generational issues arose repeatedly at the June 1957 CC plenum. Voroshilov poked a member of the CC delegation sent to interrupt the Presidium proceedings and said, "Is it you, little boy, whom we should give explanations to? First learn how to wear long pants."[159] Voroshilov tried to defend himself: "The situation is unprecedented, and you are young people." When the hall erupted, he said, "Wait, wait. You are young people; you have not yet happened to experience such things. Life is a very complicated and long thing; you will have to fight every type of struggle."[160] One CC member complained that Voroshilov treated them like Pioneers (essentially, Soviet Boy Scouts).[161] When Molotov at the plenum described the CC as the "leading political center," a CC member countered, "As for us, we have been doing party work for twenty years, and you see us wearing short pants. Why do you treat us contemptuously?"[162] One CC member joked that the old guard still saw the CC members as "youth" even though they already had grandchildren: "We are not afraid. We are not who we used to be."[163] Gromyko said that it was not the fault of his generation that they were fifteen years younger than members of the anti-party group; rather, it was "more the fault of [their] mothers and fathers."[164]

Khrushchev clearly played up these antagonisms. One CC member reported Khrushchev saying, "Our old revolutionary cadres have much revolutionary pathos, but they understand concrete life poorly; they do not know those cadres, the backbone of the party, who now organize the execution of the party's directives and have borne all the difficulties of the previous period on their own shoulders, and some think that these people walk around as before, in undershorts."[165] Khrushchev refused to allow Molotov the moral high ground with respect to seniority: "Now Molotov depicts the matter as if he was the only one defending the interests of the Old Bolsheviks. Molotov is one of the culprits in the annihilation of many thousands of old revolutionaries."[166]

Revealingly, the first public undermining of Molotov's authority within Soviet society centered on the issue of ideology-as-authority, as opposed to ideology-as-policy.[167] In February 1955, Molotov said that in the Soviet Union, "the foundations of socialist society are already built." However, in September of that year, *Kommunist* published a letter by Molotov in which he apologized for this "fallacious formulation": "I consider my formulation . . . to be theoretically erroneous and politically harmful." Molotov's viewpoint was depicted in *Pravda* and *Kommunist* as a way of thinking consigned "to a stage passed long ago." Technically, Molotov was right, but, more importantly, the debate had no practical implications whatsoever. As Samuel Kucherov perceived at the time, Molotov's public reversal was "aimed at something other than the correction of an alleged ideological blunder."[168]

Khrushchev manipulated Zhukov's historical antagonisms toward Stalin and his former comrades.[169] In Khrushchev's Secret Speech to the Twentieth Party Congress, in the section in which he criticized Stalin as a military leader (which Khrushchev personally wrote), he stated, "As a result of Stalin's suspiciousness, by slanderous accusations, a high number of army commanders and political workers were annihilated," which "naturally had an effect on the beginning of the war."[170] At the very first Presidium meeting that discussed taking a more serious line against Stalin's cult of personality, Khrushchev emphasized the death of officers: "Cadres were killed. The military ones" (*Kadry perebili. Voennye*).[171] At the Presidium meeting on March 27, 1957, when Khrushchev clashed with Molotov on industrial reform, he made the following remarks: "Molotov has completely lost touch with reality. About the Virgin [Lands policy] he does not agree, about foreign policy he does not agree, about this [issue] he does not agree. At the plenum he did not speak, but most likely he was against it even then. Now he proposes a commission—in order to delay. He hurried during collectivization; *he hurried when the generals were repressed.*"[172]

At the Presidium meeting on April 25, the political bickering continued to heat up. The Presidium decided to posthumously reinstate into the party the Soviet officers Iakir, Tukhachevskii, and Uborevich, who had been killed during the height of the Great Terror. Khrushchev did not let the opportunity to take a swing at his competitors go to waste, saying, "Let the old members of the Politburo say how they solved the problem of bringing Iakir to justice, how this first step was prepared." Kaganovich tried to defend himself: "The matter was like this: the report was made, we made decisions." This was not enough for Zhukov: "We must get clarity with regard to this question."[173] At the same meeting, Khrushchev called for the rehabilitation of a factory manager involved in the production of tanks: "In this matter my friend Georgii Malenkov played an unseemly role. Rubinchik is a victim of palace intrigue."[174]

Brezhnev probably referred to this meeting when he stated the following at the plenum: "At one of the last meetings Com[rade] Khrushchev expressed this idea: 'Look, comrades, we are reviewing materials; we are posthumously rehabilitating executed communists who were innocent. How should we treat the culprits of these shootings; will we return to this issue, or will we continue to be silent about this before the party?' "[175]

The use of compromising material, especially in the hands of Zhukov, ultimately played a crucial role in the counterattack on the anti-party group.[176] In the words of Shepilov, "Zhukov supported Khrushchev. And this decided the fate of Molotov's group."[177] When Khrushchev was finally confronted, Zhukov was the first to speak against Khrushchev's opponents and declared them responsible for the worst crimes of the Stalin era.[178] When the Presidium refused to accept Khrushchev's proposal for a plenum, deciding instead that Khrushchev should first be removed from his position as first secretary, Zhukov later described his behavior thus: "I saw an exit from the situation only in decisive actions. I stated: 'I categorically insist on immediately summoning a CC plenum. The issue is much broader than the group suggests. I want to put before the plenum the issue of Molotov, Kaganovich, Voroshilov, and Malenkov. I have in my hands material on their bloody atrocities with Stalin in 1937–1938, and they have no place in the CC Presidium and even in the CC CPSU.'"[179]

Averkii Aristov, a CC secretary, at the plenum confirmed that after the anti-party group's criticisms of Khrushchev, Zhukov counterattacked using compromising material.[180] At the July 2 meeting of the Ministry of Defense apparat and Moscow garrison, Zhukov frankly admitted that he saved Khrushchev: "In order to win time, to more deeply figure out their thoughts and intentions, to attempt to split the group, which was joined by Saburov (7–4), a supplementary question was raised by me with regard to the responsibility of Malenkov, Kaganovich and Molotov for the abuse of power."[181]

At the CC plenum, Zhukov began by describing the last Presidium meetings and accusing Khrushchev's opponents of exploiting deficiencies in the party's leadership to destroy unity. But then he changed the tone of the debate entirely. Later, Marshal Meretskov told the Ministry of Defense and Moscow garrison that "the direction of the debate in actuality was determined by Comrade Zhukov. He directly raised the question that people in the past committed crimes, and now they want to cause a split and seize power."[182]

Zhukov noted that at the Twentieth Party Congress, Khrushchev had spoken of the mass repressions and shootings but did not name Malenkov, Kaganovich, or Molotov as "the main culprits of the arrests and shootings of party and Soviet cadres." He questioned why these "comrades" did not admit their guilt when the new CC was selected, postulating that if they had done so, they would not have been elected to the next Presidium. He claimed that they had not committed crimes under pressure from Stalin but "of their own initiative." Zhukov then quoted specific documents and accused Molotov and Kaganovich of giving permission to execute 38,679 individuals. According to one former chekist, these documents were provided to Khrushchev by the head of the KGB, Serov, who also destroyed those documents that would have compromised Khrushchev. For Zhukov, Malenkov was even guiltier than Kaganovich or Molotov, as his party task had been to manage the NKVD. Zhukov told the plenum that Bulganin showed him documents from Malenkov's private safe. These documents were fifty-eight volumes of conversations among individuals such as Budennyi, Timoshenko, Zhukov, Konev, and Voroshilov: all marshals of the Soviet Army. Zhukov concluded, "And this material was preserved in his personal safe and was taken out incidentally, when the MVD needed to arrest his personal secretary." He proposed that the plenum demand explanations from Malenkov, Kaganovich, and Molotov. Zhukov was followed by the head of the MVD, Nikolai Dudorov, who continued the attack with even more compromising material. Malenkov spoke next, wryly beginning his speech by remarking, "Comrades Dudorov and Zhukov, having done quite a bit of preparation, apparently, and spent a long period of time collecting documents, have informed the CC plenum of facts with regard to different periods of my career." While Malenkov tried to defend himself, Zhukov interrupted him repeatedly. Twice Zhukov asked him why he did not report to the Presidium about the documents that included compromising material on the marshals. When Malenkov said, "I absolutely at no time had any relation to the organization of surveillance over marshals, eavesdropping on anyone, as I myself was eavesdropped upon," Zhukov stated flatly, "That is untrue." Khrushchev jumped into the fray and criticized Malenkov for portraying himself as suffering from surveillance just like Marshals Zhukov and Timoshenko.[183]

When Kaganovich began listing examples of Khrushchev violating the principles of collective leadership, Zhukov tried to change the subject: "Let's talk about responsibility for the crimes, the shootings."[184] After Zhukov told Kaganovich that he should be held for criminal charges, Kaganovich started to remind the audience that he was not the only one with blood on his hands, asking Khrushchev, "And did you really not sign papers on shooting in Ukraine?"[185]

Khrushchev and his supporters took their cue from Zhukov and played up fears that the anti-party group would return to the Terror. They could now portray the move against Khrushchev as an attempt to avoid responsibility for the killings. Khrushchev said, "You wanted to form a group; there was a plot. You wanted to remove [me] in order to get the material you need and destroy evidence of crimes."[186] Mikoian stated that during the Presidium meetings, Molotov accused Khrushchev of falling into a "rightist deviation": "This is simply a dogmatic, scholastic comparison and an attempt to find an offensive label to compromise members of the Presidium." Mikoian raised the possibility that Molotov "wanted to return to a number of Stalin's bad methods."[187] Brezhnev stated that the "seizure of power by these conspirators would inevitably regenerate those fanatical methods toward cadres of the party and state that they used a while ago": "We did not forget and will not forget that massive repressions, shootings took place at your dirty hands."[188]

Despite the clear complicity of members of the anti-party group in some of the greatest political crimes of the twentieth century, the use of compromising material against them was part of a dirty political game. Serov claimed to have been told by the head of the General Department, Vladimir Malin, that documents proving Khrushchev's role in the Terror had been destroyed. Serov pointed out that everyone wanted to use compromising material against each other, but only Khrushchev personally controlled the KGB, MVD, and procuracy.[189] Everyone was complicit, but at the same time, everyone had been dominated by Stalin. Kaganovich remarked, "Com[rade] Zhukov dragged out the names of only two or three that signed the documents, and he does not mention others—this is a factionalist maneuver. Here is where the factionalism is."[190]

Yet the tactic was used to devastating effect. In a letter to the CC written in the mid-1960s, Molotov acknowledged the power of such charges when they were again made at the Twenty-Second Party Congress: "In my opinion, this is nothing other than an attempt to scare the delegates of the Congress. And I affirm that this attempt was successful to a certain degree, as, indeed, during the time of the so-called cult of personality of Stalin there were relatively widespread facts of arbitrariness and lawlessness."[191]

Hypothesis 2a versus 2b

The Deliberations

The inability of the anti-party group to present the CC with a fait accompli was the crucial failure that allowed Khrushchev to emerge triumphant. Before the CC finally convened, Khrushchev carefully ensured that the plenum would not conduct a serious, open discussion of what had happened in the Presidium. Instead, the plenums were conducted more like mass criticism sessions than deliberations.

For many high-ranking figures, their calculus was not so much which group they thought was right but instead who had the initiative. Khrushchev later told Fidel Castro, "I trust [Mikoian] least of all. He's a shrewd fox from the east; you can't count on him. In both 1953, when we arrested Beria, and in 1957 with the 'anti-party group,' I was more nervous about Mikoian's position than anyone else's."[192] Serov writes in his memoirs that "some members of the CC were waiting to see which way the wind was blowing and did not sign [the letter demanding a plenum session]." After the incident, Zhukov and Serov would remark many times on the "confusion of certain members of the Presidium in those days and the two-faced nature of many members of the CC who would say neither yes nor no."[193]

By the time the CC plenum finally began, the fate of the anti-party group had been sealed. Zhukov was so aggressive during Molotov's speech that the latter labeled the marshal's words a threat that violated party rules.[194] The transcripts show that CC members regularly yelled or made other disruptive noises when members of the anti-party group tried to defend themselves. At one point, the transcript ceases to provide a verbatim account of what was said and instead describes what happened: "Voroshilov very explosively reacts to the expression 'anti-party group'; in the midst of a continuous noise in the hall, he says something; only the following words are intelligible: this is an abomination, fiction, there is no anti-party group. He addresses Khrushchev: Why are you silent? You are the chair; say that there is no group!" Khrushchev replied, "Kliment Efremovich, it turns out that you are a temperamental person; you accused me of my temper, and now you are no better than me in this regard."[195]

The Decision-Making Body

If the Presidium had the final say, Khrushchev would have lost. A clear majority on that body had decided that they needed to rein in Khrushchev. If a delegation from the CC had not suddenly appeared and demanded a full session, Khrushchev would have been finished. The game was not about fighting for support within a defined group but achieving an interpretation of the rules that empowered one body and not another.

Khrushchev's opponents on the Presidium were clearly a majority. As Malenkov put it, "The group consists of seven members of the Presidium—it is necessary to consider this."[196] However, Mikoian discounted the idea that the matter was a simple vote. Contrary to the economic model, Mikoian stated, "They were in a big hurry; they got carried away with arithmetics [meaning the Presidium majority]. We made a warning: do not get carried away with arithmetics. However, voices rang out that arithmetics is no small matter in politics."[197] In his memoirs, he acknowledges, "The whole matter was about which way the CC plenum would be informed: as a decision already made by the Presidium or as a dispute in the Presidium. In the former case [Khrushchev]'s song would have been sung. The plenum would have, without a doubt, approved the decision: the Stalinist traditions were strong even long after his death."[198]

The Presidium deliberations were interrupted by a group of fifteen to twenty CC members who demanded to join the meeting. They were repeatedly denied entry. Then Serov suggested to Konev, "Let's the two of us go in without invitation."[199] According to Mukhitdinov, once inside, Serov complained that for the last three days the CC had not been informed about what was going on: "Not one issue falling into the competency of the plenum [CC] should be decided here. We will not leave without a clear answer!"[200]

Legitimacy of Behavior

Although formally the CC was a more authoritative institution than the Presidium, the idea that the CC could actually override the Presidium was revolutionary. Kaganovich writes that "several members of the Presidium furiously reacted to this act of summoning members of the CC to Moscow without the permission of the CC Presidium as an act of usurpation on the part of the CC secretariat and, of course, Khrushchev himself." Saburov allegedly screamed, "I thought, Comrade Khrushchev, that you were as honest a man as ever lived. Now I see that I was mistaken—you are a dishonest person, allowing yourself to act divisively [*po-fraktsionnomu*], behind the back of the CC Presidium organizing this meeting in Sverdlov Hall."[201]

According to Ivan Serov, even Khrushchev was unsure about the legality of the plenum option. Serov writes in his memoirs of his response to Khrushchev telling him that the plotters wanted to remove him as well: "I answered: 'No matter what they want, but given such quarrels in the CC Presidium, I will not surrender the KGB to anyone without the permission of a CC plenum.' Zhukov says: 'That's right, Ivan, I also will not give up the Ministry of Defense.' Khrushchev said to this: '*The Presidium has the right to make such a decision.*' I answered: 'Well, it's better to let the CC plenum decide.'"[202]

Hypothesis 3a versus 3b

Views of Power Ministries

Hypothesis 3a predicts that the positions of the military and KGB would not have a decisive impact on the power struggle. However, we see more support for Hypothesis 3b: both sides fought especially hard for the support of Zhukov and Serov, and their support of Khrushchev had a decisive influence.

Shortly before the showdown at the Presidium, Zhukov attended the wedding of Khrushchev's son, which Molotov, Malenkov, Kaganovich, and Bulganin demonstratively left together to go to Malenkov's dacha. Kirichenko, a Khrushchev supporter, then approached Zhukov and said, "We are counting on you. You have tremendous authority in the army; with one word the army will do everything that is needed." Zhukov felt that "Kirichenko did not say these words incidentally, that it was not his idea."[203] When the Presidium meetings began, Zhukov was attending a military exercise. When he finally arrived at the Kremlin, Brezhnev said to him, "Whose side are you on; are you on their side or not? The decision will be based on this."[204]

The anti-party group also clearly sought Zhukov's support. At one point, Kaganovich slapped Zhukov on the shoulder during a trip to a dacha and said that it was time for him to become a member of the Presidium.[205] Zhukov was playing a double game. Khrushchev told the plenum, "We always knew that Zhukov visited Molotov, visited Malenkov many times, and that he also visited Voroshilov. We were always in touch with Zhukov and told him that he should go, that he should speak, first, to clarify [what was going on] and, second, to find out what was motivating them [*chem oni dyshat*]."[206] Whether Zhukov was truly that loyal to Khrushchev or this was a story made up to assuage doubts among plenum members that Zhukov was also skeptical about Khrushchev's increasingly despotic leadership style may always remain a mystery.[207]

Serov, head of the KGB, was also a key figure. The anti-party group fought hard for his support.[208] However, Serov had worked with Khrushchev in Ukraine and remained loyal to him, probably because he was compromised by his crimes during the Stalin era and knew that his position was highly dependent on Khrushchev.[209]

The relationship between Serov and Khrushchev was troubling for others on the Presidium and probably played a significant role in why they decided Khrushchev needed to be removed. Shortly before the showdown, Bulganin asked Serov to his office and demanded to know why he was not informed about some small issue. When Serov responded that he addressed all of his memoranda to the CC, which then distributed the documents to members of the Presidium, Bulganin exploded, "What, I'm not the CC? Am I a dog's cock [*khren sobachii*], is that it?" Bulganin accused Serov of sending information only to Khrushchev. Serov argued that this was a formal decision of the Presidium and that it made sense for information sent "to the CC" to go first to Khrushchev as first secretary.[210]

At the Presidium meetings, members of the anti-party group demanded the KGB submit to the Presidium as a whole (as opposed to just Khrushchev) and that a special committee be established to observe the KGB's work. They apparently hoped to replace Serov with Bulganin.[211] Kaganovich explained that "the KGB, which should be subject to the entire Presidium, was essentially subject only to him [Khrushchev]."[212]

Threat of Coercion

Without the support of the military, Khrushchev would not have been able to successfully summon a CC meeting, and his fate would have instead been sealed in the Presidium. The reactions of Khrushchev's opponents clearly demonstrate that they believed that the ways the military and KGB were behaving implied a physical threat.

As described earlier, the group that demanded a full plenum session was led by Serov and Konev—the head of the KGB and a top military officer. In fact, their whole group was mostly military officers and members of the KGB and MVD. Konev's presence, as Brian Taylor points out, would have contributed to the sense that Khrushchev was supported by the military. The military even used its own planes to bring CC members to Moscow.[213]

Khrushchev's opponents clearly believed that the military was implying the possible use of force. At the plenum, Saburov admitted to saying at the Presidium, "today military officers, and tomorrow tanks," implying that if they did not obey Zhukov's oral demands, then violence would be next. Khrushchev corrected him: "You said it like this: I now see what kind of person you are; they came today, and then we will be encircled by the tanks."[214] On the afternoon of June 18, Zhukov flatly stated, "The army will not support removals from the leadership of the CC." Everyone exchanged glances, as this sounded like a threat.[215]

How Did Institutions Matter?

Institutions, although weak, were not entirely irrelevant. Both sides went to great lengths to try to convince the CC they were adhering more closely to the rules. When members of the anti-party group realized the game was up, they did not refuse to follow the decision for the sake of party unity.

Khrushchev did not use the most forceful option available to him. During a meeting with Suslov, Mukhitdinov, Zhukov, and Furtseva, Khrushchev asked whether he should fight back. Zhukov answered, "You do not need to leave the post of first secretary. As for them, I will arrest them; everything is prepared." Suslov was skeptical: "Arrest them for what? Moreover, what crimes could we accuse them of?"[216] Serov recounted an exchange between Khrushchev and Zhukov on the second day of the Presidium proceedings that suggested they were worried about acting too blatantly: "Then Khrushchev says that 'recently Molotov called him and said why are tanks being mobilized at night.' Zhukov replied to this, cursing, 'This was done by the commander of the MVO [Moscow Military Region], Colonel General Moskalenko, idiot, I already scolded him.' Khrushchev also scolded Moskalenko, that he should not have done that."[217] In any case, both the Mukhitdinov and Serov accounts indicate that Khrushchev recognized that he was playing with fire with regard to the rules and was reluctant to violate them too obviously. But the authority model still has more explanatory power, as Khrushchev very clearly broke all prior tradition to achieve victory.

Implications

Khrushchev had indeed achieved a miraculous triumph. A majority of the Presidium, including several legendary figures, had been overruled. For the first and only time in Soviet history, the greatest criminals of the Stalin era had come as close as they ever would to a trial. Khrushchev could now pursue his own agenda without having to contend with the opinions of powerful men such as Molotov.

Yet the origin, course, and outcome of the crisis all demonstrated the fundamental failure of the principle of collective leadership. Khrushchev simply could not tolerate measured discussion of any policies. It was too hard not to interpret caveats or suggestions as anything more than an incipient challenge. What could have been measured discussions were transformed into warring platforms for the purposes of political struggle.

As this chapter demonstrates, understanding this story requires a sensitivity to both the broader political environment and Khrushchev's style as a political leader. Khrushchev undoubtedly felt threatened by the possibility that individuals such as Molotov, whose authority was formidable, might make a bid for greater power. Recognizing the problems the USSR faced, Khrushchev also could have concluded that a powerful leader, unconstrained by expectations for deliberation, was necessary. Therefore, Khrushchev had reasons to believe that an aggressive posture of exclusion was appropriate.

Crucially, however, certain other figures not only hoped for collective leadership but believed that a consensus-based approach would benefit them. Khrushchev's choice was indeed a risky one. If Khrushchev had died after the purge of Beria, it is possible that Malenkov would have survived as primus inter pares. However, we still have strong reasons to believe that collective leadership would have remained brittle—other potential competitors, like Khrushchev, might have seen similar reasons and opportunities to make a bid for autocrat.

When Khrushchev's opponents finally decided to move against him, neither side could act in a way that truly followed party rules—the rules were too inherently ambiguous. Khrushchev's opponents could not arrest the Soviet leader's destruction of collective leadership without acting in a way that was at least somewhat "factionalist." To ensure ultimate victory, Khrushchev had to push the rules harder than the anti-party group had ever believed possible.

As will be described in the following chapters on China, the power struggles after the deaths of Stalin and Mao had striking parallels. In both cases, the new leadership was shaped more by consensus on policy than differences, and the positions of competitors were often misrepresented to devastating effect. Historical antagonisms and mistrust had paramount implications. Leadership selection was not a democratic process but one marked by underhanded maneuvers. The ultimate arbiter of political power was universally seen as control over the power ministries.

Yet in one crucial respect, the Soviet Union and China were very different. In the Soviet Union, an attempt by the older generation, albeit with the support of younger leaders as well, to continue to play a prominent role was crushed. By the Twenty-Second Party Congress in 1961, only 0.6 percent of the delegates were considered "old guard."[218] In China, the Cultural Revolution was largely about forging and empowering a successor generation that would prove more "revolutionary" than the old comrades who had helped Mao found the PRC. Yet, paradoxically, in the Chinese case, it was members of the revolutionary generation who reasserted their power over the beneficiaries of the Cultural Revolution—a puzzle that will be explained in the following two chapters.

CHAPTER FOUR

The Gang of Four

Introduction: Mao's Legacy and the Chinese "Khrushchevites"

The Cultural Revolution was launched by Chairman Mao Zedong in part as a reaction to the story told in the previous chapters—Nikita Khrushchev's defeat of his opponents and his ascension to the leadership of the CPSU. "Mao's last revolution" explicitly targeted "Khrushchevs" taking over China.[1] However, on October 6, 1976, less than a month after the death of Mao, four individuals inextricably tied to the Cultural Revolution, the so-called Gang of Four, were arrested in Beijing. To resist this act, the Gang's allies in Shanghai prepared material for dissemination to the entire country "on how Khrushchev came to power."[2] But even Shanghai ultimately swallowed the decision. The official *Ninety Years of the Chinese Communist Party*, published in 2016, describes the arrest of Jiang Qing, Zhang Chunqiao, Yao Wenyuan, and Wang Hongwen as an event that "saved the party, saved the nation, and saved China's socialist development from disaster."[3]

Pathbreaking work by Roderick MacFarquhar, Michael Schoenhals, Li Xun, Shi Yun, Li Danhui, Li Haiwen, and especially Frederick C. Teiwes and Warren Sun and a large number of newly available memoirs and original documents allow for a social-science interpretation of this event that links historical evidence with theory. This chapter argues that politics at the end of the Cultural Revolution was not so much a grand struggle between two clear, mutually incompatible political visions in the hands of aggressive and defined groups as a court politics of push and pull, historical antagonisms, difficult personalities, underhanded political machinations of dubious legitimacy, and the threat of violence. For the first time, this chapter will provide an analysis focused primarily on the Gang, including their tactics, beliefs, and backgrounds. In other words, the chapter tries to answer the call to take Jiang Qing "seriously"—a rare approach in the study of Chinese elite politics.[4]

As in the Soviet chapters, the evidence in this chapter is categorized by whether it supports or detracts from two different conceptualizations of politics. Hypothesis 1a predicts that the Gang lost because they failed to co-opt key groups within the leadership. This hypothesis is similar to the many official Chinese accounts that claim that the Gang were highly aggressive and exclusionary. Evidence of the Gang's great ambitions is certainly present in the historical record. However, this chapter will show that the Gang's behavior included *both* aggression and co-optation. The Gang were far from relentlessly antagonistic, and primary sources suggest that on multiple occasions they extended olive branches to the old guard that had been purged during the earlier period of the Cultural Revolution. Their most obviously aggressive behavior can almost always be blamed on Mao. Furthermore, the Gang, especially near the end of the Cultural Revolution, were not operating as a coordinated, close-knit faction. Ultimately, Hua Guofeng decided to reject the Gang's hopes for a post-Mao collective leadership system.

Hypothesis 1a also predicts that the Gang had real policy differences with their enemies. While it would be a mistake to deny that the Gang were associated with "leftist" positions opposed by many among the elite, the evidence shows that the divisions were much less fundamental than is portrayed in official accounts. The Cultural Revolution was primarily a political struggle about status and hierarchy, not about whether the system would be fundamentally changed. The Gang did not support anarchism, and they appreciated the importance of economic development. The most famous theoretical ideas associated with Zhang Chunqiao and Yao Wenyuan were not especially ambitious. In any case, the defeat of the Gang was not immediately characterized as the end of the Cultural Revolution but rather as one of its triumphs. The Gang had no real strong policy viewpoints of their own, and they were only carrying out whatever they thought Mao wanted.

Hypothesis 1b predicts that dispositional or sociological characteristics constitute the Gang's most important strengths and weaknesses. The evidence strongly supports this hypothesis. Mao probably would have preferred to nominate one of the Gang as his successor, and if he had done so, the ensuing power struggle would have probably been much more destabilizing or protracted. However, the Gang's lack of major historical contributions to the party, their association with historical antagonisms created by the Cultural Revolution, and in some cases their gender or personal corruption meant that a clearly disappointed Mao understood that they would not last as his successor. These characteristics not only weakened their authority among the elite but made them vulnerable to compromising material. Their strongest asset was their connection to Mao—an asset that disappeared after Mao's death.

Hypothesis 2a predicts that the removal of the Gang would take place in a single, defined selectorate according to established rules. Powerful evidence again indicates that *which* political body made the ultimate decision would have a crucial impact—Hua decided simply to have the Gang arrested because he was concerned that he did not have enough votes in the CC. By executing a fait accompli, Hua could force individuals who were skeptical about the decision to fall into line by using questionable evidence about the Gang. Choosing to arrest the Gang instead of solving the problem with a "meeting," Hua picked the less politically legitimate procedure because it promised a more predictable outcome.

Hypothesis 3a predicts that the threatened or actual use of force would have no independent effect outside the enforcement of a fully legitimate political decision. However, the evidence strongly contradicts this assessment. Despite the Gang's official positions in the armed forces, they were obviously concerned that they lacked authority in the PLA. To make up for this deficiency, they tried to build up militia forces in Shanghai. The palace guard in the hands of Wang

Dongxing executed the plan to arrest the Gang even though there was no full Politburo vote, and the military served as a critical backup.

Hypothesis 1a versus 1b

Political Style

In July 1977, a party plenum finally approved Hua's purge of the Gang (nine months after the arrest took place). The plenum's official statement accused the Gang of being a "counterrevolutionary conspiratorial clique" that sought to overthrow Hua Guofeng, Zhou Enlai, and a group of leading comrades.[5] However, the evidence in this section provides a much more complicated picture. The Gang combined both exclusion and co-optation, or as it is called in Chinese, "hitting" and "pulling," and, generally, the "pulling" would be stronger unless Mao intervened. The historian Li Haiwen, an individual who was close to Hua Guofeng and has no love for the Gang of Four, admits, "The 'Gang of Four' knew many high-ranking cadres were dissatisfied with them, and they knew that the masses were dissatisfied about the 'Criticize Lin Biao and Confucius' campaign. They tried to pull this and that person, but they were not even able to pull over [the young Politburo member] Chen Guixian."[6]

After the death of Minister of Defense Lin Biao in 1971, Mao sought to engineer a condominium between the old cadres and those individuals who had benefited from the Cultural Revolution. Mao believed that this was necessary to the future of the PRC because of the age of the old revolutionaries, including himself. In November 1974, he said to Zhou Enlai, "Your health is not good; mine is also not good. Marshal Ye's health is not good, Old Kang [Sheng]'s is not good, Liu Bocheng's is not good, and Zhu De's is also no good. It will be difficult."[7] By September 1975, he was even more direct: "We now have a leadership crisis."[8]

In October 1971, Jiang Qing, Zhang Chunqiao, and Yao Wenyuan, as well as another key figure in the Cultural Revolution, Kang Sheng, met to discuss the implications of Mao's decision to no longer attack the 1967 "February Adverse Current." Mao's act was highly significant, as the "February Adverse Current" was a label used to attack the behavior of the old revolutionaries who had criticized some elements of the Cultural Revolution. Jiang Qing said she disagreed with the decision and would express her opinion to Mao. Kang argued back, "But the Chairman did not blame us; why bring trouble upon ourselves?" Zhang Chunqiao agreed, "What Old Kang says is very reasonable; if we go to talk to the Chairman about it, it will seem like we have a problem about this issue." In other words, at least Zhang did not believe that he should take the blame for the criticism. Even Jiang Qing tried to prove her innocence in the affair by seeking evidence that she never actually used the phrase "February Adverse Current."[9]

The memoirs of the former Beijing party boss Wu De claim that the Gang did their best to frustrate rehabilitations in 1974 and 1975, but they were often outmaneuvered by Zhou Enlai.[10] However, according to another account, Zhou was often able to gain permission for some rehabilitations from the Politburo without anyone from the Gang actively interfering. When Zhou was persistent in the face of Jiang's criticisms, she would ultimately accept his decision.[11] Whatever the Gang's positions, however, many old revolutionaries returned to work, including Deng Xiaoping.

Powerful evidence also suggests that the Gang tried to seek a condominium with the rehabilitated cadres. In conversations with the American scholar Roxane Witke, Jiang Qing criticized "ultra-leftism," claimed to have opposed "unnecessary bloodshed," and denounced the attacks on Zhou Enlai and the destruction of the office of the British chargé d'affaires.[12] Jiang Qing explicitly stated that "the leaders held no lasting grudges against such 'tempered officials,'" meaning the old revolutionaries who had been persecuted during the Cultural Revolution. According to Witke, Jiang Qing was even somewhat self-critical: "Justice was not always dispensed evenhandedly by persons who held power. . . . When the power to render justice was wrested from the hands of Chairman Mao and those closest to him, such comrades were wrongly attacked from both the right and the Ultra Left. . . . Both the Chairman and the Premier tried to protect those unfairly attacked. Despite their efforts, some fell under the impact of the Cultural Revolution."[13] Jiang Qing told Witke that "fighting had its good points" but also noted that "open warfare" had eased, adding "cheerily" that this was "a good thing."[14] In June 1974, Jiang Qing told two writing groups that "many problems can be solved through discussion," and she referred to two dynasties that had triumphed in history because they were able to unite the most people. She argued that during the Qing dynasty, the father of the famous author Cao Xueqin was sent to the south to convince both young and old from the previous dynasty to join in a "united front."[15]

Jiang Qing's friendliness extended to high-ranking military figures. At a large meeting with the Guangzhou leadership in the early 1970s, she said that the Wuhan July 20 Incident of 1967, which had led to the purge of several key military leaders, had been a mistake, and she placed the blame on two former members of the Central Cultural Revolution Group. The vice commissar of the Guangzhou MR was moved by her comments.[16] General Ding Sheng writes in his memoirs that Jiang tried to establish a personal relationship with him when he was commander of the Guangzhou MR.[17] In January 1975, during a meeting of the National People's Congress (NPC), Jiang Qing visited the PLA delegates. When she met with General Liao Hansheng, a man who had been purged but rehabilitated, she shook his hand and said, "Ah, you suffered! But it made you stronger" (哎呀，你吃苦了！不过，这也是受锻炼嘛). After shaking hands with others present, Jiang returned to General Liao and said in a loud voice, "I protected both you and [General] Yang Yong." In April 1976, Jiang had another encounter with General Liao when the Politburo summoned to Beijing members of the Jiangsu Party Committee and the Nanjing MR, where General Liao was commissar. Jiang criticized General Liao for "bullying" someone. When he became upset, someone at the meeting said, "She was just joking." Then Jiang Qing changed her tune and said, "Ah, it was just a joke; we are old friends. Your unit fought very well in the battle of Shajiadian."[18]

Wang Hongwen actively participated in the rehabilitation of old cadres.[19] In January 1974, he gave a crucial speech to a study session that summarized and evaluated the Cultural Revolution. The report can be read as an olive branch to the old revolutionaries. Wang praised the Cultural Revolution for cultivating a new generation of successors and stated, "It should be said that old cadres are our party's precious treasure; in the past they fought throughout the entire country and some were injured; but they did not believe that this allowed them to separate from the masses, and they did not believe they could put on airs. Instead they actively participated in the Cultural Revolution. When they discovered their shortcomings and mistakes, they conducted self-criticisms and made contributions to the Cultural Revolution. There are more than one or two such old cadres; there is a whole group of them." Wang also had words of advice for younger cadres: "Now young cadres must be humble and careful, and they must not be arrogant or shake their tails; they must respect the old cadres and study the old cadres."[20] Wang deeply respected many old cadres, especially those in the military. He repeatedly tried to see his old commander, the military theorist Song Shilun, but Song refused to meet him.[21]

The Gang's relationship with Zhou Enlai now seems to have been more complicated than earlier appreciated. At the beginning of the Cultural Revolution, Jiang Qing and the Premier were exceptionally close. Wang Dongxing, former head of the Central Party Office, later remarked, "The relationship between Jiang Qing and the Premier was rather close, it was not ordinary; his relationship with her was different from that of other leaders." Zhou even told Jiang Qing that "the Chairman and Vice Chairman Lin take the helm, and they will set the course, while we will take care of the practical work.[22] Zhou played a critical role in building up Jiang's authority; in turn, Jiang warned others not to attack Zhou.[23] According to the memoirs of Qi Benyu, a member of the Central Cultural Revolution Group, Zhou and Jiang Qing agreed more than 80 percent of the time during the early period of the Cultural Revolution.[24] Zhou treated Jiang so courteously that he once even stopped a Politburo meeting to address her complaint that her toilet seat was too cold.[25]

But by the end of the Mao years, their relationship was certainly not friendly, and Zhou clearly felt threatened. When he was heading into surgery for the fourth time in September 1975, he signed a document rejecting that he was a traitor, and he told his wife that he was not a member of the "surrender faction." In November 1975, he dictated a statement affirming his loyalty to Mao, the party, and the people, and, once again, he denied he was a member of the "surrender faction."[26]

However, when Jiang Qing did level serious attacks against Zhou after Mao turned on him in 1973, Wang Hongwen tried to remain neutral, and sometimes he even tried to calm her down.[27] In 1972, when Zhou went to repair his watch in Shanghai, Wang brought him a tray of watches to pick a new one.[28] Similarly, Zhang Chunqiao avoided creating the impression that he was competing with Zhou Enlai to be the primary mentor to Wang, who at the time of the Tenth Party Congress was still Mao's most likely successor. Zhang declined to outwardly express his support for Wang, and he also turned down the task of writing the Tenth Party Congress political report, in which he would have had to discuss Wang at length. Speaking of Zhou, Zhang said, "The Premier understands the writings in a number of countries; only he can organize the translation of documents. Even if I were to spend my life studying, I would never be able to achieve his erudition, experiences, capability, and character; you have to respect him. . . . Some people say that I, Zhang Chunqiao, want to grasp this and that, as if I were ambitious, but actually, if I have any ambition, my life's greatest ambition is to write a biography of Mao Zedong." According to Zhang's daughter, Zhang Chunqiao told Zhou Enlai, "The Duke of Zhou supported the king [referencing support of Wang Hongwen as Mao's successor]; the credit all went to the Duke of Zhou; why don't you be the Duke of Zhou[?]"[29]

Conventional accounts generally claim that the "Criticize Lin Biao and Confucius" campaign was engineered by the Gang and directed at Zhou Enlai. Yet the humiliating criticisms of Zhou within the party elite in late 1973 were related to the Chairman's own firm belief that Zhou was skeptical of the Cultural Revolution and that a great number of old cadres supported the Premier.[30] The public "Criticize Lin Biao and Confucius" campaign was the result of statements by Mao.[31] Significantly, individuals involved in the campaign deny that it was targeted against Zhou Enlai.[32] In any case, the organizers of the 1980 trial against the Gang decided that this campaign could not be blamed entirely on Jiang Qing or the others.[33]

At Zhou's funeral on January 10, 1976, Zhang Chunqiao ostentatiously embraced Zhou's widow, Deng Yingchao, and she held his hand for a prolonged period of time. Zhang's action was broadcast on television, and Deng Yingchao believed that Zhang was making some kind of gesture.[34] According to one investigator, during postarrest investigations, the Gang flatly disavowed that they had opposed Zhou. Wang Hongwen said, "I absolutely would not oppose Premier Zhou."[35] Jiang Qing told a criticism group after her arrest, "I always respected the Premier."[36]

Relations between the Gang and Ye Jianying, a key elder who held much sway in the military, were also more complicated than previously understood. In January 1976, Ye told a friend and colleague that Jiang had stated at several Politburo meetings that she had two enemies: Deng and Ye.[37] But Jiang seems to have combined pressure with outreach. Jiang invited Ye to events, visited him at his home, and even sent him a photograph.[38] One of Ye's family members told the historian Ye Yonglie that, as late as 1976, when Ye was feigning to be sick, Jiang called to invite him to a meal, leading Ye to say, "Oh, it's that 'three drops of water [Jiang Qing]' again; she wants to pull me to her side [想拉我一把]!"[39]

The relationship between Ye and Wang Hongwen is particularly significant. When Zhou Enlai communicated Mao's intention to make Wang Hongwen a vice premier, Ye strongly supported his decision: "When we were army commanders and division commanders, some were not even twenty years old; now Comrade Wang Hongwen is already thirty-eight, and I support Chairman Mao's nomination."[40] Ye not only constantly invited Wang to drink but also sometimes asked other high-ranking generals to party with Wang as well.[41] Wang sent Ye quails, and Ye told an old colleague in January 1976, "Wang Hongwen is always asking me to go hunting and fishing; he has two feet on two different ships. It's possible he is putting out feelers; he is different from the other three."[42]

Nor does Jiang seem to have actively opposed Deng Xiaoping's rehabilitation, getting along with him passably until at least October 1974.[43] In March 1976, she claimed that when Deng returned to work, "at first he was very good" to her: "In fact, I thought that Deng Xiaoping was a reasonable person, someone with whom one could have a heart-to-heart."[44] Curiously, in 1984, Hu Yaobang told the famous martial arts novelist Jin Yong that when Jiang Qing, then in prison, saw Deng on television, she said, "I never had any big differences with Deng Xiaoping, just differences on some small issues."[45]

In response to the announcement in March 1973 that Deng would return to work, the telegram affirming the decision sent from Shanghai to the party center referred to Deng's relationship with the disgraced Liu Shaoqi. Zhang Chunqiao was furious, saying to the Shanghai leadership, "What the hell were you doing? You even raised the issue of his being a capitalist headquarters conspirator.... You are truly stupid; couldn't you have just written a telegram simply affirming support of the decision? Deng himself will see it; what will he think when he sees it?"[46]

Deng and Jiang did clash in October 1974 during the so-called *Fengqing* Incident. The *Fengqing* was a domestically produced ship, but on its maiden voyage, the ship's political commissar wrote a report in favor of imported ships. At a Politburo meeting, Jiang demanded that Deng express his position on her criticism of the report. Deng, who had not yet expressed an opinion either way, did not appreciate the pressure and lost his temper. In response, Wang Hongwen traveled to Wuhan to warn Mao about Deng's behavior.[47] Official Chinese accounts portray this act as a conspiracy by the Gang against Deng. Teiwes and Sun, however, strongly qualify the event. First, the incident was not planned beforehand by the Gang, and both sides were probably surprised by the outcome of the meeting. Second, Deng's behavior raised questions about his loyalty to the Cultural Revolution, which suggests the Gang were acting defensively. Third, Wang's trip to Wuhan probably had limited goals— alerting Mao to Deng's behavior—and was probably the result of "pique and frustration," as opposed to a real plan to remove Deng. The Gang already knew that Mao had made a decision on Deng's promotion. Moreover, "it quickly blew over as an issue." Fourth, the event was probably about personalities—the two "steel factories," Deng and Jiang.[48]

After the *Fengqing* Incident, the Gang showed an understanding that they needed to co-opt more members of the Politburo, in particular by ensuring their participation in the study sessions intended to affirm the legacy of the Cultural Revolution. That task became especially important in 1975, when Deng Xiaoping started making serious progress rectifying some of the worst problems caused by the Cultural Revolution. On April 8, 1975, Jiang invited Su Zhenhua, Politburo member and commissar of the navy, to her home at Diaoyutai and told him, "Recently, I discussed matters with Wang Hongwen; we split up to meet with different members of the Politburo to discuss the issue of leadership; I am in charge of meeting with Comrades [Ji] Dengkui, [Chen] Xilian, and you. Comrade Hongwen will meet with the old comrades and young comrades on the Politburo." In other words, Jiang's mission was to win over the midgeneration Cultural Revolution beneficiaries who were not closely tied to the Gang, while Wang Hongwen was assigned to work on the older and younger generations. Jiang told Su that she was dissatisfied with Deng for two reasons: first, she disagreed with China's policy toward Japan and Portugal; and second, she was upset Deng had told her that the General Staff was too busy to create the material and maps she wanted to study the "international situation." Jiang remarked, "The Chairman says Comrade Xiaoping is easy to work with when his line is correct, but he is difficult to cooperate with when his line is incorrect. [Deng] previously committed the error of making his own independent kingdom." She encouraged Su to participate in selecting for publication Mao's theoretical articles on the dictatorship of the proletariat from the First to the Third International and to find relevant quotes from Marx, Engels, and Lenin. After Su refused, Jiang sent Su a poem and three pieces of study materials. On April 14, Wang Hongwen met with Politburo members Su Zhenhua, Ni Zhifu, and Wu Guixian and made similar requests. Although Su rejected the approach and even reported these two conversations to Zhou Enlai, Deng Xiaoping, and Ye Jianying, the conversations did demonstrate that the Gang were attempting to win over other members of the Politburo.[49]

At about the same time that Jiang and Wang were meeting with Politburo members, an ideological study campaign began. This campaign coincided with when Deng began his rectification efforts. Mao's purpose was to guarantee the historical legacy of the Cultural Revolution while moving away from it in practice. Elements of this campaign, especially an article written by Yao Wenyuan and a speech by Zhang Chunqiao on political work in the military, included criticism of "empiricism," which had often been interpreted to mean an attack on old cadres.

However, the implications of this campaign should not be overstated. According to one party historian, Wang Hongwen believed that the criticism of empiricism was only intended to warn (敲打)

those old revolutionaries who were dissatisfied with the Cultural Revolution.[50] Zhu Yongjia, a Shanghai intellectual, believes that the campaign was not an attack on Deng but rather a result of Mao's desire for a study of ideology to run parallel with Deng's practical rectification efforts.[51] Moreover, Zhang Chunqiao's speech included praise of the old revolutionaries: "I think that we have so many old comrades; they have rich experience." Zhang seems to have been making the case that the old revolutionaries needed to study Mao's directives and affirm the Cultural Revolution, not that the old revolutionaries were inherently problematic.[52]

Why did the relationship between Deng and the Gang deteriorate in 1975 and 1976? Teiwes and Sun conclude, "From Jiang's perspective, despite her earlier support (based on the fact that she understood Mao's backing of Deng), Deng had betrayed her in the spring by somehow getting the Chairman's ear and turning him against her."[53] Even Ye blamed Deng for being too aggressive in 1975, when his rectification attempts went too fast and incurred Mao's wrath: "This person is always like that; he is presumptuous [自以为是], he does not listen to the opinions of other people, he likes to take over the world by himself, and he does not stop until he hits a wall."[54] When Deng refused to write a history of the Cultural Revolution, Zhou asked him, "Couldn't you just be a little conciliatory?" (你就不能忍一忍?).[55] In December 1975, Wang Hongwen did not criticize Deng for rehabilitating old cadres but rather for not supporting younger cadres.[56]

Crucially, Mao's turn against Deng in 1975 was probably due not to the Gang's machinations but to those by Mao's nephew Mao Yuanxin—as well as those by an even more surprising individual, Li Xiannian, an "old comrade" who had survived most of the Cultural Revolution by convincing Mao of his support for the movement. According to the Shanghai politician Xu Jingxian, around the time of Chinese National Day (October 1, 1975), after a meeting with foreign dignitaries Li had brought to meet Mao, Li complained to the Chairman that Deng was not talking enough about the Cultural Revolution. Li's warning allegedly deeply concerned Mao.[57] One senior party historian interviewed for this book argues that Xu's story is partly corroborated by the official *Chronology of Mao Zedong,* which confirms that Li spoke with Mao on October 19 after they met with the wife of the president of Mali. This was the first time Mao expressed worries about Deng's actions.[58]

Despite setbacks for Jiang Qing in the summer of 1975, when Deng's power started to be felt, she still signaled friendly intentions to the old revolutionaries. On a trip to Xiyang in September 1975, she continued to interrupt a speech by Deng, saying, "Vice Chairman Deng was sent here personally by Chairman Mao" and "the Chairman wants Vice Chairman Deng to say a few words."[59] On September 17, 1975, Jiang said, "The Chairman says as long as they are not Kuomintang members, we must unite with them. Even if they are KMT members who surrendered to the Chinese Communist Party, we must unite with them."[60] Next fall, on a trip to Tsinghua University, Jiang stated, "During the Cultural Revolution, the Premier wanted to defend XXX [name redacted], but his words had no effect, so he had Old Kang [Sheng] come find me and I approved it. During the Cultural Revolution, Red Guard Kuai Dafu and others wanted to engage in anarchism, and they collected a lot of material; I told them that I did not believe their material."[61]

The limited extent of the Gang's direct attacks on Deng is revealed by a phone call that Zhang Chunqiao made to Ye Jianying after Deng came under attack. In response to Zhang's criticism of Deng, Ye said, "You all say that this and that is a problem; why didn't you say anything at the time? Saying it now, aren't you intentionally trying to cause harm?"[62] In other words, Zhang's criticisms of Deng before Deng was in trouble were probably limited.

Even after Deng's political position started to collapse, the Gang made signs that they were willing to recognize some of the mistakes of the Cultural Revolution. In November 1975, Yao Wenyuan told the leadership of *Red Flag* (a Chinese theoretical journal under the party CC), "The socialist new things that have appeared since the Cultural Revolution may have some deficiencies; it is necessary to review them and during the path ahead gradually remove these deficiencies." Yao affirmed that the policy of "treating the sickness to save the patient" should be applied to both new and old cadres who had made mistakes. Yao called for unifying with 95 percent.[63] In February 1976, when Yao Wenyuan was presented with the choice of either explicitly criticizing Deng by name or only making indirect criticisms in the Chinese media, Yao chose the latter option.[64] During that same month, Jiang Qing told General Ding Sheng, "some people oppose Chairman Mao; you old comrades have to protect Chairman Mao," thus implying that Deng was different from other old comrades.[65]

In March 1976, during a meeting with regional political and military leaders, Jiang apologized for some of the excesses of the Cultural Revolution:

> Our Chairman said that 70 percent of the Cultural Revolution was good and 30 percent was bad. I said this last time, and I won't repeat it. I will think more about the 30 percent; you comrades who were attacked should think more about the 70 percent. The Chairman says that the 30 percent must also be treated objectively [三也要一分为二]. With regard to the 30 percent, originally I had thought that it simply was not my fault. Knocking down everything, doubting everything, I sent Chairman Mao a report; those were [the ideas of] Tao Zhu [former Central Cultural Revolution Group adviser]; also the State Council had a document saying people should be burned to a crisp at every level [层层烧透]. At that time Wang [Li], Guan [Feng], and Qi [Benyu] [all members of the Central Cultural Revolution Group] wanted to use this [document]. I sent a report to the Chairman, but the Chairman said not to use it; it was necessary to defend the Premier and Vice Premier. I simply had nothing to do with all-out civil war. . . . After the Chairman's analysis, I then thought that even though it was not my fault, it had occurred during the Cultural Revolution, I was first vice head of the Central Cultural Revolution Group, so it was necessary to think about the experiences and lessons.

Jiang also blamed Deng for implying that she was opposed to old cadres: "[Deng] fomented discord while executing all of the policies set forth by the Chairman. He said that each campaign hurt those old workers with experience, hurt those cadres with experience. . . . He engaged in inciting people against each other, and he created rumors and engaged in libel." Jiang hinted that she did not believe that the removal of Deng should entail a major purge, stating that she did not believe that people, "including some of his old comrades," would follow Deng.[66]

During that same month, two articles appeared in *Wenhui bao* that were interpreted as Gang of Four attacks on the late Zhou En-lai. However, a former journalist at the newspaper provides evidence that this was a misinterpretation based on mistakes caused by the newspaper staff. According to his account, the Gang even subsequently increased their control over the paper to ensure that no more mistakes created similar misunderstandings.[67]

On October 1, again at Tsinghua University, Jiang once again blamed the early excesses of the Cultural Revolution on other individuals. She emphasized the importance of acknowledging the mistakes of the Cultural Revolution: "Here I will only talk about its shortcomings, and I will have other people talk about its achievements." Jiang remarked that even if she had not committed mistakes, she was willing to research and acknowledge the problems of the campaign: "Even if they were not done by us, it is necessary to regard them as an experience; you should all do a good job of reviewing them."[68]

On the same day, at Tsinghua's agriculture satellite campus, Jiang blamed the 1967 slogan "grab a small handful in the military," which had caused widespread instability in the PLA, on Chen Boda, former formal head of the Central Cultural Revolution Group. According to Jiang, she had opposed the slogan, characterizing it as "destroying our Great Wall." Jiang stated, "Old cadres are a treasure. . . . The Chairman said that it was necessary to have mercy on the leftist rebels because the old have all the power; the leftist rebels do not. . . . The Chairman wanted to protect both, suggesting combining old, middle, and young. Deng Xiaoping wanted old, old, old; he did not understand the objective rules of life; as soon as a person is born they contain the cause of their death."[69] In other words, Jiang was not arguing for the elimination of the old cadres but calling for their help to ensure a stable succession that included the beneficiaries of the Cultural Revolution.

The Gang's attitude toward Hua Guofeng, who became Acting Premier in February 1976 and, therefore, Mao's designated successor, was also mixed. Hua told a colleague in 1999 that the Gang both attacked him and tried to win him over (又打又拉).[70] In 1985, on multiple occasions, Hua told a historian that it took him time to understand the nature of the Gang (有一个认识过程).[71]

The Gang were certainly not especially close to Hua. At a Politburo meeting on May 31, 1976, when Jiang Qing criticized the creation of a fertilizer factory in Daqing, Hua noted that the decision had been approved by Mao. Zhang Chunqiao said, "I simply oppose this technique of yours; at every turn you use Chairman Mao to put pressure on us!"[72] Mao's nephew Mao Yuanxin told the authorities in 1980 that Hua did not shake Jiang Qing's hand at Mao's funeral, leading her, perhaps in a fit of pique, to say, "Who acknowledges he is the Chairman? It has not yet been determined who the Chairman is. . . . It is necessary to look a bit [还要看一看]."[73]

Ultimately, however, the weight of evidence suggests that the Gang planned to support Hua, although they expected that he would consider their concerns. In other words, they looked forward to collective leadership. In September 1976, Zhang Chunqiao told Wang Hongwen's secretary, "The Chairman is no longer around; it looks like in the future it is only possible to rely on collective leadership."[74] After Mao's funeral, Yao Wenyuan ordered that television footage and photographs should not focus too much on any one person but instead should "emphasize collective leadership."[75] On September 21, Zhang Chunqiao told Xu Jingxian, one of the leaders in Shanghai, "In the future, work will meet some difficulties; mainly collective [leadership] will be relied upon."[76]

But collective leadership did not mean undermining Hua Guofeng. A document written by Zhang Chunqiao in early 1976 is often used as evidence that Zhang was unhappy when Hua was installed as Acting Premier. However, in 2015, the Chinese historian Li Xun revealed that this document was a draft of a letter sent to Xiao Mu, one of Zhang's colleagues in Shanghai. The letter contained the phrase "exchanging the old symbol for a plum," which Xiao interpreted as meaning that "this new plum Hua Guofeng has replaced the old symbol Deng Xiaoping; do you not see that the situation is getting better?" In other words, the letter was interpreted to mean the exact opposite of what was intended. Xiao also overheard Zhang telling Xu Jingxian to improve the economic situation in Shanghai, which Xiao interpreted as Zhang asking Xu to help Hua.[77]

According to Xiao, on February 3, Zhang told him, "After Deng Xiaoping has fallen, it appears the big struggle has passed. In both peaceful and coercive times, sometimes it is tense, sometimes less so [文武之道，一张一弛]. After some unfinished matters of struggling, criticizing, and changing, *next will be the issue of doing construction well*. Chairman Mao's plans [meaning making Hua Acting Premier] means it is possible to achieve true unity and victory."[78]

Zhang explicitly called on his colleagues in Shanghai to support Hua. In February 1976, Zhang told Ma Tianshui, another Shanghai leader, "Now Comrade Guofeng just started to come out and manage work; it is necessary to support him; I cannot go back [to Shanghai]." Ma Tianshui referred to this event on October 12, 1976, after the Gang's arrest, when he tried to explain to Hua Guofeng, "We believed that [Zhang] stood on the same side as Comrade Guofeng."[79] At a Politburo meeting two days after Mao's death, Jiang called for removing Deng from the Chinese Communist Party (CCP). When Ye countered by saying that the most important task at hand was unity, Zhang Chunqiao and Yao Wenyuan repeatedly responded, "Yes, yes, yes!"[80] According to an account by a family member of Ye, Wang Hongwen and Zhang Chunqiao agreed with Ye Jianying's assertion that the most important goal at the time was to unite under Hua Guofeng.[81]

On October 10, after the Gang were arrested, *People's Daily* published an editorial stating that "anyone who engages in revisionism, splittism, or conspiracies is doomed to fail." Some of the Shanghai leadership, including Xu Jingxian and Wang Xiuzhen, believed that the editorial was criticizing Hua Guofeng and that the Gang were on the same side as Hua.[82] When Xu arrived in Beijing, he was not convinced by the evidence presented to him that allegedly showed that the Gang were plotting against Hua.[83]

Jiang Qing, despite her harassment of Hua at Politburo meetings, also seems to have generally supported Hua. At a Politburo meeting soon after Mao's death, Jiang said that everyone should unite and work together and that if anyone damaged the unity, they would be forced to leave.[84] At Tsinghua University on October 1, when a reporter tried to take her picture, Jiang said, "Don't hurt by trying to help [你们不要帮倒忙]; it is necessary to protect the unity of the party center; comrade Hua Guofeng is the first vice chairman of the party and premier of the State Council; this was suggested by the Chairman. The Chairman spoke very clearly; don't you understand?"[85]

The most aggressive of the Gang's behavior was when they acted according to how they understood Mao's wishes. At times the Gang certainly went farther than Mao had intended, such as their characterizing the criticism of Zhou Enlai as the eleventh line struggle (meaning a fundamental contradiction, like how previous clashes had been characterized) in 1973, adding "using the back door" to the "Criticize Lin Biao and Confucius" campaign in 1974, and their theoretical attack on "empiricism" in early 1975. However, throughout the Cultural Revolution, the Gang's behavior was generally a reaction to comments made by Mao, and the Chairman's criticism of the Gang was over details, not over the basic nature of their actions.[86]

Jiang did use the Cultural Revolution to indulge in some grudges, but these acts did not target major party figures. The historian of the Cultural Revolution Wang Nianyi writes, "Lin and Jiang certainly did bad things during the Cultural Revolution, but they were all done under Mao's 'great strategic deployment.' . . . With regard to arresting a maid or arresting a chef, these were little cases of mischief [小打小闹], and they did not determine the course of the Cultural Revolution."[87] During the trial against the Gang, no evidence was found that Jiang was personally responsible for directly ordering anyone to be physically persecuted or killed.[88]

Holding the Gang exclusively responsible for the excesses of the Cultural Revolution is not entirely fair. For example, new evidence now shows the extent to which Zhou Enlai in particular played an enormous role in the persecution of high-ranking cadres. Zhou controlled the infamous "special case groups," and he refused to defend major party figures such as Marshal He Long.[89] Jiang hinted at this fact when she complained to her lawyers that she was not in charge of the "special case groups" but that, according to the charges, it looked like it was her.[90] In fact, during her trial, Jiang said that the reversal of the verdicts on Liu Shaoqi and Peng Zhen was "opposing Premier Zhou."[91] While preparing for the trial of the Gang, Peng, who knew that Zhou signed many documents approving persecution, somewhat lamely said that Zhou was a case of "good people making mistakes," while the case of the Gang was "bad people doing bad things."[92]

Policy

To what extent did real policy differences determine the Gang's fate? The Cultural Revolution is often described as a radical attempt to change the very nature of human society, but by its end, it had morphed primarily into an extension of Mao's fear about his own historical reputation after his death.[93] Given the absolute dominance of Mao, the Gang did not dare develop their own policy agenda. Politics were fundamentally not conducive to real policy formulation or debate.

To understand the limited import of policy differences at the end of the Mao years requires an appreciation of the extent to which the political model of the early years of the Cultural Revolution had already been rejected. As one major Chinese historian writes, "Although in the press there were numerous articles about the victory of the Cultural Revolution, in his heart Mao Zedong knew that his original intention of the Cultural Revolution had as a whole failed."[94] In November 1975, as mentioned earlier, Mao himself had admitted that the Cultural Revolution was 30 percent wrong.[95]

One of the key elements of the Cultural Revolution was the idea that the masses would have the right to criticize cadres. However, practically speaking, the period in which the masses had the ability to make decisions about cadres ended in 1967, when the Revolutionary Committees were established.[96] The period of "great democracy" ended in 1968 as people faced intense pressure to ensure that their thinking was in accordance with the official line.[97] In Andrew Walder's words, "A campaign that began by encouraging students and workers to challenge bureaucratic authority ended in an orgy of repression conducted by a newly militarized bureaucracy."[98]

But even during the most radical part of the Cultural Revolution, the system itself was never challenged. The leftist rebels "did not criticize the cadres as a group, and even more so they were not criticizing the whole system. . . . [They] primarily understood the campaign based on their own experiences and situation, and, therefore, many personal grudges could be involved."[99] In fact, the "rebel workers did not address more general political issues with respect to the relationship of labor to the state or the vital issue of class relations in Chinese socialism."[100] Xu Youyu writes that the primary reason the leftist rebels criticized cadres was because they opposed Mao or because they were engaged in revisionism, while "bureaucrats enjoying privileges or repressing the masses were only a secondary reason."[101]

The Cultural Revolution was less a fight against such privileges and more a fight over a cadre's personal history, especially a history from before the revolution. Li Xun concludes that the campaign "very quickly moved away from the possibility of criticizing the system and became purely political criticism. With regard to criticizing the 'capitalist' faction, the simplest and most direct method was to look for problems in the cadres' political history, to use 'historical problems' to tarnish them. . . . The criticism of cadres' bureaucratism, special privileges, and habit of separating from the masses, or in other words, monitoring the power of the cadres, actually became of secondary importance."[102]

The Cultural Revolution, in other words, only removed the special privileges of those who had been overthrown. For those who remained in power, the privileges of status remained the same. Leftist rebels who quickly climbed the ranks soon began to enjoy the perks of their new lifestyles.[103] As the Cultural Revolution historian Yin Hongbiao demonstrates, the party directed the masses away from criticizing bureaucratic perks and instead to emphasizing struggle within the party. Individuals who sought to construct a different society were labeled extreme leftists and were repressed.[104] Zhang Chunqiao harshly, but ineffectively, scolded the leftist rebels for leading corrupt lives so soon after seizing power.[105] These dynamics are probably what led the major revolutionary elder Chen Yun in November 1981 to discount the ideological aspect of the Cultural Revolution, characterizing it as a "political struggle" used by conspirators.[106] One of the key reasons that the Red Guards, especially those in Beijing, lost faith in Mao was because they started to believe that the Cultural Revolution was just a "palace struggle."[107]

Even the famous 1967 January Revolution that saw the fall of the Shanghai Party Committee fit unclearly in the Cultural Revolution's ideology. Zhang Chunqiao originally intended to write a "January Revolution Summary" to justify the event theoretically. However, the intense factional infighting soon led the regime to emphasize unity, and Zhang never wrote the piece. In other words, the Shanghai experience never gained the explicit ideological justification necessary to become an important model for future reference.[108]

By the end of the Cultural Revolution, even Mao himself explicitly criticized "doubting everything" and "knocking down everything." After 1970, the Chairman no longer talked about "democracy"; instead, he focused on "the dictatorship of the proletariat."[109] According to a document delineating Mao's directives between November 1975 and January 1976, he called for the current campaign to be restricted to universities and not to affect industry, agriculture, commerce, or the military. Mao described the Red Guards such as Kuai Dafu and Nie Yuanzi as "anarchists," and he emphasized the importance of party leadership. Now "old comrades" would not be purged, and instead they would be "given a heads-up" and "helped." In other words, Mao was rejecting the core elements of the Cultural Revolution. According to Shi Yun and Li Danhui, when Mao was emphasizing the "70 percent" correct part of the Cultural Revolution, in actuality he "only meant the later revolution in education and a few leftover superficial ideological elements."[110]

The Cultural Revolution, moreover, was not about economic principles. Leftist rebels avoided making materialist demands because they were worried that they would appear to be rebelling for selfish reasons.[111] In the words of the party historians Shi Yun and Li Danhui, "With regard to economic work, Mao Zedong did not have any special interest, and the Jiang Qing clique was also unwilling to take on this thankless burden that required a great effort."[112] The late Chinese politician Deng Liqun argued that the Cultural Revolution was "supposed to solve ideological problems," as opposed to economic ones, which in Mao's view had already been solved.[113]

The Gang were often accused of having no interest in "production," referring to economic work in general. Yet members of the Gang often denied that they opposed "production," and they blamed shortages on sabotage caused by old cadres who opposed the Cultural Revolution. Early during the Cultural Revolution, Zhang Chunqiao demonstrated that he understood that any delays in production would hurt the campaign: "Chairman Mao sent us to Shanghai; as soon as we arrived, we felt that the economic situation was serious. The CC did not expect it would have reached such a serious of a level. . . . If this situation continues, it will create an extremely large obstacle to deepening the Cultural Revolution."[114] Zhang believed that leftist rebels should not be involved in specific decisions and concrete policy work; instead, they should limit themselves to criticism and monitoring. For Zhang, "seizing power" meant seizing power to hold the cadres accountable, not to run the economy.[115]

Zhang Chunqiao was no anarchist. In February 1967, he stated that the idea of "doubting everything, knocking down everything" was "reactionary."[116] At about the same time, he criticized the idea that "we can do without leading cadres"—"if we turn a city such as Shanghai or a province such as Jiangsu over to workers, they would find it very difficult to manage because of their lack of experience." Moreover, the "power seizures" were largely the result of the chaos and the need to restore order and production.[117] Soon after the January Revolution, when leftist rebels took over Shanghai, Zhang sought to enlist old cadres such as Ma Tianshui to help with production: "It really is necessary for old cadres who understand the situation to come grasp work a bit."[118]

Late in the Cultural Revolution, even after criticizing Deng, Zhang made comments that displayed his pragmatism. In December 1975, he attacked a local Shanghai official who had complained about the "Criticize Lin Biao and Confucius" campaign being shut down too quickly. Zhang took responsibility and asked, "Do we not have enough lessons in this regard?"[119] In June 1976, Zhang gave a speech in which he emphasized that making class struggle a part of work entailed "never causing work stoppages or delays." In the same speech, he criticized leaders who did nothing to stop the chaos and who arrested enemies who were affecting production, thus failing to "use the party organization as a castle for doing battle" (发挥不出党组织是战斗堡垒的作用). In Zhang's mind, leaders should dare to "execute dictatorship" over bad people who damaged production. Moreover, although Zhang urged that ideological study was still an important element, he emphasized the importance of leadership (as opposed to the masses), and he demanded that, even when dealing with enemy cadres, "one cannot rush to deal with them; it is necessary to first get permission." In words that sound nothing like a radical, Zhang said, "But even in conditions in which the main trends are good, there will still be some problems; these problems must be solved and cannot be ignored, such as the spread of anarchism that causes efficiency to be low or causes delays, leading to a year's worth of projects not completed. . . . When we are criticizing the mistake of using production to suppress politics, cadres absolutely must not because of this give up on production."[120]

These comments were not limited to Zhang. On October 1, 1976, Jiang said, "I need to think deeply about the '30 percent wrong' [of the Cultural Revolution]; the Chairman summarized the experience. So when criticizing Deng this time, one is not allowed to engage in revolutionary networking [串连], stubbornly work, grasp revolution, promote production, or walk the 5-7 [May 7] road; otherwise bad people will jump up and never sit their butts down [不然坏人拱起来屁股就坐不住]."[121]

And while members of the Gang made these seemingly "rightist" statements, Zhou Enlai, the alleged quintessential "moderate," was no stranger to "leftist" language. In a conversation with the Soviet ambassador in November 1970, Zhou displayed a dogmatic view of political economy. He stated that capitalist countries were in a state of crisis and excluded any possibility of studying the organization of production in capitalist countries, as "this is an issue that relates to the superstructure." Zhou argued, "when you say that we can borrow something from Western countries in the area of technology, I want to express doubt."[122]

Mao is famously associated with the idea that the party could not be allowed to develop into a new class divorced from the masses. His concern was how certain economic mechanisms created "bourgeois privilege." But by the end of the Cultural Revolution, even on this key social and economic issue, Mao no longer demonstrated utopian thinking. In October 1974, Mao had complained to the Danish premier, "The eight-level salary system, distribution according to work, currency exchange—these things are not significantly different from those in the old society. The only difference is the system of ownership."[123] According to one party document containing Mao's directive on theory, "Currently our country is a commodity system. The salary system is not fair; there are four levels of salary, and so on. This can only be restricted [that is, not eliminated] under the dictatorship of the proletariat."[124]

We have no evidence that the Gang had a different opinion than Mao on this issue. In February 1975, Yao Wenyuan told leaders of *Red Flag* magazine, "right now do not raise the issue of getting rid of commodities" and "we are not eliminating distribution according to work"—commodities and distribution according to work should only be "restricted." In fact, Yao picked a Goldilocks position, criticizing both Sun Yefang, normally seen as a "rightist," and Chen Boda, who in 1958 had wanted to completely remove commodities.[125] In Zhang's famous article "On Exercising All-Round Dictatorship over the Bourgeoisie," he referred to Mao's comment that policies like the commodity and wage systems "can only be restricted," and he affirmed, "This state of affairs that Chairman Mao pinpointed cannot be changed within a short period." In a private conversation with a colleague, Zhang once explained, "Of course, the CCP accepts a certain amount of hierarchy; according to the size of a person's contribution, there should be a definite difference in income." Zhang simply did not want these differences to be so serious as to form a "special-privilege class," whatever that meant.[126]

Even Jiang Qing had trouble determining how many commodities could be "restricted." In one speech, she criticized high salaries and praised the "supply system." The latter would mean no longer giving salaries to cadres, instead providing them with food and clothing based directly on their rank, and the eight-level salary system for workers would also be eliminated. But then she remarked, "We at Diaoyutai also have commodities. Because we planted Chinese medicine, we must sell it to the public. It was planted by me and those comrades working for me. . . . The Chairman says what is to be done? On this question, you of course cannot indulge in fantasy! One cannot reach communism in one jump. We also cannot completely separate from the old society!"[127] Jiang's answer to this dilemma was to conduct campaigns to educate the party and the population but not to fundamentally restructure society.

Yao Wenyuan told the *Red Flag* leadership in June 1975 that "bourgeois privilege is not only a way of thinking, and it is not something that can be eliminated suddenly; it requires the work of several generations. . . . Rushing is no good; this is an objective factor. Some things need to be eliminated, but some things need to be protected."[128] As Lowell Dittmer puts it, "The radicals were for the time being surprisingly prudent in their policy recommendations. Associating attempts to 'abolish' the commodity system with Trotsky and attempts to 'perpetuate [it] forever' with Bukharin, they sought to steer a middle course. . . . Even the masses seem to have been puzzled by a campaign so ambitious in theory yet so modest in intent."[129]

The Gang's attacks on "bourgeois privilege" did not translate into utopian policies. After Zhang Chunqiao's famous March 1975 article was published, he asked his Shanghai colleagues to estimate just how much it would cost to run the city on a "supply system." The result of the investigation indicated that such a system would cost the government several times more than providing salaries. Once Zhang understood that a "supply system" was economically impossible, he dropped the idea.[130]

Agricultural policy was another area where the Gang had little sway and unclear policy preferences. Jiang did attempt to make Xiaojinzhuang village a model for the entire country. However, as Jeremy Brown demonstrates, the model was in fact entirely for show and did not represent a serious policy concept. Xiaojinzhuang "trumpeted the notion that cultural advances supposedly lead to improvement in material life, but everyone in the village knew that the harvest required outside assistance in order to take place at all." Observers wondered whether the village was merely an inspiration for poetry and song. By 1976, Xiaojinzhuang only meant criticizing Deng, opposing market activity, and defending the legacy of the Cultural Revolution. In other words, it was only "a political tool." Even the original real innovations at Xiaojinzhuang were stolen by Jiang and should not be considered her own ideas.[131] Teiwes and Sun write, "There is little to suggest that the radicals, who had no bureaucratic responsibilities in this area, had any serious program for agriculture."[132]

The Gang also do not seem to have had much familiarity with foreign policy. During a meeting criticizing Zhou Enlai in late 1973, the Gang lambasted the Premier's actions in the foreign-policy realm. But, according to the account of one attendant at the meeting who worked in the Foreign Ministry, "At the time, the members of the Politburo, including the Gang of Four, simply did not understand foreign policy; they could not even state clearly what the situation was, and they never touched the true content of foreign policy."[133]

It also bears remembering that when the Gang were eliminated, the victory was not heralded as a defeat of radical politics. For example, at a meeting in November 1976, Hua Guofeng argued, "It is necessary to keep class struggle in mind; exposing and criticizing the Gang of Four is class struggle." Hua even explicitly stated, "Do not reject the Cultural Revolution."[134] That same month, propaganda workers were told that the Gang of Four were extreme rightists who "opposed and damaged the new things of the Cultural Revolution and socialism." The propagandists were instructed to emphasize the importance of supporting the "new things" of the Cultural Revolution, restricting bourgeois privilege, and integrating the old, middle-aged, and young. The "education revolution, Cultural Revolution, hygiene revolution, and technology line revolution," sent-down youth, economic self-dependence, and criticism of Deng were all to continue.[135]

In February 1977, Hua blamed the breakdown of collectivism in the countryside and the growth of small trading on the Gang of Four.[136] After the Gang were purged, Ye Jianying repeatedly referred to Mao's comments that he had only accomplished two things in life—taking over the country and the Cultural Revolution—to emphasize the importance of the campaign. Ye even refuted Mao's statement that the Cultural Revolution was 30 percent wrong by sticking up his thumb and saying, "The Cultural Revolution is 100 percent this!" (文化大革命是这一份的!).[137] When Deng officially returned to power in July 1977, he remarked, "If not for the Cultural Revolution started by Chairman Mao, if not for big-character posters, speaking out freely, airing views freely, and holding great debates [known as the "four bigs," these four types of criticism are now synonymous with the Cultural Revolution excesses], making us see things clearly, I would have really allowed Liu Shaoqi to lead me around by the nose; what does this show? . . . So the achievements of the Cultural Revolution fundamentally guarantee the nature of our party and guarantee that the rivers and mountains do not change color."[138] When the Gang were removed, the leadership still had no clear idea of a "reform" platform. Even at the famous Third Plenum in 1978, thinking about reform was still extremely murky.[139]

At the same time, many of the changes commonly associated with the reform era actually began during the late Mao years—when the Gang were still in power. Odd Arne Westad, for example, argues that the late Maoist era "held some of the seeds of the reforms that were accepted after Mao's death in 1976."[140] The late Cultural Revolution era was not exclusively "leftist." For example, with regard to economic relations with the outside world, long before Mao's death, he explicitly approved large-scale international trade.[141] Christian Talley shows that an emphasis on Deng's role in the later reforms "often crowds out a more extended examination of trade relations during the 1973–78 period and the progress made therein."[142] The fall of the Gang was important, but the significance of the moment has been overstated in historiography.

The notion that the Gang represented a coherent worldview is also challenged by the fact that almost no real policy discussion took place under Mao's leadership. The Gang were primarily motivated by shifts in Mao's own views. Therefore, the Gang are best understood as a group of political opportunists inferring what Mao wanted and executing his wishes better than others, not as a cohesive group with their own policy platform.[143]

A Shanghai colleague of Zhang and Yao believes that after seeing the fall of Mao's previous "pens," the two men concluded that they could never go beyond simply conveying the Chairman's views. Zhang repeatedly told his family, "I do not say anything the Chairman does not tell me to say; if the Chairman doesn't tell me to move, I don't move."[144] Zhang Chunqiao once complained to his wife, "This person Jiang Qing has a lot of ideas; if today one idea appears, tomorrow it is completely denied; it's like what she said previously was never even said. I suppose this is possible because she hears some wind from the Chairman so she immediately changes her position. But she refuses to admit that earlier she was wrong."[145]

After the Gang of Four were purged, the Gang's allies in Shanghai were accused of considering a famous 1975 article by Zhang as a manifestation of "Zhang Chunqiao Thought," a dangerous "new contribution" to Mao Zedong Thought. However, according to one of those individuals, at the time they had no concept of "Zhang Chunqiao Thought," which would have been taboo given the Mao-centric political environment.[146]

The Gang of Four so slavishly followed the will of Mao that when preparing the trial against them, it was exceedingly difficult to separate them from the Chairman. In May 1977, Wang Dong-xing responded to an article criticizing one particular idea by say-ing, "What fucking theory does the 'Gang of Four' have; they are merely criticizing Chairman Mao."[147] Jiang said during her trial, "I don't have any of my own guiding principles [纲领]; everything that I do is in order to execute and defend the directives and policies of Chairman Mao and the party center. . . . I am Chairman Mao's dog. . . . You are not putting me on trial but Chairman Mao!" Her death note after her suicide said, "Chairman, your student is com-ing to join you!" (主席，您的学生跟随您去了！).[148] Zhang Chunqiao told his daughter that he considered himself only Mao's "secretary," nothing more.[149]

Finally, the Gang did not always act as a coherent group, which also discounts the idea that they fought together as a faction for a cohesive ideological platform.[150] While in jail, Wang Hongwen claimed, "Before Mao's death, we already were relatively separated from each other" (我们已经是比较松散的了).[151] According to Jiang's former secretary, after the Ninth Party Congress, the other three members of the Gang started to sometimes refuse Jiang's invitation to watch movies with her. On one occasion in June 1973, all three of them declined on the same night, leading Jiang to accuse her sec-retary of trying to cause dissension among the Gang by lying about their responses to her invitation.[152] In June 1975, Mao told Deng, "Jiang Qing also does not like [Wang Hongwen]; she came specifi-cally to complain to me about him."[153] Zhang Hanzhi, a translator at the Foreign Ministry, claimed that by September 1975 the Gang did not dare spend time with one another and that Jiang had basically disappeared.[154]

The so-called leftist rebels outside the Politburo, moreover, regularly failed to work in concert with the Gang. Teiwes and Sun conclude, "Broad common interests did not generally translate into local activities being orchestrated by the Politburo radicals."[155] Sim-ilarly, the sociologist Joel Andreas states that the protests that took place during the campaign against Deng in 1976 "depended on factory-based informal networks and employed work unit resources, but none enjoyed formal support from above."[156] One "leftist rebel" leader in Hunan complains in his memoirs about how Wang Hongwen refused to support him during the "Criticize Deng" campaign. He writes, "The pitiful leftist rebels shouted every day to defend Mao Zedong, to defend Mao Zedong's Cultural Revolution line, but not a single person in Mao Zedong's party center reported to them the true seriousness of the situation at the time, and even more did not take organizational methods to make the leftist rebels achieve power."[157]

The Gang also seem to have been highly sensitive to claims that they were "leftists." In September 1975, Jiang said, "Recently, people have been making rumors about me, saying that I made a mistake, was sent down to labor, killed myself. They also say that in the center there is a leftist deviation, that there is a radical leftist faction; they say I am head of the radical leftist faction."[158] According to the Shanghai politician Xu Jingxian, "[Zhang Chunqiao] said: 'People are already saying we are a "Shanghai Gang!"' He then angrily said: 'One time at a meeting with foreigners in Beijing, they actually sat us all together; at that time I told my opinion to the Premier.'"[159] In June 1974, a report appeared in a New China News Agency publication intended for internal circulation. The report referred to an overseas observer who believed that Chinese elite politics were divided by a "radical faction with Jiang Qing in command and a moderate faction with Zhou Enlai in command." Xie Jingyi, who had a close relationship with Jiang Qing, told a writing group that such a claim was "bullshit."[160]

The preceding evidence should be understood as a qualification, but not a wholesale rejection, of the idea that the Gang were ideological radicals separated from more pragmatic figures. By the end of the Cultural Revolution, the rebel camp in factories had subscribed to the "socialist new things," such as shrinking the gap between mental and manual labor and ending temporary employment programs, although they "combined these incendiary ideas with relatively modest proposals for reform."[161] Political study campaigns affirming the Cultural Revolution were still a distraction from work and affected production. The demonstrations on Tiananmen Square in April 1976 helped convince Hua Guofeng that people were tired of these campaigns. The Gang's reticence to allow criticism that implied a full rejection of the Cultural Revolution meant significant restrictions on rectification efforts. Zhang Chunqiao admitted to his daughter that he often argued with Deng about policy, although Zhang did claim to respect Deng and he maintained that their debates did not involve any sense of personal antagonism.[162]

Moreover, the elite were conscious of differences within the Politburo. Deng was no fan of the leftist propaganda against "bourgeois privilege"—allegedly arguing in March 1975 that restricting bourgeois privilege needed a material basis and asking, "Why do we describe everything as bourgeois right? Isn't it right to receive more for more work done? Should this be called bourgeois right?"[163] According to one account, the majority of a central study group was disappointed to hear Wang Hongwen support the criticisms of the piece-rate system used at a port in Guangzhou, and Hu Yaobang fell asleep during a discussion of articles by Zhang and Yao on bourgeois privilege.[164] In September 1975, Hua criticized the Shanghai method of conducting science, expressed opposition to criticism of primary research, and supported specialists and the reading of foreign material. These comments helped persuade Ye Jianying, who played a crucial role in the Gang's arrest, that Hua was not a radical.[165]

However, the preceding evidence weakens the argument that the fall of the Gang was purely about rejecting their political positions. The earlier failures of the Cultural Revolution meant that the Gang were basically accepting of rectification. The Gang had a limited policy agenda beyond political education, and they showed no independence from Mao. Beyond a concern for remaining loyal to Mao's legacy in at least nominal terms, given the chance, the Gang might have been at least somewhat flexible on policy issues. The move against the Gang was not initially characterized as a rejection of any political position. As will be shown in the remainder of this chapter, a complete explanation of the Gang's fall requires attention to their dispositional characteristics, how their removal was arranged, and the importance of force.

Historical Legacies and Compromising Material

Why did Mao not select one of the Gang as his successor? The Chairman's choice of Hua was generally a surprise—Ye Jianying, for example, was shocked when he learned that Mao had selected Hua, not any member of the Gang.[166] If Mao had allowed a member of the Gang to become the top leader, such clear imprimatur, plus the formal trappings of office, would have made an attack against them much riskier. But Mao understood that no member of the Gang was strong enough to assume that position. Their weaknesses, which are also crucial for understanding why they were defeated so soon after Mao's death, were primarily related to their histories and personal characteristics. The Gang had not made serious contributions to the party before 1949, and they were particularly susceptible to compromising material and character assassinations. The Gang had poor personal skills and lacked charisma. Their linkage to Mao was a double-edged sword—it helped them reach the pinnacle of Chinese politics, but the Chairman's death meant that this advantage would not last past September 9, 1976. Their association with the Cultural Revolution made them the target of individuals with negative memories of that era. Therefore, Wang Dongxing accurately summarized the Gang's fall at a meeting in November 1976: "The Gang of Four were extremely ambitious; why were they not able to succeed? First, they had no prestige, and second, they created a huge number of grievances."[167]

Every member of the Gang struggled against compromising material, but Jiang Qing's entire life was a struggle against character assassination. Roxane Witke, who spent days interviewing Jiang, writes, "A persistent theme of her reconstruction of the past is how, throughout her life, she had been plagued by the sorts of gossip to which women who strive for political effect inevitably are subject."[168] Jiang's history in Shanghai during the 1930s as an actress was particularly sensitive. According to a woman close to Jiang at the time, most of the media coverage about Jiang referred to her scandals, not her acting skills.[169] The atmosphere for celebrities in Shanghai in the 1930s was toxic—the tabloids led several actresses to commit suicide and led the famous author Lu Xun to write a piece called "Gossip Is a Fearful Thing."[170] Jiang later told Witke to read that essay: "for in it you will find clues to my own life."[171]

Also during Jiang's time in Shanghai, she was at one point allegedly arrested, which later led to questions about whether she had betrayed the CCP while in prison. In 1954, she received an anonymous letter that referred to her scandalous past and supposed betrayal of the CCP while in jail.[172] One document disseminated to the party after the Gang were arrested includes circumstantial evidence supporting this viewpoint.[173] However, these accusations are untrue—the evidence has no documentary proof, and the portions based on oral sources were forced. Xu Mingqing, a woman who knew Jiang Qing for decades, was placed under intense physical and emotional pressure to say that Jiang was a traitor. She later recanted.[174] Even the individual who was supposedly with Jiang Qing when she was arrested, a man named Le Yuhong, later claimed that the arrest itself never even happened—although shortly after the Cultural Revolution, he too was forced to say that it did.[175]

Jiang Qing joined the party in 1933 and left Shanghai in 1937–38 for the much-less-comfortable Communist base camp of Yan'an, which meant that she did not entirely lack credentials. But Mao said to a Politburo meeting in 1975 that Jiang "did not participate in a big half of the party's history," including the Long March and the struggles against leaders such as Chen Duxiu or Qu Qiubai.[176] Moreover, when Jiang arrived in Yan'an, she did not enjoy the prestige of the earlier cohort of feminist woman leaders who had participated in the May Fourth movement.[177] According to one credible account, while in Yan'an, when the top leaders would go to the theater, they would all bring their wives who would appear publicly. However, Jiang would merely sit in the back and not act prominently—she would not dare to act like the wives of Zhou Enlai, Zhu De, Zhang Wentian, or Li Fuchun.[178]

Jiang's status as an actress whose personal life had been covered extensively in the tabloids contrasted strongly with that of Mao's previous wife, He Zizhen, who had participated in the Long March. According to a former head of the Chinese Public Security Ministry, when Xiang Ying, commissar of the New Fourth Army, heard that Mao was going to marry Jiang, he ordered an investigation into Jiang's history in Shanghai. Xiang then sent the report to Yan'an and flatly stated that Jiang was not an appropriate wife for Mao.[179] So many senior party members opposed the wedding between Mao and Jiang that Zhang Wentian, who was formally head of the party at the time, was forced to communicate their feelings to Mao. While the widespread rumor that the party forced Mao to prevent his new wife from participating in politics is almost certainly false, the party center did announce that Jiang would focus on tending to Mao's personal life.[180]

Jiang's continuing concern over compromising information was clearly apparent during the Cultural Revolution. Zhou Enlai and Jiang Qing sent a general to Shanghai to detain a Red Guard who had been spreading compromising material about Jiang's past during the 1930s.[181] Jiang also ordered archived material about her history to be destroyed to eliminate the possibility of a full investigation of her past.[182] Zhou Enlai not only explicitly discounted anti-Jiang compromising material in public but also participated in the destruction of relevant documents.[183] During the Cultural Revolution, Jiang mercilessly persecuted individuals who were familiar with her past in the 1930s.[184]

Jiang also suffered from sexist attacks. In imperial China, women rulers were considered meddlers, and emperors' wives were expected to focus on domestic matters.[185] On a trip to the countryside in June 1974, Jiang complained about sexism in Chinese culture: "'Treasuring men and discounting women' [男尊女卑] is everywhere; our Central Committee is inappropriate. . . . They are all male chauvinists; after taking government power, it all came out, and they took it all."[186]

Speech evidence from Jiang's detractors displays a clear bias against women. The Lin Biao ally Huang Yongsheng once exclaimed, "Jiang Qing is Chairman Mao's wife, but we are still Chairman Mao's soldiers!"[187] In November 1976, in one of Hua Guofeng's less-shining moments, he claimed, "Jiang Qing bought fake hair; she wanted to rival the wife of [Ferdinand] Marcos. In Tianjin, Jiang Qing made twenty-some skirts at one time."[188] During that same month, Wang Dongxing told a group of propaganda workers, "Jiang Qing is a political hoodlum; she is also a woman hoodlum."[189] Even a woman candidate member of the Politburo, Wu Guixian, suggested that women should be deferential. In 2010, Wu recounted a conversation with Zhou Enlai's wife: "Big Sister Deng said: 'Comrade Guixian, I never participated whenever anyone reported to the Premier.' This left a very deep impression on me. It made me think that if Jiang Qing had half the bearing as Big Sister Deng, the old comrades would not have been so angry with her."[190]

Jiang struggled to achieve close personal relations. Witke writes that Jiang described her life as "lonely and harsh, devoid of trust and tenderness, save for a few familial and comradely attachments."[191] Before the trial, one of the investigators mocked Jiang by asking her why she did not have any friends. Jiang screamed, "I still have friends; I have true friends!" She refused to name them, arguing that giving their names would lead to their arrest.[192] Jiang suffered nightmares in which the ghosts of Lin Biao and Ye Qun demanded her life.[193] She was extremely isolated—Jiang refused to see visitors whom she did not summon, and she brushed them off by saying, "[Can't they go see] the Premier or Xiaoping?"[194]

Mao understood Jiang's problems. In November 1974, Mao told Li Xiannian that Jiang "cannot help but fall out with many people; she looks down on everyone."[195] Mao himself was forced to tell her staff, "Jiang Qing is sick, her temper is bad; do it for me, do not fight with her. I apologize to you."[196]

Therefore, Jiang's personality was a double-edged sword in Mao's estimation: she was dogged on attack but unable to work with others. Mao once said to members of the Politburo, "Jiang Qing's fighting spirit is strong, her class position is unshakable; here she and I are the same. She is not two-faced, but she does not understand tactics; she does not understand how to unite people, so she suffers. If she had a good adviser by her side, she could be a great standard-bearer."[197]

Zhang Chunqiao's historical record left him exposed to criticism as well. After arriving in Yan'an, Zhang claimed to have joined the CCP in Shanghai in April 1936. However, Zhang had actually joined an organization created independently by party members who had lost contact with the central party organization. This organization was illegitimate, and, therefore, Zhang technically did not join the party at this time. The reason Zhang so desperately wanted his party membership to date from April 1936 was almost certainly because individuals who joined the party before July 1937 were considered to have had much more prestige and authority than those who joined later. That date marked the beginning of the war against the Japanese and the second united front with the KMT, which meant a great deal less danger for party members.[198] In other words, even though Zhang was famous for challenging the legitimacy of the old revolutionary figures, he too was acutely sensitive to the importance of party seniority. When Zhang was made a member of the Politburo Standing Committee (PSC) in 1973, his daughter asked him how he felt. Zhang told her, "I don't feel anything. Which base area was started by me? Which military unit was created by me? Which campaign was fought by me?"[199]

Zhang's wife, Wen Jing (née Li Shufen), was another vulnerability. In 1943, shortly after marrying Zhang, Wen was captured by the Japanese. After six months of torture, she revealed her status as a CCP member and subsequently wrote anti-Communist material for a Japanese propaganda organization. After the Japanese were defeated, Wen returned to Zhang, who, somewhat surprisingly given his political aspirations, accepted her back. Over the years, Zhang hid his wife's history and placed her in sensitive political positions.[200] In 1973, despite Zhang's affection for his wife, he ultimately divorced her to firewall himself from her political problems.[201]

Zhang was widely seen as a former traitor within the Chinese political elite. In 1969, Huang Yongsheng told a colleague, "Glasses [meaning Zhang Chunqiao] is a traitor; the material has already been sent to Chairman Mao."[202] Lin Biao's son, who planned a coup against Mao, called for Zhang's arrest and announced in the famous "571 Project Summary" that he was a traitor. This document was published openly.[203]

Like Jiang, Zhang was extremely aggressive in his attempts to fight against compromising material. The rumors infuriated him: "I was never arrested; how could I be a traitor?"[204] Two individuals who discovered his wife's history were sent to jail for eight years, and his wife's documents were moved to a more secure location. In 1970, Zhang threatened to kill anyone who used compromising material against him. Enemy cadres were arrested and isolated in a dormitory, and they were tortured by being forced to listen to loud broadcasts of their family members crying. The pressure was so intense that some had a mental breakdown or killed themselves. When the Public Security Ministry created a special case committee on the Shanghai cultural sphere in the 1930s, Zhang was concerned it would find compromising information about him, so he demanded that all the material be placed under his direct control. When Jiang Qing complained that the ministry had a "special archive" on her, Zhang immediately sent one thousand people to search the ministry's collection, steal over fifty pieces of material on Jiang, seal up fifteen thousand books and journals, and also take a large collection of material related to Zhang and Yao. Zhang refused to allow doctors to treat one archivist whom he had thrown in jail, and the archivist was eventually persecuted to death. Zhang had 137 public security officials thrown in jail and tortured—the screaming grew so intense and lasted so long that nearby citizens could no longer stand it.[205]

Also similar to Jiang, Zhang's personality frustrated his political ambitions. Throughout his career, he was seen as arrogant and conniving. The head of the Shanghai Party Committee, Chen Pixian, believed Zhang was "sometimes open, sometimes sinister, hard to get along with."[206] When Mao Zedong asked his nephew Yuanxin for his opinion of Zhang, Yuanxin said that Zhang was thoughtful and capable, but "he cannot unify cadres; no one ever knows what he is thinking; he is a little sinister."[207] Another ally, Zhu Yongjia, noted that Zhang's habits of never talking about anything other than work and having no private interactions with colleagues gave Zhang a nefarious air and also isolated him.[208]

Zhang's historical "problems," personality, and inextricable links with the unpopular Cultural Revolution weakened his standing. As Shi Yun and Li Danhui argue, "The materials could not prove the earlier claim that Zhang was a 'traitor'—because Zhang had never been captured. Even defining him as a 'KMT agent' was not accurate. These are all just personal historical problems. But in that era when special case investigations defined people, personal history problems became a major issue that could affect a decision on the succession and change the entire history of the party and nation."[209]

Of all the members of the Gang, Wang Hongwen was perhaps the strongest candidate to be Mao's successor. Mao repeatedly said that Wang "once planted a field, was a soldier, was a worker. Worker, peasant, soldier are all there. Later, he was a cadre. His résumé is relatively perfect."[210] Mao even told Zhang Chunqiao,

"[Wang's] background is better than both of ours."[211] Wang's personality also separated him from the other members of the Gang. Wang would stick up for those who he felt had been wronged, and he got along easily with others.[212] Another key advantage for Wang was that, at least compared to Zhang and Jiang, the young man had not created nearly as many grudges on his way to the top. After the arrest of the Gang, even Hua Guofeng said, "If Wang Hongwen had always been bad, he would not have been able to enter the party center."[213] Zhu Yongjia later wrote that Wang was "different from Zhang Chunqiao; Zhang was at the front line of the Cultural Revolution, and he offended too many people; perhaps [Wang] could be a buffer zone between the Cultural Revolution faction and the old cadres."[214]

However, Wang too was held back by personal problems. Despite his obvious skills during the early stage of the Cultural Revolution, he lacked the ability to effectively work in the party center. The new power went to his head, and he lived an increasingly extravagant lifestyle. One Shanghai radical wrote an angry letter to Zhang Chunqiao and Yao Wenyuan, complaining that Wang led a life of dissolution, treating friends to French food, seeking out the best cars and clothes, and never talking about the works of Marx or Mao.[215] Another radical wrote a letter warning about Wang's participation in wasteful parties organized by Ye Jianying.[216] By 1976, Wang did not even pass through a doorway until a servant had moved the curtain for him.[217] Wang would even chew on a dumpling but not eat it, just to experience the taste.[218] This behavior seriously damaged his reputation. Mao allegedly told Wang Dongxing, "if we allow Wang Hongwen to be in command, no one will be able to eat well except him."[219] In a postarrest rant, Wang Dongxing claimed that Wang Hongwen "could not leave alcohol, could not leave pornography."[220]

Despite Wang's formal qualifications as someone with a peasant, soldier, and worker background, in a political system that valued seniority, his youth put him at a disadvantage. At a Politburo meeting before the Tenth Party Congress, Zhou nominated Wang as a vice premier, second only to Zhou Enlai and ranking ahead of Kang Sheng and Ye Jianying. After a period of silence, General Xu Shiyou said Wang was too young. The Politburo needed convincing. This incident left a deep impression on the thirty-eight-year-old Wang.[221]

Wang's weak willpower also lessened Mao's evaluation of him. Mao liked tough individuals. When asked why Zhou was an unacceptable successor, Mao made a cutting motion with a knife and said the Premier lacked this characteristic.[222] At a Politburo meeting in May 1975, Mao said to Wang, "Don't do this," and waved his hand in a way that suggested wavering.[223] Mao often praised Deng's toughness, but Wang could not escape Jiang Qing's domination.[224]

The Gang did have one powerful advantage over their competitors: their linkage to Mao Zedong. However, this characteristic was a double-edged sword. Jiang Qing struggled to balance reliance on Mao with attempts to establish her own authority. She often contrasted herself with the wives of other comrades who only relied on their husbands.[225] When she received a letter addressed to "Wife of Chairman Mao," she became angry. But she was delighted when she received a letter addressed to "Politburo Member Jiang Qing."[226] However, Jiang would inevitably begin speeches by saying that she represented Mao.[227]

Relying entirely on Mao was problematic. As Chen Boda said, "If it had not been for her relations with Chairman Mao, who would have taken her seriously?"[228] In a political world in which familial relations conveyed power, even the details of courtship were important—when Lin Biao wanted to hurt Jiang's authority in the eyes of his generals, he said, "In Yan'an, it was Jiang Qing who pursued the Chairman. . . . She had to fight tooth and nail to court Chairman Mao; only then did they marry."[229] Mao understood that her power was inextricably linked to his own: "She hardly respects anyone, just one person, herself. In the future, she will fight with everyone. Right now, people are just pretending to respect her [敷衍她]. After I die, she will stir up trouble."[230]

After Mao's death, the Gang hoped that their association with Mao would continue to help them. And indeed, Mao exerted an influence even from the grave. After Mao's death, Yao Wenyuan noted that people were starting to distance themselves from Jiang Qing. But Yao wrote in his diary, "I cannot do this; I must do my best to help her, support her. Otherwise, I will let down the Chairman."[231] After

Wang Hongwen was arrested, he said, "I didn't expect you would be so fast!" Similarly, Mao Yuanxin remarked, "The Chairman's corpse is not yet even cold, and you already . . ." Although Hua, Ye, and Wang Dongxing were acting against Mao's wishes, after the fall of the Gang of Four, they even went to Mao's corpse to report to him.[232]

The Gang's legitimacy was also tied to their "contributions" during the Cultural Revolution. In 1969, Yao Wenyuan justified that Jiang Qing specifically be one of Mao's successors because she was a "standard-bearer" of the Cultural Revolution.[233] Jiang understood that her fate was tied to the Cultural Revolution, and at least once, she referred to herself in this context as "a pawn that crossed the center of the board" (过了河的卒子).[234] At the same meeting when Mao first warned Jiang, Wang, Zhang, and Yao not to form a Gang of Four, he also praised Jiang Qing for her role during the Cultural Revolution.[235]

As Li Xun writes, before the Cultural Revolution, status was determined by when someone had joined the CCP and by their loyalty to the new regime. During the Cultural Revolution, however, the leftist rebels tried to institute a new system: status was then conferred by how early someone had joined the Cultural Revolution and whether they "dared to rebel."[236] Li and Perry identify the irony of this situation: "Despite their claim to be making a radical break with traditional values, the rebels embraced a familiar notion of social hierarchy based upon seniority."[237]

But this status readjustment faced serious difficulties. On the one hand, Mao was the force behind the Cultural Revolution, and his authority was absolute. On the other hand, the consequences of the Cultural Revolution were loathed. In 1969, General Xu Shiyou told Mao, "Our party's biggest problem is that the old cadres are unhappy with the leftist rebels; they are unhappy, but they find it difficult to speak out. All the old cadres were forced to suffer by the leftist rebels. With regard to this issue, the only reason the old cadres do not cause trouble is because they obey Chairman Mao. The old cadres do not oppose the Cultural Revolution, but they do oppose the leftist rebels!"[238] Mao clearly understood that the old cadres were unhappy. Almost begging them to have mercy on the younger generation, he said, "Some people were attacked; they were unhappy, and they took offense. This is understandable and can be forgiven. But [one] cannot be angry with the majority."[239] Therefore, in the words of Dittmer, "The Four ultimately backed away from their anarchist implications, but as the most salient beneficiaries of the Cultural Revolution they were blamed for the movement's every excess by die-hard opponents of the whole notion of mass criticism of authority."[240]

Hypothesis 2a versus 2b

The Deliberations

Behind the backs of the Gang of Four, Hua secretly met with members of the leadership to plan their arrests. Since those conversations were conspiratorial in nature, and the Gang could not defend themselves against the charges, this was hardly a serious, comprehensive review of elite preferences. As can be expected based on the evidence presented earlier, Hua had little material that was truly explosive and fatal for the Gang's prospects. When presented with evidence of the Gang's "crimes" after the four were already arrested, not everyone was impressed. Yet, with the arrests revealed as a fait accompli, the purge was ultimately accepted.

By 1976, Hua had been privy to power struggles at the top of the CCP hierarchy, and he had learned a great deal from those experiences. For example, he watched closely as Mao and Zhou managed the fallout after Minister of Defense Lin Biao died fleeing China in 1971. They arrested and held Lin's comrades incommunicado while they were investigated. Hua concluded, "Of course it is necessary to be extremely careful, to proceed in steps with a plan, to take the initiative."[241]

Just like prior to the moves against Beria and Khrushchev in the Soviet Union, the conspirators met individually or in small groups. Although a significant number in the leadership had been made aware that something was afoot, only a small number knew exactly what that was. Individuals who thought the issue of the Gang had to be addressed still disagreed about who should be targeted or how they should be managed. Many people thought it would be best to leave Jiang Qing free; she, after all, was Mao's widow. Only a tiny group participated in the actual planning of the arrest.[242]

Had the Gang been given the chance to defend themselves, they would have had good responses against the accusations. The most crucial evidence against them consisted of Mao's criticisms of them. On October 6, the night of the Gang's arrest, Ye Jianying presented the action as fulfillment of Mao's wishes.[243] Later, at a Politburo meeting in January 1977, Hua remarked, "Document No. 16's use of several of Chairman Mao's criticisms [of the Gang] was what had power. Didn't Jiang Qing repeatedly say that she was appearing to represent Chairman Mao? We used Chairman Mao's words to expose her; Chairman Mao had said she cannot represent Chairman Mao. It was the use of Chairman Mao's criticisms and exposure of the 'Gang of Four' that had a big effect. So we achieved a victory."[244] However, Mao's criticisms of the Gang never betrayed any sense of urgency. About the Gang, the Chairman actually said, "I do not believe this is a big problem; do not make a mountain out of a molehill. . . . If it cannot be solved in the next half year, then solve it in the next half year; if it cannot be solved this year, then solve it next year; if it cannot be solved next year, then solve it in the year after that."[245]

Another charge used to justify the arrest of the Gang was that they had been planning a coup. On the night of the Gang's arrest, Wang Dongxing told the Politburo, "For a period of time after Mao's death the 'Gang of Four' were preparing to execute a coup, so we were forced to act first."[246] This may not have been a conscious lie—Hua and the other plotters may have believed that the Gang were indeed up to something. However, as Sun and Teiwes and Shi Yun and Li Danhui emphatically demonstrate, the Gang were not in fact plotting an attack.[247]

When the Gang's Shanghai allies were shown evidence of all the Gang's "crimes," they were far from convinced. After being shown the supposed evidence during a meeting in Beijing on October 7, Ma Tianshui complained,

> The persuasiveness of this material is not strong. Chairman Mao has not even been dead for a month; how could they have gone bad so quickly? I do not agree with this method of arresting them; even if they made a mistake, it should be treated as a contradiction among the people. Give them an

opportunity to do a self-criticism! Did all four of them really make the same mistakes? . . . This material is not enough. The material relating to Jiang Qing is mostly about her lifestyle, and there is no material on Wang, Zhang, or Yao. This is simply a sudden attack, a palace coup. I think it is about first grabbing them and then finding material![248]

When on October 13 the full Shanghai leadership was informed of the decision to arrest the Gang, some members said the material used to justify the arrest was false. One person questioned, "Just this little bit was enough to purge the 'Gang of Four'?"[249] One of the radicals threw a document with Mao's criticisms of the Gang onto a table and said, "I thought you would bring back some real bombshells! Turns out it's just these few things. There's no heads or tails to it; anyone could use this if they got their hands on it!" Others reasonably asked why Mao himself did not purge the Gang if he had criticized them as early as 1974.[250] But the fait accompli meant that a real consideration of the evidence was impossible.

The Decision-Making Body

The fall of the Gang of Four had interesting parallels with the case of the anti-party group in 1957 in the Soviet Union. In the case of the Gang of Four, the possibility existed that, if given the opportunity, the CC would have rejected the charges against the Gang. Drawing explicitly on the Soviet experience in 1957, Hua and his allies went to great lengths to bypass the CC to ensure that the body did not come to the Gang's rescue. Instead, the power struggle was confined to a single decision-making body: a subset of the conspirators within the Politburo.

At the time of Mao's death, the PSC was made up of Hua Guofeng, Ye Jianying, Zhang Chunqiao, and Wang Hongwen. In other words, half of the PSC was controlled by the Gang of Four. Moreover, before Mao's death, he had taken steps to weaken Ye's political power, such as deciding in February 1976 that Chen Xilian would take care of the daily affairs of the Central Military Commission (CMC) while Ye was "sick."[251]

Of the thirteen Politburo members in Beijing, the Gang confronted a problem of political math. The Gang itself of course had at least four votes. One member, Liu Bocheng, was an invalid. Hua Guofeng, Ye Jianying, Li Xiannian, Wang Dongxing, Wu De, and Chen Xilian knew about the plot and supported it. Chen Yonggui, Wu Guixian, and Ji Dengkui probably supported Hua, but the evidence is ambiguous.[252]

In a simple vote, the Gang would have had four votes, and the plotters would have had at least six votes and possibly more. But Hua realized that if the struggle were to be played out in the Politburo—what the plotters called the "meeting-solution"—it is likely that the Gang would have called for a CC meeting to judge the split, and this situation would have been more dangerous for Hua. The party elder Chen Yun carefully looked at the membership of the CC and decided that using legal means to remove the Gang during the upcoming Third Plenum of the Tenth Party Congress was not a guaranteed victory. Ye and Chen did the math on the CC membership multiple times before deciding that using force was better than legal means.[253]

A close colleague of Ye believed that, as of September 22, Ye's original plan had been to wait for a period of time after Mao's funeral and then call an enlarged Politburo meeting to criticize the Gang. Ye believed that at this meeting the Politburo would decide to send people such as Zhang first to a lower position and then outside of Beijing, whereas Jiang would be allowed to remain as a figurehead.[254] On September 23, Wang Dongxing provided Hua Guofeng with written records of Mao's comments for use against the Gang at a meeting.[255] According to a party historian with a close personal relationship to Hua Guofeng, at the time many people thought that the problem would be best solved by calling a Politburo meeting or a CC meeting.[256]

Hua, however, believed, "The 'Gang of Four' have lackeys in every province and department. They also control the media. If a CC meeting were to be held, it would be chaos. A Politburo meeting also would not be good. The 'Gang of Four' would create chaos; there would be an open split, and it would get out of hand. If only three of the Gang were arrested, it would be no good. Jiang Qing must also be arrested; otherwise it will not solve the problem."[257]

On December 17, 1977, Hua told Hu Yaobang that if a meeting had been held to solve the Gang of Four problem, it would have been "no good," as the Gang controlled the media, Shanghai, and Liaoning. Hua said, "If matters had been allowed to continue as they were [要是放任自流], there definitely would have been a civil war. They definitely would have failed, but the losses would have been too great."[258]

Of even greater concern was the possibility of the move backfiring, such as the case in the Soviet Union. When, on September 26 or 27, Wu De, a Politburo member, expressed support for the "meeting-solution" option, Li Xiannian asked him, "Do you know how Khrushchev came to power?" Wu claims to have said, "Of course, I know. Khrushchev was in the minority in the Presidium; Molotov and Malenkov were in the majority. Khrushchev used Zhukov's support, and he used military planes to bring the CC members from all over to convene a CC meeting. At the CC meeting, Khrushchev had a majority, and Molotov and Malenkov were defeated. They were turned into an anti-party clique."[259]

Legitimacy of Behavior

Chinese historians such as Shi Yun and Li Danhui acknowledge that using force to defeat the Gang did not fit the party's rules (不合程序). Moreover, even those who executed the move against the Gang were aware of the legitimacy problem. According to a former vice editor of *People's Liberation Army Daily*, Ye Jianying once said that the act was "an exceptional method that had to be used in an exceptional time": "This is the last time in our party's history that such an exceptional method will be used."[260] Chen Yun was reluctant to accept the use of force.[261] Indeed, according to the party charter passed by the Tenth Party Congress, the Congress and the CC are the highest organs of party leadership, and the CC picks the Politburo and the PSC.[262] When Jiang Qing was arrested, she seemed to think that a coup was taking place, and she promptly wrote a letter to Hua Guofeng: "Comrade Guofeng, people here, claiming to act according to your order, declare that I be put under isolated investigation. I don't know whether this is a decision of the Central Committee."[263]

Hypothesis 3a versus 3b
Views of Power Ministries

Force, or the implicit threat of force, is necessary to understand the ultimate defeat of the Gang. All sides understood that the PLA had the capacity to play a decisive outcome in any potential power struggle, and everyone fought to develop their own capacity for violence. The Gang of Four "could not help but acknowledge that they lacked the key source of power—the military did not obey their orders. This was a fundamental shortcoming that they could not overcome."[264]

The top military hierarchy had no respect for four individuals who had contributed little to the victory in 1949. Lin Biao had once told his generals, "Zhang and Yao are nobodies; I don't know where they came from; they never did any big work; they are just journalists."[265] General Wu Faxian's distaste for the more intellectual Gang was obvious in the description of his attitude toward Zhang: "Vice Chairman Lin is the successor personally picked by Mao after the test of fighting during decades of war and political struggle. Could you, Zhang Chunqiao, and your ilk handle him? If Lin Biao were knocked down, could you, Zhang Chunqiao, fight a war and defend the nation?"[266]

Jiang Qing did have a significant and undeniable credit in her personal history: when the leadership fled Yan'an in 1947, she was the only wife who stayed behind.[267] Jiang understood the importance of this history. She had spent between ten and twenty hours explaining to Roxane Witke her role in fighting in the Northwest.[268] At her trial, Jiang screamed, "During the war, when we fled from Yan'an, I was the only female comrade to stay at the front lines with Chairman Mao. Where did you all hide?"[269] In November 1970, on a trip to Hainan Island, Jiang Qing brazenly asked the PLA forces there to seize the Paracel Islands, which were not yet controlled by China. When one officer explained that they would need an order from the CMC, Jiang said, "You need to know that I am also a member of the military. I used to be a soldier; it is just I did not keep my insignia. . . . I commanded in the Northwest during the War of Liberation. At that time I commanded with the great leader Chairman Mao. . . . I also learned how to fight."[270]

But Jiang had trouble asserting her military credentials—her statement at the trial made the audience laugh.[271] Witke vividly describes Jiang's difficulty wearing the military mantle: "The chance to speak authoritatively on warfare, historically a male prerogative, was uneasily taken, for at moments she acted surprisingly feminine. In the course of the evening's discussion of some seven hours she would suddenly break off her narration of military history and turn with a sparkling smile to blown-up examples of the Chairman's calligraphy adorning the walls, or toy nervously with tiny wreaths of jasmine and orchid blossoms attached to her fan, or adjust the blossoms she had attached to mine."[272]

At the time of Zhang Chunqiao's arrest, he was a member of the CMC Council, head of the GPD, and commissar of the Nanjing MR and the Shanghai Garrison. But these formal positions did not translate into any real political or military power. At an investigation meeting of a general in 1973, Zhang had complained, "You all libel me and say I oppose the military."[273] At a meeting in Shanghai, Zhang stood up, banged on the table, and said, "Some people don't respect me as commissar [of the Nanjing MR and the Shanghai Garrison], but you must respect this!" He then pointed to the insignia on his military uniform: "Don't think you have a strong patron. I still have Chairman Mao!"[274]

When Deng Xiaoping promoted a number of military officers in July 1975, Wang Hongwen complained, "Comrade Chunqiao and I did not know who these people were; we had no idea what their situation was. We could not think of a reason to oppose, so the [promotions] could be passed," and "[Zhang Chunqiao said his position as] head of the General Political Department is only a rubber stamp."[275] When Zhang was made head of the GPD, he had told his daughter, "If I were to go there to give a talk, who would listen?"[276] During the protests on Tiananmen Square in April 1976, Zhang asked, "What if the armed forces were to turn their guns around, at us? Then what?"[277]

Only Wang Hongwen had actually served in the PLA; but he did not rise in the ranks, and after returning to China from the Korean War, he played a clarinet in a military band.[278] Mao's shuffling of the military commanders in late 1973 and his launch of the "Criticize Lin Biao and Confucius" campaign in early 1974 were almost

certainly related to his concerns about the military's loyalty to the
Cultural Revolution after his death.[279]

The Gang were clearly troubled that they lacked real authority
in the military despite their formal positions. In August 1976, one
Shanghai radical, Wang Xiuzhen, wanted research to be carried out
on how Khrushchev had used the military to rise to power.[280] Yao
Wenyuan wrote in his diary in February 1976, "I have no iron in
my hand, just a pen."[281] Occasionally, members of the Gang would
try to make inroads with the military by writing letters to certain
units, and in at least one case, the Nanjing MR supported the study
of one of Jiang Qing's letters.[282] Knowing that the military was not
under their control, the Gang sought to create a militia force to
balance against the PLA.[283] On multiple occasions, Wang Hongwen
discussed urban warfare with his Shanghai colleagues, even having
them watch US movies that included footage of such warfare.[284] Ma
Tianshui stated that the Shanghai militia was given weapons after
Mao's death because he feared that a civil war would soon erupt.[285]

Beginning with Lin Biao and his generals, the PLA took steps to
prevent Jiang Qing from gaining inroads in the military.[286] Numerous top-ranking military figures urged Ye Jianying to do something
about the Gang.[287] In January 1975, during a CMC discussion meeting, Marshal Ye met individually with the top military leaders to secretly show them a written record of Mao's criticism of the Gang of
Four.[288] That same month, when Vice Commander of the General
Staff Yang Chengwu was summoned by Jiang Qing, Deng Xiaoping
told him to see her only if it was unavoidable: "Don't listen to her
formula; even the Chairman does not see her."[289] Between April and
June 1975, General Su Yu traveled throughout the country to warn
old comrades to "be careful of those people from Shanghai." Afterward, he informed Deng and Ye that the military was in reliable
hands, leading Deng and Ye to say, "Now we can relax."[290] At an
enlarged CMC meeting in the summer of 1975, Ye abandoned the
text of his official speech to add an implicit warning about allowing
the Gang to expand influence in the PLA.[291]

Hua Guofeng and his allies were clearly concerned about the
Gang's potential capacity for violence. Hua demanded that Wang
Dongxing come up with a plan to arrest the Gang as quickly as pos-
sible, partly because Hua was worried that "a minority of people

in the military have been co-opted by them."[292] In July 1976, at Ye Jianying's first personal meeting with Hua, he primarily emphasized his worries about the Shanghai militia.[293] Wang and Ye used connections in Macao to import guns for their personal defense.[294] On September 21, Marshal Nie Rongzhen told General Yang Chengwu about concerns that Deng would be assassinated and Ye would be placed under house arrest.[295] Hua told a colleague in 1999 that at the time he was worried about Zhang Chunqiao's younger brother interacting with a tank division near Beijing and about the release of weapons to the Shanghai militia.[296]

Threat of Coercion

Without the support of Wang Dongxing's palace guards, Hua's plans would have been impossible to execute. Moreover, although the PLA did not participate in the arrests, Hua would almost certainly not have dared such a risky act if military support as a critical backup were not guaranteed. Ye's support played a crucial role in giving Hua confidence to act.

To defeat the Gang, as discussed earlier, Hua decided to use force, not a meeting. The logistical planning for the arrest of the Gang was arranged by the Central Guards Bureau under Wang Dongxing's direction.[297] They left nothing to chance—when asked what to do if Wang Hongwen were carrying a gun during the arrest, Ye said, "Beat him to death; give him a little brutality!" (往死里打, 给他一点厉害!).[298] With regard to the actual move against the Gang, Wang Dongxing and his forces deserve the lion's share of the credit.

Ye was the informal leader of the old marshals and generals.[299] His support was so necessary that Hua even offered to give him the party chairmanship immediately after the Gang's arrest. As Shi Yun and Li Danhui argue, "It can be said that in order to destroy the 'Gang of Four,' without Ye it would not have been absolutely impossible, but after their destruction, without Ye it would have been absolutely impossible for Hua to consolidate his authority and stabilize society."[300]

The PLA actively prepared to support a move against the Gang. Before Mao's death, Ye spoke individually with the heads of the army, navy, and air force, warning them to maintain stability. To prepare for any eventualities, Ye told Zhang Tingfa, commissar of the air force, to leave the hospital and return to his post.[301] On October 5, Ye told Yang Chengwu to stay by the phone and control (掌握好) the three general departments, army, navy, air force, and coastal defenses. Ye said, "As long as the military has no problem, there is nothing to worry about!"[302] Members of the Beijing Garrison participated in the seizure of the central radio and television stations, and the vice commissar of the Beijing MR, Chi Haotian, led the occupation of *People's Daily*.[303]

Control over the PLA also helped prevent a 1957 anti-party-group scenario. The Gang's best hope was that their allies in Shanghai would hold out long enough to force a review of the decision to arrest the Gang. When the allies in Shanghai learned of the arrest, some wanted to use violence to resist the decision. Zhu Yongjia said, "They fear the masses; they fear Shanghai will become paralyzed. If we can hold out for three or five years and shut down the ports, it will create influence all over the world. At this time, even if we fail like the Paris Commune, we can use blood to educate the next generation." Another radical said, "If we fight, we'll fall; if we don't fight, we'll fall. I would rather struggle to the death than surrender."[304] But ultimately the balance of power persuaded the Shanghai leadership to capitulate. On October 13, when one Shanghai radical was still urging the use of force to resist the "coup" in Beijing, Ma Tianshui stated flatly, "The military is not in our hands. The militia simply cannot resist the military."[305]

Shanghai immediately concluded that force was involved in the Gang's disappearance. After the arrest but before it was announced publicly, one individual close to the Gang suspected a military coup, asking, "Have a few marshals or commanders of a few military regions struck?" Xu Jingxian answered, "Many signs indicate something has happened in the party center; it is extremely possible that a military coup has taken place."[306] Others, however, believed that Wang Dongxing and the security services were more likely to be the culprits. Wang Hongwen's secretary Liao Zukang stated, "Unit 8341 is extremely powerful [很厉害的]; it obeys Director Wang [Dongxing]. Without the command of Director Wang, it would not have been easy to quickly knock down [the Gang of Four]."[307]

How Did Institutions Matter?

First, as in the Soviet cases, the new leadership went to great lengths to demonstrate the legitimacy of its victory. However, the evidence shows that, just as in other cases, the new leadership only pursued outcomes it could dictate with certainty. At first, the party leadership wanted to engage in struggle sessions against the Gang. But the results were unsatisfactory, and the sessions were swiftly brought to an end.[308] Most famously, the leadership decided to exert enormous time and energy in preparing a major trial that would examine only the Gang's *legal* crimes, as opposed to their mistakes as party members. However, key elements of the trial were unfair. Alexander Cook writes, "The selective prosecution of politically palatable defendants, the retroactive application of laws, the numerous procedural irregularities, the widespread assumption of guilt, the limited opportunities for defense, the strongly pedagogical tone—these elements rightly contributed to the impression that the Gang of Four trial used the barest of legal trappings to conceal a raw demonstration of political power."[309]

The most important consideration was to secure convictions that would stand the test of time—this meant separating the Gang's actions from the policies of Mao and the party. The leadership was most concerned about what the Gang would say given the opportunity to defend themselves. The decision to hold an open trial was made only once the leadership was convinced it had enough powerful evidence.[310]

Second, as in the other cases in this book, the military was a crucial part of the story but not the whole story. Previous scholarship overemphasized the role of Ye Jianying.[311] However, as Teiwes and Sun argue, Hua Guofeng's position as head of the party was critical.[312] Ye told Hua, "You are first vice chairman of the party; you run the daily affairs of the party. You are also premier of the State Council. If you had not given the go-ahead, it would have been difficult to proceed! It is precisely because you made up your mind and made the decision that doing this became relatively easy."[313] Hua repeatedly emphasized to a party historian the importance that Ye was not the first person to suggest arresting the Gang: Hua first raised the issue, which was then supported by Ye.[314] Wu De said on October 21,

1976, that if Hua had not had the status of "first" vice chairman at the time of Mao's death, "it would have been unbelievable!" (不加上 '第一' 两个字, 就不得了啊!).[315]

Finally, party discipline helped ensure that Hua's fait accompli was successful. After the Cultural Revolution, the resilience of this discipline was remarkable—in October 1965, Mao had even suggested that the military should prepare to spread out production in case of civil war, warning, "If the party center acts incorrectly, and I don't mean a little incorrectly but very incorrectly, if a Khrushchev appears, with the small third line, it will be easy to rebel."[316] But this came to nothing—when a "Khrushchev" did finally appear in Beijing, the party did not split.

Implications

During the sensitive period after Mao's death, it is easy to imagine why Hua might have kept the Politburo united to help guarantee stability. The arrest of Jiang Qing sat uncomfortably with the leadership's decision to unite around Mao's memory. With more preparation, Hua might have been able to work with the CC to engineer a more graceful exit for the Gang. But Hua was in a hurry—as discussed earlier, he decided to move against the Gang almost immediately after Mao's death.

Certainly, one reason for the rush was concern about the Gang's intentions. But another factor had more to do with Hua's own vision for China. The Cultural Revolution had deepened China's backwardness, and the leadership felt pressed to rapidly improve the situation.[317] In a conversation with members of the Shanghai leadership on October 7, 1976, Hua, when justifying the arrest of the Gang, stated, "It is intolerable to wait another year; the national economy cannot wait" (再拖半年受不了, 国民经济也受不了).[318] At a meeting in 1977, Hua argued that economic growth was the top priority: "If the speed of our economic development is not as fast as that in Japan, South Korea, and Vietnam, and if the gap with the Soviet revisionists increases, if we say how great our Marxism is, how can anyone be persuaded?"[319]

Hua was almost certainly concerned that if the Gang of Four had remained in the leadership, reforms would not have been nearly as smooth. In 1977, when Deng stated that one particular plan would have been impossible with the Gang still around, Hua concurred: "Last year when the Politburo discussed the issue of Daqing importing a large chemical fertilizer, the 'Gang of Four' attacked. I said, this was approved by Chairman Mao; it cannot be criticized too much. Zhang Chunqiao talked back to me, saying, 'You all always use this to intimidate people.' "[320] Most importantly, it was apparently Jiang Qing's personal political style that pushed Hua to take an extreme step. Hua repeatedly complained in powerful terms to his biographer about Jiang's habit of causing trouble at Politburo meetings by taking over discussions and having temper tantrums. Removing Jiang from the equation would make change much easier.[321]

Although a move against the Gang would have threatened to destabilize the regime, ultimately leaving the Gang on the Politburo would have required at least some attention to their concerns. In 1969, Jiang Qing had stated, "There should not be one successor to Chairman Mao; we must take all those whom Chairman Mao trusts the most and put them in the core leadership."[322] But Hua and his allies had little confidence in the Gang's leadership—for all the reasons discussed earlier, the Gang were not easy to trust or to like, and Jiang's extremely antagonistic political style made serious Politburo discussions difficult. Chen Xilian, who was running the daily affairs of the military on the eve of the move against the Gang, complained to Li Xiannian, "As soon as a Politburo meeting starts, fighting erupts. Jiang Qing takes the lead, making the Politburo unable to function normally."[323] Only a quick solution would create a political atmosphere conducive to moving forward quickly after Mao's death.[324]

CHAPTER FIVE

The Fall of Hua Guofeng

Introduction: Return of the Old Comrades

At the time of Mao's death on September 9, 1976, Hua Guofeng sat at the top of the party, state, and military structures. Mao was forced to name Hua as his successor because Deng Xiaoping was under house arrest, having disappointed Mao for the last time. When Premier Zhou Enlai's legendary administrative talents began to fail due to his debilitating cancer, Mao had summoned Deng, who had been purged at the beginning of the Cultural Revolution, to bring the country back to its feet. But by the end of 1975, Deng's rectification goals were on the ropes, and, by April 1976, he was removed from all of his positions. The news that the Gang of Four had been purged, which Deng's daughters relayed to him in the toilet while the water was running to prevent eavesdropping, came as a relief to the already elderly and still incarcerated statesman. "It looks like I can spend my last days in peace," Deng said.[1]

Yet by 1981, Deng had fully eclipsed the younger Hua as paramount leader, thus inaugurating what would become known as the era of "old person politics."[2] Mao's attempt to pass the baton to a younger generation had been thwarted. Unlike in the Soviet Union, the transition in China ended with a reassertion of power by the old comrades. The Cultural Revolution proved to be a hiatus before traditional systems of authority were reestablished.

The historiographical consensus on this period fits neatly with the principles of the economic model introduced in chapter 1. According to this narrative, Hua, although not as aggressive as the Gang of Four, still adhered to a dogmatic and radical ideology. He attempted to block the rehabilitation of old revolutionaries who had been purged during the Cultural Revolution, including Deng Xiaoping. He surrounded himself with his own faction, known as the "whateverists." His anti-reform policies were defeated at the famous work conference before the Third Plenum. These unpopular qualities made him an exceptionally weak figure whose fall would be inevitable. The military did not play a decisive role. Lowell Dittmer, in 2011, wrote that "as a beneficiary of the Cultural Revolution (and Mao's personal benediction), Hua felt obliged to continue the heaven-storming policies of radical Maoism, thereby losing the support of the moderates who had helped him dispose of the Gang." Dittmer describes this viewpoint as "consensually accepted by the scholarly community."[3]

These characterizations range from outright fabrications to gross simplifications. This chapter presents a different view of the events of 1976–81 based on primary source material from the Hubei Provincial Archives, the database History of Contemporary Chinese Political Movements, the Service Center for Chinese Publications, the Fairbank Center Collection of Harvard's H. C. Fung Library, official publications, memoirs, history journals, and history books published on the mainland or in Hong Kong, as well as pathbreaking work by Li Haiwen, Han Gang, Frederick C. Teiwes, and Warren Sun.

With regard to the first hypothesis on the economic and authority model, we find support for the latter in the following ways. First, the economic model predicts that the most democratic, consensus-oriented figure will win a political contest due to their superior ability to co-opt threats. These adjectives fit Hua closely; but the winner, Deng Xiaoping, had an autocratic, dictatorial personality and he was not given to compromise. In fact, Hua hoped to co-opt the old revolutionaries, including Deng, but these attempts did not secure his power. Instead, the entire history was a one-sided contest, as Hua did nothing to fight back against Deng's growing power. Second, no real policy differences separated Hua and Deng. Rather, the most important divide separating Hua from Deng was that between their generations and their differing roles during the Cultural Revolution.

Hua's departure from the leadership was not the result of a structured discussion within the party about his strengths and weaknesses. Deng acted in a conspiratorial fashion to weaken Hua's position. Hua was a popular individual among many of the party members, and his defeat was primarily the result of Deng's choices, not a broad consensus within the party that Hua should be punished. Hua's most serious political setbacks resulted from highly irregular interpretations of party rules. Most famously, the work conference before the Third Plenum in late 1978 took the initiative from the PSC. Deng not only allowed but sometimes even manipulated political pressure from lower levels of the party to bend the rules to his benefit.

The role of the military during this period is especially interesting, as Hua's ultimate defeat cannot be understood without careful attention to the PLA. Yet the armed forces never acted in an operational sense as described in the other chapters of this book. Simply put, Deng's behavior in the immediate post-Mao era reveals the extent to which he saw control over the PLA as the real source of power. When Deng concluded that the reform process was creating doubts and opposition within parts of the PLA, he not only took special care to reassert his authority there but also intensified his aggressive posture toward Hua. Deng's use of the military to advance the "practice is the sole criterion of truth" campaign, as well as his decision to attack Vietnam, demonstrated to the elite that the PLA ultimately obeyed Deng.

Hypothesis 1a versus 1b

Political Style

According to Hypothesis 1a, the leader best able to aggregate interests and co-opt threats will emerge victorious. If this were the case, then Hua, who was consensus-oriented, should have easily emerged the victor. Instead, we see support for Hypothesis 1b, whereby the more dictatorial personality, Deng Xiaoping, prevailed over Hua.

The evidence is overwhelming that Deng had little interest in collective decision-making. During a December 1973 meeting with the military high command, Mao said of Deng, "Some people are afraid of him; he deals with matters rather resolutely. . . . You [Deng], people are a little afraid of you; I will describe you with a few words [我送你两句话]: toughness inside softness, a needle wrapped in cotton. On the outside you are a little gentle, but inside you are a steel factory."[4] Mao's conclusions were shared by many others. On October 31, 1976, Marshal Ye Jianying told an old friend, "This man Xiaoping, he never takes things easy; he monopolizes power [擅权]; as soon as he comes back, he will steal the show, and it will be impossible for Hua to show his stuff."[5] The party intellectual Li Honglin remarked, "I discovered that Deng Xiaoping was a true 'steel factory,' an absolute autocrat [一言堂]. Even when Hu Yaobang [then party general secretary] went to him, he, let alone other people, could not talk back." As opposed to Mao, who when interacting with people would tell jokes and chat, "if [you] were in front of Deng Xiaoping, you could only accept his commands totally obediently."[6]

If Deng was the "ass-kicker," as the late China watcher Michel Oksenberg wrote in a memo to Zbigniew Brzezinski in May 1978, then Hua was the "reconciler."[7] Mao described Hua very differently from Deng: "Comrade Guofeng, I understand him very well; he has integrity and is honest; he can care for the masses; he can conduct investigations; and he can unite comrades." Marshal Ye agreed: Hua was "modest, careful, sincere; he has a democratic style." Li Xiannian, a PSC member, believed that Hua was "extremely principled."[8] Deng Liqun, then vice president of the Chinese Academy of Social Sciences, in one of his speeches on party history remarked, "This person Hua Guofeng was very cunning, but it should be said that he did not engage in conspiracies. . . . It should be said that Hua Guofeng's life was just and honest."[9] According to the historian Xiao Donglian, Hua "was honest, and his style was relatively democratic."[10]

Even when the party needed to rally around Hua soon after the defeat of the Gang, he took steps to ensure that he did not become the center of a new personality cult. The man in charge of broadcasting in China, Zhang Xiangshan, informed his colleagues that although Hua's status as successor should be emphasized, "at the same time it should not be overdone. The goal is not to exaggerate but to seek truth from facts, reasonably and correctly convey the image of the new chairman, the new leader." However, on November 12, one top leader (unnamed but probably Wang Dongxing) complained to a meeting of propagandists that praise of Hua should be toned down or it would have the opposite effect and hurt Hua's image.[11] People other than Hua, especially Marshal Ye, built up Hua's authority in a way that some people misinterpreted as Hua engaging in personality-cult behavior.[12] When Hua said that he did not want the title of "wise leader" (英明领袖), even the Deng ally Wang Zhen stood up and said, "I checked the dictionary; *yingming* means *mingjun* [enlightened king]. I think it's okay!"[13] Later criticisms of Hua as a despotic ruler were intended to undermine the broad sentiment that Hua was democratically oriented.

Hua's tenure was in fact a golden era of collective leadership. Hua told a group preparing his official biography, "After the fall of the 'Gang of Four' and when I was chairman, collective leadership was very strongly emphasized, democratic centralism. It was not one or two people who could make decisions; collective leadership was needed. If the leadership was collective, matters would be dealt with well. The party center all lived at Yuquanshan together, and stabilizing measures were all discussed collectively. All of my speeches were discussed by the Politburo collectively."[14] According to the former editor of *People's Daily* Hu Jiwei, "[Unlike Mao,] when Hua Guofeng made mistakes, he could be criticized. . . . He did not exert strict control; his methods were not cruel."[15] Hua was a consensus builder. In April 1978, when the propaganda apparatus put pressure on Hua to speak out on controversial ideological issues, Hua refused, saying that as party chairman, speaking out too quickly would unfairly cause any debate to be stillborn.[16] To his credit, his decision not to rely on his formal position to fight tooth and nail against his removal speaks to his consensual and democratic personality. Speaking to one interviewer about his resignation, Hua said, "If the party were to have another internal struggle, the regular people would have suffered. I stubbornly resigned from all positions. I told Marshal Ye before I did it. Some said that I was a fool. Some said that I was too honest, but I do not regret it."[17]

Shockingly, two highly credible sources told the author of this book that on June 1 or 2, 1980, Ye Jianying even asked Hua whether they should "do another smashing of the Gang of Four"—or, in other words, execute a coup against Deng. Hua refrained.[18] Hu Jiwei later reflected on how strange it was that a leader would choose not to label his opponents as counterrevolutionaries or engage in "brutal struggle and cruel attacks." Hua's tolerance for criticism was revolutionary, writes Hu Jiwei: "This was one of the most civilized changes in leadership positions in the history of our party."[19]

Hypothesis 1a predicts that the loser in a power struggle would be the competitor who was either unable or unwilling to co-opt their political challengers. At first glance, this might seem to explain why Hua lost. Ezra Vogel argues that Hua "did not support the full-scale return of senior officials who had been brought back to work under Deng's leadership."[20] Harry Harding similarly concludes that Hua tried "to prevent the reemergence of more senior leaders who might threaten his political dominance."[21] This is an important point to evaluate because Hua's alleged lack of respect for his elders, including Deng, was identified as one of his principal crimes.

Instead we see more support for Hypothesis 1b: Hua did try to co-opt his potential challengers, but he was still removed from the leadership. As the historian Han Gang points out, Hua took a personal interest in the rehabilitation of important cadres such as Hu Yaobang, Hu Jiwei, and Zhang Aiping, all of whom had been purged along with Deng near the end of the Cultural Revolution. Hua also played an important role in solving the infamous "Inner Mongolia" and "61 Traitor Clique" cases. Hua's attitude was conciliatory: "Why is it that some old cadres cannot come out [be liberated]? Why can't there be reciprocal forgiveness? Isn't it good that Xi Zhongxun and Song Renqiong have come out? Zhou Hui wants to go to Inner Mongolia. Some old cadres have been on the sidelines for many years; why aren't they allowed to come out? There is a fear not to use talents that are not presently serving the country [怕举逸民]. They are all proletarian hermits."[22] Prior to the work conference

before the Third Plenum, Hua had already been preparing to rehabilitate the "61 Traitor Clique," Peng Dehuai, and Tao Zhu.[23]

When Ye affirmed Hua's leadership of the country after the
fall of the Gang of Four, he listed Hua's respect for old comrades
(along with his youth, honesty, democratic sensibility, and work experience) as among his most important positive qualities.[24] Shortly
before Hua was officially removed from the party chairmanship, Li
Xiannian admitted that Hua did not block the rehabilitation of the
veteran comrade Wang Renzhong and the "61 Traitor Clique."[25]

Surprisingly, it was not Hua but Deng who opposed the other
major old revolutionary, Chen Yun, from returning to work. Hua
revealed in June 1981, "At the First Plenum of the Eleventh Party
Congress everyone suggested that Comrade Chen Yun, Comrade
Deng Yingchao, and Comrade Wang Zhen should join the Politburo; at the Politburo when I spoke and mentioned this situation,
it was not I who opposed it. At the time, it really was discussed.
Comrade Xiaoping first suggested that wouldn't it be better if no
changes were made at that time." When Deng Xiaoping finally suggested that Chen become a vice chairman at the Third Plenum, Hua
immediately accepted Deng's proposal.[26] Hua also supported the ascension of another major elder, Peng Zhen, to the PSC, but he was
blocked by both Deng and Chen.[27]

During a meeting dedicated to criticizing Hua, he did a self-
criticism about the "two whatevers," leftism in economics, and the
creation of his own personality cult. But among all of the trumped-up
charges, he flatly refused to admit that he had blocked the rehabilitation of old revolutionaries: "You say that I blocked the return of
old cadres; whom did I block exactly? I am not going to say any
more. Say whatever you want!"[28]

What was Hua's view of Deng in particular? Richard Baum
writes that Hua and his loyalists "adamantly opposed" Deng's rehabilitation.[29] New evidence decisively rejects this conclusion. As early
as October 26, 1976, two Politburo members, Su Zhenhua and Ni
Zhifu, told Deng that he would return to work.[30] On December 10,
Deng was allowed to visit a PLA hospital to treat an infected pros-
tate. Soon after that, Deng was allowed to read classified materials.[31]
During this time, Deng took a trip to Yuquanshan to listen to Hua
give an account of the fall of the Gang of Four.[32] All of these devel-

opments were signs of a political loosening.[33] Deng, therefore, had to know that sooner or later he would be rehabilitated.

Hua's speech to the Politburo on January 6, 1977, is crucial evidence that he never opposed Deng's return to work and that he had already approved Deng's return at an appropriate time. Hua said, "The issue of Deng Xiaoping was considered repeatedly while managing the 'Gang of Four' issue. . . . The issue of Comrade Deng Xiaoping will be solved, and actually it is already being solved. . . . The issue of returning to work should be a matter of time." Hua also provided a rationale for this timing:

> Now there are people who propose not doing it this way; they propose that after knocking down the "Gang of Four," Deng Xiaoping should come to work immediately. If Deng Xiaoping were to come to work immediately after the fall of the "Gang of Four," it is possible we would be falling into a big trap. . . . If we hastily and in a big hurry [急急忙忙] were to suggest that Deng Xiaoping return to work, then Documents No. 4 and 5, those issues that Chairman Mao managed, would they still count? Then wouldn't people say that this is overturning the verdict on Deng Xiaoping? Wouldn't this mean we are not carrying out the unfulfilled wishes of Chairman Mao?

Hua even expressed confidence that Deng would understand the need for some delay.[34] In November 1980, Deng admitted that he was aware of this rationale. But he was still rankled—he rhetorically asked why he could not have become premier and then emotionally said he would not have taken the position anyway.[35]

Although Ye Jianying has traditionally been identified as supporting Deng's swift rehabilitation, Ye shared Hua's view that the process of Deng's return should be managed carefully. Ye wanted to protect Hua Guofeng's status but also to bring Deng back to work, which meant he was "caught between two difficulties" (有一个两难).[36] On October 31, 1976, Ye told an old friend, "Deng will return to work, but it will be a little later. When a car turns too quickly, it will turn over. The matter of Xiaoping was raised by Chairman Mao; the Politburo decided to leave him in the party to watch him, to see if the offender mends his ways; it is not good [不行] if [he] all of a sudden were to return to work. There must be a process. Otherwise, it would really be a palace coup."[37]

Policy

The consensus view is that Hua and Deng differed on major policy issues. Hypothesis 1a assumes that the victor in a political power struggle is the one whose policy or patronage platform is more popular. Hypothesis 1b, on the other hand, allows for the possibility that power struggles can occur when policy differences are minimal and those differences are inflated for political purposes. New evidence emphatically demonstrates the greater explanatory value of Hypothesis 1b. Deng in fact cooperated with Hua on a whole host of issues. According to Deng Liqun, "Deng [Xiaoping] and Chen [Yun] were united on some issues with Hua, and they conflicted on other issues; there was unity within the struggle [斗争中间 有统一], and it certainly was not the case that they opposed Hua Guofeng on every issue."[38]

For scholars of Chinese politics, Hua is perhaps most famously known for the "two whatevers," a political slogan interpreted to mean that Mao's political line would be continued without any changes. Indeed, this slogan was seen by many high-ranking cadres at the time as an attempt to block Deng Xiaoping from returning to work, a refusal to reverse the verdict on the Tiananmen Incident of 1976, and an affirmation of extremist ideology. The first issue is addressed in the previous section that demonstrates that Hua actually sought to co-opt Deng. The two other perceived implications are policy related. On these issues, did Hua actually have a different view from that of Deng?

Powerful evidence can now put to rest the accusation that Hua resisted changing the verdict on the 1976 Tiananmen Square Incident.[39] Zhou Enlai died in January 1976, and in April, wreaths commemorating him covered Tiananmen Square, sparking a political crisis. The Politburo decided to remove the crowds from the square. On April 5, Mao labeled the Tiananmen disturbances a "counterrevolutionary rebellion," allowed the use of force, and said that Deng should be placed under investigation because of his alleged role in the affair.[40] Following Mao's death, the issue of whether to reverse the verdict on the Tiananmen Square Incident was particularly sensitive, and it was made more complicated by the fact that it was broadly seen to be related to Deng's status in the post-Mao political world.

However, as early as the Politburo meeting on January 6, 1977, Hua signaled that he would not adopt a hard line on the Tiananmen Square issue, although, at first, he did not want to spur controversy by saying that Mao had made a mistake. Hua noted that the issue "really was suppressed by the 'Gang of Four'" and that "the Tiananmen Incident was forced" (implying that the Gang of Four's behavior was a cause of the incident). Hua counseled patience: "If there are some other opinions, it is not a big deal; they must be guided."[41]

The Chinese scholar Xu Qingquan, drawing on extensive interviews, has demonstrated that Hua slowly continued to prepare the ground for a different appraisal of the Tiananmen Incident. In August 1978, *People's Daily* published an article accusing the Beijing party boss Wu De of blocking the reversal of the Tiananmen verdict. By the time of the work conference before the Third Plenum, the top party leadership, including Hua, had already decided to support a full rehabilitation.[42]

New evidence now shows that the origin of the "two whatevers" had nothing to do with political or economic orthodoxy. The historian Han Gang writes, "According to official accounts, the 'change in emphasis' [重点转移] was a historical change that occurred after the 'Cultural Revolution,' and Deng Xiaoping was the first to suggest this strategy. Some accounts even say that this was the result of a struggle against the 'two whatevers,' which in direct or indirect ways draws a line between Hua Guofeng and Deng Xiaoping. Actually, it was nothing like this."[43] After Hua left the leadership, he told an interviewer that if he had really engaged in the "two whatevers," he would not have smashed the Gang of Four.[44]

The dominant view is that Hua was an economic dogmatist who made major economic mistakes. Richard Baum, for example, refers to the "unswerving public devotion [of Hua and his supporters] to whatever Mao said or did."[45] Although Harry Harding writes that Hua "seemed to recognize the country's need for a period of political normalcy and economic development," he also concludes that

Deng "had become convinced of the need for much more sweeping political and economic reforms than Hua Guofeng was willing to undertake." Harding believes that Deng had "an attractive alternative program."[46]

Recently, however, this argument has been under attack by historians. Alexander Pantsov, with Steven Levine, writes that Hua was convinced "of the need to reexamine the most odious of the Maoist directives" on economics and was "increasingly convinced of the need for rapid modernization."[47] Hua in fact began taking steps toward economic reform that are most commonly associated with Deng. As Teiwes and Sun show, on economic issues, Hua was not an ideologue, and to the extent that his policies were a failure, Deng was equally culpable. Teiwes and Sun write, "On all key dimensions—the overambitious drive for growth, a newly expansive policy of openness to the outside world, and limited steps toward management reform—Hua and Deng were in basic agreement."[48] They also demonstrate that Deng did not support key agricultural reforms as quickly as Hua and that, moreover, this issue had no bearing on their relative authority.[49] Hua, not Deng, was the individual in the party center who played the most important role in supporting the Special Economic Zones.[50]

Chinese historians have also participated in changing to this new view of Hua. Cheng Zhongyuan provides a series of examples of Hua challenging party dogma on economic issues, including emphasizing production as a key element of revolution and advocating the provision of material benefits in exchange for hard work.[51] Hua took the initiative to improve the treatment of scientists, and it was he who first called for, and presided over, a major conference on reform of science and technology that was held in March 1978.[52] He also played a crucial role in the July–September 1978 "State Council Conference to Discuss Principles," a meeting that set the stage for major breakthroughs on a slew of economic issues at the Third Plenum.[53]

In fact, as early as January 1977, only three months after the Gang of Four were eliminated, Hua displayed an open mind. That month, Xiang Nan, then working at the First Ministry of Machine Building, reported to the top leadership about a trip to the United States. After the meeting, Hua asked Xiang to stay behind. Xiang emphasized that inequality was more severe in China than it was in the United States and that it was necessary to study capitalism's achievements. After a moment of silence, Hua remarked, "I believe that what you have said is true," but he also warned Xiang not to speak of such matters publicly.[54] In his later years, when Hua saw a television report on reform and opening that emphasized Deng's role, he muttered, "Reform and opening was first suggested by me."[55]

What, then, did the "two whatevers" actually mean, and why did so many individuals in the elite misinterpret the expression? The key to understanding this puzzle is that the immediate challenge facing Hua was how to show his flexibility on the Deng and Tiananmen issues without raising concerns that he was moving too quickly to reject the Maoist legacy. Unfortunately for Hua, he handled this problem in a particularly clumsy way, and it was this clumsiness, as opposed to political dogmatism or opposition to Deng, that led to the "two whatevers."

In January 1977, Wang Dongxing, the PSC member in charge of propaganda work, told the party writer Li Xin to draft two speeches for Hua. One of those speeches was intended for a meeting of the top leadership in the party, government, and military to announce that Deng would return to power once the situation had stabilized. When Li Xin met his work group, he told his assistants to include criticism of rumors and "splittist" talk, which was a code for discussions about Deng and Tiananmen. Li suggested that one way to prevent the Deng and Tiananmen issues from becoming explosive was to emphasize the big picture. The most obvious way to do this was to rally around Mao. Therefore, when on January 21, the first draft of Hua's planned January speech was completed, the following phrase appeared: "Whatever policies Chairman Mao raised, they must be protected; they cannot be violated; whatever language and behavior damages Chairman Mao's image, they must be controlled; they cannot be tolerated." Li Xin later explained why he included these words:

In the process of writing the draft, the most difficult matter to manage was, under the circumstances of the time, stabilizing the situation, which meant raising high the banner of Chairman Mao. It was impossible to say Chairman Mao made mistakes; it could not be said that "criticize Deng, counterattack the rightist verdict-reversal wind" was a mistake; at the same time, it was necessary to say that Deng Xiaoping's return to work was correct and necessary. Therefore, writing the draft was extremely difficult; no matter what was said, it was imperfect. Because I emphasized raising high the banner of Mao Zedong and stabilizing the situation, the expression "two whatevers" appeared in the second draft of the speech.

By the time that the fourth draft of Hua's January speech was completed, the situation had changed. Instead of a meeting for leading cadres in the party, government, and military, a work meeting of the CC would take place—but later. On February 3, Li Xin informed his group that the speech would be delayed, and instead first an editorial would be published. On February 6, the editorial, called "Study the Documents Well and Grasp the Key Link," was read on the radio, and it was published in *People's Daily* the following day. This editorial contained the infamous "two whatevers": "We will resolutely uphold whatever policy decisions Chairman Mao made and unswervingly follow whatever instructions Chairman Mao gave."[56] The "two whatevers," therefore, was not, as Vogel argues, the result of Hua "direct[ing] his supporters to prepare a theoretical article to show his commitment to the Maoist legacy."[57]

Both the appearance of the "two whatevers" and the delay in more broadly announcing the plan to rehabilitate Deng had disastrous long-term political repercussions for Hua. Some in the top leadership interpreted this phrase as a dogmatic statement. Geng Biao, for example, remarked, "Publishing this article is the equivalent of not smashing the 'Gang of Four.'"[58] Deng Liqun saw the "two whatevers" as an attempt to prevent Deng Xiaoping from returning to work. A few days later, Wang Zhen lambasted the "two whatevers" at a meeting of the National Defense Industry Office of the State Council. Then Wang told Deng Xiaoping about how he and Deng Liqun had interpreted the "two whatevers."[59]

A terrible misunderstanding had occurred. The historian Han Gang writes,

The planning at the top to solve the Deng Xiaoping issue was unknown to the outside world, and even the majority of the membership of the party, including senior members [党内大多数人包括资深人士], did not understand; so it was difficult to avoid giving the impression of a "delay." . . . But when the "two whatevers" appeared, matters did not move in the direction hoped for by its creators but instead created an unforeseen reaction. It seemed that they had created a political restriction for more deeply exposing and criticizing the "Gang of Four" and that the creators had not fundamentally understood the connection between the "Cultural Revolution" and Mao Zedong's mistakes in his later years and, therefore, they could not solve or completely eliminate the mistakes of the "Cultural Revolution."[60]

Despite the assertions by many Chinese scholars that figures such as Chen Yun had tried but failed to persuade Hua to allow Deng to return to work at the party meeting in March 1977, it was in fact at this meeting that the decision to allow Deng to return to work (already made) was revealed publicly.[61] Hua seems to have understood that the delay, and especially the "two whatevers," had raised suspicions about his intentions. He tried to explain himself:

Recently within the party and among the masses there has been no small amount of debate around the issues of Deng Xiaoping and the Tiananmen Incident. . . . With regard to Deng Xiaoping, everyone knows that "criticizing Deng and opposing the rightist reversal of cases" was decided by the great leader Chairman Mao. Criticism is necessary, but how the Gang of Four criticized Deng was different; they violated Chairman Mao's order. . . . This was an important part of their plan to take over the party and seize power. . . . When the center solved the problem of the Gang of Four anti-party clique, it believed that the issue of Deng Xiaoping should be solved correctly and that it should be done in phases, as part of a process; the center's decision to continue to "criticize Deng and the rightist reversal of cases" was considered multiple times; by doing it in this way, it would fundamentally destroy and excuse the Gang of Four and its remnants and other counterrevolutionary powers from using this issue to provoke counterrevolutionary activity, thereby stabilizing the entire country. . . . Some comrades did not really understand and do not really support the center's decision, believing that once the Gang of Four was defeated, it was necessary to immediately have Comrade Deng Xiaoping return to work. This position did not consider the question from the perspective of the struggle on a comprehensive level. . . . It has now been demonstrated by investigation that a small group of counterrevolutionaries had a counterrevolutionary policy of calling for Comrade Deng Xiaoping to return to work to force the center to take a position and then to attack us for violating the last wishes of Chairman Mao, thereby overthrowing the party Central Committee.[62]

Hua declared that an official decision for Deng to return to work would be made at the Third Plenum of the Tenth Party Congress.[63] In a speech at the March work meeting, Ye Jianying argued that Mao had shown that party "revisionists" could be defeated with another Cultural Revolution, apparently trying to quell fears that Deng's return to power would imply a victory of revisionism.[64] Even Chen Yun, who is described in many sources as unhappy with Hua's policies at this time, said, "I strongly support having Comrade Deng Xiaoping return to work when the time is ripe."[65]

Deng was upset about the "two whatevers." On May 24, he had an important meeting with Wang Zhen, Deng Liqun, and Yu Guangyuan.[66] Deng said it was impossible to explain why the verdict on him was reversed or why the Tiananmen Incident was not a counterrevolutionary incident under the "two whatevers."[67] Hua seems to have immediately taken Deng's criticisms to heart. In 1978, Zhao Ziyang, who would later become party general secretary, pointed out that Hua very quickly moved away from the "two whatevers" and accepted Deng's terminology:

I believe that the "two whatevers" spoken of at the March work conference of last year were a result of the historical conditions at the time; it is understandable. That's because the Gang of Four had just been destroyed and it was necessary to decrease the amount of guessing going on in other countries, and, moreover, the solving of everyone's thinking needed to go through a process. At the Third Plenum of the Tenth Party Congress [July 1977], Chairman Hua and Vice Chairman Deng suggested a comprehensive and accurate understanding of Mao Zedong Thought, and practically speaking, this was a clarification and already the issue was solved.[68]

At the end of the November 1978 work conference, the landmark meeting that signified an important defeat for Hua, he did a self-criticism for the "two whatevers," explaining that they were intended to encourage unity and protect Mao's image, not to attack Deng:

> At the time, my intention was that while giving a free hand in mobilizing the masses to start the great struggle to expose and criticize the "Gang of Four," it was absolutely imperative not to damage the glorious image of Chairman Mao. This was an important issue I was always considering in theoretical terms immediately after the smashing of the "Gang of Four." Later, I discovered that the first part [of the "two whatevers"] was too absolute and the second part really did need to be emphasized. But I did not clearly say how to restrict this. At the time, I did not consider these two expressions completely enough. Reflecting now, if only I had not raised the "two whatevers," things would have been fine.[69]

But the concept of the "two whatevers" was pinned to Hua, and later Deng would even use this expression against him.

Other than the "two whatevers," Hua is often accused of opposing Deng's view that "practice is the sole criterion of truth" and that the appearance of the "practice" position was originally a reaction to Hua's "two whatevers." If Hua truly opposed the popular "practice" position because of his dogmatic viewpoints and was punished politically for it, this would support Hypothesis 1a. However, newly

available evidence shows that for several reasons this characterization is extremely misleading. This evidence supports Hypothesis 1b:
Deng gained the upper hand against Hua by turning the "practice"
issue into a political tool.

The "practice" debate was originally not about ideology in general but rather about a much narrower topic: how to reverse verdicts on cases that had been personally approved by Mao, which, as
discussed earlier, were supported by Hua. Therefore, the issue was
much narrower than general accounts suggest, and it certainly had
nothing to do with Maoist policies in economics. The problem was
that in order to reverse political verdicts on purged cadres, Mao's
personal orders would somehow have to be addressed.[70] In December 1977, Hu Yaobang, then vice dean of the Central Party School,
gave a speech on how to study history in which the phrase "practice
is the sole criterion of truth" was first used, and the context was
clearly about wrongful cases from the Cultural Revolution. Hu said,
"With regard to history during the last ten-plus years, do not just
use one document or one speech by a comrade; it is necessary to
conduct an analysis with practice as the criterion."[71]

In May 1978, an article that used the phrase "practice is the sole
criterion of truth" appeared in *Guangming Daily* and again the next
day in *People's Daily* and *People's Liberation Army Daily*. This article
argued that if theories failed to achieve their intentions, they should
be changed in the face of experience. Crucially, this article was not
written at the direction of any top-ranking leader.[72] Moreover, before Yang Xiguang, the editor of *Guangming Daily*, mentioned the
phrase "two whatevers" at a meeting on April 13, neither the author
nor the man who commissioned the article had ever heard the expression before. Although they were conscious of the "two whatevers" as a negative influence that should be countered in the next
stage of revisions, the newspaper took careful steps to make sure
that the article did not too obviously criticize Hua's formulation
from the year previously.[73]

Negative reaction to the article was swift. Late at night on
May 12, Wu Lengxi, who was working for a committee editing Mao's
documents, called Hu Jiwei, a deputy chief editor at *People's Daily*.
According to Hu, Wu said, "This article made a fundamental mistake. In theoretical terms it is a mistake; in political terms the prob-

lem is even bigger. It is very bad, very bad." Wu said that the article rejected both the relativity of truth and the universal truth of Marxism. He pointed out that Lenin made theoretical predictions before they came to pass, but that did not mean they were not theories before the events transpired. One did not have to wait many years to realize that the Eleventh Party Congress was truth. In Wu's mind, the article called for a philosophy of doubting everything: "Mao Zedong Thought is the basis for our unity; if we go and suspect the Chairman's directives are wrong, if we think they should be revised, if everyone goes and debates which ones are wrong and which ones need to be changed, can our party still maintain unity?"[74]

Top officials in the propaganda apparatus did their best to prevent a broader discussion of the principles in the *Guangming Daily* article. On May 17, Wang Dongxing asked, "Which party center is this the opinion of? It must be investigated, people must be taught a lesson, thinking must be unified, and this must not set a precedent."[75] On May 18, Wang Dongxing told the editor of *Red Flag* that the article was opposed to Mao and it was not the thinking of the party center.[76]

Wang's tough reaction threatened to end any discussion of "practice." The historian Shen Baoxiang writes, "If powerful support was not available, this discussion of the criterion of truth that had just begun would have been stopped and forced down." But suddenly the discussion was given a boost by Deng, who was beginning to make a political issue of it.[77] Therefore, the historian Long Pingping is correct to argue that "the authors and organizers of the article did not plan beforehand and did not even think that the article's publication would cause a big discussion. The reason that it could turn into a big discussion on a national scale that would last for a prolonged period of time and develop into a thought movement, fundamentally speaking, is because Deng Xiaoping started and led it."[78]

Hua's plan for managing the situation remains somewhat mysterious, but he very obviously did not try to quash the debate. Many of the anecdotal accounts about Hua's attitude came after he had already been identified by party historians as an opponent of "practice." Moreover, Hua even provided some of his own language to justify moving on to new things, like "new period, new situation, and new topic" and "studying new things and studying old things."

In about August, one old revolutionary, Wang Renzhong, asked Hua about the "practice" position. Hua's response was that it was an important question that needed to be clarified but that it should begin and end with unity.[79]

In some ways, Hua even directly expressed support for "practice." He twice read an article published in June 1978 in the theoretical journal *Lilun dongtai* that implied support for the "practice" argument by criticizing individuals who during the Cultural Revolution only sought to support the position of the Gang of Four, thus leading real Mao Zedong Thought to disappear.[80] When the magazine *China Youth* resumed publication in 1978, the first issue included both an article implying support for "practice" and poems from the Tiananmen Incident of 1976. Wang Dongxing canceled the issue and demanded that it be retracted. When the editors protested, Wang met the leadership of the journal on September 14 and revealed that "Chairman Hua says: if they dare to publish, what is there to be afraid of? If it is published, it is published. Let them do it, if they dare [只要他们敢干就干吧]." This permission signified that Tiananmen and "practice" were no longer off-limits.[81] When the old revolutionary Tan Zhenlin tried to include support for the "practice" position in an article in *Red Flag*, the editors of the journal, who had been instructed not to participate in the debate, asked the top leadership how to proceed. Hua was the first one to express support.[82]

In Hua's closing speech at the November 1978 work conference, he gave the following account of his actions:

> On May 11 of this year *Guangming Daily* published and on May 12 *People's Daily* and the PLA newspaper reprinted this article on practice being the sole criterion of truth. Because at the time I had just returned from North Korea, there were many issues that had to be dealt with. So I did not have time to read it in June or July. Several members of the PSC told me in succession what they had heard about this. At that point I learned that there were different viewpoints on these two articles; when the members of the Standing Committee of the Politburo held a meeting, they discussed this issue. They believed that the topic of the article was good, but they did not specifically go and research the multiple

articles that came out later. There were many domestic and international reactions. Marshal Ye believed that the State Council theory meeting went well, so he suggested having a theory working meeting with all the comrades together, ... have everyone with different opinions express them, on the basis of democratic discussion unify thinking and solve this problem, and all Standing Committee members agreed with this. Because I wanted all Standing Committee members to be present to solve this problem, when Comrade Xiaoping went on a business trip, there was no time to have this [theory meeting] before the work conference started.[83]

Wang Dongxing did have conservative ideological views, and Hua was unfairly associated with them. Hua Nan, then editor of *People's Liberation Army Daily*, later admitted that although Hua Guofeng, as the top leader, had to take responsibility for the "two whatevers," "in reality Comrade Wang Dongxing was the direct executor and creator of the 'two whatevers.'"[84] The historian Han Gang writes, "At the time certainly not all of the Standing Committee members thought the article was good. There is no evidence that shows whether Hua liked the topic—but there is also no evidence that he attempted to end the debate. At most, Hua was cautious and simply did not want to express a position on the theoretical issue; this simply cannot be compared with Wang Dongxing's quashing and criticism."[85]

Hua was not only not a "whateverist" who defied "practice." At the November 1978 work conference, he also did not oppose changing the party's "key link" from "class struggle" to economics. The idea that Deng somehow triumphed over Hua on this issue is wrong. During Hua's tenure, "class struggle" did not have the same meaning that it had during the Cultural Revolution. Then it meant the campaign to expose and criticize the Gang of Four. As the historians Cheng Zhongyuan, Wang Yuxiang, and Li Zhenghua explain, "At the time it was thought that the contradiction between socialism and capitalism, the contradiction between the proletariat and the bourgeoisie, and the contradiction between Marxism and revisionism were collectively manifested as the contradiction between the Chinese Communist Party and the 'Gang of Four.'"[86]

At the Eleventh Party Congress in 1977, the plan of Hua and the top leadership was to finish the "ferreting-out" (清查) phase of exposing and criticizing the Gang of Four within the year or a little longer. At the Fifth National People's Congress in February and March 1978, Hua said that the "ferreting-out" campaign was basically finished on a national scale.[87] For some unclear reason, the top leadership never officially declared an end to the campaign, but the evidence is clear that Hua never intended for class struggle as the "key link" to mean a continuation of the Cultural Revolution or for it to last forever.

Deng has been credited with opposing "class struggle" as the "key link." However, his statements in this spirit were exclusively in regard to the situation in the military. If the military was focused on purging "Gang" elements, then it could not do what it was supposed to do: prepare for war.[88] Deng, therefore, had reason to support a different timetable for the military than he did for the rest of the party.

In September 1978, during a trip to the Northeast, Deng spoke with the top leadership of the Shenyang MR and expressed dissatisfaction with the length of the "ferreting-out" campaign. He said, "With regard to the campaign, you can research it. How does it end? There is never a complete victory. The campaign can't really go on like this, right? When campaigns go on too long, people get sick of them. It is a little superficial, there is no goal, and it's formalism."[89] The next month, Deng met with Hu Qiaomu, president of the Academy of Social Sciences, and Deng Liqun. Deng Xiaoping told them, "This time in the Shenyang Military Region I discussed the issue of exposing and criticizing the 'Gang of Four.' I said there must be an end to the campaign to expose and criticize the 'Gang of Four'; we certainly cannot continue it for another three or five years!"[90]

We now know that Hua did not oppose Deng on this matter. On October 9, Hua met with members of a committee working on Mao's writings. Hua told them that when Deng was in Shenyang, the head of the Shenyang MR, Li Desheng, had said that officers at the grass-roots levels were sick of the campaign. Hua also said that Deng had raised five criteria for ending the campaign in the military. Hua suggested that the November work conference discuss this issue, a proposal that was approved by the Politburo.[91]

On the night before the work conference meeting, Hua told some speechwriters, "It should be clear that the change [away from class struggle as the "key link"] will be made on January 1. Stubbornly change. The opinions of local governments have been sought out, the Standing Committee has discussed [it], the Politburo has talked [about it], everyone supports this; if again change does not occur, work will be delayed." Hua did want the "change in emphasis" to still fall under the slogans of "class struggle is the key link" or "expose and criticize the 'Gang of Four' as the key link." By approaching the matter in this way, "liberating thinking" would not in any way be presented as contradicting Mao Zedong Thought. According to Han Gang, "With regard to [the work conference before the Third Plenum], it was only on this little point that Hua's opinion was slightly different from Deng's."[92]

Strikingly, Hu Yaobang credits Hua, not Deng, for the breakthrough that finally happened at the Third Plenum. On November 25, 1978, Hu Yaobang returned home and told his son, "The pain and disaster suffered by the Chinese people caused the awakening of the entire people today. What is the meaning of 'having foresight' [先知先觉]? Actually, there is only one meaning; it's that thinking comes first, actions take a first step, and those who originally do not want to step forward also come along. . . . Hua Guofeng in one swipe of the pickaxe broke a hole in the dyke; just how big the flow of history will make that hole is completely up to the power of the people."[93] Hu Yaobang once told his secretary, "Our party did not have any 'whateverist faction!' . . . Making a leader of the whateverist faction is for nothing other than for getting rid of Comrade Guofeng."[94]

Pinning conservative "leftist" or "radical" views on Hua is also problematic for another reason. Just a few months after the work conference, Deng announced the extremely conservative "Four Cardinal Principles." Intellectuals who had helped defeat the "two whatevers" were shocked, feeling that the values of the Third Plenum were being reversed and that now the emphasis would be on attacking the Right, not the Left.[95] Deng had used intellectuals and calls for greater democracy outside the party to improve his position, but once they were no longer needed, and indeed once he saw that they were threatening broader stability, he immediately turned on them. The Chinese intellectual Su Shaozhi concludes, "While the sound of Deng Xiaoping's assault on the 'whateverist faction' was still ringing in one's ears, he himself also 'whatevered' up to Mao Zedong and Mao Zedong Thought."[96]

Historical Legacies and Compromising Material

If Hypothesis 1a is not able to answer what cleavage separated Hua from Deng, what really happened? The more important forces shaping Hua's fall were historical legacies, personal antagonisms, and worries about whether individuals close to Hua might use compromising material as a weapon. To overcome Hua's significant popularity within the party, Deng deliberately misrepresented Hua's tenure as leader and even engaged in character assassination.

Hua was a member of the "took-the-stage" group (上台派): individuals who had somehow avoided being purged.[97] One way or another, these cadres had survived while countless numbers of their compatriots had fallen. The "took-the-stage" group was skeptical of the broader purges and often harbored more pragmatic sympathies. Many of these individuals who benefited from the purges but did not participate in them directly also cooperated in Deng's brief rectification campaign in 1975. They had a complicated relationship with the old revolutionaries; this was also known as the "fell-off-the-stage" group (下台派) because of their downfall during the Cultural Revolution.

The "fell-off-the-stage" group was suspicious of the "took-the-stage" group for several reasons.[98] First, the old revolutionaries had lost their jobs to these younger counterparts. The "took-the-stage" group often saw their careers skyrocket to the top, a type of career development that was later referred to by their detractors as "helicoptering." As Ji Dengkui later noted, "Because I was liberated early, I was on the stage for a long time; [the old comrades] hoped I would help them, but I was not able to help."[99] Second, those who benefited from the Cultural Revolution, by simply remaining in power for such a long time in an environment like the Cultural Revolution, often had no shortage of skeletons in their closets. Third, the old revolutionaries, who had spent decades leading the Communist Party to victory against the Japanese and the Nationalists, had little respect for individuals who had joined the party later or who had played smaller roles in those earlier times. Shortly before the move against the Gang of Four, Hua asked Ye, "My credentials are weak; can the old comrades respect me?" (我资历浅，老同志能看得起我吗?).[100] In the words of Vogel, "Hua lacked Mao's and Deng's heroic revolutionary past."[101] Fourth, many of the old revolutionaries knew they could not take out their anger on Mao's memory, but they still felt the need to punish someone. Finally, these arrivistes had come to power during the Cultural Revolution, a time that the old revolutionaries hated. The old guard suspected that the "took-the-stage" group still harbored sympathies for those dark old days. In the words of Teiwes, "Hua's decline essentially had nothing to do with policy disputes: it had everything to do with historical status in the CCP."[102]

Beyond these historical antagonisms, the old revolutionaries were also concerned that compromising material might be used against them again in the future. Wang Dongxing, Ji Dengkui, and Wu De, all members of the "took-the-stage" group, were in charge of the notorious "special case committees" (专案组) set up during the Cultural Revolution to investigate purged cadres.[103] Many old comrades returned to work before their cases were officially rehabilitated and, as a result, felt as if a sword was still hanging over their heads.

Dissatisfaction with the "took-the-stage" faction in general and the issue of compromising material in particular, not differences in policy or ideology, is what led to the surprise outcome of the November 1978 work conference. Hua began the meeting with a speech that announced four topics for discussion: agriculture, economic growth for the next two years, a speech Li Xiannian had recently given to the State Council, and the "change in emphasis."[104]

But many old revolutionaries instead addressed historical issues and attacked prominent "took-the-stage" group members such as Wang Dongxing. Tan Zhenlin revealed that Luo Ruiqing, the former secretary general of the CMC who had recently died, had urged the dissolution of three special case committees. Luo called these committees "a ticking time bomb" because of the compromising material they controlled. On the second day of the meeting, the old general Lu Zhengcao suggested that the three special case committees be turned over to the Organization Department because they were "keeping secrets," which was equivalent to "keeping secrets for Lin Biao and the Gang of Four."[105] This demand to settle accounts is what led to the Third Plenum and the significant rise in power and stature of the old revolutionaries, especially Deng.

Even after the Third Plenum, Hua was still formidable. Hypothesis 1a predicts that Deng would seek to further weaken Hua by co-opting members of Hua's group or by canvassing for support with a more popular set of policies. Instead, Deng resorted to rewriting history and to skillfully using compromising material. His chosen method is the reason why, even today, Hua's tenure as leader is widely misunderstood. As Hua himself put it, "Writing history, writing true history, is very, very difficult. Official history writers [史官] walk with the emperor; [the Han Dynasty historiographer] Sima Qian wrote *Records of the Grand Historian*; [Emperor] Han Wudi did not disseminate a single chapter."[106]

Justifying the removal of Hua from the leadership demanded character assassination. As Xiao Donglian puts it, "In the eyes of the people, Hua did not have high prestige, he was not particularly wise, and it was difficult for him to manage the three top positions. But by capturing the 'Gang of Four' he had made a major contribution, and he had not made any unforgivable mistakes; he was honest, his style was relatively democratic, and there was no reason to definitely knock him off his horse. This type of domestic opinion and feeling could not be ignored."[107]

In February 1980, right before the Fifth Plenum of the Eleventh Central Committee when a number of the "took-the-stage" group lost their positions, an official photographer informed the deputy chief editor of *People's Daily* about a picture he had taken three days after the death of Mao. This picture, taken next to Mao's dead body, included not only the Gang of Four but also Hua Guofeng, Wang Dongxing, Chen Xilian, and Mao Yuanxin (Mao's nephew). The picture was sent to Chen Yun with the implication that Hua had a closer relationship with the Gang and a weaker relationship with Ye Jianying than had been previously understood. The accusation was outrageous.[108]

According to Xiao Donglian, although an issue like the "gang-of-eight picture" could not be written into official documents, "it was enough to put Hua Guofeng into an even more passive position."[109] In June 1981, Chen Yun said that the picture was a useful way to convince people that Hua was not a good person. At the same meeting, Hua pointed out that the picture was taken *after* he had already set plans in motion to destroy the Gang of Four. Li Xiannian and Hu Yaobang criticized the use of the picture and defended Hua.[110]

In particular, Hua's role in the arrest of the Gang of Four and his status as Mao's chosen successor had to be undermined. In July 1981, Feng Wenbin, first vice chairman of the CCP Central Office, gave a speech to the Central Party School in which he explained the decisions of the June 1981 Sixth Plenum of the Eleventh Central Committee. Feng noted that "some people see the fall of the 'Gang of Four' entirely as the sole contribution of Comrade Hua Guofeng; they say something like not letting him become chairman is supposedly 'crossing the river and burning the bridge.'" According to Feng, Hua only sought out Ye's support after he learned that the Gang of Four were about to move against him. Moreover, "everyone knows that at the time, if not for the support of the military, would [the move against the Gang] have worked? No." Feng told the group, "According to the way Comrade Chen Yun put it, Comrade Hua Guofeng did something that a Communist Party member should have done."[111]

Finally, Hua's relationship with Mao also had to be addressed. In August 1980, Deng famously gave a speech criticizing "feudal practices and calling for an institutionalized political system. The speech is often interpreted as a programmatic statement in favor of political reform."[112] However, that is a fundamental misreading of the speech's origins and implications. Criticisms of feudalism and calls for political reform were not a real platform but rather an ideological justification for Hua's removal from the leadership. Deng clearly stated what he meant by "feudal" in an interview with an Italian journalist: "A leader who picks his own successor on his own is an extension of a type of feudal practice."[113] As Deng Liqun freely admitted, "This speech by Comrade Xiaoping in actuality was directed against Hua Guofeng; it was preparation for Hua to leave his position, to find a theoretical justification."[114] When a friend pointed out that this speech was a reason why many people believed that Deng Xiaoping supported real inner-party democracy and institutionalization,

Zhao Ziyang discounted this analysis, saying, "At this time, Deng was primarily addressing Hua Guofeng; he was struggling against Hua Guofeng."[115]

Hypothesis 2a versus 2b

The Deliberations

Hypothesis 2a predicts that effective institutions enabled the party to balance the pros and cons of Hua as a leader and that a clear majority of the party supported one individual. However, neither of those predictions is accurate. Deng met conspiratorially with other figures in the elite to discuss the need to remove Hua. Hua still enjoyed significant popularity not only in the middle and lower levels of the party but even at the very top. Deng's decision to remove Hua was essentially a fait accompli, one that Hua accepted to avoid open struggle within the party. Counterintuitively, the pressure to remove Hua became stronger as his popularity increased. If Hua's position could have been put to an open vote, he would not have been removed in the way that he was in 1980 and 1981.

In November 1979, Hua made a trip to western Europe. Party historians claim that while Hua was gone, Deng used the opportunity to widely complain about Hua and to make demands for changes in the top leadership. The number of people Deng met with is disputed, with one historian suggesting he met up to a hundred people and another expressing skepticism he would be so brazen. After Hua returned, both Ye Jianying and Peng Zhen warned him about Deng's behavior and even suggested that Hua should meet with the people Deng had contacted. Hua refrained, however, once again referring to the danger of the party splitting if such behavior were to occur.[116]

Before and during Hua's absence, Deng focused his efforts on the military in particular to replace the country's leadership. Deng had already placed Marshal Nie Rongzhen in charge of planning for the next leadership in the General Departments, armed services, and main military regions.[117] According to Ye's official chronology, on July 13, Ye received a letter from Nie that included details on a reorganization of the top leadership in the military regions, which

Ye had approved.[118] On July 17, when Zhou Genlong of the General Political Department's Cadre Bureau reported to Marshal Xu Xiangqian on personnel changes, the discussions were still ongoing.[119] Curiously, after that meeting, no evidence suggests that the leadership returned to this issue until October 11, when Zhou Genlong again reported to Marshal Xu. Xu then called Geng Biao, secretary general of the CMC, to ask how the other marshals felt.[120] The next day, October 12, Hua left on his trip to Europe and would not return until November 10.

On the same day that Hua departed, Xu met with Zhu Yunqian, vice head of the GPD, and Zhou Genlong to talk about personnel issues. Xu was in a curious rush: immediately after the conversation ended, he called Geng Biao and said he wanted to discuss matters as quickly as possible. Geng suggested they go see Deng together. Xu said it would be best to set a time within two or three days, saying, "talking early is best." However, the next day, Geng's office reported that Deng wanted to pick another time to meet (谈是谈一次，另定时间). Then, only three days later, a major meeting on military personnel was held that included Ye Jianying, Deng Xiaoping, Nie Rongzhen, Geng Biao, Wei Guoqing, Xu Xiangqian, and several other important leaders. On October 21, after reading a report by Zhou Genlong on personnel matters, Xu wrote two separate letters: one to Deng and another to Nie Rongzhen and Geng Biao, in which he said that he took responsibility for the personnel changes personally in front of Deng (说明班子调整是在邓面前承担了责任的). On October 23, Deng responded, "Comrade Xiangqian, I completely agree; please manage everything." Xu then, "according to Vice Chairman Deng's notification," called for a meeting at Sanzuomen on October 24. On October 29, with Hua still out of the country, Geng Biao reported that the CMC vice chairmen had agreed that a CMC Office meeting (军委办公会议) would be set up under the leadership of the CMC Standing Committee. That meeting would include Geng Biao, Wei Guoqing, Yang Yong, Wang Ping, Wang Shangrong, Liang Biye, Hong Xuezhi, and Xiao Hongda: a group with many historical ties to Deng. Geng also reported that the CMC (nonvoting) Standing Committee (军委列席常委) would no longer meet. Meanwhile, challenges to the PLA personnel decisions were springing up. Between October 31 and November 2, several military commanders complained about the proposed changes, either because they did not want to move or because they thought other personnel changes were inappropriate. On November 4, Deng put the entire process of rearranging the top leadership on hold (大军区班子，邓副主席说暂缓).[121] Despite this temporary retreat—only three major changes were made before the end of 1979—the PLA followed through with the changes in January and February 1980.[122]

Sometime between November 6 and December 18, Feng Wenbin went to report to Ye Jianying, then in Guangzhou, on personnel changes. Feng was almost certainly reporting on the plan to remove the so-called whateverists from the top leadership at the Fifth Plenum of the Eleventh Central Committee in February 1980. Yet Ye again defended both Hua and Wang Dongxing, noting that if any one of them had spilled the secret of the plot against the Gang of Four, "there would have been a big problem." Therefore, "their contribution cannot be forgotten."[123] When Ye returned to Beijing later that month, he also warned Hua about Deng's behavior.[124] Yet, despite Ye's remonstrations, Wang and the other "whateverists" were removed from the top leadership at the plenum.

Not only did Deng sometimes engage in conspiratorial methods, but his choice to remove and punish Hua was essentially a fait accompli. Hua did not even attempt to campaign for support within the party to defeat Deng's machinations, which meant the CCP never seriously and collectively made a careful evaluation of the relative merits of Deng and Hua. As early as August 1980, around the time of Deng's famous speech against feudal practices within the party, Hua expressed his willingness to resign.[125] When Deng made up his mind, no one resisted, even Hua, despite the fact that Deng was not even the formal party leader.

If Hua wanted to fight, he almost certainly would have lost, but he could have drawn on significant support. Hua was Mao's handpicked successor, had defeated the Gang of Four, was moving China toward reform, and was humble and capable of listening to the opinions of others. Moreover, others must have certainly realized that a move against Hua could be destabilizing after years of political chaos, and they recognized that Hua had helped solve the succession crisis in generational terms. Although he did not deliberately cultivate this belief, Hua became increasingly popular among the middle and lower ranks of the party as the reform process accelerated. Leftist attitudes were powerful after the Third Plenum, and Hua stood to benefit. Of the thirty-eight million members who had joined the party by 1980, twenty million had joined during the Cultural Revolution. Xiao Donglian writes, "Just from open reports it could be felt that in all regions a new and serious blocking force had appeared when executing all the policies of the Third Plenum. In Shanghai, there was a popular expression among cadres: 'The Third Plenum cut down the flag [of Mao Zedong Thought]; the change in emphasis left the line [重点转折离了线], liberating thought went off the rails, and developing democracy caused a disaster.'"[126] Conservative, leftist forces were using the opportunity to blame Deng for the chaos.[127] In essence, Hua was proven right: moving too quickly and carelessly on ideological issues would prove to be destabilizing.

Regional officials displayed their fealty to Hua in significant ways well into 1980. As Xiao Donglian puts it, "Among local officials who were not in the know, Hua still had significant influence. . . . The methods of these regional officials were certainly not according to Hua Guofeng's wishes, but Hua clearly did not stop them." Counterintuitively, Hua's popularity accelerated the preparations to remove him: "Whether he wanted to use this to restore his decreasing influence is impossible to know, but the result was the opposite. Hua was criticized even more, and pressure against him increased."[128] As late as July 1981, Deng Liqun was still complaining about wide swaths of the party not believing that Hua should be removed: "Among high-ranking cadres, this issue [of removing Hua] has been solved, at least for the vast majority of cadres. But among medium and lower levels, and among some of the masses, this matter has yet to be solved well. What kind of issue is this?"[129]

Despite Deng Liqun's comments, Hua was popular at the top of the party leadership as well. Heavyweights such as Peng Zhen, Li Xiannian, and Ye Jianying had positive inclinations toward him. Hua wanted to bring Peng, an individual whose party seniority was comparable to that of Deng Xiaoping and Chen Yun, into the leadership as a counterweight against those two men, and Peng would later indirectly express indignation at how Hua was treated.[130] Li Xiannian, another major elder, had no reason to oppose Hua, as the two had closely together planned the arrest of the Gang of Four.[131] Although Li seems to have gone along with the decision to remove Hua from the party chairmanship in June 1981, at a meeting immediately prior to Hua's dismissal, he also summoned the courage to speak a few words in Hua's favor.[132]

At a May 1981 enlarged Politburo session, "a majority of comrades," already under intense pressure from Deng, agreed to criticize Hua by name in a forthcoming document on party history. However, several important figures opposed this public criticism (Huang Kecheng, Han Xianchu, Deng Yingchao, Ulanfu, and Xu Xiangqian).[133] In June 1981, at a small group meeting during the Sixth Plenum, when Hua was to be formally stripped of his power, Xu even praised Hua, saying that without Hua's permission, it would have been impossible to remove the Gang of Four: "If the 'Gang of Four' were in charge, then we would have lost our heads [掉脑袋]; first it would have been Ye and Deng, then us."[134]

Hu Yaobang, who replaced Hua as formal head of the party, also opposed the change. Hu, who had worked with Hua in 1964, disagreed with Deng's assessment that Hua was really a "leftist rebel" (造反派) who had "helicoptered" to the top of the party.[135] Hu believed that Hua could have adopted his position on "practice" but that unfortunately he had been led poorly by individuals like Wang Dongxing.[136] In Hu's speech to the Politburo on November 19, 1980, he admitted that up until two or three months earlier, he had only spoken of Hua's strengths.[137] Hu revealed to his son that Zhao Ziyang and Hu Qili also opposed the move: "The new thinking in my opinion is a risky move; me, Zhao [Ziyang], Hu [Qili?] are all not very supportive. . . . Making personal issues [人事] the most important issue, not principles, is no good!" In Hu's mind, this would have been a good opportunity to create a "Chairmen Presidium" (主席团) with multiple chairmen. Each of them would have one vote: "In the top leadership we would simply create a completely democratic leadership, a completely collective leadership." Deng, however, opposed such an institutionalized system.[138]

According to a Chinese journalist who interviewed people about their true feelings on the history decision that criticized Hua, dissatisfaction with the charges was ubiquitous. Everyone (各界

在学习讨论中，一致认为) apparently believed that Deng was only exacting vengeance (算总账) because Hua was made first vice chairman and premier during the "criticize Deng" campaign. In their minds, all other explanations for Hua's removal were outrageous (莫须有的裁赃).[139]

The new PSC established in June 1981 included, in rank order, Hu Yaobang, Ye Jianying, Deng Xiaoping, Zhao Ziyang, Li Xiannian, Chen Yun, and Hua Guofeng. Of this group, only Deng and Chen had unambiguously negative opinions of Hua. Deng, in other words, was able to force the decision on the party despite Hua's popularity and at precisely the moment when large swaths of the party were rallying under Hua's banner.

The Decision-Making Body

Hypothesis 2a predicts that rules on leadership selection are standardized and formal. Yet throughout Hua's tenure as leader, Deng repeatedly allowed authority to shift to lower levels of the party when it suited his interests to hurt Hua. In other words, Deng only tolerated the interpretation of ambiguous rules when it worked to his advantage. Famously, the November 1978 work conference removed the initiative from the PSC and damaged Hua's political standing. In 1980, without the permission of the PSC, Deng manipulated discussion of the decision on CCP history to ensure that the decision mentioned Hua in a negative light.

As discussed earlier, Hua and Deng were united on almost all the key political and economic issues. That begs the question, if the party was united on the question of reforms, then how is it possible that the work conference before the Third Plenum suddenly took the initiative away from the PSC? The answer is not, as many scholars previously understood, that the work conference opposed Hua's dogmatic policy agenda. Instead, what surprised the PSC was the sudden emphasis on historical verdicts from the Cultural Revolution.

On the eve of the work conference, the PSC had five members: Hua Guofeng, Ye Jianying, Deng Xiaoping, Wang Dongxing, and Li Xiannian. Wang and Ye were definitely loyal to Hua, and Li was an old revolutionary who had remained in power during the Cultural Revolution and was friendly toward Hua. For Hua and Wang to suffer a political setback, pressure had to come from outside the PSC.

As discussed earlier, when Hua made his introductory remarks at the work conference, he listed four subjects for discussion. Yet, as Han Gang points out, "After the meeting started, the participants went beyond the original agenda; they raised demands to resolve unsolved historical cases. Not only did Hua Guofeng not expect this; it is likely that other members of the PSC did not expect this as well." Wang Dongxing, Ji Dengkui, Chen Xilian, and Wu De, all high-ranking beneficiaries of the Cultural Revolution, were also criticized. Wang and Ji were under special suspicion because of their direct role in managing cases from the Cultural Revolution. Those spontaneous attacks, especially because they included a member of the PSC, were unprecedented and almost unimaginable at the time.[140]

The work conference then turned to the Third Plenum of the Eleventh Central Committee to make sudden unplanned changes to the leadership. Old revolutionaries such as Chen Yun, Deng Ying-chao, and Wang Zhen were added to the Politburo. Chen Yun not only became a member of the PSC but also assumed the position of vice chairman of the party, and he replaced Wang Dongxing as the man responsible for reviewing old cases.[141] Hua was not explicitly criticized, but Deng Xiaoping was clearly a major beneficiary of the outcome, as he rode the wave of the shifting political tide and determined the final decisions of the meeting.

In one important sense, then, the work conference had a remarkable similarity to the June 1957 plenum in the Soviet Union: a shift not in policy but in leadership. The outcome was predicated on the initiative to make an unprecedented shift in authority to a new body. Han Gang argues, "With regard to this work conference and the Third Plenum, the authorities and academia both have made many judgments, and together, their judgments can be summarized as 'executing a change in emphasis.' I, however, believe that the most important result of this meeting was not so much a 'change in emphasis' as a shift in the center of authority."[142]

Yet this new role for the CC did not last. Ultimately, Deng's attitude toward such moments of "inner-party democracy" was clear: he only supported them when they favored him. The chief editor of *People's Daily* Hu Jiwei recalls how surprised he was by Deng's reaction to a speech he gave at a meeting of the National People's Congress in June 1979. In his speech, Hu criticized Wang Dongxing for corruption and suggested that Wang should be removed from the chairmen group (主席团) of the NPC. Hu was supported by other delegates, but Deng exploded, "This is a list determined by the Politburo; do you still dare to give an opinion?!" According to NPC rules, Hu had every right to discuss something the Politburo had proposed. Moreover, Wang was in fact a political enemy of Deng and would be removed shortly thereafter in February 1980.[143] Deng's inclination, in other words, was to support discussion at lower levels when he was ready for it and could direct it.

And that is exactly what happened again between October and November 1980, when discussions about party history began among more than four thousand top-ranking cadres.[144] One major question for the history document was whether to cover the time period after the Cultural Revolution (meaning the Hua era). In late September, Hu Qiaomu, with Deng's support, wrote a new fourth section for the document that included criticisms of the "two whatevers" and Hua. This was done without a discussion within the PSC. When this section was submitted to the PSC, Hua expressed his opposition, pointing out that the document on history written at the Seventh Party Congress in 1945 did not cover the war against Japan since the war was still ongoing. A decision was made that the fourth section would only be included if the four thousand cadres decided it was necessary.[145]

However, the four-thousand-plus party members did not have an entirely democratic discussion. As Xiao Donglian puts it, "On the eve of the four-thousand-person discussion, Deng Liqun made a hint [把风放了出去]. When the draft seeking opinions was distributed, Deng Liqun and others required that everyone express an opinion: Should this section be written?"[146] Subsequently, Deng Liqun gave two speeches, on October 15 and 18, to the Chinese Academy of Social Sciences in which he delineated Hua's alleged crimes. Thus, a theoretical justification was being provided to the party for why

Hua should be removed, and the hint was that everyone should support including this reason in the historical decision.[147]

Legitimacy of Behavior

The November 1978 work conference represents a new precedent in CCP history. Moreover, certain aspects of the way in which Deng Xiaoping engineered Hua's exit, such as character assassination, the disregard for Hua's popularity, and dirty tricks, were all seen as deeply unfair and unjust.

During most of CCP history, power had flowed downward, not upward. The PSC, or more likely the top leader, made the decisions, which were then executed. Therefore, the work conference truly was a unique moment in Chinese politics. In particular, the criticisms of Wang Dongxing, a party vice chairman, were extraordinary. As Han Gang writes, "In the past, unless it was the party chairman criticizing a vice chairman, criticizing a vice chairman by name at a central meeting was almost totally unimaginable."[148] Everyone understood that something new had occurred.

However, not only was Deng's method of going after Hua unpopular at the time, some individuals who participated later regretted their actions. Hu Jiwei later expressed remorse for his role in the "gang-of-eight picture."[149] Deng Liqun's role in creating pressure to include criticisms of Hua in the history decision was seen as dishonest. Some party members even wondered if Deng Liqun's actions had been approved by the entirety of the top leadership, "and if not, it is nonorganizational activity [非组织活动]; there are ulterior motives, and it should be investigated."[150] Deng Liqun later did a self-criticism for his behavior: "Now looking back, my evaluation of Hua Guofeng at the time included several not entirely justified opinions. It can be put like this, I suppose: in order to purge someone [拱倒], no matter whether it is a big figure or a small one, you list all of his mistakes together; it is all right to include some that in fact are not issues of political principle but are issues of things that were taken too far [但讲得过于上纲了]."[151] In the words of General Zhang Aiping, "Comrade Hua Guofeng is an honest man. I have always been grateful to him. He was treated unjustly."[152]

Hypothesis 3a versus 3b

Views of Power Ministries

Hypothesis 3a does not expect that the military will serve any special function in a power struggle, except as voting members of a selectorate. However, the evidence is overwhelming that the military played a role in the denouement of Hua's tenure as leader. After the Cultural Revolution, the old guard was worried about who held ultimate control over the military. Deng Xiaoping's sense that Hua was expanding his influence in the PLA was the first trip wire that led Deng to dramatically undermine Hua's authority. When unease about the speed of reform became more prominent after the Third Plenum, Deng was primarily focused upon the situation in the military, and he spearheaded his response within the PLA. In 1980, Deng's concern that Hua was continuing to curry favor in the armed forces, as well as a shocking small insurrection, led him to speed up the process of Hua's removal and subject Hua to even more severe criticism.

Deng's own personal authority was inextricably linked to his history as a major military figure.[153] Deng had extensive war-fighting experience and saw himself primarily as a military man: "I am a soldier; my true profession is fighting wars."[154] In 1937, he was promoted to vice head of the GPD of the entire Red Army, and by 1938, he was political commissar of the legendary 129th Division (one of three political commissars at the time), which later became the Second Field Army.[155] In the war against the KMT after the defeat of the Japanese, Deng led a joint committee that commanded both the Second and Third Field Armies in the decisive Huaihai campaign.[156] Not only was Deng secretary of the Front Committee, but Mao had told him that he had the power to command.[157]

Hua was officially chairman of the CMC, yet he spent little time on military issues, with the curious exception of the nuclear weapons program, in which Deng apparently exerted little influence.[158] Ye, who was in charge of managing the daily affairs of the CMC, gave Deng great leeway as chief of staff. After Deng announced that he would assist Ye in managing the CMC's daily affairs, Ye allowed documents submitted to the CMC for approval to be first sent to Deng.[159]

Because the PLA had played such a critical role in helping to start the Cultural Revolution, the question of who controlled the gun was an extremely serious matter. Chen Yun, for example, believed that Ye was a bulwark against a potential political coup by the "took-the-stage" group. At the November–December 1978 work meeting, Chen said, "Because Marshal Ye is old, people are afraid there will be an incident; they are afraid that Deng Xiaoping will be purged again."[160]

The evidence clearly shows that the contest between Hua and Deng revolved to a decisive extent around the PLA. Han Gang argues, "After the smashing of the Gang of Four, these two men, Hua Guofeng and Deng Xiaoping, generally speaking, cooperated, and their relationship was largely positive. Then why was it that later there was a power transition? In 1978, there were many incidents, and these incidents, in my opinion, were an extremely important factor for why Deng developed suspicions about Hua; they were a crucial point [关节点]."[161]

The three factors identified by Han are a navy leader (Su Zhenhua) complaining to Hua after being criticized by Deng, Hua's decision to visit the navy without telling the CMC, and criticism of Deng's comments by a member of the PLA's GPD—all military-related issues. These three incidents together explain why Deng decided not only to support the "practice" position but also to turn it into a discussion that would weaken the authority of Wang Dongxing and, to a lesser extent, that of Hua. Moreover, by doing so, Deng clearly violated the spirit of civilian control over the military. As Han Gang concludes, "These three incidents [Su complaining to Hua, the navy inspection, and criticisms of the "Political Work Decision"] occurred within one month exactly, so Deng Xiaoping supported 'practice.'"[162]

On March 9, 1978, an explosion occurred on ship "160" at 8:40 p.m. in Zhanjiang harbor in Guangdong province.[163] The ship, an elite missile destroyer, sank at 10:55 p.m., killing 134 and wounding 28. An electrician who was upset that he had been punished for an illicit sexual relationship was at fault.[164] According to the official *Biography of Luo Ruiqing*, Deng criticized Navy Commissar Su Zhenhua for the "160" Incident, but Su ignored him and went to meet Hua on April 12 to complain. Hua allegedly expressed support for

Su and told him that he would go to Dalian for a naval inspection after a trip to North Korea. Su then went to tell the navy high command that Hua supported them, that they should not be nervous, and that they would not be purged. Su, demanding complete secrecy, told a few naval vice commanders to prepare 120 ships and 80 planes. When Yang Guoyu, head of the Navy General Staff, suggested that Navy Commander Xiao Jingguang should know about this exercise, Su agreed. But when Yang suggested telling Deng's General Staff as well, Su said that there was no need to since Hua had already expressed his approval. When on April 13 Yang reported this to Xiao, Xiao told him to report to Luo Ruiqing. On April 15, Yang Guoyu supposedly again told Su that it was necessary to report to the CMC and the General Staff, and otherwise it would be impossible to move the ships. Su finally approved. When Luo Ruiqing met Yang on April 17, Luo allegedly asked why it was necessary at that time to have such a large military maneuver and what kind of effect this would "have on the international and domestic situation." Luo also expressed puzzlement as to why this was only being reported then if the decision had been made on April 12. Luo said, "I will report this to Vice Chairman Deng; whether or not this is okay, I will contact you by phone later." According to Luo's biography, Luo expressed his personal opposition to Su's plans to Deng, who agreed.[165]

An addendum to the decision that stripped Hua's position as party chairman and CMC chairman, distributed in July 1981, contained the following account of the incident:

When a navy ship exploded and sank, Comrade Xiaoping criticized Comrade Su Zhenhua, but Su was unhappy so he went to Comrade Hua Guofeng to complain. They spoke for five hours, and Hua Guofeng said to Su: "The navy only had a '160 Incident'; what are you afraid of, you won't be knocked down." In order to express his support for Su, Hua also decided that when he returned from a visit to North Korea, he would go to Dalian to inspect the navy. Su manipulated Hua's support, did not care about the serious influence and political implications domestically or internationally, did not get permission from the Operations Department of the navy, and did not get permission from the General Staff and the CMC. He still prepared to move 120 destroyers and 80 airplanes for a training exercise. This matter was blocked by Comrade Luo Ruiqing. Before Su returned to Beijing from Shanghai, he told people that Chairman Hua wanted him to return to Beijing so he could help Chairman Hua control the military.[166]

What are we to make of these two accounts? Other evidence suggests Su Zhenhua might not have actually acted so brazenly. Qiao Ya, a secretary who had worked for both Su Zhenhua and Xiao Jingguang, argues that Xiao played a role in a smear campaign against his own commissar. According to Qiao's account, Xiao was a politically astute man who held long grudges and liked to exact vengeance on those who crossed him, and Su and Xiao had crossed swords multiple times throughout the history of the PLA Navy.[167]

In 1998, Su's wife asked Hua Guofeng about the incident. Hua revealed that after the fall of the Gang of Four, he was busy and did not have time to pay much attention to the military. At the beginning of 1978, Ye and the Standing Committee members of the CMC told Hua to familiarize himself with military affairs. Therefore, he, along with most of the CMC leadership, first watched an air force demonstration in Yangcun. Hua began to consider a trip to the navy. This created an opportunity when Su Zhenhua came to report to Hua. After Su's report, Hua used the opportunity to say he wanted to inspect the navy. Hua claimed, however, that he ended up not having time to attend the inspection. But he also said, "At the time, I was chairman of the CMC, and going to take a look at naval units was absolutely acceptable. When people say that Su Zhenhua came to me to complain [about Deng], that is simply not true."[168]

The historian Yu Ruxin points out that the navy commander, Xiao Jingguang, should have taken primary responsibility for the ship that exploded, especially because at the time Su's main bailiwick was Shanghai, where Su had been sent to stabilize the situation after the fall of the Gang. Yu writes, "Was it Luo's report that blocked Hua's inspection, or was it Hua taking the initiative not to go? Both of these arguments are suspicious. Let's hypothesize another possibility: Luo reported to Deng, without expressing his own opposition, but Deng Xiaoping did not want to give Hua this opportunity, using the excuse that Luo was opposed; and then he went to persuade Hua not to go. Of course, we emphasize that this is only a hypothesis; there is no direct evidence, but it fits the historical background and personality of the characters." Yu remarks, "Hua Guofeng was correct: as CMC chairman, why couldn't he inspect the navy?"[169] Yu only hints at the answer, but he seems to suggest that Hua's attempt to manage military affairs was seen as a violation by Deng. Therefore, analysts of this period, such as Yang Jisheng and Han Gang, are probably correct to point to the navy incident as the turning point at which Deng decided that Hua somehow had to be brought to heel.[170]

Soon after the navy incident, another event further incensed Deng. On March 12, the GPD sent two documents to Deng for examination: a "report" to be given by the head of the GPD, Wei Guoqing, and a "Political Work Decision." During a meeting with the GPD leadership on March 20, Deng argued that the "Decision" should include more about the nature of political work "under the new historical conditions" (现在处在新的历史条件下).[171] However, some members of the group in charge of the draft refused to use that language.[172]

On April 27, Liang Biye, vice head of the GPD, announced that, according to the GPD party committee, the "Decision" would have to be edited based on the spirit of Deng's instructions. However, those who opposed the new terminology refused to obey. On May 2, the draft "Decision" was submitted to the various working committees for discussion. At this time, the differences between Wei's report, which hewed to Deng's position, and the draft "Decision" became obvious to the committee. In order to overcome opposition to this change, Wei had the GPD create a third group (in addition to the two groups in charge of writing Wei's report and the "Decision").[173] Yet the individuals on the "Decision" draft committee argued that Deng's "new historical conditions" differed too strongly from the extant formulation, "new historical period" (新的历史时期). They also criticized the expression "the PLA has a proletarian nature." According to them, Mao had only said that the PLA was "the people's army."[174]

The meeting became so heated that Liang sent everyone home. That evening, when the discussions continued, they were even more intense. Li Mancun, head of the Propaganda Department of the GPD and one of the drafters of the "Decision," suggested that if opinions were different, then they should ask the party center for advice. Liang said that Wei's report was written according to Deng's wishes. Li then suggested that the GPD Party Committee discuss the issue, to which Liang responded that the GPD Party Committee had already done so. When Wei returned from Guangzhou on May 19, he said that such a situation should have never been allowed to happen: "This is not a coincidence; it should raise serious concern." He agreed to the demand of the head of the "Decision" draft committee to go to Deng on May 20. Deng, of course, supported Wei.[175]

On May 30, Deng met with officers from the GPD and Hu Qiaomu. Deng told them about the debate on the two different expressions, concluding about those who opposed his wording, "In summary, the opinion is this: As long as the words you speak are different from those of Chairman Mao, and different from those of Chairman Hua, they are not all right. It is not all right if you say what Chairman Mao did not say or what Chairman Hua did not say. How can this be acceptable? You must copy completely what Chairman Mao said and what Chairman Hua said. This is not an isolated phenomenon; this is a reflection of a type of contemporary thinking."[176]

Deng gave a major speech to the political work meeting on June 2. Although he did not use the exact terms "practice is the sole criterion of truth," as discussed earlier, it was clearly intended to give a boost to that debate. Deng also took a not-so-subtle swipe at the "two whatevers": "In essence, their view is that one need only parrot what was said by Marx, Lenin, and Comrade Mao Zedong— it is enough to reproduce their words mechanically."[177] Some parts of the speech were so inflammatory that they were not included in collections of Deng's official works but can be read in the Hubei Provincial Archives: "At this military-wide political work meeting, certain individual comrades did not support us in discussing the 'new historical conditions,' saying that this is different from a 'new era of development,' and they do not support discussion of 'maintaining the proletarian nature of our military,' saying this is different from 'maintaining the nature of the people's army.' And, therefore, this led to a debate."[178]

On June 15, Wang Dongxing, at a meeting of the top leaders in the Department of Propaganda and news agencies directly subordinate to the top of the party, criticized coverage of Deng's speech at the PLA political work meeting: "*People's Daily's* news coverage of the military political work meeting also has problems; it was correct to headline that Deng insightfully elaborated on Mao Zedong Thought. But why weren't the speeches by Chairman Hua and Vice Chairman Ye headlined as 'insightful elaboration'? Can it be that the speeches by Chairman Hua and Vice Chairman Ye did not insightfully elaborate on Mao Zedong Thought? Doesn't this mean there is some significance to the headline?"[179]

Deng's speech was not the only way the military moved the "practice" debate forward. Around May 20, Hua Nan, editor of *People's Liberation Army Daily*, and Yao Yuanfang, deputy editor, went to Luo Ruiqing to discuss the upcoming political work meeting. Luo told them that he had heard that some individuals were opposed to the *Guangming Daily* article and that it was necessary to convince them otherwise. Luo clearly told them that the military-wide political work meeting was intended to spread the "ideological line" (思想路线) of seeking truth from facts. Luo also told them that *People's Liberation Army Daily* should propagate this message as this was part of "an important struggle" to eliminate the influence of the "two whatevers" from the military.[180]

Immediately after Deng's speech to the political work meeting, Luo Ruiqing told *People's Liberation Army Daily* to quickly write an editorial to affirm Deng's message. On June 7 or 8, Yao Yuanfang told Luo about an article written by Wu Jiang, a member of Hu Yaobang's group at the Central Party School. Luo began discussions with Hua Nan on this piece on a daily basis. On June 10, Luo said that he approved of the article but that it had to be strengthened, in particular by using Mao's own words and quotes from Deng's speech to the military political work meeting.[181]

Without this support from the military, Hu Yaobang would not have been able to push forward the discussion of "practice." The propaganda apparatus had already refused to allow the Party School newsletter to continue the discussion, and *Guangming Daily* and *People's Daily* had also been put on notice. After realizing that Deng's speech at the military political work conference was opposed to the "two whatevers," Wu Jiang decided to go to the military for help, knowing that no other media organ would dare publish it. Wu even suggested using a "specially invited *People's Liberation Army Daily* commentator" to increase the importance of the article. This was the first time the newspaper ever used such a byline.[182]

Deng's speech and the *People's Liberation Army Daily* article were critical for communicating the nature of the struggle between Deng and Hua more broadly. Deng had artificially manufactured an ideological debate that he could turn into a political debate. Prior to that, the "two whatevers" was not something on the minds of most individuals. General Chen Heqiao reminisces, "When the great debate on the issue of the criterion of truth first started, a few of us in the military could not immediately figure out the political and ideological significance of this great theory. . . . After Deng Xiaoping's speech to the military-wide political work meeting, and Chief of Staff [*sic*] Luo Ruiqing became personally involved in organizing an article to support discussion of the criterion of truth, all of the big units throughout the military also expressed support."[183] According to Zhang Guanghua, who was studying at the PLA Political Work Academy, "As far as we students go, including myself, if we had not heard and seen the speeches and articles by Deng Xiaoping and other comrades, we would not have known that the 'two whatevers' was incorrect; actually, it is possible we would have very naturally accepted the viewpoint of the 'two whatevers.'"[184]

Deng had successfully used the PLA to advocate "practice" and undermine Wang Dongxing and, to a lesser extent, Hua. But that was not the end of the role of the military. As discussed earlier, many individuals within the party, as well as in the military, were confused by the rapid changes in the country. Younger officers who had been indoctrinated with the leftist ideals of the Cultural Revolution were concerned that Deng was leading China down a path of de-Maoification. High-ranking officers who realized the disastrous nature of the Cultural Revolution were fully aware that the new winds of reform were undermining their ability to discipline these young leftist officers.[185]

For example, in April, the Nanjing MR conducted a theory training course in which two hundred officers participated. The meeting did not proceed smoothly. Some officers disputed that either "leftism" or "rightism" as described by Deng existed. Others complained about propaganda directives that they felt were leading people to criticize Mao. With young people returning to the cities from the countryside and class labels being removed, officers questioned whether class struggle had really ceased to exist. Some officers worried that "liberating thinking" was a mistake and that the real task ahead was to properly execute the four cardinal principles. They explicitly criticized the Third Plenum for adopting the wrong policies.[186]

Crucially, the Third Plenum had not eliminated Hua's prestige in the military among younger individuals who had been promoted during the Cultural Revolution. According to Zhang Guanghua, the general sense during discussions about the plenum was that the "mistakes" made by Hua and Wang were forgivable: "Especially Hua Guofeng, he clearly had the honest and frugal moral character of many offspring of Chinese peasants; he could not have raised the 'two whatevers' in order to protect his personal position. In actuality, it was very likely that it was done to protect the authority of Chairman Mao and on behalf of the interests of the project started by Chairman Mao."[187]

In the spring of 1979, a student at the PLA Political Academy claimed at a small meeting that one-third of the people at the school opposed the Third Plenum. Afterward, a reporter from the military newspaper agency drafted a confidential report based on the words of this student.[188] On July 9, Deng wrote comments on an internal newsletter saying, "This material is very important; please ask the Central Committee Office for a few copies to be sent to the members of the Standing Committee, members of the Politburo, and the CMC for them to take a look; everyone should consider this matter a bit."[189]

Deng was clearly deeply worried about these developments. On July 12, he told Hu Qiaomu and Deng Liqun that "in the [PLA] Political Academy one-third of the people do not understand, doubt, or are dissatisfied with the Third Plenum and with the policies determined by the party center since the Third Plenum." Hu Qiaomu remarked that someone at the Chinese Academy of Social Sciences also said that everywhere there was a problem of one-third of the cadres opposing the Third Plenum. But Deng did not care about these other units nearly as much as he cared about the military.[190]

According to two interviewees who were deeply familiar with the PLA Political Academy at this time, Deng was overreacting to what were only minor grumblings.[191] A self-published memoir by Zhang Guanghua affirms this viewpoint. Zhang writes that the investigator concluded that one-third of the students completely supported the Third Plenum; one-third basically supported it but had trouble understanding certain issues; and the final third disagreed with specific issues, such as rehabilitating rightists, restoring individual plots, and reversing the verdicts on the Tiananmen Square Incident and Liu Shaoqi, but they did not oppose the plenum as a whole. When a colleague asked Zhang Guanghua whether the situation was as serious as Deng described, Zhang replied, "It would be accurate to say that about one-third were resentful about or did not understand this or that specific policy, but saying that they opposed [the Third Plenum] is an exaggeration. . . . We cannot say that people who do not adequately understand a few issues after the Third Plenum are opposed to the line of the Third Plenum."[192]

We can only hypothesize about why Deng reacted the way he did. Deng had a tendency to perceive small grumblings as representative of broader, more serious problems—a habit he shared with Mao. Deng may also have been particularly sensitive to problems in the military because he viewed the armed forces as a key source of political power. Finally, he may have believed that emphasizing alleged opposition to the Third Plenum would help justify an assertion of his power.

On May 20, 1979, the GPD released a document, "An Opinion Regarding Deepening the Study of the Third Plenum and Work Conference Spirit," that called for unifying around the Third Plenum.[193] The first salvo in public was an article in *People's Liberation Army Daily* on May 21 complaining that in many units the study of "practice" had not really been executed and many comrades had not truly understood its importance. The article called for a "review" of practice as the sole criterion of truth and demanded that the military study the documents from the Third Plenum more closely.[194]

Deng turned up the heat by giving an important speech to an enlarged session of the Navy Party Committee on July 29. One significant section of this speech was cut from the official *Selected Works of Deng Xiaoping*. The redacted words again show Deng's concern that a third of the military was not completely under his control: "Using the mistakes of Chairman Mao and upholding the 'two whatevers' is the same as still upholding that business of Lin Biao and the 'Gang of Four' but just changing one's face; this kind of person makes up about a third of all units [单位]. This is a reflection of the entire country."[195] Deng also reminded the committee about what had happened to those who supposedly resisted him by making a disparaging remark about Su Zhenhua, saying that in the last year he had to "embarrass a general" (将了一军) for not addressing problems as earnestly as the air force did.[196]

Perhaps the most interesting aspect of Deng's "review" activities is that his speeches on the matter were not publicized or distributed officially through party channels. Instead, in September and October, Deng's words were communicated through confidential Xinhua reports. Because this was done in such a manner, some people started to doubt whether they actually had to participate. Xiao Donglian writes, "This shows that whether or not the 'review' should be executed throughout the entire party, whether the debate against the 'two whatevers' should be brought up again, was debated both at the center and in the provinces." Even before the September Xinhua report, the "review" had already started in the military. In August and September, the Ji'nan, Shenyang, Nanjing, Guangzhou, Beijing, Chengdu, Lanzhou, and Urumqi MRs, as well as the air force, navy, and Second Artillery, had all already conducted "review" sessions.[197]

Deng was employing a familiar trick: using the military, his natural place of dominance, to expand a broader campaign intended to strengthen his own position. The "review" was not only about bringing the military around to support the Third Plenum but also about gaining control of the gun. Xiao Donglian summarizes:

These facts show that changing the thinking among military officers and soldiers was a serious problem; making them accept the guidelines and policies of the Third Plenum still faced significant trouble; it also shows that Hua Guofeng still had significant support in the military, especially at the lower levels, and that this was not because he had any historical relationship with the military but because he was the successor picked by Mao Zedong. In the military, Deng

Xiaoping's prestige was not absolute. This caused Deng Xiaoping to decide to solve the problem in the military, and the topic he picked was to review practice as the sole criterion of truth in the military. *At a fundamental level, this was a matter of solving whose commands the military would obey and whom it would follow.*[198]

During the final push against Hua over the course of 1980, the PLA again played a crucial role in politics. The "review" campaign had not extinguished Hua's support within the military. Deng continued to worry about morale in the PLA as the reforms deepened, and he explicitly tied instability in the armed forces to Hua's continuing presence within the leadership. Deng once again used a military issue—this time a debate over an old slogan—as a key wedge to justify Hua's defeat.

Between April 18 and 30, 1980, a military-wide political work meeting was held in Beijing. At this meeting, Hua gave a speech in which he used a Cultural Revolution–era slogan: "Supporting the proletarians and annihilating the capitalists." Wei Guoqing, head of the GPD, agreed that the military should "actively expand the education and struggle of 'supporting the proletarians and annihilating the capitalists.'"[199]

Some observers reached the conclusion that Hua was attempting to rally leftist forces in the military to his side.[200] The CIA believed that Hua was seeking support from the military: "Faced with an emerging and unfriendly majority in both the party and the government, Hua turned to the military for support. The PLA had its own reservations about Deng's reform policies." Most interestingly, the CIA concluded, "In any case, we believe Hua's turn to the PLA was the last straw insofar as Deng was concerned."[201] According to Ruan Ming, the use of this leftist phrase was a direct rejection of the "review": "Dogmatists in the military dug in behind the 'Four Cardinal Principles' in order to shut the door on this debate."[202] However, senior party historians in China find the idea that Hua was trying a counterattack to be fanciful. Instead, they believe that Deng simply chose to make Hua's words a bigger deal than they really were.[203]

When Deng Liqun saw that the phrase "supporting the proletarians and annihilating the capitalists" had reappeared, he criticized it at a number of venues, arguing that it was a Cultural Revolution–era slogan. When Wei Guoqing heard about this, he became angry. He told members of the military that the report on using this slogan had been approved by Deng Xiaoping himself. Wei personally complained to Deng Xiaoping about Deng Liqun.[204] Yet on May 31, Deng Xiaoping stood by Deng Liqun, telling him and Hu Qiaomu, "In my opinion, this slogan has some drawbacks, and it is not complete. I myself am not involved with this meeting of the PLA's General Political Department. I have asked Comrade Deng Liqun to tell Comrade Hua Nan of the General Political Department not to overpropagandize this slogan. It is important to interpret its contents correctly and apply them accordingly."[205]

On August 10, Hua offered his resignation. That same month, "several PSC members" argued at an enlarged Politburo session that Hua should no longer be head of the CMC.[206] The close chronological proximity of these events hints strongly that the calls for Hua's removal were linked to Deng Xiaoping's attack on Hua's behavior toward the military. On August 18, in the speech described earlier in which Deng cynically attacked "feudal" tendencies in the party to theoretically justify Hua's removal, Deng stated, "Not long ago, in order to educate people in the revolutionary outlook, the People's Liberation Army again raised the slogan 'foster proletarian ideology and eliminate bourgeois ideology.' I read the relevant documents of the General Political Department and didn't find anything wrong at the time. As I see it now, however, this slogan is neither comprehensive nor precise enough."[207]

The pressure to swiftly remove Hua and provide as strong a reason as possible drastically increased in November. That month, a temporary worker at a People's Armed Forces Department in Hebei's Jize County named Gao Huaiming stole a gun and went to an artillery regiment in the Sixty-Sixth Army near Tianjin to declare himself "a special emissary from the new Central Committee." Gao said it was time to "establish a new People's Republic of China." Most troublesome were Gao's claims, supported by some officers, that some in the party wanted to overthrow Hua. The commissar of the regiment, Zhu Fuxiang, opened two meetings for regimental and battalion leaders to listen to Gao's words. Shockingly, all but one of the officers in the regiment and battalions expressed support for Hua.[208]

Deng was furious. After listening to a report of the event on January 17, 1981, Deng said, "The problem in the artillery regiment is a serious trend in the Beijing Military Region, and it is also a serious trend in the entire military; it is imperative that it raises serious concern, and it cannot be treated lightly." Deng called for a special investigation into the event. On the follow-up report, Deng wrote, "This is an extremely serious incident that has occurred in the military; it is a blatant counterrevolutionary political incident, and it is a sparrow that should be dissected carefully."[209] On March 4, during a discussion with leaders from the Beijing MR, Deng said, "This is not a problem within a single regiment but a problem with universal characteristics. The entire military has underappreciated this phenomenon."[210]

The stage was set for Hua's official removal from the party and CMC chairmanships. On June 22, at a preparatory meeting for the Sixth Plenum of the Eleventh Central Committee, Deng justified criticizing Hua in the special document on party history by emphasizing that leftist forces were rallying behind Hua, regardless of whether Hua had any such intentions to lead them or not. Deng was particularly worried about the consequences of these political trends in the military: "The remnants of the 'Gang of Four' and dissidents, whose flag do they wave? The two incidents, in the Sixty-Sixth Artillery regiment and [the navy] in Dalian, both use the name of another center to send people to start activities. And this center is Hua Guofeng's center. . . . Of course, there is another center; we count as another center." Wang Renzhong responded, "Reactionary posters in Xinjiang say 'return Hua Guofeng to us.'" Deng continued, "There are not only officers in the regiment; there are commanders at the army level; they truly believe there is such a center. [General] Qin Jiwei, is this not correct? Why did they not dare to immediately stop this? . . . If the center is not united, if matters are dealt with poorly, we will burn ourselves. There are some slogans, including those that want to overthrow me, also [slogans such as] the 'new Gang of Four' [Deng Xiaoping, Zhao Ziyang, Hu Yaobang, and Chen Yun]; these people all support Hua Guofeng." General Qin Jiwei, head of the Beijing MR, then said, "The officers [at the very top] of the Sixty-Sixth Army are also guilty. He [the commander] knew that those words were false, but he did not dare deny them.

Why? He believed it was like when the Gang of Four were captured, that you were all taken; that is why he believed it."[211]

Top military leaders worried about destabilization at the lower levels of the military if their subordinates perceived a rupture between Deng and Hua.[212] On June 30, Marshal Nie Rongzhen drafted a letter to Deng Xiaoping, Hu Yaobang, and Chen Yun in which he blamed the recent public security crises throughout the country on Hua not being strong enough in his purge of the remnants of the Gang of Four. Nie wrote, "These people, when opposing the current center and leading comrades, also all bring out [use] Comrade Hua Guofeng; this is a unique point of the current struggle." Therefore, it was necessary to "clarify the muddled thinking toward Hua Guofeng."[213] Deng had Marshal Nie's letter distributed to every participant in an ongoing work conference.[214]

Ji Dengkui referred to these incidents in the military and their effect on Hua in a conversation with his son: "If some [of your subordinates in the military] get a little excited and do things sloppily, soldiers carry weapons; if God forbid there is some trouble, you will be the one held responsible. Hua Guofeng simply did not understand the seriousness of this issue; later there was a 'Third Artillery Regiment Incident.' When things like that blow up, it will only make your punishment worse." When Ji's son asked whether positions in the military were really that sensitive, his father responded that "holding military power and being a civilian are of course different." Ji declared, "In peacetime, holding military power is playing with fire!"[215]

Threat of Coercion

The preceding section clearly demonstrates the extent to which Deng prioritized control over the military during his competition with Hua. The position of the military also had implications for how the nonmilitary elite interpreted the situation. Deng's ability to demonstrate that the military listened to him, and not Hua, influenced calculations within the leadership. Two cases in particular reveal how this dynamic worked: the military's role in the "practice" debate as described earlier and the decision to attack Vietnam.

The *People's Liberation Army Daily*'s publication of the "practice" article on June 24, 1978, was not only important because the military newspaper was the only top publication not controlled by Wang Dongxing. The publication also signaled the military's support for the idea, which led others to fall in line. As Hu Yaobang explained to his confidential secretary, Liang Jinquan, "There's a way, going to [找] a senior general [大将], going to Senior General Luo [Ruiqing]." Liang asked why. Hu said, "Senior General Luo says he wants to publish. If it is published there [in *People's Liberation Army Daily*], the weight is very different. Senior General Luo's prestige in the party is high, he has a lot of influence, he is strong in theoretical terms, and it is impossible to use our own publication [the Central Party School journal] now." Luo's influence, Hu implied, was derived from his position in the military.[216] When the article appeared on June 24, people, in the words of one party intellectual, "believed that the gun had spoken, so all areas started in succession to express their position."[217]

The key was the byline: a *"People's Liberation Army Daily* specially invited commentator." Wang Dongxing had criticized the use of "specially invited commentators," leading Luo to make the sarcastic comment, "Isn't there someone who despises 'specially invited commentators'? That's why *People's Liberation Army Daily* will publish this article under the name of a 'specially invited commentator.'"[218] Luo was fully aware of how dangerous his behavior was. On July 18, as Luo was getting on a plane to undergo surgery in East Germany, he told the heads of the *People's Liberation Army Daily*, "It is possible that some people will oppose that article; I take responsibility. If someone is to be flogged, flog me [打板子 打我]." Before leaving, Luo also called the deputy chief editor of *People's Daily*, Hu Jiwei, to tell him that if someone was to be punished for the article, he was willing to be caned five times.[219]

The decision to attack Vietnam was more evidence for the country's top leadership that Deng controlled the military. Among the elite, Deng was isolated in his support for attacking Vietnam, and the ultimate decision to attack was, therefore, a key signal of his authority within the PLA. This outsized effect on the political situation is evidence for Hypothesis 3b.

Three interpretations of the evidence are possible. First, Deng had strategic reasons for wanting to attack Vietnam, and the political benefits, which showed that the military followed his wishes, was a side benefit. Second, Deng had both international and domestic reasons for engineering the attack on Vietnam. Third, Deng chose an issue on which he knew others in the elite would differ from him in order to assert his dominance and demonstrate that the military obeyed his wishes. We cannot decisively identify which interpretation is correct. One senior party historian is fully confident of the third hypothesis, while other historians say the evidence is still not decisive, although they allow for the possibility of all three.[220] However, all three theses, albeit to a greater or lesser extent, are supportive of Hypothesis 3b, which suggests that demonstrations of dominance over the military are of critical importance for political maneuvering in Leninist regimes.

Deng was clearly one of the few in the top leadership who supported the attack. In the words of Teiwes, "It is difficult to find any areas of significant policy differences between Hua and Deng, with the possible exception of the invasion of Vietnam where Hua, as well as many civil and military leaders, apparently initially doubted Deng's venture."[221] Deng Liqun's account is the following: "At the time I did not hear Marshal Ye or Wang Zhen say anything. Was there anyone else in the military who also held a contrary position? It is difficult to say. At the time, Comrade Xiaoping's position on this issue was very difficult [在这个问提上处境难], so he went to seek out Chen Yun's help." Chen Yun sought out many generals to discuss the issue and then told Deng Xiaoping that the most dangerous outcome of a war against Vietnam was Soviet involvement. Chen explained that if the Soviets decided to intervene, the result would be a large, medium, or small war. Chen argued that the Soviets would not have time to start a big war (大打); if the fight were wrapped up in less than half a year, then even a medium war (中打) would be easily managed. Chen expressed support for the war.[222] Chen's chronology confirms that Deng asked him to consider the advantages and disadvantages of an attack and that Chen supported the war and made suggestions, but the account provides no extra details.[223] Yet Chen had an extremely consistent record of opposing any actions that would drain the budget.[224] He also never had an especially close relationship with the military.[225] However, we do know that Chen was extremely upset with Hua during this time. This suggests that if Deng's decision to attack Vietnam was connected to weakening Hua's position, then Chen's curious behavior might have been the result of a tactical alliance with Deng. Later, Chen and Deng would enter into such an alliance on economic policy, despite somewhat differing preferences, to undermine Hua.[226]

Beyond Deng Liqun's account, other evidence hints at broad skepticism within the military about an attack on the scale that Deng Xiaoping was suggesting. On March 16, 1979, at a conference reviewing reports on the war in Vietnam, Deng himself admitted that there was broad opposition to the war: "Everyone knows that it was difficult for the party center and the CMC to make this decision. Only after repeated considerations during about two months was this decision made. Among our party and among our people, many people worried about this issue—whether it could be done well, how big the chain reaction would be, whether it would influence our four modernizations, and whether it would be fought well."[227] Several high-ranking generals were skeptical. In June 1977, Ye Jianying argued that it did not make sense to continue struggling with the Vietnamese (斗争要适可而止).[228]

According to interviews conducted by Xiaoming Zhang, Ye opposed the war against Vietnam for some reason related to a family member. He also points out that Ye did not attend an important expanded Politburo meeting on New Year's Eve.[229] According to General Wang Shangrong, Ye said that Deng was the "main director" (总导演) of the war against Vietnam.[230] Warren Sun was told in his own interviews that Ye's position was ambiguous, as opposed to those of Marshals Xu Xiangqian and Nie Rongzhen, who opposed fighting and spoke out.[231] The Taiwanese historian Chung Yen-lin was told by a mainland party historian that General Su Yu also opposed attacking Vietnam.[232] A secret report disseminated on July 4, 1981, included eleven examples intended to show that it was "old comrades," and especially Deng, *not* Hua, who were most responsible for positive changes since the death of Mao. According to point 8, "Between October 1978 and January 1979, Comrade Xiaoping visited Japan, America, and again Japan, began to open the foreign-policy general pattern [总格局] of united opposition to hegemony, and at the same time made a decision for a defensive counterattack against Vietnam. This matter is extremely important; without any boldness, without any strategic thinking, [one would] not have dared to start the defensive counterattack."[233]

The final decision to attack was made on November 23, placing the decision sometime right in the middle of the November–December work conference—a key moment in Hua's shifting political fortunes. According to Zhou Deli, a staff officer in the Guangzhou MR, Deng had already determined the plan of attack, which was much larger in scale than the draft that Zhou had seen at the meeting in September. Zhou writes, "Because this was an issue decided by the head of the General Staff, none of our opinions were raised again, and we did not reveal them to others."[234]

Within a few months, the PLA would invade Vietnam. Several pieces of evidence raise the strong possibility that the war was intended to have an effect on the political situation at home: Deng's decision to enlist the unlikely ally Chen Yun to rally support, Hua's absence from the planning, the timing of the decision so soon after the spat over the navy military exercise, and the collapse of Hua's authority around the time of the final decision. As Pantsov, with Levine, points out, "Some observers in China believed that Deng, who was then chief of the PLA General Staff, insisted on war and then directed the entire operation only so he could establish his own total control over the military in order to gain unlimited power."[235] And indeed, the understanding that Deng used Vietnam for domestic political purposes appears to be widespread among the Chinese elite. According to David Lampton, "Some 'supreme' leaders, at the start of their terms, use external conflicts to shore up their positions with both the military and the populace, exerting more control over the PLA and external relations once they have consolidated power. As one knowledgeable senior person explained, it is like Deng Xiaoping coming back and then in 1979 pursuing a strike against Vietnam. 'Do something to control the army, and indeed Jiang Zemin did this in 1995–1996 regarding Taiwan.' "[236]

How Did Institutions Matter?

The preceding sections strongly indicate that institutionalization was not robust. But it was not entirely absent. Most obviously, the leadership took steps to make it seem as if the removal of Hua was justified. That helps explain both the use of compromising material and the decision to keep Hua in office for so long. Hua's humiliation was prolonged: he was not removed from his party chairmanship position until June 1981, and he was still kept on as a vice chairman until the Twelfth Party Congress in September 1982. Stunningly, the decision to criticize Hua in the document on party history and to introduce the worst of the compromising material occurred *after* Hua had already agreed to resign. Hua in fact first offered to resign in August 1980.[237] Finally, Deng wanted to keep the real reasons for the split hidden. In the words of Ezra Vogel, "Deng's informal authority would trump Hua's formal authority, but Deng, like his colleagues, tried to avoid any public dissension."[238]

In a mockery of the power of formal authority, Hua had been forced to stay on as party chairman in a fake show of unity while the history decision was being prepared and more compromising material was being introduced. Disgusted by this treatment, Hua refused to show himself at a New Year's gathering, placing the top leadership in a difficult position.[239] Marshal Ye, having initially agreed to have Hua removed on the condition that Deng declare himself chairman of both the party and the CMC, was not impressed by Deng's "playing the good guy" for not taking up the party chairmanship.[240]

Institutions also mattered to Hua, and he obviously hewed more closely to a democratic interpretation of party rules. When he realized that his position was under attack from Deng, he chose not to put the party through yet another power struggle. Therefore, Hua deserves credit not only for being involved in the beginning of the reform process but also for respecting the party enough not to damage it by subjecting it to another political crisis.

Had Chinese elite politics been more clearly defined by robust institutionalization, power dynamics would not have been nearly so deeply affected by pro-Hua elements in the military, nor would it have been possible for Deng to have been so successful at using the military to improve his own political position. However, the evidence provided here indicates that the political dynamics of the time did not revolve entirely around the armed forces. Moreover, it is absolutely clear that this was not a military figure marching into a Politburo meeting to arrest the head of the party. This was not a case of naked aggression by the power ministries against the party leadership.

The story of the military in Hua's ultimate defeat is much subtler. Deng did not command the military to physically isolate Hua or even to help him maneuver during a moment of intense political crisis. Instead, he took steps that made his personal authority in the PLA obvious, and he used the PLA to push political discussions in directions that benefited him politically. Deng did not need to execute a coup for others in the party, especially Hua, to appreciate that he controlled the most powerful coercive organization in politics.

Implications

For a brief moment, the PRC had experienced a triumvirate. Led by Hua, Ye, and Deng, China achieved major breakthroughs in reform across a number of different issue areas. Yet gradually, for reasons that had nothing to do with differing opinions about those reforms, Hua and Ye were gradually sidelined. During this transition, Deng demonstrated characteristics that would continue to manifest themselves throughout his tenure as top leader: a pattern of interpreting challenges where none probably existed; a belief that China was served best by one leader with absolute authority; an extremely hierarchical view of party discipline; a habit of making decisions on major personnel changes without a meaningfully deliberative process; and an understanding that control over the military would always prove decisive in any leadership contest.

At the conclusion of the Hua era, Deng chose not to assume the top formal positions in the party. He did not even rank first on the PSC. Yet he did decide to accept the position of chairman of the CMC. In the words of a former *People's Daily* chief editor,

> Deng Xiaoping inherited the key of Mao Zedong's control over power: to closely guard control over the military, to definitely hold the position of CMC chairman. . . . Deng Xiaoping could let Hu Yaobang or Zhao Ziyang serve as general secretary, but Deng closely guarded control over the position of CMC chairman. Hu Yaobang and Zhao Ziyang in actuality were only "big secretaries"; they could not move a single unit. Thereby, Deng Xiaoping, using his position as CMC chairman as a shield [后盾], could use a group of cohesive

elders raised by Mao Zedong, and a few elders could have a meeting and Hu Yaobang and Zhao Ziyang could be fired.[241]

As Hua made his exit, the new general secretary, Hu Yaobang, made clear that he was serving only at Deng's request. At the closing session of the Sixth Plenum, Hu remarked,

> According to the wishes of the vast majority of comrades in the entire party, Deng Xiaoping should be the chair of the party. Other than Comrade Deng Xiaoping, from the perspective of talent, ability, or prestige, there are many other old comrades more suitable than I am. . . . I have the responsibility to tell the plenum that two things have not changed: one is that the role of the old revolutionaries has not changed, and the other is that my qualities have not changed. . . . Even foreigners know that Comrade Deng Xiaoping is the main decision-maker in China's party to-day [现今中国党的主要决策人]. . . . The members of the old revolutionary generation are still the core figures who play the main role in the party. Can this situation be told to the entire party? I think that it is not only appropriate but that it even should be done.[242]

Deng was pleased: "Just now [Hu] gave a short speech; I think that this speech also proves that our decision was correct."[243] The Hua era was officially over: "old man politics" had arrived, and such a state of affairs, not true collective leadership, would define the 1980s and early 1990s.[244]

CHAPTER SIX

Conclusion

The Chinese and Russian revolutions represent two of the most ambitious political experiments in human history. After the tumult of Stalin and Mao, all of their successors worried that significant political changes were necessary to regime survival. Yet the post-Stalin and post-Mao leaderships were internally splintered by historical antagonisms and lack of trust. Aspiring leaders waged wars of intrigue against each other using compromising material, twisted interpretations of rules, and explicit or implicit threats of force. The winners were not those individuals who were best able to co-opt potential challengers but the ones with the most aggressive political styles.

The historic failure of the Soviet Union and China to truly institutionalize politics even within their own ruling parties is one of the many tragedies of these grand political projects. The path dependencies created at several moments of transition after Stalin and Mao, as well as the flawed characteristics of elite politics that those struggles revealed, had profound implications for the long-term political trajectories of these states.

Soviet Union

Soon after Khrushchev's defeat of the anti-party group, he swiftly turned against his former ally Marshal Zhukov. Zhukov generally supported Khrushchev's policies, but the power that Zhukov had demonstrated during the transition distressed the Soviet leader. With the new civilian leadership now fully behind Khrushchev, Zhukov was incapable and unwilling to fight for his political career.

Khrushchev not only refused to enter into a collective leadership arrangement with legendary figures such as Molotov or Zhukov but also refused to deliberate with the new members of the Presidium. He regularly humiliated the other members of the elite.[1] Despite Khrushchev's behavior, his comrades acted obsequiously. In a letter to the CC in the mid-1960s, Molotov asked, "Where, in which materials after 1957 and all the way up to October 1964, can be found even the slightest opposition to Khrushchev? It is not on a single one of the thousands of pages published over all these years from the CC CPSU plenums, party congresses, the dozens and hundreds of meetings at the highest level of both the all-union and republic scale."[2]

Khrushchev was indeed removed in 1964. Yet that was hardly a victory for collective leadership.[3] Soviet leaders withstood years of abuse and egregious behavior by Khrushchev before he finally fell. At a Presidium meeting in August 1964, Khrushchev, after a dispute with Deputy Premier Dmitrii Polianskii, asked Aleksandr Shelepin, who ran the State Control Commission, to stick a memorandum into Polianskii's nose. Polianskii pleaded, "Don't put it in my nose. I'm a human being." When Khrushchev responded that he too was a human being, Polianskii asked, "How can anyone speak with you? When an opinion is expressed by someone, immediately there is conflict. Perhaps you have such an attitude toward me?" Khrushchev was blunt: "Apparently yes, I do not deny it. . . . I cannot rely on you."[4]

Just as in 1957, the plotters fought not to execute a new policy platform but to save themselves. Khrushchev's colleagues on the Presidium feared that their days were numbered. The available evidence now supports Anastas Mikoian's analysis: "Now I think that Khrushchev himself provoked them, having promised after vacation to introduce suggestions on making the Presidium younger."[5] In other words, only fear for their political careers persuaded the plotters to risk a move against Khrushchev.

Instead of holding a meeting to give Khrushchev an opportunity to revise his ways, the plotters acted in conspiratorial fashion. When Ukrainian party boss Petro Shelest suggested that instead of a coup the leadership simply meet and discuss the situation, Leonid Brezhnev almost screamed, "I already told you, I do not believe in open conspiracies. Whoever speaks first will be the first to be hurled out of the leadership."[6] Up until the very end, a strong possibility persisted that Khrushchev would emerge triumphant. If one more meeting had been held at which Khrushchev could have shaken up the leadership, he would have stabilized his position. When Brezhnev got word that Khrushchev might have learned about the plot, he started crying and said, "He will shoot all of us." Brezhnev's colleague had to bring him to a sink and tell him to clean himself up.[7] When one speech at the Presidium meeting showdown went on too long, Aleksei Kosygin interrupted: "It is necessary to not talk so long; otherwise we will end up with what we got in 1957, the members of the CC will come and carry us all out of here."[8]

Although Brezhnev was subtler than Khrushchev, he too jealously guarded his authority as top leader. Brezhnev once told an assistant, "If necessary, I can strike so hard that, whatever happens to the other person I would strike, I would remain sick myself for three days."[9] Over the years, he either undermined or removed previous allies such as Shelest, Shelepin, Polianskii, Moscow party boss Nikolai Egorychev, chairman of the Council of Ministers of the Russian Soviet Federative Socialist Republic Gennadii Voronov, Premier Aleksei Kosygin, and chairman of the Soviet Presidium Nikolai Podgornyi. Even when Brezhnev started to decline, power did not revert to the full Politburo. Instead, if the *troika* of Iurii Andropov, Dmitrii Ustinov, and Andrei Gromyko made a decision and obtained Brezhnev's support, that was the equivalent of a fait accompli, and no other individuals dared to express opposition.[10] When Mikhail Gorbachev complained about Brezhnev falling asleep at a meeting, Andropov said that "the stability of the party, country and even the world" meant everyone had to "support Leonid Il'ich."[11]

China

The current consensus in historiography on China during the Deng era depicts a golden era of political and economic progress, with the notable exception of the 1989 events in Tiananmen Square. In particular, Deng is credited with creating institutions to prevent the rise of any future Mao-like figure and ruling in conjunction with other powerful figures.[12] One recent book describes the PSC in the post-Mao era as "an unelected board of directors . . . which governs by consensus" and argues, "China has had no despots."[13] That assessment has become heavily politicized in the current Xi Jinping era, during which Xi's detractors accuse him of departing from Deng's reformist line.[14] Even Xuezhi Guo, one of the few scholars who acknowledge that Deng became an autocrat, believes that Deng at least briefly promoted "institutionalization and formal politics."[15] Yet, as this book shows, the hints of what Deng would become were already apparent in the immediate aftermath of Mao's death.

And, indeed, the Deng era was emphatically one of continued strongman rule. Tragically, the Mao era had not been overcome. Lu Zhichao, a leftist party intellectual, concludes,

> But [Deng's detractors] also had some defects, one that was cultivated by the Chinese Communist Party over many years; beginning with the Communist International the constraining effects of the passive tradition were large, which meant that in party struggles it was necessary to take special care to follow the rules, in particular to keep the big picture in mind, to be very weak, and to very easily compromise. Previously under Mao Zedong, and now under Deng Xiaoping, it was always like this; no one dared to have a different opinion; no one dared to "rebel" or to rely on the party's collective power to struggle with mistakes. This also had to do with a lack of inner-party democracy.[16]

Wang Xiaozhong, who worked in the Central Advisory Commission, a body of old revolutionaries that Deng created to ease generational turnover, concurs:

Especially leaders such as Bo Yibo, Wang Zhen, and Song Renqiong, they followed Deng's positions and plans as if they were his own shadow; they followed him slavishly. Even though the elders had different ways of thinking, and splits and contradictions in opinions, and some elders even had different political positions and viewpoints, generally speaking, even if they were "left" or "right," they were progressive or retrogressive, the basic position and attitude of the Central Advisory Commission as a collective was to always follow the ideas of Deng Xiaoping. . . . After a life of difficulties and turbulence, especially the catastrophe of the "Cultural Revolution," the elders reflected and even criticized the personality cult and superstition of the Mao Zedong era, and they all believed that this was the most painful historical lesson. But a new personality cult and superstition were again quietly appearing around Deng Xiaoping.[17]

A lack of real institutionalization meant that it was easy for Deng to ignore dissenters, even senior party elders such as Chen Yun. During both the Hu and Zhao eras, the PSC met irregularly. Hu Yaobang told Li Rui that "PSC meetings are held rarely. . . . Xiaoping said: 'Can't come to an agreement, so don't hold a meeting. I go to Chen's home once a year.'" Zhao Ziyang informed the historian Yang Jisheng, "When I was acting general secretary, Chen Yun wanted me to hold a meeting; Xiaoping said not to do so. Chen Yun wanted a meeting as a place to talk, but Xiaoping opposed a meeting because in this way he could talk directly to us. When I did not hold a meeting, Chen Yun asked me: 'Why don't you hold a meeting?' I said: 'I am just a big secretary. To hold a meeting, you and Comrade Xiaoping have to agree first.' Chen Yun then repeated under his breath: 'just a big secretary.'"[18]

Chen Yun, who was allegedly Deng's greatest competitor, never constituted a serious threat. Throughout his life, Chen was sickly, devious, and cowardly.[19] Mao Zedong once complained that Chen was "the type of person who is afraid that a falling leaf will hurt his head."[20] According to Deng Liqun, "Comrade Chen Yun always took the big picture and put Comrade Deng Xiaoping first."[21] On May 26, 1989, in a speech intended to rally support for martial law,

Chen even referred to Deng in his speech as *touzi* (头子), a term per-haps best translated as "capo." In the public version of his remarks, that phrase is turned into "core" (核心), probably because of the word's mafia-like connotations.[22]

As Xuezhi Guo powerfully demonstrates in one of the few works that acknowledge China's failure to institutionalize in the 1980s, "core" was the term that Deng used to characterize his own thinking on authority.[23] Deng believed that "any leadership collective must have a core; without a core the leadership is unreliable."[24] It was the characteristic of strong centralized leadership, in Deng's mind, that made the CCP so effective. Zhao Ziyang recalled, "I remember an instance, sometime in the early 1980s, when the topic of the Soviet invasion of Afghanistan came up, Deng said, I think that America is inferior to the Soviet Union—all the Soviet Union had to do was hold a meeting of the Politburo [to make the decision to invade]. Could America achieve such a thing?"[25]

Deng regularly made decisions without widespread consulting and, in some cases, despite widespread opposition. In May 1988, Deng suddenly suggested that it was necessary to achieve rapid progress in price reform. Li Peng and Yao Yilin, two PSC mem-bers, were aware that Chen opposed the idea, but they did not even convey Chen's position to the PSC, Politburo, or the leading small group on finance. Li and Yao understood that if they had done so, that "would mean they clearly stood on the side of Chen Yun and they were directly challenging Deng Xiaoping's authority."[26] The choice led to inflation and severely delayed China's reforms.

In 1987, Deng, without going through the appropriate protocol, removed Hu Yaobang from his position as general secretary. Deng's complete disregard for party rules during this incident was widely reviled within the leadership. When Jiang Zemin replaced Zhao Ziyang as leader in 1989, Jiang worried that he would be installed in the same unpopular fashion.[27] But perhaps most crucially for the fate of the PRC, Deng engineered a violent solution to the protests centered in Tiananmen Square in the spring of 1989. Deng was able to force this decision despite widespread opposition in the party, state, and military.[28]

This state of affairs meant that Deng could rule not only with-out fear of resistance but also without formalized restrictions on his behavior. According to Lu Zhichao, the spying, use of compromising material, lying, and plotting that were characteristic of the 1980s often reached levels reminiscent of the Cultural Revolution and were also a direct result of the lack of institutionalization. Lu writes in his memoirs that Deng "did not achieve unity by using methods of collective leadership in the party or the principles of democratic centralism or by using democratic life in the leadership core; instead, he used the special old method of past emperors, the result of which was to spark left-right factional struggles."[29]

Deng was probably China's last best chance for real institutionalization. Ren Zhongyi, the late reformist leader of Guangdong province, once sadly told an interviewer that "Comrade Xiaoping's main deficiency was that he did not use his lofty authority at the right time to execute the political reform for which he expressed support."[30] The CCP has gone to great lengths to keep the true nature of Deng's rule secret. In March 2003, the newspaper *21st Century Global Report* published an interview with the party elder Li Rui in which Li stated,

> It is said that during the leadership transition to the third generation Xiaoping said three things: When Mao was around, Mao had the final say. When I am around, I have the final say. When you have the final say, I'll be at ease. . . . I believe that Xiaoping firmly and correctly grasped the economy. . . . But in terms of the political structure and the leadership structure, he thought that China was so big and had so many people that if everyone spoke at once, without an authority, that would be intolerable. With regard to a capitalist political structure, the so-called separation of powers, he was stubbornly opposed. . . . Why was [Deng Xiaoping's August 1980 speech] disregarded? Ultimately, other than the influence of Hu Qiaomu, it was that he himself could not escape the old understanding, the old habits.

Li explained that he raised these ideas in a report to the Fifteenth Party Congress in order to "avoid repeating the same mistake again."[31] *21st Century Global Report* was immediately shut down, and the contents of its website were deleted.

Post-Strongman Transitions in
Comparative Perspective

Trotsky

Having finished this book, readers familiar with communist history may wonder, but what about Lev Trotsky? Trotsky's prestige as a revolutionary was second only to Lenin—indeed, most people saw Trotsky as the "second man" in the party precisely because of his contributions to early victories. Trotsky had been a prominent figure for many years before 1917 and then played a prominent role in the October Revolution. Moreover, during the Civil War, he was people's commissar of military and naval affairs, which meant he had proven his mettle on the battlefield as well. In 1922, Trotsky was almost as popular with the delegates at the Eleventh Party Congress as Lenin was: both won the exact same number of votes, with Lenin's name consistently appearing first in the filled-out voters' forms.[32] This begs an obvious question: Why was it that Trotsky did not pull a "Deng Xiaoping" against Stalin's "Hua Guofeng"? The commonalities are clear: before Lenin's death, he had promoted the lesser-known Stalin to general secretary, just as Mao had made Hua head of the party, state, and military. So why, after Lenin's death, did authority relations not naturally revert to a proper reflection of revolutionary legacies, as they did in China?

This question is particularly pertinent because, as J. Arch Getty points out, Trotsky's defeat is generally explained as the result of Stalin's superior ability to forge policy coalitions and by "plant[ing] his supporters in the provincial party committees, who in turn sent delegates to the national party meetings and who supported him and not others"—a "circular flow of power."[33] Trotsky himself famously claimed that Stalin was the political representative of the interests of the bureaucracy. This classic understanding of Stalin's rise clearly subscribes to the economic model. However, the latest generation of historiography suggests a rather different picture—one that more closely hews to the authority model.

As Getty points out, the "circular flow of power" theory fails to recognize that Stalin did not pick delegates to the Party Congresses—those representatives were still being elected democratically. Therefore, he concludes, "It is difficult to posit massive provincial delegate support based on gratitude or loyalty for giving them their jobs."[34] In the words of the Russian historian Oleg Khlevniuk, "All power flowed downstream from the Politburo."[35]

Ideas were, naturally, important, especially in the cultural milieu of Bolshevism. Ideological propriety was a key to power, and Stalin understood that he had to provide a coherent vision as part of any claim to top leader.[36] However, the *contest* for power was not primarily about competing political platforms. The opposition's critiques lacked practical details, and "often it was not principled programmatic differences that spawned conflict but ties of friendship, sore feelings, or ambition."[37] In fact, Getty argues that "provincial party leaders saw the struggle in Moscow as non-principled and non-ideological. . . . Trotsky's and Zinoviev's critiques of Stalin's policy on the Chinese and German revolutions, their hairsplitting about theories of permanent revolution or 'primitive socialist accumulation,' must have seemed wholly irrelevant to the provincial parties."[38] As one delegate put it, "We are constructing socialism, and will construct it in the future, and the task of the theoreticians of our party is to theoretically justify what we are doing in practice."[39] Hiroaki Kuromiya similarly concludes that "the delegates [to the Fourteenth Party Congress] suspected that the opposition's true concern was power, and not substantive policy issues."[40] Stephen Kotkin characterizes Trotsky's position in 1923 as "strikingly narrow" and a "sterile program."[41]

In a more forgiving political environment, Trotsky might have been able to draw on real concern about the New Economic Policy (NEP). As one Bolshevik said in 1923, if the NEP had been proposed by anyone other than Lenin, that person would have been labeled "a flabby compromiser, if not an insidious traitor and betrayer."[42] Yet even colossal foreign-policy failures such as the collapse of the General Strike in 1926 or the KMT crackdown on the CCP in 1927 also failed to arrest Stalin's rise to dominance.[43] By then, "politics had become a matter not of ideology and debate but of faith and loyalty."[44] Just as in the previous cases in this book, politics was not about competing policies or punishing failures.

Trotsky's contributions during the October Revolution and the Civil War were undeniable. Just as the authority model predicts, those legacies proved to be Trotsky's most formidable weapon. When Lenin's health completely collapsed, the first salvo in the ensuing struggle was in the form of an article by Karl Radek, a Trotsky ally, in *Pravda*: "Lev Trotsky—Organizer of Victory." The article argued that the only institution that functioned well after the Revolution was the Red Army, which was led by Trotsky.[45] But unlike Deng, Trotsky also had very serious historical problems. Crucially, Trotsky spent many years as a Menshevik and only allied with Lenin in 1917, which led the Old Bolsheviks to "view him with suspicion as a Johnny-come-lately."[46] Trotsky's Jewish heritage was probably also a strike against him.[47]

As part of Trotsky's claim to political power, he tried to portray himself as both a close friend to Lenin but also an individual who had sometimes *corrected* the late leader. Those claims were not persuasive, however, and Trotsky was vulnerable to the clear evidence that he had often quarreled with Lenin. Stalin's allies used access to Lenin's archives to find the choicest remarks Lenin had made about Trotsky. Kompromat was ubiquitous—Trotsky was regularly subjected to attack by "underground" works such as *What Il'ich Wrote and Thought about Trotsky*.[48] Trotsky, therefore, can be roughly compared to Molotov in 1957: both enjoyed authority and prestige related to their history in the party, but that narrative was susceptible to the effective use of compromising material.

Although the Russian historian Valentin Sakharov believes that Stalin and Trotsky were separated by real policy differences, his book on Lenin's "Testament" demonstrates that the succession struggles were still largely dominated by questions about the nature of the competitors' relationships with Lenin before the Soviet leader's death, and, to a dramatic extent, this debate was shaped by the strategic use of compromising material. Sakharov concludes that the most powerful weapon in the hands of Stalin's opponents were comments, falsely attributed to Lenin, about Stalin's style of leadership, which even included a call for his departure from the position of general secretary. One of Stalin's greatest achievements was his ability to cleverly address those accusations while still affirming his closeness to Lenin.[49]

Both Stalin and Trotsky, just like Deng, only supported inner-party democracy *when it suited them*. This extremely cynical and opportunistic approach to party rules led members of the party to conclude that Trotsky was motivated by personal ambitions when he later claimed, opportunistically, that his ideas were not given sufficient attention. Ultimately, the dangers of factionalism and fears of a party split made it easy for Stalin to prevent a serious discussion of competing policy proposals.[50] Stalin could effectively shut down meaningful debate by portraying any attack against him as a criticism of the party itself.[51] Significantly, and curiously, this characteristic was a clear difference with Hua, who deliberately refused to shut down party debate by declaring potential opponents factionalists.

Stalin could also prevent serious deliberation by manipulating which groups were allowed to make decisions. Between 1923 and 1925, key decisions were deliberately made among a small group before full Politburo meetings to avoid giving Trotsky an opportunity to exert influence.[52] At the Thirteenth Party Congress in 1924, Stalin had Lenin's alleged testament discussed among delegations, not during plenary sessions, which allowed Stalin to better guide the course of the deliberations.[53] Often, the party did not even know what Trotsky really thought. For example, in 1927, "control of the party apparatus enabled the majority to conceal the proposals of the opposition not only from rank-and-file Communists but also from the Central Committee members."[54] Stalin also used "joint plenums" to determine membership of key decision-making sessions. As Kotkin writes, at one decisive meeting at which Trotsky suffered a serious setback, "the room had already been prepared."[55] Stalin even allegedly stated, "Who votes how in the party is totally unimportant. What is extremely important is who counts the votes and how."[56] The game was clearly rigged.

Trotsky's opponents were cognizant of the possibility that he would use his relationship with the military in the power struggles.[57] Yet, by late 1923, Trotsky no longer ran the daily affairs of the military, and Stalin had been able to use the party to exert greater power over the Red Army.[58] Perhaps most famously, however, the political police were fully in Stalin's hands, and Stalin also used his special relationship with them to exert terrific pressure on Trotsky's allies.[59]

Kim Jong-il

Readers of this book may also wonder whether the authority model can explain the rise of Kim Jong-il. After all, at the time of Kim Il-sung's death in 1994, some of the guerrillas that had fought with him in Manchuria against Japan during the 1930s were still alive.[60] Why, then, was Kim Jong-il, a man with no military experience, able to emerge triumphant? The answer to this question is especially interesting given the content of this book, as scattered evidence suggests that Kim Il-sung's preparation for the succession was at least in part inspired by what had happened in the Soviet Union and China.

Kim Il, a partisan who was especially close to Kim Il-sung, allegedly pointed to the succession crises in the Soviet Union after Stalin and Lin Biao's fall in China when expressing support for Kim Jong-il as successor, although we are still unable to confirm this comment.[61] Kim Jong-il seemed a better prospect to the old marshals than Kim Il-sung's wife, Kim Song-ae. One analyst believes that the partisans supported Kim Jong-il because they were afraid of Kim Song-ae's growing power, which they saw as similar to Mao's wife, Jiang Qing.[62] One version based on defector accounts argues that, in contrast to Kim's wife, "who attempted to reduce privileges to the old partisans, Kim Jong-il doggedly took care of them. . . . Sin Kyong-wan [a defector] reports that elders of the first generation of the revolution pushed for Kim Jong-il to be chosen as the successor."[63]

Troubling outcomes in neighboring countries and prolonged worries about a stable succession help to explain one of the standout characteristics of the succession in North Korea: the amount of time Kim Il-sung spent preparing the succession before his death. The CIA dated the decision to groom Kim Jong-il to 1973, while Kong Dan Oh believes the preparation for the succession began as early as 1971.[64] At the time, Kim Il-sung's power was overwhelming. During the 1950s and 1960s, he had purged from the top leadership all but his closest associates from the Manchurian period.[65] The CIA concluded in October 1978 that Kim's ability to install his son as successor was high because of Kim's great personal power, the lack of any obvious challengers, and political indoctrination.[66]

Although correlation is not causation, the timing of some of the key moments in the succession suggests the import of events in

China. The earliest reports of Kim Jong-il's status as possible successor come around the time of the death of Lin Biao—Mao's chosen successor. Kim Il-sung apparently accelerated the formal installation of his son after the fall of the Gang of Four (which included Mao's own wife) and the removal of Hua Guofeng (Mao's chosen successor at the time of the Chairman's death). In 1980, Kim even expressed concern to the Chinese leadership that Hua's departure from the leadership would damage the PRC's stability.[67]

Extant scholarly analysis and intelligence reports all support the same conclusion: the old partisans strongly supported Kim Jong-il as the successor. In 1983, the CIA concluded that "there seems little doubt now that the son has crossed the first hurdle—the veteran guerrilla leaders of Kim Il-sung's generation."[68] Kim Jong-il was smart enough to respect the old guard, declaring that "to respect the revolutionary seniors is a noble moral obligation of all revolutionaries" and that "the revolutionary achievements of old guards must be inherited and protected."[69] Kim showed a deep appreciation of both the potency of martial contributions as a propaganda tool and the emotional sensitivity that the old generals felt to the way their martial accomplishments were portrayed. He helped establish a propaganda system in which the partisan experience and familial succession were fundamentally intertwined.[70]

Why did Kim Il-sung and the old partisans decide that Kim Jong-il was the safest choice to guarantee a stable succession? Mao's behavior in his late life provides clues. The Chairman had at least briefly seriously considered Jiang Qing as his successor. When he decided against her, he then started developing his nephew Mao Yuanxin as a potential successor. According to Yao Wenyuan, "I always had the feeling that maybe Chairman Mao was cultivating Mao Yuanxin." In October 1975, Mao, having lost faith in everyone else, entrusted Mao Yuanxin to become a "liaison" with the Politburo, but, in practice, this position far surpassed its innocuous-sounding title. If Mao's own son had not died in the Korean War, Jiang had made fewer enemies, and Mao Yuanxin was a little older, the post-Mao succession may have looked much closer to what happened in North Korea.[71]

The recognition that family ties can help guarantee stable successions has now entered the third generation in the form of Kim

Jong-un. According to Kim Jong-il's oldest son, Jong-nam, who may have been assassinated because of his heritage, Kim Jong-il originally opposed a third generation of dynastic succession but ultimately changed his mind because of its ideological power: "My own understanding is that for the Korean people who only trust and serve the so-called Paektusan bloodline, if someone's 'blood' is not 'pure' enough, it is possible that it will cause the nation much trouble. I judge that even if in the future Korea moves toward a collective leadership system, if its core is not the 'Paektusan bloodline,' then the ruling elite will not be able to continue."[72] In other words, the coin of the realm in North Korea's succession politics is, once again, not political exchange but historical prestige, here in the form of familial relations with the founder of the regime.

Foreign Policy

This book focuses primarily on domestic politics. But what import do the findings of this book have on the study of foreign policy? Political scientists have recently grown increasingly interested in how the structure of elite politics in dictatorships affects decisions on war and peace. The basic insight of this literature is that dictators, just as leaders in democratic regimes, might be punished politically if they fight a losing war. Jessica L. P. Weeks, for example, argues that authoritarian leaders in certain types of systems are more susceptible to domestic pressures ("audience costs") than others, and this helps explain whether or not they choose risky or ambitious policies.[73]

A fine-grained, in-depth examination of these contests reveals several surprising, perhaps counterintuitive nuances to these dynamics that previously were unappreciated by the political science literature. First, for audience costs to have an effect, there must be real policy differences within the elite. As this book shows, this is very often an unrealistic assumption. After Stalin's death, the Soviet leadership was united in the hope for better relations with the West. One of the most crucial foreign-policy decisions of the Khrushchev era, the decision to invade Hungary, was a consensus position within the elite. It was not an issue at the 1957 June plenum that saw the defeat of the anti-party group.

Second, for audience costs to be important, policy differences not only have to exist but also have to matter. This book is full of examples in which the individual with even the less popular policy position is ultimately able to emerge victorious through some mix of personal prestige, rule manipulation, and reliance on coercive organs. Even when a leader's foreign-policy blunder "matters" in the sense that it somehow damages their political position, they have plenty of tricks at their disposal to discount its importance. When removed from power, Khrushchev was criticized for the debacle of the Cuban missile crisis. But to say that this was the single most decisive factor in his removal would be historically inaccurate. Deng's political position was damaged by the disastrous war in Vietnam. But he continued as the most powerful leader for many years thereafter.

Third, researchers should be very careful when interpreting policy differences that are "revealed" as part of a political power struggle. For example, Khrushchev very obviously overstated his foreign-policy differences with Molotov as a political weapon to weaken his opponent. Strikingly, the creation of any sort of political cleavage was so useful to Khrushchev that it hardly mattered whether the "opposing" viewpoint might have been more popular. As suggested throughout this book, when leaders are removed, the victors have every incentive to lie and exaggerate about the crimes of their predecessors so as to make their own victory appear to be more legitimate.

Fourth, prestige as a successful military leader is identified in this book as an especially important quality for political competitors. We might expect that some leaders would adopt deliberately risky and ambitious foreign policies so as to contribute to their status in this regard, especially when other forms of authority are particularly weak. No cases of such behavior are identified in this book, but some analysts believe that North Korea's recent behavior might be partially explained by such thinking.[74]

Fifth, the case of China's invasion of Vietnam is potentially an important example of a leader pursuing an unpopular policy precisely because the adoption of such a position would be a clear indicator of his dominance. This is a concept that has not previously been identified within the literature on audience costs, and indeed it strongly differs from the themes emphasized in that literature.

Sixth, loyalty to the party as an organization is a clear theme throughout this book. Removing a leader during either a major international crisis or in the aftermath of a crisis that had a disastrous outcome would very obviously be a damaging blow to party unity. Under such conditions, we would be much more likely to see unity as a primary concern.

Lessons and Future Directions

Unfortunately, one takeaway for readers of this book should be the difficulty that not only outside analysts but even party insiders face when trying to understand elite politics in Leninist regimes. Sinologists have always struggled to see inside the "black box," and the track record is not strong.[75] Yet getting history right is immensely important, as the past is one of the few places that allow us to understand structural features that might persist. In particular, critical junctures are moments when politics are at their most "visible," and thus they allow us to theorize about limitations and possibilities for the future.[76] For example, in January 2017, drawing on the findings of the research presented here when it was still in dissertation form, I published a short article in the *War on the Rocks* blog about what Deng Xiaoping's legacy might tell us about Xi Jinping. Since Deng had not actually achieved real institutionalization, I suggested that Xi would probably not face real constraints if he decided to break "tradition" and not choose a successor at the forthcoming Nineteenth Party Congress—a prediction that proved accurate.

Just like the continuities from the Mao to the Deng era that are described in this book, we are now seeing parts of the Deng legacy manifest themselves in the Xi era. Despite a regular focus on the "vulnerabilities" of dictators, the CPSU and CCP have usually proven to be quite favorable to leaders—the lieutenants generally have much more to worry about than their superiors. And indeed Xi's leadership has persisted despite severe attacks on high-ranking figures and a number of policy decisions that have led some critics to question his judgment.[77]

If continuities are strong, in the unlikely situation that conspirators make a move against Xi, they will probably not be acting because they have different policy preferences. It is more likely that the plotters will have concluded that Xi had completely escaped any constraints or that they had decided that they had to move first to save their own skins. Hopes that the party will somehow "select" a leader with a different policy platform, an act of "elite revolt," will only come true if the continuities identified in this book are weak.[78] Generally speaking, policy differences do not determine the outcome of elite contestation, and, in any case, Xi is in a strong position to manipulate party rules and direct the military and the political police.

However, in several important ways Xi faces a different set of challenges than Mao's immediate successors did. The leadership may not be divided by the antagonisms that were present after the Cultural Revolution, but Xi does not enjoy the kind of personal prestige that Deng had as a legend of the wars against the KMT and the Japanese. Perhaps for this reason, Xi has cared more than Deng did about formal authority, day-to-day decision-making, and prominence in party propaganda. Deng never assumed the position of party chairman, which led to complaints that he "reigned from behind the curtain." Deng preferred to direct leaders on the "first line" and to avoid PSC meetings at which dissenters might have a chance to express their opinions. He cared deeply about his public image and wanted people to understand that when it counted, he was in charge. Xi's decision to more aggressively and obviously arrogate power speaks more to his weakness than to his strength.

Given Xi's dominance, the extent of the purges conducted under his tenure, and the controversial choices he has made with regard to policy, his successors, whenever and however they might appear, will face a complex set of challenges. How such tensions will be resolved is impossible to say. But whatever may come, the victor will not necessarily be the most "popular" individual who beats their opponents by playing by the rules.

Chronology

October 16, 1952	CC plenum. Stalin attacks old revolutionaries and proposes the creation of a new leadership body of young men who had played no role in the October Revolution.
March 5, 1953	Stalin dies.
March 13, 1953	Beria orders the creation of special investigative groups to reevaluate the Doctors' Plot, the arrests of former members of the Ministry of State Security, officers in the General Artillery Department, and Georgian party officials.
April 4, 1953	Beria distributes a document that criticized the use of torture in the past and explicitly forbids its use in the future.
May 6, 1953	Beria writes a memorandum to the Presidium rehabilitating Kaganovich's brother.
May 8, 1953	Beria writes a note to the Presidium blaming the failure to defeat the insurrection in Lithuania on the lack of Lithuanians in the republic's MVD and draws attention to the absence of ethnic Lithuanians in the party leadership of the republic.
May 13, 1953	Beria proposes an end to restrictions on where Soviet citizens can live within the USSR and suggests greater restrictions on

	the extrajudicial Special Council, which was responsible for many of the abuses of the Stalin era.
May 16, 1953	Beria submits to the Presidium a memorandum on Ukraine pointing to the lack of ethnic Ukrainians in leadership positions in western Ukraine.
May 27, 1953	Discussion in the Soviet leadership on the crisis in the GDR.
Summer 1953	Beria proposes the arrest of former secretary of the CC and minister of state security S. D. Ignat'ev and arrests M. D. Riumin, former head of the investigative unit for particularly important cases and a man who can make accusations against Malenkov and Khrushchev.
June 8, 1953	Beria submits a proposal to the Presidium in which he suggests the removal of the Belorussian party chief Patolichev in favor of an ethnic Belarusian.
June 1953	Khrushchev writes a memorandum about Latvia that touches on the same themes as Beria's memos on Ukraine, Belorussia, and Lithuania.
June 26, 1953	Beria's arrest.
June 29, 1953	New state procurator Rudenko is ordered by the Presidium to identify and investigate the facts of hostile anti-state, anti-party activities of Beria through his entourage.
July 1, 1953	Beria writes a letter to Malenkov on the reform proposals he made as head of the MVD. He does not deny that he asked the MVD to collect information on non-Russian cadres.
July 2, 1953	Beria writes pleas to the Presidium to investigate his affair, but his wishes are denied.
July 2–7, 1953	CC plenum. Malenkov accuses Beria of single-handedly ordering preparation for the first test explosion of a hydrogen bomb. Malenkov is described as Stalin's successor; he states that he is not the sole successor.

August 1953	Malenkov's speech to the fifth session of the Supreme Soviet appeals to the peasant masses.
February 8, 1954	Presidium meeting. Kaganovich says that after the July 1953 plenum, the MVD is "behaving passively" and suggests writing a "motivating document." The leadership establishes a Committee of State Security that entails greater control than a Ministry of State Security.
Fall 1954	Soviet delegation goes to China. When asked by the Chinese, they fail to identify a single top leader, claim they function as "collective leadership." Bulganin attacks Mikoian for the latter's position on Beria's arrest.
February 1955	Malenkov is removed from premiership.
July 4–12, 1955	CC Plenum. Molotov is severely criticized over foreign policy toward Yugoslavia. He denies having fundamentally different positions on any issue.
November 5, 1955	Presidium meeting. Discussion of how to commemorate the anniversary of Stalin's birth.
End of 1955	Khrushchev humiliates Kaganovich by secretly developing a railways plan that he knows Kaganovich will oppose.
January 1956	Led by Molotov, the Soviet Foreign Ministry drafts a document that acclaims the steps taken by the socialist camp to ease international tensions, including improving relationships with Yugoslavia, Austria, Finland, and West Germany.
February 1, 1956	Presidium meeting. Molotov does not deny Stalin's mistakes but insists that the latter still be recognized as a great leader.
February 9, 1956	Everyone in the leadership agrees to tell the Party Congress the "truth" about Stalin. Some believe these truths should include not only Stalin's wrongdoings but triumphs as well.

February 14–25, 1956	Twentieth Party Congress. Molotov supports the introduction of "peaceful coexistence" into the party platform.
April 1956	Molotov speaks with the Chinese ambassador, admits there is no fatal inevitability of war. The CC distributes a letter to the party that restricts discussion of Khrushchev's Secret Speech.
May 1, 1956	Khrushchev says at a reception that no differences on Stalin exist within the leadership.
May 26, 1956	Presidium meeting. Khrushchev attacks Molotov and suggests the latter be removed from his position as minister of foreign affairs.
June 29, 1956	A CC document takes an official position on Stalin that is much more positive than in Khrushchev's speech.
December 6, 1956	Presidium approves the draft of a letter to be sent in the name of the CC to all party organizations on ending attacks by anti-Soviet and enemy elements.
January 1957	Khrushchev gives a speech at the Chinese embassy, describes Stalin as a man who devoted his whole life to the victory of the working class and socialism, and continues to publicly play the pro-Stalin card.
March 27, 1957	Presidium meeting. Bulganin, Pervukhin, and Malenkov complain that Molotov's memo on industrial reform threatens party unity. Molotov claims he was operating within a broad consensus on the issue, states that Khrushchev misrepresented him and did not disagree with the decisions of the February plenum.
April 25, 1957	Presidium meeting. Decision is made to posthumously reinstate into the party Soviet officers killed during the height of the Great Terror.
May 19, 1957	Khrushchev attacks Molotov at a meeting with intellectuals.

June 1957	The anti-party group tries to remove Khrushchev from his position as first secretary of the CPSU.
July 2, 1957	Meeting of the Ministry of Defense apparat and Moscow garrison. Zhukov frankly admits that he saved Khrushchev.
October 28–29, 1957	October plenum. Zhukov is purged.
April 1–24, 1969	Ninth Party Congress ratifies the political purge of Deng Xiaoping and elevates the military and Mao's radical allies to power. Lin Biao is chosen as "the close comrade-in-arms of Chairman Mao" and Mao's successor.
September 13, 1971	Death of Lin Biao in plane crash over Mongolia in attempt to flee to the Soviet Union.
1972	Jiang Qing talks to the American scholar Roxane Witke.
March 1973	Announcement that Deng Xiaoping will return to work.
August 24–28, 1973	Tenth Party Congress. With support of Mao, the Gang of Four manage to secure leading party positions.
December 1973	Mao refers to Deng Xiaoping as a "needle wrapped in cotton": on the outside he is a little gentle, but inside he is a steel factory. Deng is reappointed to the Politburo.
January 1975	Fourth National People's Congress abolishes positions of president and vice president of China, according to the suggestion of Chairman Mao Zedong as part of the Cultural Revolution. Second Plenum of the Tenth Central Committee appoints Deng Xiaoping as a vice chairman of the Politburo Standing Committee.
September 1975	Zhou Enlai signs document rejecting that he was a traitor.

November 1975   Mao Zedong admits that the Cultural Revolution is 30 percent wrong.

January 8, 1976   Death of Zhou Enlai.

February 1976   Hua Guofeng becomes acting premier.

April 1976   Protests in Tiananmen Square labeled "counterrevolutionary rebellion"; Deng Xiaoping is removed from all positions.

September 9, 1976   Death of Mao Zedong.

October 6, 1976   Arrest of the Gang of Four.

January 6, 1977   Hua Guofeng's speech to the Politburo confirms that he never opposed Deng's return to work and that he had already approved Deng's return at an appropriate time.

February 6, 1977   Editorial called "Study the Documents Well and Grasp the Key Link" contains "two whatevers": "We will resolutely uphold whatever policy decisions Chairman Mao made and unswervingly follow whatever instructions Chairman Mao gave."

July 21, 1977   Communiqué of the Third Plenum of the Tenth Central Committee formally reinstates Deng Xiaoping and approves of Hua's purge of the Gang of Four.

August 1977   Eleventh Party Congress announces plan of Hua and the top leadership to finish the "ferreting-out" (清查) phase of exposing and criticizing the Gang of Four within the year or a little longer.

December 1977   Hu Yaobang's speech on how to study history first uses the phrase "practice is the sole criterion of truth," referring to the wrongful cases from the Cultural Revolution.

February–March 1978   Fifth National People's Congress. Hua announces that the "ferreting-out" campaign is basically finished on a national scale.

March 9, 1978   Explosion on ship "160" in Zhanjiang harbor in Guangdong province.

May 1978	*Guangming Daily*, *People's Daily*, and *People's Liberation Army Daily* use the phrase "practice is the sole criterion of truth."
June 1978	Deng gives major speech at a military-wide political work meeting, giving a boost to the "practice is the sole criterion of truth" debate.
July–December 1978	State Council Conference to Discuss Principles sets stage for major breakthroughs on a slew of economic issues at the Third Plenum.
July 24, 1978	*People's Liberation Army Daily*'s publication of the "practice" article signals the military's support for the idea and leading others to fall in line.
November 23, 1978	Final decision to attack Vietnam.
November–December 1978	Work Conference before the Third Plenum.
December 1978	Third Plenum of Eleventh Central Committee. Significant rise in power and stature of the old revolutionaries, especially Deng Xiaoping, and the verdicts on a number of major military officials reversed, even though many of them had already returned to work.
February–March 1979	Chinese invasion of Vietnam, providing more evidence for the country's top leadership that Deng controlled the military.
March 16, 1979	Deng admits broad opposition to war in Vietnam.
March 30, 1979	Deng introduces the Four Cardinal Principles.
May 20, 1979	The military's General Political Department releases a document, titled "An Opinion Regarding Deepening the Study of the Third Plenum and Work Conference Spirit," that calls for unifying around the decisions of the Third Plenum.

July 29, 1979	Deng's speech to an enlarged session of the Navy Party Committee indicates his concern that one-third of the military was not completely under his control.
October–November 1979	Hua Guofeng's trip to western Europe.
February 1980	Fifth Plenum of Eleventh Central Committee dismisses a number of the "took-the-stage" group, including Wang Dongxing, Ji Dengkui, Wu De, and Chen Xilian.
April 18–30, 1980	Hua Guofeng's speech at a military-wide political work meeting uses a Cultural Revolution–era slogan: "Supporting the proletarians and annihilating the capitalists."
August 1980	Deng gives speech criticizing feudal practices and calling for an institutionalized political system as an ideological justification for Hua's removal from the leadership. Hua expresses his willingness to resign. Several Politburo Standing Committee members argue at an enlarged Politburo session that Hua should no longer be head of the Central Military Commission.
October–November 1980	Discussions about party history begin among more than four thousand top-ranking cadres.
October 15, 18, 1980	Deng Liqun gives two speeches to the Chinese Academy of Social Sciences in which he delineates Hua Guofeng's alleged crimes, thus justifying why Hua should be removed.
June 1981	Sixth Plenum of Eleventh Central Committee. Hu Yaobang replaces Hua Guofeng as party chairman. Hua is reduced to vice chairman. The new Politburo Standing Committee includes, in rank order, Hu Yaobang, Ye Jianying, Deng Xiaoping, Zhao Ziyang, Li Xiannian, Chen Yun, and Hua Guofeng.

July 1981	Deng Liqun complains about wide swaths of the party not believing that Hua should be removed.
November 1981	Trial of the Gang of Four.
September 1982	Twelfth Party Congress. Political position of Hua Guofeng is reduced to membership on the Central Committee.

Notes

Chapter 1. Theory

1. Zhang Sheng, *Cong zhanzheng zhong zoulai: Liang dai junren de duihua* [Returning from War: A Conversation between Two Generations of Military Men] (Beijing: Zhongguo qingnian chubanshe, 2008), 412.

2. The top party decision-making body in the Soviet Union from 1952 to 1966 was called the "Presidium." Before and after that time, it was called the "Politburo." Throughout the book, I use whichever term applied at the time under discussion.

3. "Plenum TsK KPSS. Iiun' 1957 goda. Stenograficheskii otchet. Zasedanie pervoe (22 iiunia)" [CC CPSU Plenum. June 1957. Transcript. First Session (June 22)], in *Molotov, Malenkov, Kaganovich. 1957. Stenogramma iiun'skogo plenuma TsK KPSS i drugie dokumenty* [Molotov, Malenkov, Kaganovich. 1957. Transcript of the June CC CPSU Plenum and Other Documents], ed. A. N. Iakovlev (Moscow: MFD, 1998), 33–42.

4. Paul Pierson, "Power and Path Dependence," in *Advances in Comparative-Historical Analysis*, Strategies for Social Inquiry, ed. Kathleen Ann Thelen and James Mahoney (New York: Cambridge University Press, 2015), 123.

5. Sheena Chestnut Greitens, *Dictators and Their Secret Police: Coercive Institutions and State Violence* (Cambridge: Cambridge University Press, 2016), 6–7.

6. Bruce Bueno de Mesquita and Alastair Smith, *The Dictator's Handbook: Why Bad Behavior Is Almost Always Good Politics* (New York: PublicAffairs, 2011), 14.

7. Carl Minzner, *End of an Era: How China's Authoritarian Revival Is Undermining Its Rise* (New York: Oxford University Press, 2018); and Elizabeth Economy, *The Third Revolution: Xi Jinping and the New Chinese State* (New York: Oxford University Press, 2018).

8. Dong Daling, *Deng Xiaoping bu ke gaoren de mimi* [Untold Secret of Deng Xiaoping] (Deer Park, NY: Mingjing chubanshe, 2013), 31.

9. J. M. Barbalet, "Power and Resistance," in *Max Weber: Critical Assessments*, ed. Peter Hamilton, vol. 2 (London: Routledge, 1991), 388.

10. David Miller, "Deliberative Democracy and Social Choice," *Political Studies*, no. 40 (1992): 55; and Christopher H. Achen and Larry M. Bartels, *Democracy for Realists: Why Elections Do Not Produce Responsive Government* (Princeton, NJ: Princeton University Press, 2016), 24.

11. Ronald Wintrobe, *The Political Economy of Dictatorship* (Cambridge: Cambridge University Press, 1998); and Milan W. Svolik, *The Politics of Authoritarian Rule* (Cambridge: Cambridge University Press, 2012).

12. Bueno de Mesquita and Smith, *Dictator's Handbook*, 25.

13. Daron Acemoglu and James A. Robinson, *Economic Origins of Dictatorship and Democracy* (Cambridge: Cambridge University Press, 2006), xii.

14. Susan L. Shirk, *The Political Logic of Economic Reform in China* (Berkeley: University of California Press, 1993).

15. Anthony Downs, *An Economic Theory of Democracy* (New York: Harper, 1957).

16. Bueno de Mesquita and Smith, *Dictator's Handbook*, 5.

17. Robert V. Daniels, "Political Processes and Generational Change," in *Political Leadership in the Soviet Union*, ed. Archie Brown (Basingstoke, UK: Macmillan, 1989), 96–126.

18. Samuel P. Huntington, *Political Order in Changing Societies* (New Haven, CT: Yale University Press, 2006), 194.

19. Bueno de Mesquita and Smith, *Dictator's Handbook*, 8.

20. Roger B. Myerson, "The Autocrat's Credibility Problem and Foundations of the Constitutional State," *American Political Science Review* 102, no. 1 (February 2008): 125–39; and Bueno de Mesquita and Smith, *Dictator's Handbook*.

21. Barbara Geddes, "What Do We Know about Democratization after Twenty Years?," *Annual Review of Political Science* 2, no. 1 (1999): 115–44; Jason Brownlee, *Authoritarianism in an Age of Democratization* (Cambridge: Cambridge University Press, 2007); and Beatriz Magaloni, *Voting for Autocracy: Hegemonic Party Survival and Its Demise in Mexico* (Cambridge: Cambridge University Press, 2008).

22. Wolfgang Streeck and Kathleen Ann Thelen, "Introduction: Institutional Change in Advanced Political Economies," in *Beyond Continuity: Institutional Change in Advanced Political Economies*, ed. Wolfgang Streeck and Kathleen Thelen (New York: Oxford University Press, 2005), 10–11.

23. Bruce J. Dickson, *Wealth into Power: The Communist Party's Embrace of China's Private Sector* (Cambridge: Cambridge University Press, 2008); and Philip Selznick, *The Organizational Weapon: A Study of Bolshevik Strategy and Tactics* (Santa Monica, CA: RAND, 1952).

24. Reinhard Bendix, *Max Weber: An Intellectual Portrait* (Berkeley: University of California Press, 1977), 295.

25. Peter A. Hall and Rosemary C. R. Taylor, "Political Science and the Three New Institutionalisms," *Political Studies* 44, no. 5 (December 1996): 941.

26. Dan Slater and Sofia Fenner, "State Power and Staying Power: Infrastructural Mechanisms and Authoritarian Durability," *Journal of International Affairs* 65, no. 1 (Fall 2011): 15–29.

27. Terry M. Moe, "Power and Political Institutions," *Perspectives on Politics* 3, no. 2 (2005): 221.

28. Paul Pierson, *Politics in Time: History, Institutions, and Social Analysis* (Princeton, NJ: Princeton University Press, 2004), 34.

29. Bendix, *Max Weber*, 294.

30. For a theoretical investigation of the nature of informal rules, see Gretchen Helmke and Steven Levitsky, "Informal Institutions and Comparative Politics: A Research Agenda," *Perspectives on Politics* 2, no. 4 (2004): 725–40.

31. Svolik, *Politics of Authoritarian Rule*. This book has important similarities and differences with Svolik's impressive work. Both Svolik and the analysis presented here emphasize the lack of an external arbiter as a defining characteristic of authoritarian regimes. Svolik understands leadership struggles as a contest between the dictator and elites who want to prevent him from seeking "power." Absolute dominance occurs when other members of the elite, suffering from collective action problems and terror of failure, fail to stop the dictator from grasping too much of this power. Svolik does not explicitly theorize what this "power" is or why the most loyal courtiers would not ultimately change their mind and decide to oppose their benefactor after his other competitors are eliminated.

32. Amos Perlmutter and William M. LeoGrande, "The Party in Uniform: Toward a Theory of Civil-Military Relations in Communist Political Systems," *American Political Science Review* 76, no. 4 (December 1982): 787.

33. Brian D. Taylor, *Politics and the Russian Army: Civil-Military Relations, 1689–2000* (Cambridge: Cambridge University Press, 2003).

34. Hans Joachim Morgenthau, *Politics among Nations: The Struggle for Power and Peace*, 3rd ed. (New York: Knopf, 1960); and Kenneth Neal Waltz, *Theory of International Politics* (Reading, MA: Addison-Wesley, 1979).

35. Hedley Bull, *The Anarchical Society: A Study of Order in World Politics*, 3rd ed. (New York: Columbia University Press, 2002).

36. Stacie E. Goddard, "When Right Makes Might: How Prussia Overturned the European Balance of Power," *International Security* 33, no. 3 (Winter 2008–9): 110–42.

37. Thomas M. Franck, *The Power of Legitimacy among Nations* (New York: Oxford University Press, 1990); Thomas M. Franck, *Fairness in International Law and Institutions* (Oxford, UK: Clarendon, 1995); and Omar M. Dajani,

"Shadow or Shade? The Roles of International Law in Palestinian-Israeli Peace Talks," *Yale Journal of International Law* 32, no. 1 (Winter 2007): 61–112.

38. John Dunn, "Situating Democratic Political Accountability," in *Democracy, Accountability, and Representation*, ed. Adam Przeworski, Susan C. Stokes, and Bernard Manin (New York: Cambridge University Press, 1999), 342–43.

39. Kenneth Jowitt, *New World Disorder: The Leninist Extinction* (Berkeley: University of California Press, 1992); Selznick, *Organizational Weapon*; Nathan Leites, *The Operational Code of the Politburo* (Santa Monica, CA: RAND, 1950); and A. James McAdams, *Vanguard of the Revolution: The Global Idea of the Communist Party* (Princeton, NJ: Princeton University Press, 2017).

40. Geddes, "What Do We Know about Democratization after Twenty Years?"; and Jennifer Gandhi and Adam Przeworski, "Authoritarian Institutions and the Survival of Autocrats," *Comparative Political Studies* 40, no. 11 (January 2007): 1279–301.

41. Robert Conquest, *The Great Terror: A Reassessment* (New York: Oxford University Press, 1990), 113.

42. Jin Chongji and Pang Xianzhi, *Mao Zedong zhuan 1949–1976, xia* [Biography of Mao Zedong 1949–1976, Volume 2] (Beijing: Zhongyang wenxian chubanshe, 2003), 1594.

43. Taylor, *Politics and the Russian Army*.

44. Perlmutter and LeoGrande, "Party in Uniform."

45. Bueno de Mesquita and Smith, *Dictator's Handbook*, 5.

46. Jessica L. P. Weeks, *Dictators at War and Peace* (Ithaca, NY: Cornell University Press, 2014), 40.

47. Alice Miller, "The PLA in the Party Leadership Decisionmaking System," in *PLA Influence on China's National Security Policymaking*, ed. Phillip C. Saunders and Andrew Scobell (Stanford, CA: Stanford University Press, 2015), 58–83; Carl Minzner, "China after the Reform Era," *Journal of Democracy* 26, no. 3 (June 2015): 129–43; Susan L. Shirk, "The Return to Personalistic Rule," *Journal of Democracy* 29, no. 2 (April 2018): 22–36; and Economy, *Third Revolution*.

48. Valerie Bunce, "Leadership Succession and Policy Innovation in the Soviet Republics," *Comparative Politics* 11, no. 4 (July 1979): 380–81; and Grey Hodnett, "Succession Contingencies in the Soviet Union," *Problems of Communism* 24, no. 2 (March–April 1975): 1–21.

49. Geddes, "What Do We Know about Democratization after Twenty Years?"

50. Barbara Geddes, Joseph Wright, and Erica Frantz, *How Dictatorships Work: Power, Personalization, and Collapse* (Cambridge: Cambridge University Press, 2018), 2.

51. Victor C. Shih, "Contentious Elites in China: New Evidence and Approaches," *Journal of East Asian Studies* 16, no. 1 (March 2016): 3.

52. Jason Seawright, "Regression-Based Inference: A Case Study in Failed Causal Assessment," in *Rethinking Social Inquiry: Diverse Tools, Shared Standards*, ed. Henry E. Brady and David Collier, 2nd ed. (Lanham, MD: Rowman and Littlefield, 2010); Michael Shalev, "Limits and Alternatives to Multiple Regression in Comparative Research," *Comparative Social Research* 24 (2007): 261–308; David Freedman, *Statistical Models and Causal Inference: A Dialogue with the Social Sciences*, ed. David Collier, Jasjeet Singh Sekhon, and Philip B. Stark (Cambridge: Cambridge University Press, 2010); Rocío Titiunik, "Can Big Data Solve the Fundamental Problem of Causal Inference?," *PS: Political Science & Politics* 48, no. 1 (January 2015): 75–79; and Thad Dunning, *Natural Experiments in the Social Sciences: A Design-Based Approach* (New York: Cambridge University Press, 2012).

53. Nicholas Sambanis, "A Review of Recent Advances and Future Directions in the Quantitative Literature on Civil War," *Defence and Peace Economics* 13, no. 3 (2002): 215–43; and Mark S. Bell, "Examining Explanations for Nuclear Proliferation," *International Studies Quarterly* 60, no. 3 (2016): 520–29.

54. Stephan Haggard and Robert R. Kaufman, "Inequality and Regime Change: Democratic Transitions and the Stability of Democratic Rule," *American Political Science Review* 106, no. 3 (2012): 495–516; Marcus Kreuzer, "Historical Knowledge and Quantitative Analysis: The Case of the Origins of Proportional Representation," *American Political Science Review* 104, no. 2 (2010): 369–92; Bruce Morrison, "Channeling the 'Restless Spirit of Innovation': Elite Concessions and Institutional Change in the British Reform Act of 1832," *World Politics* 63, no. 4 (2011): 678–710; Dan Slater and Benjamin Smith, "Economic Origins of Democratic Breakdown: The Redistributive Model and the Postcolonial State," University of Chicago Department of Political Science Working Paper Series, June 2012; Mary Gallagher and Jonathan K. Hanson, "Authoritarian Survival, Resilience, and the Selectorate Theory," in *Why Communism Did Not Collapse: Understanding Authoritarian Regime Resilience in Asia and Europe*, ed. Martin K. Dimitrov (New York: Cambridge University Press, 2013), 185–204; and Marc Trachtenberg, "Audience Costs: An Historical Analysis," *Security Studies* 21, no. 1 (January 2012): 3–42.

55. Dani Rodrik, *Economics Rules: Why Economics Works, When It Fails, and How to Tell the Difference* (New York: Oxford University Press, 2015).

56. Giovanni Capoccia and Daniel Ziblatt, "The Historical Turn in Democratization Studies: A New Research Agenda for Europe and Beyond," *Comparative Political Studies* 43, nos. 8–9 (August 2010): 934, 939, 942, 943.

57. Kathleen Thelen, "Historical Institutionalism in Comparative Politics," *Annual Review of Political Science* 2, no. 1 (1999): 378.

58. Ian Shapiro and Alexander Wendt, "The Difference That Realism Makes: Social Science and the Politics of Consent," in *The Flight from Reality in the Human Sciences*, ed. Ian Shapiro (Princeton, NJ: Princeton University Press, 2005), 40.

59. Ira Katznelson, "Structure and Configuration in Comparative Politics," in *Comparative Politics: Rationality, Culture, and Structure*, ed. Mark Irving Lichbach and Alan S. Zuckerman (Cambridge: Cambridge University Press, 1997), 99.

60. Amel Ahmed and Rudra Sil, "When Multi-Method Research Subverts Methodological Pluralism—or, Why We Still Need Single-Method Research," *Perspectives on Politics* 10, no. 4 (December 2012): 935–53; and Gary Goertz and James Mahoney, *A Tale of Two Cultures: Qualitative and Quantitative Research in the Social Sciences* (Princeton, NJ: Princeton University Press, 2012).

61. Berth Danermark, Mats Ekström, Liselotte Jakobson, and Jan Ch. Karlsson, *Explaining Society: Critical Realism in the Social Sciences* (London: Routledge, 2002).

62. Xiao Donglian, "Guanyu gaige kaifang shi yanjiu de ruogan wenti" [Regarding a Few Issues on the History of Reform and Opening], *Zhonggong dangshi yanjiu*, no. 2 (February 2020): 95.

63. J. Arch Getty, *Practicing Stalinism: Bolsheviks, Boyars, and the Persistence of Tradition* (New Haven, CT: Yale University Press, 2013); Frederick C. Teiwes, "The Paradoxical Post-Mao Transition: From Obeying the Leader to 'Normal Politics,'" *China Journal*, no. 34 (1995): 55–94; and Xuezhi Guo, *The Politics of the Core Leader in China: Culture, Institution, Legitimacy, and Power* (Cambridge: Cambridge University Press, 2019).

64. Steven Levitsky and Lucan A. Way, *Competitive Authoritarianism: Hybrid Regimes after the Cold War* (New York: Cambridge University Press, 2010), 26.

65. Dan Slater, *Ordering Power: Contentious Politics and Authoritarian Leviathans in Southeast Asia* (Cambridge: Cambridge University Press, 2010), 5.

66. Elisabeth Jean Wood, "The Social Processes of Civil War: The Wartime Transformation of Social Networks," *Annual Review of Political Science*, no. 11 (2008): 539–61; Elisabeth Jean Wood, *Insurgent Collective Action and Civil War in El Salvador* (Cambridge: Cambridge University Press, 2003); and Jeremy M. Weinstein, *Inside Rebellion: The Politics of Insurgent Violence* (Cambridge: Cambridge University Press, 2007).

Chapter 2. The Defeat of Beria

1. Joshua Rubenstein, *The Last Days of Stalin* (New Haven, CT: Yale University Press, 2017), 35–51.

2. Nuriddin Mukhitdinov, *Gody, provedennye v Kremle: Vospominaniia veterana voiny, truda i Kommunisticheskoi partii, rabotavshego so Stalinym, Malenko-*

vym, Khrushchevym, Brezhnevym, Andropovym [Years Spent in the Kremlin: Memoirs of a Veteran of War, Labor, and the Communist Party Who Worked with Stalin, Malenkov, Khrushchev, Brezhnev, Andropov] (Tashkent: Izdatel'stvo narodnogo naslediia im. A. Kadyri, 1994), 82–83.

3. Nikita Khrushchev, *Memoirs of Nikita Khrushchev*, vol. 2, *Reformer, 1945–1964*, ed. Sergei Khrushchev (University Park: Pennsylvania State University, 2006), 109–11, 116.

4. A. V. Pyzhikov and A. A. Danilov, *Rozhdenie sverkhderzhavy. 1945–1953 gody* [The Birth of a Superpower. 1945–1953] (Moscow: OLMA-PRESS, 2002), 208–10.

5. RGANI, fond 2, opis 1, delo 23, listy 1–5, Harvard Cold War Studies Collection.

6. Zh. A. Medvedev, "Zagadka smerti Stalina" [The Mystery of Stalin's Death], *Voprosy istorii*, no. 1 (2000): 83–91.

7. E. Iu. Zubkova, "Malenkov i Khrushchev: Lichnyi faktor v politike poslestalinskogo rukovodstva" [Malenkov and Khrushchev: The Personal Factor in the Politics of the Post-Stalin Leadership], *Otechestvennaia istoriia*, no. 4 (July–August 1995): 106.

8. V. P. Naumov, "Bor'ba N. S. Khrushcheva za edinolichnuiu vlast'" [N. S. Khrushchev's Struggle for Sole Power], *Novaia i noveishaia istoriia*, no. 2 (March–April 1996): 12.

9. L. M. Kaganovich, *Pamiatnye zapiski rabochego, kommunista-bol'shevika, profsoiuznogo, partiinogo i sovetsko-gosudarstvennogo rabotnika* [Notes of a Worker, Communist-Bolshevik, Professional Union, Party and Soviet State Official] (Moscow: Vagrius, 1996), 503. According to Kaganovich, Malenkov made the proposal without discussing it with other members of the leadership during a break between plenum sessions. When Kaganovich later asked him why he had done this, Malenkov explained that Bulganin told him to do so: "Otherwise, I will make this proposal myself." Malenkov did not think Bulganin would act alone, so he nominated Khrushchev for the position. Kaganovich recounts that the others reservedly accepted this decision not because they were afraid of opposing it but simply because if a first secretary was to be chosen, there was no other option.

10. William Taubman, *Khrushchev: The Man and His Era* (New York: Norton, 2003), 240.

11. Sergei Kremlev, *Beriia. Luchshii menedzher XX veka* [Beria. The Best Manager of the Twentieth Century] (Moscow: Iauza, 2008).

12. L. P. Beriia, *"Stalin slezam ne verit." Lichnyi dnevnik 1937–1941* ["Stalin Does Not Believe in Tears." Personal Diary 1937–1941] (Moscow: Iazua-Press, 2011).

13. For superb historical accounts, see Mark Kramer, "Leadership Succession and Political Violence in the USSR Following Stalin's Death," in *Political Violence: Belief, Behavior, and Legitimation*, ed. Paul Hollander (New York: Palgrave Macmillan, 2008); Taubman, *Khrushchev*, 244–57; and Amy

Knight, *Beria: Stalin's First Lieutenant* (Princeton, NJ: Princeton University Press, 1993).

14. F. I. Chuev and V. M. Molotov, *Molotov Remembers: Inside Kremlin Politics: Conversations with Felix Chuev*, ed. Albert Resis (Chicago: Ivan R. Dee, 1993), 237.

15. Ibid., 324.

16. I. G. Zemtsov, *Litsa i maski: O vremeni i o sebe: V 2 kn. Kniga 1* [Faces and Masks: About the Time and Myself: In 2 Books. Book 1] (Moscow: Terra, 2008), 117.

17. "Zapiska L. P. Berii v Prezidium TsK KPSS o reabilitatsii M. M. Kaganovicha. 6 maia 1953 goda" [L. P. Beria's Memo to the CC CPSU Presidium on Rehabilitation of M. M. Kaganovich. May 6, 1953], in *Lavrentii Beriia. 1953. Stenogramma iiul'skogo plenuma TsK KPSS i drugie dokumenty* [Lavrentii Beria. 1953. Transcript of the July Plenum of the CC CPSU and Other Documents], ed. A. N. Iakovlev (Moscow: MFD, 1999), 42.

18. Nikita Khrushchev, *Khrushchev Remembers* (Boston: Little, Brown, 1970), 324–25.

19. RGANI, fond 2, opis 1, delo 23, list 7, Harvard Cold War Studies Collection.

20. A. I. Mikoian, *Tak bylo. Razmyshleniia o minuvshem* [It Was. Reflections on the Past] (Moscow: Tsentrpoligraf, 2014), 628.

21. Chuev and Molotov, *Molotov Remembers*, 334–35.

22. Khrushchev, *Memoirs of Nikita Khrushchev*, 2:186.

23. "Stenogramma iiul'skogo (1953 g.) plenuma TsK KPSS. Zasedanie 2 iiulia" [Transcript of the July (1953) CC CPSU Plenum. July 2 Session], in Iakovlev, *Lavrentii Beriia*, 94.

24. "Pis'mo L. P. Berii v TsK KPSS. 1 iiulia 1953 g." [L. P. Beria's Letter to the CC CPSU. July 1, 1953], in Iakovlev, *Lavrentii Beriia*, 72–78.

25. "Prikazanie ministra vnutrennikh del SSSR L. P. Berii o sozdanii sledstvennykh grupp po peresmotru sledstvennykh del. 13 marta 1953" [Order of the USSR Minister of Internal Affairs L. P. Beria on Creation of Investigative Groups to Reevaluate Criminal Cases. March 13, 1953], in Iakovlev, *Lavrentii Beriia*, 17–18.

26. "Prikaz ministra vnutrennikh del SSSR L. P. Berii 'O zapreshchenii primeneniia k arestovannym kakikh-libo mer prinuzhdeniia i fizicheskogo vozdeistviia.' 4 aprelia 1953 g." [Order of the USSR Minister of Internal Affairs L. P. Beria "On Prohibition of Any Measures of Enforcement and Physical Coercion with Regard to the Arrested." April 4, 1953], in Iakovlev, *Lavrentii Beriia*, 28–29.

27. "Zapiska L. P. Berii v Prezidium TsK KPSS ob uprazdnenii pasportnykh ogranichenii i rezhimnykh mestnostei" [L. P. Beria's Memo to the CC CPSU on the Abolition of Passport Restrictions and Restricted Areas], in Iakovlev, *Lavrentii Beriia*, 43–46.

28. "Zapiska L. P. Berii v Prezidium TsK KPSS ob ogranichenii prav Osobogo soveshchaniia pri MVD SSSR. 15 iiunia 1953 g." [L. P. Beria's Memo to the CC CPSU on Restriction of Rights of the Special Council at the USSR MVD. June 15, 1953], in Iakovlev, *Lavrentii Beriia*, 62–64.

29. K. Simonov, "Strashnyi chelovek" [Terrible Person], in *Beriia: Konets kar'ery* [Beria: End of Career], ed. V. F. Nekrasov (Moscow: Politizdat, 1991), 188–89.

30. Kramer, "Leadership Succession and Political Violence," 74.

31. "Stenogramma iiul'skogo (1953 g.) plenuma TsK KPSS. Zasedanie 3 iiulia (utrennee)" [Transcript of the July (1953) CC CPSU plenum. July 3 (Morning) Session], in Iakovlev, *Lavrentii Beriia*, 136.

32. Ibid., 137.

33. D. T. Shepilov, *The Kremlin's Scholar: A Memoir of Soviet Politics under Stalin and Khrushchev*, ed. Stephen V. Bittner, trans. Anthony Austin (New Haven, CT: Yale University Press, 2007), 261.

34. V. F. Nekrasov, "Final (Po materialam sudebnogo protsessa)" [The Finale (From Materials of the Court Process)], in Nekrasov, *Beriia*, 410.

35. R. J. Service, "The Road to the Twentieth Party Congress: An Analysis of the Events Surrounding the Central Committee Plenum of July 1953," *Soviet Studies* 33, no. 2 (1981): 232–45.

36. Kramer, "Leadership Succession and Political Violence," 72, 80.

37. "Pis'mo L. P. Berii v TsK KPSS. 1 iiulia 1953 g.," 73 (emphasis added).

38. Ibid.

39. A. M. Filitov, "SSSR i GDR: God 1953-i" [USSR and GDR: The Year 1953], *Voprosy istorii*, no. 7 (2000): 123–35.

40. Mark Kramer, "The Early Post-Stalin Succession Struggle and Upheavals in East-Central Europe: Internal-External Linkages in Soviet Policy Making (Part 1)," *Journal of Cold War Studies* 1, no. 1 (1999): 3–55; Mark Kramer, "The Early Post-Stalin Succession Struggle and Upheavals in East-Central Europe: Internal-External Linkages in Soviet Policy Making (Part 2)," *Journal of Cold War Studies* 1, no. 2 (1999): 3–38; Mark Kramer, "The Early Post-Stalin Succession Struggle and Upheavals in East-Central Europe: Internal-External Linkages in Soviet Policy Making (Part 3)," *Journal of Cold War Studies* 1, no. 3 (1999): 3–66; Filitov, "SSSR i GDR," 123–35; and A. M. Filitov, *Germaniia v sovetskom vneshnepoliticheskom planirovanii, 1941–1990* [Germany in Soviet Foreign Policy Planning, 1941–1990] (Moscow: Nauka, 2009).

41. Filitov, "SSSR i GDR," 124.

42. Filitov, *Germaniia*, 192–95.

43. "Protokol doprosa L. P. Beriia. 11 iiulia 1953 g." [Protocol of L. P. Beria's Interrogation. July 11, 1953], in *Delo Beriia. Prigovor obzhalovaniiu ne podlezhit* [The Beria Affair. The Verdict Cannot Be Appealed], comp. V. N. Khaustov (Moscow: MFD, 2012), 85–86.

44. RGANI, fond 2, opis 1, delo 127, list 121, Harvard Cold War Studies Collection.

45. "Stenogramma iiul'skogo (1953 g.) plenuma TsK KPSS. Zasedanie 3 iiulia (utrennee)," 147.

46. Kramer, "Leadership Succession and Political Violence," 77–78.

47. G. K. Zhukov, "Riskovannaia operatsiia" [Dangerous Operation], in Nekrasov, *Beriia*, 281–83.

48. Transcript of Pavel Sudoplatov interviews, Pavel Sudoplatov, Box 1, Hoover Institution Archives, Stanford University, Stanford, CA.

49. William J. Tompson, *Khrushchev: A Political Life* (New York: St. Martin's Griffin, 1997), 118–20.

50. RGASPI, fond 82, opis 2, delo 896, listy 135–42.

51. Ibid., 143–50.

52. RGASPI, fond 82, opis 2, delo 898, list 132.

53. "Postanovlenie Prezidiuma TsK KPSS o politicheskom i khoziaistvennom sostoianii zapadnykh oblastei Ukrainskoi SSR. 26 maia 1953 g." [Resolution of the CC CPSU Presidium on the Political and Economic Condition of Western Regions of the Ukrainian SSR. May 26, 1953], in Iakovlev, *Lavrentii Beriia*, 49; and "Postanovlenie Prezidiuma TsK KPSS o polozhenii v Litovskoi SSR. 26 maia 1953 g." [Resolution of the CC CPSU on the Situation in the Lithuanian SSR. May 26, 1953], in Iakovlev, *Lavrentii Beriia*, 52.

54. Zubkova, "Malenkov i Khrushchev," 107; and RGANI, fond 5, opis 30, delo 6, listy 20–29. I thank Simon Miles for finding this document for me.

55. Geoffrey Swain, *Khrushchev* (London: Palgrave, 2016), 64.

56. "Pis'mo L. P. Berii v TsK KPSS. 1 iiulia 1953 g.," 73.

57. "Protokol doprosa L. P. Beriia. 9 iiulia 1953 g." [Protocol of L. P. Beria's Interrogation. July 9, 1953], in Khaustov, *Delo Beriia*, 38.

58. Iakovlev, introduction to *Lavrentii Beriia*, 8.

59. "Chernovaia zapis' vystupleniia G. M. Malenkova na zasedanii Prezidiuma TsK KPSS. 26 iiunia 1953 g." [Malenkov's Draft Speech at a Session of the CC CPSU Presidium. June 26, 1953], in Iakovlev, *Lavrentii Beriia*, 70.

60. "Stenogramma iiul'skogo (1953 g.) plenuma TsK KPSS. Zasedanie 2 iiulia," 89.

61. "Stenogramma iiul'skogo (1953 g.) plenuma TsK KPSS. Zasedanie 3 iiulia (utrennee)," 110.

62. "Plenum TsK KPSS. Iiun' 1957 goda. Stenograficheskii otchet. Zasedanie pervoe (22 iiunia)" [CC CPSU Plenum. June 1957. Transcript. First Session (June 22)], in *Molotov, Malenkov, Kaganovich. 1957. Stenogramma iiun'skogo plenuma TsK KPSS i drugie dokumenty* [Molotov, Malenkov, Kaganovich. 1957. Transcript of the June Plenum of the CC CPSU and Other Documents], ed. A. N. Iakovlev (Moscow: MFD, 1998), 47.

63. Ibid., 43.

64. Sudoplatov to Volkogonov, November 18, 1990, Reel 8, Volkogonov Papers, Library of Congress, Washington, DC, 2.

65. "Protokol doprosa B. A. Liudvigova. 4 iiulia 1953 g." [Protocol of B. A. Ludvigov's Interrogation. July 4, 1953], in Khaustov, *Delo Beriia*, 25.

66. "Protokol doprosa L. P. Beriia. 10 iiulia 1953 g." [Protocol of L. P. Beria's Interrogation. July 10, 1953], in Khaustov, *Delo Beriia*, 49.

67. Pavel Sudoplatov, *Special Tasks: The Memoirs of an Unwanted Witness—a Soviet Spymaster* (Boston: Little, Brown, 1995), 359.

68. Shepilov, *Kremlin's Scholar*, 265.

69. Khrushchev, *Memoirs of Nikita Khrushchev*, 2:191–94.

70. F. I. Chuev, *Tak govoril Kaganovich: Ispoved' stalinskogo apostola* [Thus Spoke Kaganovich: Confession of Stalin's Apostle] (Moscow: Otechestvo, 1992), 65–66.

71. I. A. Serov, *Zapiski iz chemodana. Tainye dnevniki pervogo predsedatelia KGB, naidennye cherez 25 let posle ego smerti* [Notes from the Suitcase. The Hidden Diaries of the First Chairman of the KGB Found Twenty-Five Years after His Death] (Moscow: Prosveshchenie, 2016), 430.

72. Chuev and Molotov, *Molotov Remembers*, 345; and N. S. Khrushchev, "Aktsiia" [The Act], in Nekrasov, *Beriia*, 277.

73. Brian D. Taylor, *Politics and the Russian Army: Civil-Military Relations, 1689–2000* (Cambridge: Cambridge University Press, 2003), 180.

74. Chuev, *Tak govoril Kaganovich*, 66.

75. Mikoian, *Tak bylo*, 634.

76. "Chernovaia zapis' vystupleniia G. M. Malenkova na zasedanii Prezidiuma TsK KPSS. 26 iiunia 1953 g.," 70.

77. Khrushchev, *Memoirs of Nikita Khrushchev*, 2:197–98; and K. S. Moskalenko, "Kak byl arestovan Beriia" [How Beria Was Arrested], in Nekrasov, *Beriia*, 286: according to Moskalenko, Malenkov said to make the arrest "in the name of Soviet law."

78. F. M. Burlatskii, *N. Khrushchev i ego sovetniki—krasnye, chernye, belye* [N. Khrushchev and His Advisers—Red, Black, White] (Moscow: EKSMO-Press, 2002), 24–25.

79. "Iz vospominanii Sukhanova D. N., byvshego pomoshchnika Malenkova G. M." [From the Recollections of D. N. Sukhanov, Former Assistant to G. M. Malenkov], n.d., Reel 8, Volkogonov Papers, Library of Congress, Washington, DC, 19–22.

80. Burlatskii, *N. Khrushchev i ego sovetniki*, 27.

81. Moskalenko, "Kak byl arestovan Beriia," 286.

82. S. Bystrov, "Zadanie osobogo svoistva" [Mission of a Special Nature], *Krasnaia zvezda*, no. 65 (March 19, 1988): 6.

83. "Stenogramma iiul'skogo (1953 g.) plenuma TsK KPSS. Zasedanie 4 iiulia (vechernee)" [Transcript of the July (1953) CC CPSU plenum. July 4 (Evening) Session], in Iakovlev, *Lavrentii Beriia*, 191.

84. "Stenogramma iiul'skogo (1953 g.) plenuma TsK KPSS. Zasedanie 3 iiulia (utrennee)," 140.

85. "Stenogramma iiul'skogo (1953 g.) plenuma TsK KPSS. Zasedanie 2 iiulia," 98.

86. "Stenogramma iiul'skogo (1953 g.) plenuma TsK KPSS. Zasedanie 3 iiulia (vechernee)" [Transcript of the July (1953) CC CPSU plenum. July 3 (Evening) Session], in Iakovlev, *Lavrentii Beriia*, 167.

87. V. P. Naumov, "Byl li zagovor Berii? Novye dokumenty o sobytiiakh 1953 g." [Was There a Beria Conspiracy? New Documents on the Events of 1953], *Novaia i noveishaia istoriia*, no. 5 (September–October 1998): 32.

88. Taylor, *Politics and the Russian Army*, 181.

89. Khrushchev, *Memoirs of Nikita Khrushchev*, 2:191–94.

90. Ibid., 195.

91. Moskalenko, "Kak byl arestovan Beriia." Sergo claimed that his father was actually killed on June 26 at his home and that his letters and records of interrogation were forged. This argument is impossible to accept, as it would require a complete rejection of all other primary sources and memoirs. According to Sergo, shots were fired at his father's house, and a bodyguard told him that a body was carried out covered in tarp. Therefore, not even Sergo provided persuasive information that his father was killed. Sergo Beriia, *Moi otets—narkom Beriia* [My Father—Commissar Beria] (Moscow: Algoritm, 2013), 444–45.

92. "Stenogramma iiul'skogo (1953 g.) plenuma TsK KPSS. Zasedanie 2 iiulia," 88.

93. RGASPI, fond 45, opis 1, delo 23, listy 29–31.

94. RGANI, fond 2, opis 1, delo 23, list 8, Harvard Cold War Studies Collection.

95. Zemtsov, *Litsa i maski*, 1:130.

96. "Postanovlenie Prezidiuma TsK KPSS 'Ob organizatsii sledstviia po delu o prestupnykh antipartiinykh i antigosudarstvennykh deistviiakh Beriia.' 29 iiunia 1953 g." [Resolution of the CC CPSU Presidium "On Investigation of Criminal Anti-Party and Anti-State Actions of Beria." June 29, 1953], in Iakovlev, *Lavrentii Beriia*, 72.

97. "Pis'mo L. P. Berii v Prezidium TsK KPSS. 2 iiulia 1953 g." [L. P. Beria's Letter to the CC CPSU Presidium. July 2, 1953], in Iakovlev, *Lavrentii Beriia*, 79.

98. Khrushchev, *Khrushchev Remembers*, 339.

99. Elizaveta Maetnaia, "Marshal Konev revnoval budushchuiu zhenu k Marshalu Zhukovu" [Marshal Konev Was Jealous of His Wife with Regard to Marshal Zhukov], *Komsomol'skaia pravda*, no. 225 (December 5, 1997): 7.

100. A. G. Zviagintsev, *Rudenko* (Moscow: Molodaia gvardiia, 2007), 156.

101. Burlatskii, *N. Khrushchev i ego sovetniki*, 23.

102. Naumov, "Byl li zagovor Berii?"

103. "Stenogramma iiul'skogo (1953 g.) plenuma TsK KPSS. Zasedanie 2 iiulia," 89.

104. "Stenogramma iiul'skogo (1953 g.) plenuma TsK KPSS. Zasedanie 3 iiulia (utrennee)," 112.

105. Mikoian, *Tak bylo*, 633.

106. "Zapiska V. A. Makhneva o deiatel'nosti L. P. Beriia v spetskomitete. 11 iiulia 1953 g." [V. A. Makhnev's Memo on L. P. Beria's Activity in the Special Committee. July 11, 1953], in Khaustov, *Delo Beriia*, 53.

107. Andrei Sakharov, *Memoirs* (New York: Knopf, 1990), 169.

108. "Plenum TsK KPSS. Iiul' 1953 goda. Stenograficheskii otchet. Zasedanie pervoe. 2 iiulia" [CC CPSU Plenum. July 1953. Transcript. First Session. July 2], in Iakovlev, *Lavrentii Beriia*, 224.

109. "Zapiska V. Makhneva G. M. Malenkovu. 11 iiulia 1953 g." [V. Makhnev's Memo to G. M. Malenkov. July 11, 1953], in Khaustov, *Delo Beriia*, 58–59.

110. David Holloway, *Stalin and the Bomb: The Soviet Union and Atomic Energy, 1939–1956* (New Haven, CT: Yale University Press, 1994), 321. Holloway was told by someone in a position to know that key scientists speculated after the arrest "about the possibility that [Beria] might have thought about doing something like exploiting his position as head of the atomic project to seize overall power." Personal communication with author, October 2012.

111. Moskalenko, "Kak byl arestovan Beriia," 289.

112. However, in 1985, three participants of the operation wrote to the Central Committee asking that they receive the Hero of the Soviet Union award for their actions. They were refused, the reason being that they had already been awarded in January 1954 with the Order of the Red Flag. See Dmitrii Volkogonov, *Autopsy of an Empire: The Seven Leaders Who Built the Soviet Regime* (New York: Free Press, 1998), 194; and "Net neobkhodimosti govorit' o nashikh boevykh zaslugakh" [There Is No Need to Speak of Our Military Achievements], *Rodina*, no. 10 (1992): 64.

113. Moskalenko, "Kak byl arestovan Beriia," 287–88.

114. Ibid.

115. N. A. Svetlishin, *Krutye stupeni sud'by: Zhizn' i ratnye podvigi marshala G. K. Zhukova* [Steep Steps of Fate: The Life and Military Exploits of Marshal G. K. Zhukov] (Khabarovsk: Knizhnoe izdatel'stvo, 1992), 235–36.

116. Roy Medvedev, *Khrushchev: A Biography* (Garden City, NY: Anchor Books, 1984), 62–63.

117. "Plenum TsK KPSS. Iiun' 1957 goda. . . . Zasedanie pervoe (22 iiunia)," 49.

118. "Stenogramma zasedaniia Sverdlovskogo raikoma partii po voprosu iskliucheniia V. M. Molotova iz riadov KPSS. 14 fevralia 1962 g." [Transcript of the Sverdlovsk Party District Committee Session on V. M. Molotov's Expulsion from the CPSU. February 14, 1962], in *Boi s "ten'iu"*

Stalina. Prodolzhenie: Dokumenty i materialy ob istorii XXII s"ezda KPSS i vtorogo etapa destalinizatsii [The Battle with Stalin's "Shadow." Continued: Documents and Materials on the History of the Twenty-Second CPSU Congress and the Second Stage of De-Stalinization], ed. N. G. Tomilina (Moscow: Nestor-Istoriia, 2015), 372.

119. Khrushchev, *Khrushchev Remembers*, 333–35.

120. RGANI, fond 89, opis 18, delo 27, listy 1–2, Harvard Cold War Studies Collection.

121. B. V. Geraskin, *Voennaia kontrrazvedka i armiia. Zapiski veterana organov voennoi kontrrazvedki. (Vypusk 3)* [Military Counterintelligence and the Army. Notes of a Veteran of Military Counterintelligence. (Issue No. 3)] (Moscow: Izvestiia, 2016), 132.

122. A. I. Kokurin and N. V. Petrov, comps., *Lubianka: Organy VChK— OGPU—NKVD—NKGB—MGB—MVD—KGB. 1917–1991. Spravochnik* [Lubianka: Organs of the VChK—OGPU—NKVD—NKGB—MGB— MVD—KGB. 1917–1991. Directory] (Moscow: MFD, 2003), 115.

123. "Protokol No. 50. Zasedanie 8 fevralia 1954 g." [Protocol No. 50. Meeting of February 8, 1954], in *Prezidium TsK KPSS. 1954–1964. Chernovye protokol'nye zapisi zasedanii. Stenogrammy. Postanovleniia. V 3 t. T. 1: Chernovye protokol'nye zapisi zasedanii. Stenogrammy* [Presidium of the CC CPSU. 1954–1964. Draft Minutes of Meetings. Transcripts. Resolutions. In 3 Vols. Vol. 1: Draft Minutes of Meetings. Transcripts], ed. A. A. Fursenko (Moscow: ROSSPEN, 2004), 19–24.

124. R. G. Pikhoia, *Sovetskii Soiuz: Istoriia vlasti. 1945–1991* [The Soviet Union: A History of Power. 1945–1991], 2nd ed. (Novosibirsk: Sibirskii khronograf, 2000), 96.

125. N. V. Petrov, *Palachi: Oni vypolniali zakazy Stalina* [Butchers: They Executed the Orders of Stalin] (Moscow: Novaia gazeta, 2011), 14.

126. Holloway, *Stalin and the Bomb*.

Chapter 3. The Anti-Party Group

1. Charles E. Bohlen, *Witness to History, 1929–1969* (Toronto: Norton, 1973), 453–54. Bohlen did, however, correctly identify the importance of whether the decision was made in the Presidium or the CC: "It seems to have been a question of who had the majority where and when."

2. For a superb historical treatment of this event, see William Taubman, *Khrushchev: The Man and His Era* (New York: Norton, 2003), 303–24.

3. A. I. Mikoian, *Tak bylo. Razmyshleniia o minuvshem* [It Was. Reflections on the Past] (Moscow: Tsentrpoligraf, 2014), 644.

4. A. M. Filitov, *Germaniia v sovetskom vneshnepoliticheskom planirovanii, 1941–1990* [Germany in Soviet Foreign Policy Planning, 1941–1990] (Moscow: Nauka, 2009).

5. Shi Zhe and Li Haiwen, *Zai lishi juren shenbian: Shi Zhe huiyilu* [Next to a Historical Giant: The Memoirs of Shi Zhe] (Beijing: Jiuzhou chubanshe, 2015), 408.

6. Yan Mingfu, *Yan Mingfu huiyilu, shang* [Memoirs of Yan Mingfu, Volume 1] (Beijing: Renmin chubanshe, 2015), 366.

7. F. I. Chuev, *Tak govoril Kaganovich: Ispoved' stalinskogo apostola* [Thus Spoke Kaganovich: Confession of Stalin's Apostle] (Moscow: Otechestvo, 1992), 85.

8. Elena Zubkova, "The Rivalry with Malenkov," in *Nikita Khrushchev*, ed. William Taubman, Sergei Khrushchev, and Abbott Gleason (New Haven, CT: Yale University Press, 2000), 76.

9. D. T. Shepilov, *The Kremlin's Scholar: A Memoir of Soviet Politics under Stalin and Khrushchev*, ed. Stephen V. Bittner, trans. Anthony Austin (New Haven, CT: Yale University Press, 2007), 254.

10. Andrei Sakharov, *Memoirs* (New York: Knopf, 1990), 180.

11. Mikoian, *Tak bylo*, 633.

12. Emiliia Gromyko-Piradova, *A. A. Gromyko i vek peremen: Vospominaniia docheri ob Andree Andreeviche Gromyko, ego sem'e i epokhe, v kotoruiu on zhil* [A. A. Gromyko and the Age of Change: Daughter's Memoirs about Andrei Andreevich Gromyko, His Family, and the Epoch in Which He Lived] (Moscow: Sovetskii pisatel', 2009), 166.

13. S. N. Khrushchev, *Nikita Khrushchev: Rozhdenie sverkhderzhavy* [Nikita Khrushchev: Birth of a Superpower] (Moscow: Vremia, 2010), 53.

14. William J. Tompson, *Khrushchev: A Political Life* (New York: St. Martin's Griffin, 1997), 116.

15. Iu. V. Aksiutin and A. V. Pyzhikov, *Poststalinskoe obshchestvo: Problema liderstva i transformatsiia vlasti* [Post-Stalin Society: The Problem of Leadership and the Transformation of Power] (Moscow: Nauchnaia kniga, 1999), 24–25.

16. "Iz vospominanii Sukhanova D. N., byvshego pomoshchnika Malenkova G. M." [From the Recollections of D. N. Sukhanov, Former Assistant to G. M. Malenkov], n.d., Reel 8, Volkogonov Papers, Library of Congress, Washington, DC, 27.

17. "Postanovlenie Prezidiuma TsK KPSS o Malenkove G. M. 29 i 31 ianvaria 1955 g." [Resolution of the CC CPSU Presidium on G. M. Malenkov. January 29 and 31, 1955], in *Delo Beriia. Prigovor obzhalovaniiu ne podlezhit* [The Beria Affair. The Verdict Cannot Be Appealed], comp. V. N. Khaustov (Moscow: MFD, 2012), 614–16.

18. Iu. V. Aksiutin, *Khrushchevskaia "ottepel'" i obshchestvennye nastroeniia v SSSR v 1953–1964 gg.* [Khrushchev's "Thaw" and Societal Attitudes in the USSR in 1953–1964], 2nd ed. (Moscow: ROSSPEN, 2010), 67–68.

19. "Protokol No. [104]. Zasedanie 22 ianvaria 1955 g." [Protocol No. [104]. Meeting of January 22, 1955], in *Prezidium TsK KPSS. 1954–1964.*

Chernovye protokol'nye zapisi zasedanii. Stenogrammy. Postanovleniia. V 3 t. T. 1: Chernovye protokol'nye zapisi zasedanii. Stenogrammy [CC CPSU Presidium. 1954–1964. Draft Minutes of Meetings. Transcripts. Resolutions. In 3 Vols. Vol. 1: Draft Minutes of Meetings. Transcripts], ed. A. A. Fursenko (Moscow: ROSSPEN, 2004), 35.

20. A. B. Edemskii, *Ot konflikta k normalizatsii. Sovetsko-iugoslavskie otnosheniia v 1953–1956 godakh* [From Conflict to Normalization. Soviet-Yugoslav Relations in 1953–1956] (Moscow: Nauka, 2008), 364.

21. I. G. Zemtsov, *Litsa i maski: O vremeni i o sebe: V 2 kn. Kniga 1* [Faces and Masks: About the Time and Myself: In 2 Books. Book 1] (Moscow: Terra, 2008), 127–28.

22. Tompson, *Khrushchev*, 143.

23. Zubkova, "Rivalry with Malenkov," 78.

24. Yoram Gorlizki, "Anti-Ministerialism and the USSR Ministry of Justice, 1953–56: A Study in Organizational Decline," *Europe-Asia Studies* 48, no. 8 (December 1996): 1282.

25. Geoffrey Swain, *Khrushchev* (London: Palgrave, 2016), 72.

26. Tompson, *Khrushchev*, 139.

27. L. M. Kaganovich, *Pamiatnye zapiski rabochego, kommunista-bol'shevika, profsoiuznogo, partiinogo i sovetsko-gosudarstvennogo rabotnika* [Notes of a Worker, Communist-Bolshevik, Professional Union, Party, and Soviet State Official] (Moscow: Vagrius, 1996), 506.

28. I. A. Serov, *Zapiski iz chemodana. Tainye dnevniki pervogo predsedatelia KGB, naidennye cherez 25 let posle ego smerti* [Notes from the Suitcase. The Hidden Diaries of the First Chairman of the KGB Found Twenty-Five Years after His Death] (Moscow: Prosveshchenie, 2016), 435.

29. Ibid., 442–43.

30. "Protokol No. [104]. Zasedanie 22 ianvaria 1955 g.," 1:35–36; and Derek Watson, *Molotov: A Biography* (Basingstoke, UK: Palgrave Macmillan, 2005), 250.

31. F. I. Chuev and V. M. Molotov, *Molotov Remembers: Inside Kremlin Politics: Conversations with Felix Chuev*, ed. Albert Resis (Chicago: Ivan R. Dee, 1993), 350.

32. "Protokol No. 19. Zasedanie 26 maia 1956 g." [Protocol No. 19. Meeting of May 26, 1956], in Fursenko, *Prezidium TsK KPSS*, 1:137.

33. "Protokol No. 20. Zasedanie 28 maia 1956 g." [Protocol No. 20. Meeting of May 28, 1956], ibid., 1:137–38. Strikingly, Bulganin admitted at this meeting that "recently there have been fewer disputes," suggesting that at this time Molotov was even less outspoken at meetings than he allegedly had been before. Ibid., 1:137.

34. N. K. Baibakov, *Sorok let v pravitel'stve* [Forty Years in the Government] (Moscow: Respublika, 1993), 68–71.

35. "Plenum TsK KPSS. Iiun' 1957 goda. Stenograficheskii otchet. Zasedanie shestoe (utrennee, 26 iiunia)" [CC CPSU Plenum. June 1957. Transcript.

Sixth Session (Morning, June 26)], in *Molotov, Malenkov, Kaganovich. 1957. Stenogramma iiun'skogo Plenuma TsK KPSS i drugie dokumenty* [Molotov, Malenkov, Kaganovich. 1957. Transcript of the June CC CPSU Plenum and Other Documents], ed. A. N. Iakovlev (Moscow: MFD, 1998), 240.

36. Nuriddin Mukhitdinov, *Gody, provedennye v Kremle: Vospominaniia veterana voiny, truda i Kommunisticheskoi partii, rabotavshego so Stalinym, Malenkovym, Khrushchevym, Brezhnevym, Andropovym* [Years Spent in the Kremlin: Memoirs of a Veteran of War, Labor, and the Communist Party Who Worked with Stalin, Malenkov, Khrushchev, Brezhnev, Andropov] (Tashkent: Izdatel'stvo narodnogo naslediia im. A. Kadyri, 1994), 266.

37. "Plenum TsK KPSS. Iiun' 1957 goda. Stenograficheskii otchet. Zasedanie pervoe (22 iiunia)" [CC CPSU Plenum. June 1957. Transcript. First Session (June 22)], in Iakovlev, *Molotov, Malenkov, Kaganovich*, 54.

38. Ibid.

39. "Stenogramma vstrechi rukovoditelei KPSS i sovetskogo pravitel'stva s pisateliami, khudozhnikami, skul'ptorami i kompozitorami. 19 maia 1957 g." [Transcript of Meeting of the CPSU and Soviet Government Leaders with Writers, Artists, Sculptors, and Composers. May 19, 1957], in *Nikita Sergeevich Khrushchev: Dva tsveta vremeni: Dokumenty iz lichnogo fonda N. S. Khrushcheva: V 2 tomakh. T. 2* [Nikita Sergeevich Khrushchev: Two Colors of the Times: Documents from the Personal File of N. S. Khrushchev: In 2 Volumes. Vol. 2], ed. N. G. Tomilina (Moscow: MFD, 2009), 490.

40. Kaganovich, *Pamiatnye zapiski*, 515–16.

41. "Plenum TsK KPSS. Iiun' 1957 goda. Stenograficheskii otchet. Zasedanie tret'e (vechernee, 24 iiunia)" [CC CPSU Plenum. June 1957. Transcript. Third Session (Evening, June 24)], in Iakovlev, *Molotov, Malenkov, Kaganovich*, 144.

42. "Plenum TsK KPSS. Iiun' 1957 goda.... Zasedanie pervoe (22 iiunia)," 59.

43. Ibid., 54.

44. L. I. Brezhnev, *Rabochie i dnevnikovye zapisi. V 3-kh tomakh. Tom 3. Leonid Brezhnev. Rabochie i dnevnikovye zapisi. 1944–1964 gg.* [Work and Diary Notes. In 3 Volumes. Volume 3. Leonid Brezhnev. Work and Diary Notes. 1944–1964] (Moscow: IstLit, 2016), 97–103.

45. Shepilov, *Kremlin's Scholar*, 396.

46. "Plenum TsK KPSS. Iiun' 1957 goda.... Zasedanie pervoe (22 iiunia)," 52.

47. Serov, *Zapiski iz chemodana*, 515.

48. "Plenum Tsentral'nogo Komiteta KPSS. Oktiabr' 1957 goda. Stenogramma. Zasedanie tret'e (29 oktiabria)" [Plenum of the CPSU Central Committee. October 1957. Transcript. Third Session (October 29)], in *Georgii Zhukov. Stenogramma oktiabr'skogo (1957 g.) plenuma TsK KPSS i drugie dokumenty* [Georgii Zhukov. Transcript of the October (1957) CC CPSU Plenum and Other Documents], ed. A. N. Iakovlev (Moscow: MFD, 2001), 333.

49. Serov, *Zapiski iz chemodana*, 515–16.

50. Nikolai Mitrokhin, "The Rise of Political Clans in the Era of Nikita Khrushchev: The First Phase, 1953–1959," in *Khrushchev in the Kremlin: Policy and Government in the Soviet Union, 1953–1964*, ed. Jeremy Smith and Melanie Ilic (London: Routledge, 2013), 26–40.

51. Robert Service, "De-Stalinization in the USSR before Khrushchev's Secret Speech," in *Il XX Congresso del PEUS*, ed. E. A. Ambartsumov, Francesca Gori, and Fondazione Giangiacomo Feltrinelli (Milan: Franco Angeli, 1988), 299.

52. "Vystuplenie N. S. Khrushcheva na odinnadtsatom zasedanii Plenuma TsK KPSS, vosproizvedennoe po nepravlenoi stenogramme" [Reproduced Uncorrected N. S. Khrushchev's Speech at the Eleventh Session of the CC CPSU Plenum], in Iakovlev, *Molotov, Malenkov, Kaganovich*, 511.

53. Vladislav Zubok, "Soviet Policy Aims at the Geneva Conference, 1955," in *Cold War Respite: The Geneva Summit of 1955*, ed. Günter Bischof and Saki Dockrill (Baton Rouge: Louisiana State University Press, 2000).

54. Geoffrey Roberts, *Molotov: Stalin's Cold Warrior* (Washington, DC: Potomac Books, 2012), 131–74.

55. Anthony Eden, *Full Circle: The Memoirs of Anthony Eden* (Boston: Houghton Mifflin, 1960), 130.

56. "Notes from MID USSR Concerning Questions of Foreign Policy (Material for the January 6 Meeting)," in *The 1956 Hungarian Revolution: A History in Documents*, ed. Csaba Bekes, Janos Rainer, and Malcolm Byrne (Budapest: Central European University Press, 2003), 106–10.

57. "Moluotuofu tongzhi Liu Xiao dashi tanlu jilu zhaiyao" [Summary of Conversation between Comrade Molotov and Ambassador Liu Xiao], April 17, 1956, PRC FMA 109-00983-13; and AVP RF, fond 0100, opis 49, papka 410, delo 6, listy 45–53.

58. "Protokol No. 184. Zasedanie 30 ianvaria 1956 g." [Protocol No. 184. Meeting of January 30, 1956], in Fursenko, *Prezidium TsK KPSS*, 1:89. Molotov had three reservations. First, he criticized an abbreviated version of a statement originally made by Stalin. The draft report said, "Peace will be maintained and strengthened if people take the maintenance of peace into their own hands." The report did not say this was Stalin's phrase and, moreover, did not include the rest of Stalin's sentence: "and defend it to the end." Second, he emphasized that when speaking of the possible path to socialism by "parliamentary means," it was necessary also to criticize laborists and "socialists" in England, Norway, and Sweden who had been voted into power, as those parties were not bringing their societies to real socialism. Finally, he said it was necessary to criticize not only dead revisionists such as Bernstein and Kautskii but living ones as well. Ibid., 1:89. Shvernik clearly stated that "what Molotov said does not contradict the draft of the report." Ibid., 1:92. Although at this meeting Kaganovich was more critical of Western leftist parties, for which he was criticized, he was

polite: "I will try to soften my suggestions. We do not have fundamental differences. I support that the [draft] be approved in principle. I completely understand the desire of the person giving the report." Ibid., 1:93.

59. Telegram from the Embassy in the Soviet Union to the Department of State, Document 163, September 8, 1960, in *Foreign Relations of the United States, 1958–1960*, vol. 10, pt. 1, *Eastern European Region, Soviet Union*, https://history.state.gov/historicaldocuments/frus1958-60v10p1/d163.

60. Roberts, *Molotov*; and Filitov, *Germaniia*.

61. Filitov, *Germaniia*, 235–36.

62. A. Iu. Vatlin, B. S. Kotov, and A. K. Sorokin, "Avstriiskii vopros v 1945–1955 gg. Dokumenty sovetskoi epokhi" [The Austrian Issue in 1945–1955. Soviet Era Documents], in *SSSR i Avstriia na puti k Gosudarstvennomu dogovoru. Stranitsy dokumental'noi istorii. 1945–1955. Obrazy i teksty* [The USSR and Austria on the Path to State Treaty. Pages of a Document History. 1945–1955. Images and Texts], ed. V. I. Iakunin (Moscow: ROSSPEN, 2015), 20. That decision included no longer forcing the Austrians to pay for Soviet troops. According to the editor of a collection of documents on the Austrian issue, "the successors to Stalin despite all the inconsistency and contradiction of their activities tried to find new approaches to the solution of multiple international problems that were a legacy of the previous time period." Those documents indeed show a desire by Soviet diplomats to solve the Austrian situation and lessen international tensions, although their tactics evolved over time. Ibid.

63. Alexei Filitov, "The Post-Stalin Succession Struggle and the Austrian State Treaty," in *Der Österreichische Staatsvertrag 1955: Internationale Strategie, Rechtliche Relevanz, Nationale Identität, Bd. 140* [The Austrian State Treaty 1955: International Strategy, Legal Relevance, National Identity, Vol. 140], ed. Arnold Suppan, Gerald Stourzh, and Wolfgang Mueller (Vienna: Verlag der Österreichischen Akademie der Wissenschaften, 2005), 131–32.

64. V. A. Nikonov, *Molotov: Nashe delo pravoe. V 2 kn. Kn. 2* [Molotov: Our Cause Is Right. In 2 Books. Book 2] (Moscow: Molodaia gvardiia, 2016), 426.

65. Filitov, *Germaniia*, 225.

66. Filitov, "Post-Stalin Succession Struggle," 124–29.

67. Filitov, *Germaniia*, 224.

68. Watson, *Molotov*, 252–53.

69. "Vystuplenie (vtoroe) V. M. Molotova na zasedanii partkoma Upravleniia delami Soveta Ministrov SSSR. 10 fevralia 1962 g." [V. M. Molotov's (Second) Speech at a Session of the Party Committee of the USSR Council of Ministers Administration. February 10, 1962], in *Boi s "ten'iu" Stalina. Prodolzhenie: Dokumenty i materialy ob istorii XXII s"ezda KPSS i vtorogo etapa destalinizatsii* [The Battle with Stalin's "Shadow." Continued: Documents and Materials on the History of the Twenty-Second CPSU Congress

and the Second Stage of De-Stalinization], ed. N. G. Tomilina (Moscow: Nestor-Istoriia, 2015), 365.

70. RGANI, fond 2, opis 1, delo 158, listy 1, 21, 34, 43–45, 50–51, Harvard Cold War Studies Collection. When Molotov acknowledged the signing of the Soviet-Yugoslav declaration of June 2, 1955, to be a result of the Soviet delegation's good work and a big accomplishment, Khrushchev interrupted, "Which we achieved through a struggle with you." Molotov replied, "That is incorrect, of course." Ibid., 57.

71. RGANI, fond 2, opis 1, delo 161, listy 180, 185, Harvard Cold War Studies Collection.

72. Edemskii, *Ot konflikta k normalizatsii*, 237.

73. Kaganovich, *Pamiatnye zapiski*, 511.

74. T. H. Rigby, *Political Elites in the USSR: Central Leaders and Local Cadres from Lenin to Gorbachev* (Aldershot, UK: Edward Elgar, 1990); and O. V. Khlevniuk, M. Iu. Prozumenshchikov, V. Iu. Vasil'ev, Y. Gorlizki, T. Iu. Zhukova, V. V. Kondrashin, L. P. Kosheleva, R. A. Podkur, and E. V. Sheveleva, comps., *Regional'naia politika N. S. Khrushcheva. TsK KPSS i mestnye partiinye komitety. 1953–1964 gg.* [The Regional Policy of N. S. Khrushchev. The CC CPSU and Regional Party Committees. 1953–1964] (Moscow: ROSSPEN, 2009), 6.

75. "Postanovlenie Prezidiuma TsK KPSS 'O ser'eznykh nedostatkakh v rabote partiinogo i gosudarstvennogo apparata.' 25 ianvaria 1954 g." [Resolution of the CC CPSU Presidium "On Serious Drawbacks in the Work of Party and State Apparatus." January 25, 1954], in Khlevniuk et al., *Regional'naia politika*, 103–4; and "Dokladnaia zapiska otdelov partiinykh organov TsK KPSS po RSFSR i soiuznym respublikam i Upravleniia delami TsK KPSS v Sekretariat TsK KPSS o rasshirenii prav mestnykh partiinykh komitetov v reshenii nekotorykh organizatsionno-partiinykh voprosov. 2 avgusta 1955 g." [Memo by the Party Organs of the RSFSR and Union Republics Departments of the CC CPSU and the CC CPSU Administration to the CC CPSU Secretariat on the Expansion of Rights of the Local Party Committees in the Resolution of Certain Organizational-Party Issues. August 2, 1955], ibid., 123–25.

76. Khlevniuk et al., introduction to *Regional'naia politika*, 9.

77. Nikonov, *Molotov*, 2:366.

78. "Zapiska N. S. Khrushcheva 'Nekotorye soobrazheniia ob uluchshenii organizatsii rukovodstva promyshlennost'iu i stroitel'stvom.' 27 ianvaria 1957 g." [N. S. Khrushchev's Memo on "Certain Considerations on Improvement of Industrial and Construction Management." January 27, 1957], in *Prezidium TsK KPSS. 1954–1964. Chernovye protokol'nye zapisi zasedanii. Stenogrammy. Postanovleniia. T. 2: Postanovleniia. 1954–1958* [CC CPSU Presidium. 1954–1964. Draft Minutes of Meetings. Transcripts. Resolutions. Vol. 2: Resolutions. 1954–1958], ed. A. A. Fursenko (Moscow: ROSSPEN, 2006), 522–39.

79. "Protokol No. 70. Zasedanie 28 ianvaria 1957 g." [Protocol No. 70. Meeting of January 28, 1957], in Fursenko, *Prezidium TsK KPSS*, 1:221–23.

80. Yakov Feygin, "Reforming the Cold War State: Economic Thought, Internationalization, and the Politics of Soviet Reform, 1955–1985" (PhD diss., University of Pennsylvania, 2017), 116–17.

81. "Protokol No. 84. Zasedanie 22 marta 1957 g." [Protocol No. 84. Meeting of March 22, 1957], in Fursenko, *Prezidium TsK KPSS*, 1:236–39.

82. "Zapiska V. M. Molotova v sviazi s obsuzhdeniem proekta tezisov doklada N. S. Khrushcheva na Prezidiume TsK KPSS 22 marta 1957 g. 24 marta 1957 g." [V. M. Molotov's Memo with Regard to the Discussion of Draft Abstracts of N. S. Khrushchev's Speech at the CC CPSU Presidium on March 22, 1957. March 24, 1957], in Fursenko, *Prezidium TsK KPSS*, 2:613–15.

83. "Zapiska N. S. Khrushcheva po povodu zapiski V. M. Molotova, soderzhashchei kritiku tezisov [doklada Khrushcheva] 'O dal'neishem sovershenstvovanii i organizatsii upravleniia promyshlennost'iu i stroitel'-stvom, 26 marta 1957 g." [N. S. Khrushchev's Memo with Regard to V. M. Molotov's Memo Containing Criticism of Abstracts of [Khrushchev's Report] "On Further Improvement of Industrial and Construction Management." March 26, 1957], in Fursenko, *Prezidium TsK KPSS*, 2:615–19.

84. "Protokol No. 85. Zasedanie 27 marta 1957 g." [Protocol No. 85. Meeting of March 27, 1957], in Fursenko, *Prezidium TsK KPSS*, 1:240–46.

85. "Plenum TsK KPSS. Iiun' 1957 goda. Stenograficheskii otchet. Zasedanie piatoe (vechernee, 25 iiunia)" [CC CPSU Plenum. June 1957. Transcript. Fifth Session (Evening, June 25)], in Iakovlev, *Molotov, Malenkov, Kaganovich*, 214.

86. Nataliya Kibita, *Soviet Economic Management under Khrushchev: The Sovnarkhoz Reform* (New York: Routledge, 2013), 39.

87. Taubman, *Khrushchev*, 304.

88. "Plenum TsK KPSS. Iiun' 1957 goda. . . . Zasedanie tret'e (vechernee, 24 iiunia)," 144.

89. "Plenum TsK KPSS. Iiun' 1957 goda. Stenograficheskii otchet. Zasedanie vtoroe (utrennee, 24 iiunia)" [CC CPSU Plenum. June 1957. Transcript. Second Session (Morning, June 24)], in Iakovlev, *Molotov, Malenkov, Kaganovich*, 107.

90. Kibita, *Soviet Economic Management*, 40.

91. Oscar Sanchez-Sibony, "Soviet Industry in the World Spotlight: The Domestic Dilemmas of Soviet Foreign Economic Relations, 1955–1965," *Europe-Asia Studies* 62, no. 9 (November 2010): 1559.

92. Watson, *Molotov*, 244–45.

93. Polly Jones, *Myth, Memory, Trauma: Rethinking the Stalinist Past in the Soviet Union, 1953–1970* (New Haven, CT: Yale University Press, 2013), 7.

94. Swain, *Khrushchev*, 103.

95. Edward Cohn, *The High Title of a Communist: Postwar Party Discipline and the Values of the Soviet Regime* (DeKalb: Northern Illinois University Press, 2015).

96. Miriam Dobson, *Khrushchev's Cold Summer: Gulag Returnees, Crime, and the Fate of Reform after Stalin* (Ithaca, NY: Cornell University Press, 2009), 15.

97. "Protokol No. 184. Zasedanie 30 ianvaria 1956 g.," 1:94.

98. Ol'ga Shatunovskaia, *Ob ushedshem veke* [About the Past Century] (La Jolla, CA: DAA Books, 2001), 290.

99. Dobson, *Khrushchev's Cold Summer*, 80.

100. A. N. Artizov, Iu. V. Sigachev, V. G. Khlopov, and I. N. Shevchuk, comps., *Reabilitatsiia: Kak eto bylo. Dokumenty Prezidiuma TsK KPSS i drugie materialy. Tom II. Fevral' 1956–nachalo 80-kh godov* [Rehabilitation: How It Was. Documents of the CC CPSU Presidium and Other Materials. Volume 2. February 1956–Beginning of 1980s] (Moscow: MFD, 2003), 6.

101. A. N. Artizov, Iu. V. Sigachev, V. G. Khlopov, and I. N. Shevchuk, comps., *Reabilitatsiia: Kak eto bylo. Dokumenty Prezidiuma TsK KPSS i drugie materialy. V 3-kh tomakh. Tom 1. Mart 1953–fevral' 1956* [Rehabilitation: How It Was. Documents of the CC CPSU Presidium and Other Materials. In 3 Volumes. Volume 1. March 1953–February 1956] (Moscow: MFD, 2000), 10–11.

102. "Plenum TsK KPSS. Iiun' 1957 goda. Stenograficheskii otchet. Zasedanie chetvertoe (utrennee, 25 iiunia)" [CC CPSU Plenum. June 1957. Transcript. Fourth Session (Morning, June 25)], in Iakovlev, *Molotov, Malenkov, Kaganovich*, 189.

103. Serov, *Zapiski iz chemodana*, 465.

104. "Vystuplenie N. S. Khrushcheva na odinnadtsatom zasedanii Plenuma TsK KPSS," 537.

105. Shatunovskaia, *Ob ushedshem veke*, 291.

106. Michael Parks, "Soviets Complete Rehabilitation of Bukharin, Key Stalin Foe," *Los Angeles Times*, July 10, 1988, http://articles.latimes.com/1988-07-10/news/mn-9457_1_josef-stalin.

107. Nikita Petrov, *Pervyi predsedatel' KGB Ivan Serov* [First Head of the KGB Ivan Serov] (Moscow: Materik, 2005).

108. RGASPI, fond 556, opis 14, delo 54, listy 27–28, contains a letter complaining that rehabilitated Old Bolsheviks were being treated poorly by the apparat.

109. Stephen F. Cohen, *The Victims Return: Survivors of the Gulag after Stalin* (Exeter, NH: PublishingWorks, 2010), 79.

110. A. N. Artizov and Iu. V. Sigachev, introduction to Artizov et al., *Reabilitatsiia*, 2:9.

111. Vitalii Afiani, "Segodnia, 60 let nazad, zavershilsia XX s"ezd KPSS, a nakanune . . . [Today, Sixty Years Ago, the Twentieth CPSU Party Con-

gress Was Held, but on the Eve . . .]," *Novaia gazeta*, no. 20 (February 26, 2016): 14.

112. R. J. Service, "The Road to the Twentieth Party Congress: An Analysis of the Events Surrounding the Central Committee Plenum of July 1953," *Soviet Studies* 33, no. 2 (1981): 240–41. Molotov did not mention the terror, but his behavior so soon after Beria's arrest does point to flexibility on this issue.

113. Tompson, *Khrushchev*, 123.

114. V. I. Ivkin, "Kak otmeniali Stalinskie premii. Dokumenty TsK KPSS i Soveta ministrov SSSR. 1953–1967 gg." [How the Stalin Prizes Were Ended. Documents of the CC CPSU and the USSR Council of Ministers. 1953–1967], *Istoricheskii arkhiv*, no. 6 (2013): 3–49.

115. Nikita Khrushchev, *Memoirs of Nikita Khrushchev*, vol. 2, *Reformer, 1945–1964*, ed. Sergei Khrushchev (University Park: Pennsylvania State University, 2006), 209–10.

116. Chuev, *Tak govoril Kaganovich*, 44, 64.

117. "Protokol No. 167. Zasedanie 5 noiabria 1955 g." [Protocol No. 167. Meeting of November 5, 1955], in Fursenko, *Prezidium TsK KPSS*, 1:56–57.

118. "Protokol No. 185. Zasedanie 1 fevralia 1956 g." [Protocol No. 185. Meeting of February 1, 1956], ibid., 95–97.

119. "Protokol No. 187. Zasedanie 9 fevralia 1956 g." [Protocol No. 187. Meeting of February 9, 1956], ibid., 98–103.

120. Iu. V. Aksiutin and A. V. Pyzhikov, "O podgotovke zaktrytogo doklada N. S. Khrushcheva XX s"ezdu KPSS v svete novykh dokumentov" [On the Preparation of the Secret Speech of N. S. Khrushchev to the Twentieth CPSU Congress in Light of New Documents], *Novaia i noveishaia istoriia*, no. 2 (March–April 2002): 113–14.

121. "Plenum TsK KPSS. Iiun' 1957 goda. . . . Zasedanie pervoe (22 iiunia)," 68.

122. "Plenum TsK KPSS. Iiun' 1957 goda. . . . Zasedanie vtoroe (utrennee, 24 iiunia)," 110.

123. "Plenum TsK KPSS. Iiun' 1957 goda. . . . Zasedanie tret'e (vechernee, 24 iiunia)," 130.

124. Nikonov, *Molotov*, 2:394.

125. "Vystuplenie (pervoe) V. M. Molotova na partiinom sobranii partorganizatsii no. 3 Upravleniia delami Soveta Ministrov SSSR. 9 fevralia 1962 g." [V. M. Molotov's (First) Speech at a Party Meeting of Party Organization No. 3 of the USSR Council of Ministers Administration. February 9, 1962], in Tomilina, *Boi s "ten'iu" Stalina*, 348–50; "Vystuplenie (vtoroe) V. M. Molotova na partiinom sobranii partorganizatsii no. 3 Upravleniia delami Soveta Ministrov SSSR. 9 fevralia 1962 g." [V. M. Molotov's (Second) Speech at a Party Meeting of Party Organization No. 3 of the USSR Council of Ministers Administration. February 9,

1962], ibid., 350–52; "Vystuplenie (pervoe) V. M. Molotova na zasedanii partkoma Upravleniia delami Soveta Ministrov SSSR. 10 fevralia 1962 g." [V. M. Molotov's (First) Speech at a Session of the Party Committee of the USSR Council of Ministers Administration. February 10, 1962], ibid., 352–56; "Stenogramma zasedaniia partkoma Upravleniia delami Soveta Ministrov SSSR. 10 fevralia 1962 g." [Transcript of Session of the Party Committee of the USSR Council of Ministers Administration. February 10, 1962], ibid., 356–64; "Vystuplenie (vtoroe) V. M. Molotova na zasedanii partkoma Upravleniia delami Soveta Ministrov SSSR. 10 fevralia 1962 g.," ibid., 365–67; "Stenogramma zasedaniia Sverdlovskogo raikoma partii po voprosu iskliucheniia V. M. Molotova iz riadov KPSS. 14 fevralia 1962 g." [Transcript of the Sverdlovsk Party District Committee Session on V. M. Molotov's Expulsion from the CPSU. February 14, 1962], ibid., 369–82; and "Stenogramma zasedaniia biuro MGK KPSS po voprosu ob iskliuchenii V. M. Molotova iz riadov KPSS. 21 marta 1962 g." [Transcript of Meeting of the CPSU Moscow City Committee on V. M. Molotov's Expulsion from the CPSU. March 21, 1962], ibid., 383–411.

126. "Stenogramma zasedaniia biuro MGK KPSS po voprosu ob iskliuchenii L. M. Kaganovicha iz riadov KPSS. 23 marta 1962 g." [Transcript of Meeting of the CPSU Moscow City Committee on L. M. Kaganovich's Expulsion from the CPSU. March 23, 1962], ibid., 420.

127. Mukhitdinov, *Gody, provedennye v Kremle*, 171.

128. F. M. Burlatskii, *N. Khrushchev i ego sovetniki—krasnye, chernye, belye* [N. Khrushchev and His Advisers—Red, Black, White] (Moscow: EKSMO-Press, 2002), 86.

129. Veljko Micunovic, *Moscow Diary* (Garden City, NY: Doubleday, 1980), 37.

130. Aleksandr Iakovlev, *Omut pamiati* [Whirlpool of Memory] (Moscow: Vagrius, 2000), 117.

131. "Spravka Ministerstva oborony SSSR 'O reagirovanii voennosluzhashchikh i sluzhashchikh Sovetskoi Armii v chastiakh Moskovskogo voennogo okruga na doklad tov. Khrushcheva "O kul'te lichnosti i ego posledstviiakh."' Ne pozdnee 6 iiunia 1956 g." [Memo by the USSR Ministry of Defense "On Responses of the Military Servicemen and Employees of the Soviet Army in Units of the Moscow Military Region to Com. Khrushchev's Speech 'On the Personality Cult and Its Consequences.'" No Later than June 6, 1956], in *Doklad N. S. Khrushcheva o kul'te lichnosti Stalina na XX s"ezde KPSS: Dokumenty* [N. S. Khrushchev's Speech on Stalin's Cult of Personality at the Twentieth CPSU Congress: Documents], ed. Karl Eimermacher (Moscow: ROSSPEN, 2002), 540–41.

132. RGVA, fond 40894, opis 2, delo 31, list 122 oborot.

133. Micunovic, *Moscow Diary*, 34, 38.

134. "N. S. Khrushchev: 'U Stalina byli momenty prosvetleniia.' Zapis' besedy s delegatsiei Ital'ianskoi kompartii" [N. S. Khrushchev: "Stalin Had Mo-

ments of Enlightenment." Record of Conversation with the Delegation of the Italian Communist Party], *Istochnik*, no. 2 (1994): 86.

135. "Postanovlenie Prezidiuma TsK KPSS 'O vrazhdebnykh vylazkakh na sobranii partiinoi organizatsii Teplotekhnicheskoi laboratorii Akademii nauk SSSR po itogam XX s"ezda KPSS.' 5 aprelia 1956 g." [Resolution of the CC CPSU Presidium "On Hostile Actions at a Meeting of the Party Organization of the Heat-Engineering Laboratory of the USSR Academy of Sciences on the Outcomes of the Twentieth CPSU Congress." April 5, 1956], in Artizov et al., *Reabilitatsiia*, 2:63–65; "Zapiska Komissii TsK KPSS pod predsedatel'stvom P. N. Pospelova v TsK KPSS o predstavlenii proekta postanovleniia TsK KPSS 'O rabote partii po preodoleniiu kul'ta lichnosti i ego posledstvii.' 29 iiunia 1956 g." [Memo by the CC CPSU Commission Headed by P. N. Pospelov to the CC CPSU on the Submission of Draft CC CPSU Resolution "On the Party Work to Overcome the Personality Cult and Its Consequences." June 29, 1956], ibid., 2:132–46; and Jones, *Myth, Memory, Trauma*, 17–56.

136. "Heluxiaofu tongzhi zai 'wu yi' yanhui shang de tanhua qingkuang" [The Situation of Comrade Khrushchev's Speech at the "May First" Banquet], May 4, 1956, PRC FMA 109-00763-01.

137. "Pis'mo TsK KPSS 'Ob usilenii politicheskoi raboty partiinykh organizatsii v massakh i presechenii vylazok antisovetskikh vrazhdebnykh elementov.' 19 dekabria 1956 g." [CC CPSU Letter "On Strengthening of Political Work of the Party Organizations with the Masses and Curtailing Actions of Anti-Soviet Elements." December 19, 1956], in Artizov et al., *Reabilitatsiia*, 2:208–14.

138. "Protokol No. 62. Zasedanie 6 dekabria 1956 g." [Protocol No. 62. Meeting of December 6, 1956], in Fursenko, *Prezidium TsK KPSS*, 1:212–13.

139. Liu Xiao, *Chushi Sulian banian* [Eight Years as Ambassador in the Soviet Union] (Beijing: Zhonggong dangshi ziliao chubanshe, 1986), 21.

140. "Pis'mo G. K. Zhukova N. S. Khrushchevu s pros'boi oznakomit'sia s proektom ego doklada 'Sostoianie i zadachi voenno-ideologicheskoi raboty' i dat' zamechaniia. 19 maia 1956 g." [G. K. Zhukov's Letter to N. S. Khrushchev Requesting to Consider His Draft Speech "State and Tasks of Military-Ideological Work" and Provide Comments. May 19, 1956], in Eimermacher, *Doklad N. S. Khrushcheva o kul'te lichnosti*, 309–22; "Zapiska D. T. Shepilova v TsK KPSS s pros'boi oznakomit'sia s proektom doklada na predstoiashchem Plenume po ideologicheskim voprosam. 23 maia 1956 g." [D. T. Shepilov's Memo Requesting to Consider the Draft Speech at the Forthcoming Plenum on Ideological Issues. May 23, 1956], ibid., 325–42; and RGANI, fond 52, opis 1, dela 204 and 205.

141. B. T. Kulik, *Sovetsko-kitaiskii raskol: Prichiny i posledstviia* [The Sino-Soviet Split: Reasons and Consequences] (Moscow: Institut Dal'nego Vostoka RAN, 2000), 165.

142. Micunovic, *Moscow Diary*, 188, 277.

143. RGANI, fond 2, opis 1, delo 215, listy 117–18, Harvard Cold War Studies Collection.

144. National Security Archive, Box 16, Russian and Eastern European Archive Documents Database, 07.02.1957, R11697, Speeches at the Meeting, 54.

145. "Plenum TsK KPSS. Iiun' 1957 goda. . . . Zasedanie vtoroe (utrennee, 24 iiunia)," 76–77, 98, 100, 101, 113; "Plenum TsK KPSS. Iiun' 1957 goda. . . . Zasedanie tret'e (vechernee, 24 iiunia)," 128; "Plenum TsK KPSS. Iiun' 1957 goda. . . . Zasedanie chetvertoe (utrennee, 25 iiunia)," 166; and "Plenum TsK KPSS. Iiun' 1957 goda. . . . Zasedanie shestoe (utrennee, 26 iiunia)," 267 (emphasis added).

146. "Pis'mo V. M. Molotova v TsK KPSS (1964 g.)" [V. M. Molotov's Letter to the CC CPSU (1964)], *Voprosy istorii*, no. 5 (2011): 66 (original emphasis).

147. Sheila Fitzpatrick, *On Stalin's Team: The Years of Living Dangerously in Soviet Politics* (Princeton, NJ: Princeton University Press, 2015), 253, 276.

148. Khrushchev, *Memoirs of Nikita Khrushchev*, 2:106.

149. D. V. Pavlov, "Iz zapisok narkoma" [From the Notes of the Commissar], *Novaia i noveishaia istoriia*, no. 6 (November–December 1988): 125.

150. F. I. Chuev, *Kaganovich. Shepilov* (Moscow: OLMA-PRESS, 2001), 315.

151. Gromyko-Piradova, *Gromyko i vek peremen*, 164.

152. Zemtsov, *Litsa i maski*, 1:115.

153. Mukhitdinov, *Gody, provedennye v Kremle*, 268.

154. Charles S. Sampson and John Michael Joyce, eds., *Foreign Relations of the United States, 1961–1963*, vol. 5, *Soviet Union* (Washington, DC: United States Government Printing Office, 1998), 359.

155. RGASPI, fond 556, opis 14, delo 70, list 57.

156. RGASPI, fond 556, opis 14, delo 72, list 10.

157. Ibid., 70.

158. Ibid., 25–26.

159. A. I. Adzhubei, *Te desiat' let* [Those Ten Years] (Moscow: Sovetskaia Rossiia, 1989), 275.

160. "Plenum TsK KPSS. Iiun' 1957 goda. . . . Zasedanie shestoe (utrennee, 26 iiunia)," 266.

161. "Plenum TsK KPSS. Iiun' 1957 goda. Stenograficheskii otchet. Zasedanie deviatoe (vechernee, 27 iiunia)" [CC CPSU Plenum. June 1957. Transcript. Ninth Session (Evening, June 27)], in Iakovlev, *Molotov, Malenkov, Kaganovich*, 383.

162. "Plenum TsK KPSS. Iiun' 1957 goda. . . . Zasedanie vtoroe (utrennee, 24 iiunia)," 111.

163. "Plenum TsK KPSS. Iiun' 1957 goda. . . . Zasedanie deviatoe (vechernee, 27 iiunia)," 367.

164. "Plenum TsK KPSS. Iiun' 1957 goda. . . . Zasedanie piatoe (vechernee, 25 iiunia)," 229.

165. "Plenum TsK KPSS. Iiun' 1957 goda. Stenograficheskii otchet. Zasedanie vos'moe (utrennee, 27 iiunia)" [CC CPSU Plenum. June 1957. Transcript. Eighth Session (Morning, June 27)], in Iakovlev, *Molotov, Malenkov, Kaganovich*, 325.

166. "Vystuplenie N. S. Khrushcheva na odinnadtsatom zasedanii Plenuma TsK KPSS," 543.

167. Watson, *Molotov*, 253–54.

168. Samuel Kucherov, "The Soviet Union Is Not a Socialist Society (In 'Defense' of V. M. Molotov)," *Political Science Quarterly* 71, no. 2 (June 1956): 182–83.

169. Micunovic, *Moscow Diary*, 154. Khrushchev may have been seeking out military support in other ways as well: "Khrushchev told us frankly during the talks on November 2–3 that the Soviet Army has been the main factor in reaching a decision about the intervention in Hungary."

170. "Doklad Pervogo sekretaria TsK KPSS tov. Khrushcheva N. S. XX s"ezdu Kommunisticheskoi partii Sovetskogo Soiuza 25 fevralia 1956 goda" [Speech of the CC CPSU First Secretary Com. N. S. Khrushchev to the Twentieth Congress of the Communist Party of the Soviet Union on February 25, 1956], in Eimermacher, *Doklad N. S. Khrushcheva o kul'te lichnosti*, 87–88.

171. "Protokol No. 167. Zasedanie 5 noiabria 1955 g.," 1:57.

172. Roberts, *Molotov*, 181 (emphasis added).

173. "Protokol No. 93. Zasedanie 4 maia 1957 g." [Protocol No. 93. Meeting of May 4, 1957], in Fursenko, *Prezidium TsK KPSS*, 1:254.

174. Ibid.

175. "Plenum TsK KPSS. Iiun' 1957 goda. . . . Zasedanie shestoe (utrennee, 26 iiunia)," 245–46.

176. Swain, *Khrushchev*, 106–7.

177. Chuev, *Kaganovich. Shepilov*, 365.

178. "Plenum TsK KPSS. Iiun' 1957 goda. . . . Zasedanie chetvertoe (utrennee, 25 iiunia)," 183.

179. "Posle smerti Stalina. Zapis' vospominanii G. K. Zhukova [1963–1964 gg.]" [After Stalin's Death. Record of G. K. Zhukov's Memoirs (1963–1964)], in Iakovlev, *Georgii Zhukov*, 629.

180. "Plenum TsK KPSS. Iiun' 1957 goda. . . . Zasedanie chetvertoe (utrennee, 25 iiunia)," 183.

181. National Security Archive, Box 16, Russian and Eastern European Archive Documents Database, 07.02.1957, R11697, Speeches at the Meeting, 12.

182. Ibid., 86.

183. "Plenum TsK KPSS. Iiun' 1957 goda. . . . Zasedanie pervoe (22 iiunia)," 46–47.

184. Ibid., 67.

185. Ibid., 68.

186. Ibid., 60.

187. "Plenum TsK KPSS. Iiun' 1957 goda.... Zasedanie chetvertoe (utrennee, 25 iiunia)," 162–63.

188. "Plenum TsK KPSS. Iiun' 1957 goda. . . . Zasedanie shestoe (utrennee, 26 iiunia)," 246.

189. Serov, *Zapiski iz chemodana*, 465–66.

190. "Plenum TsK KPSS. Iiun' 1957 goda.... Zasedanie pervoe (22 iiunia)," 68.

191. "Pis'mo V. M. Molotova v TsK KPSS (1964 g.)" [V. M. Molotov's Letter to the CC CPSU (1964)], *Voprosy istorii*, no. 6 (2011): 72.

192. Taubman, *Khrushchev*, 581.

193. Serov, *Zapiski iz chemodana*, 511, 515. Serov puts the number of people who demanded a session at forty—still many less than even half the CC membership.

194. "Plenum TsK KPSS. Iiun' 1957 goda. . . . Zasedanie vtoroe (utrennee, 24 iiunia)," 118.

195. "Plenum TsK KPSS. Iiun' 1957 goda.... Zasedanie pervoe (22 iiunia)," 66.

196. Ibid., 53.

197. "Plenum TsK KPSS. Iiun' 1957 goda. . . . Zasedanie vtoroe (utrennee, 24 iiunia)," 154.

198. Mikoian, *Tak bylo*, 646.

199. Serov, *Zapiski iz chemodana*, 512.

200. Mukhitdinov, *Gody, provedennye v Kremle*, 272–73; and Kaganovich, *Pamiatnye zapiski*, 521. Serov, however, claimed that it was Mikoian who went out to address them.

201. Kaganovich, *Pamiatnye zapiski*, 521.

202. Serov, *Zapiski iz chemodana*, 510 (emphasis added).

203. "Posle smerti Stalina. Zapis' vospominanii G. K. Zhukova," 627.

204. "Plenum TsK KPSS. Iiun' 1957 goda. . . . Zasedanie shestoe (utrennee, 26 iiunia)," 242–43.

205. "Plenum TsK KPSS. Iiun' 1957 goda.... Zasedanie pervoe (22 iiunia)," 79.

206. "Plenum TsK KPSS. Iiun' 1957 goda. . . . Zasedanie vtoroe (utrennee, 24 iiunia)," 99–100.

207. The approaches made by members of the anti-party group toward Zhukov and their goal of removing Serov from the KGB were interpreted by at least one individual as an attempt to use force to coerce the party. The commander of the Pacific Fleet made this argument at a *partaktiv* in July 1957—clearly a double standard given Khrushchev's use of those two individuals. See RGASPI, fond 556, opis 14, delo 71, list 17. Interestingly, Zhukov's role was not obvious to the party as a whole. Some party members asked questions about how Zhukov behaved and indicated a lack of knowledge about his role. See, for example, ibid., 31.

208. Serov, *Zapiski iz chemodana*, 507.

209. Petrov, *Pervyi predsedatel' KGB Ivan Serov*.

210. Serov, *Zapiski iz chemodana*, 507.

211. "Plenum TsK KPSS. Iiun' 1957 goda. . . . Zasedanie pervoe (22 iiunia)," 54, 56.

212. Ibid., 64.

213. Brian D. Taylor, *Politics and the Russian Army: Civil-Military Relations, 1689–2000* (Cambridge: Cambridge University Press, 2003), 183–84.

214. "Plenum TsK KPSS. Iiun' 1957 goda. . . . Zasedanie vtoroe (utrennee, 24 iiunia)," 86.

215. Mukhitdinov, *Gody, provedennye v Kremle*, 267.

216. Ibid., 271.

217. Serov, *Zapiski iz chemodana*, 510.

218. T. Iu. Konova, "XXII s"ezd KPSS i problemy destalinizatsii" [Twenty-Second CPSU Congress and De-Stalinization Problems], in Tomilina, *Boi s "ten'iu" Stalina*, 33.

Chapter 4. The Gang of Four

1. Michael Schoenhals and Roderick MacFarquhar, *Mao's Last Revolution* (Cambridge, MA: Harvard University Press, 2006), 3–7.

2. Li Haiwen and Wang Shoujia, *"Siren bang" zai Shanghai yudang fumie ji: 1976.10–1979.10* [Record of the Destruction of the Remaining Cohorts of the "Gang of Four": October 1976–October 1979] (Beijing: Zhongguo qingnian chubanshe, 2015), 32.

3. Zhongguo zhongyang dangshi yanjiushi, *Zhongguo gongchandang de jiushi nian: Shehuizhuyi geming he jianshe shiqi* [Ninety Years of the CCP: The Period of Socialist Revolution and Construction] (Beijing: Zhonggong dangshi chubanshe, 2016), 629.

4. Tani Barlow, "Jiang Qing, Seriously," *PRC History Review* 2, no. 4 (October 2017): 1–3.

5. "Zhongguo gongchandang dishijie zhongyang weiyuanhui disanci quanti huiyi guanyu Wang Hongwen, Zhang Chunqiao, Jiang Qing, Yao Wenyuan fandang jituan de jueyi (jielu)" [Third Plenum of the Tenth Party Congress Decision on the Wang Hongwen, Zhang Chunqiao, Jiang Qing, and Yao Wenyuan Anti-Party Clique (excerpt)], July 17, 1977, History of Contemporary Chinese Political Movements, Chinese University Press.

6. Li Haiwen, "Zhonggong shida hou xingcheng de 'Siren bang' yu zheng-zhiju duoshu de duili" [The Formation of a Politburo Majority Opposed to the "Gang of Four" after the Tenth Party Congress], *Dangshi bolan*, no. 7 (July 2017): 41.

7. Pang Xianzhi and Feng Hui, eds., *Mao Zedong nianpu 1949–1976, diliujuan* [Chronology of Mao Zedong 1949–1976, Volume 6] (Beijing: Zhongyang wenxian chubanshe, 2013), 562.

8. Ibid., 610.

9. Yang Yinlu, *Tingyuan shenshen Diaoyutai: Wo gei Jiang Qing dang mishu* [Deep in the Diaoyutai Courtyard: I Was Jiang Qing's Secretary] (Beijing: Dangdai Zhongguo chubanshe, 2013), 95–99.

10. Wu De, *Wu De koushu: Shinian fengyu wangshi, Wo zai Beijing gongzuo de yixie jingli* [Wu De's Oral Account: Past Events during the Ten Years' Storm, Some Experiences from My Work in Beijing] (Beijing: Dangdai Zhongguo chubanshe, 2004), 177–87.

11. Gao Wenqian, *Wannian Zhou Enlai* [Zhou Enlai's Later Years], 50th ed. (Carle Place, NY: Mingjing chubanshe, 2013), 383.

12. Roxane Witke, *Comrade Chiang Ch'ing* (Boston: Little, Brown, 1977), 347–49.

13. Ibid., 362–63.

14. Ibid., 367.

15. Shi Yijun, "'Wenge' houqi de 'Liangxiao' da pipan zu" [The "Liangxiao" Criticism Group in the Late "Cultural Revolution"], *Dangshi bolan*, no. 3 (2006): 14.

16. Ding Sheng, *Luonan yingxiong: Ding Sheng jiangjun huiyilu* [Hero in Distress: Memoirs of General Ding Sheng] (Hong Kong: Xin shiji chuban ji chuanmei youxian gongsi, 2011), 230.

17. Ibid.

18. Liao Hansheng, *Liao Hansheng huiyilu* [Memoirs of Liao Hansheng] (Beijing: Jiefangjun chubanshe, 2012), 545, 570.

19. Suoliweng and Ouyang Longmen, *Xin faxian de Zhou Enlai, xia* [The Newly Discovered Zhou Enlai, Volume 2] (Hong Kong: Mingjing chubanshe, 2009), 760; and Warren Sun and Frederick C. Teiwes, *The End of the Maoist Era: Chinese Politics during the Twilight of the Cultural Revolution, 1972–1976* (Armonk, NY: M. E. Sharpe, 2007), 271–74.

20. Wang Hongwen, "Wang Hongwen zai zhongyang dushu ban de baogao" [Wang Hongwen's Report to the Central Study Group], January 14, 1974, History of Contemporary Chinese Political Movements.

21. Junshi kexueyuan jundui jianshe yanjiubu "Song Shilun zhuan" bianxiezu, *Song Shilun zhuan* [Biography of Song Shilun] (Beijing: Junshi kexue chubanshe, 2007), 493.

22. Yan Changgui and Wang Guangyu, *Diaoyutai yi wang: Jiang Qing suiyuan de zhengyan* [Remembering Diaoyutai: The Evidence of Jiang Qing's Staff Members] (Hong Kong: Tianxing jianchu chubanshe, 2013), 339–42.

23. Sima Qingyang, "Shilun wenge chuqi Zhou Enlai yu Jiang Qing yiji zhongyang wenge xiaozu de guanxi" [Discussion on Relations between Zhou Enlai and Jiang Qing, and the Central Cultural Revolution Small Group at the Beginning of the Cultural Revolution], *Huaxia wenzhai zengkan*, no. 625 (January 23, 2008), online.

24. Qi Benyu, *Qi Benyu huiyilu, xia* [Memoirs of Qi Benyu, Volume 2] (Hong Kong: Zhongguo wenge lishi chuban youxian gongsi, 2016), 674–76.

25. Zheng Huang, *Junren Yongsheng: Yuan jiefangjun zong canmouzhang Huang Yongsheng jiangjun qianzhuan* [Military Man Yongsheng: Former PLA

Chief of Staff General Huang Yongsheng, Prequel] (Hong Kong: Xin shiji chuban ji chuanmei youxian gongsi, 2010), 539–40.

26. Zhao Wei and Ling Feng, *Xihua ting suiyue: Wo zai Zhou Enlai Deng Ying-chao shenbian sanshiqinian* [Years in the Xihua Pavilion: I Was at the Side of Zhou Enlai and Deng Yingchao for Thirty-Seven Years] (Beijing: Shehui kexue wenxian chubanshe, 2009), 255–56, 266–67.

27. Zhang Hanzhi, "Zhang Hanzhi tongzhi jianghua" [Comrade Zhang Han-zhi's Talk], between 1980 and 1989. Available in the Fairbank Center Col-lection, H. C. Fung Library, Harvard University, Cambridge, MA.

28. Cheng Hua, *Zhou Enlai he tade mishumen* [Zhou Enlai and His Secretar-ies] (Beijing: Zhongguo guangbo dianshi chubanshe, 1992), 435.

29. Zheng Zhong, *Zhang Chunqiao: 1949 ji qihou* [Zhang Chunqiao: 1949 and After] (Hong Kong: Zhongwen daxue chubanshe, 2017), 654; and Xiao Mu, "Xiao Mu: Zhang Chunqiao xinlu guiji shitan" [Xiao Mu: Feeling Out the Tracks of Zhang Chunqiao's Intentions], *Difang wenge shi jiaoliu wang* (blog), July 27, 2017, http://www.difangwenge.org/read.php?tid=14950.

30. Gao, *Wannian Zhou Enlai*, 604.

31. Sun and Teiwes, *End of the Maoist Era*, 113.

32. Suoliweng and Ouyang, *Xin faxian de Zhou Enlai, xia*, 674–75.

33. Shen Guofan, *Wang Wenzheng koushu: Gongheguo da shenpan* [*Oral Account of Wang Wenzheng: Big Trial of the Republic*] (Beijing: Dangdai Zhongguo chubanshe, 2005), 224.

34. Zhang Zuoliang, *Zhou Enlai de zuihou shinian: Yi wei baojian yisheng de huiyi* [Zhou Enlai's Last Ten Years: Memories of a Doctor] (Shanghai: Shanghai renmin chubanshe, 1997), 383.

35. Wang Wenfeng, *Cong "Tong Huaizhou" dao shen Jiang Qing* [From "Tong Huaizhou" to Trying Jiang Qing] (Beijing: Dangdai Zhongguo chuban-she, 2004), 118–20.

36. Yang Yinlu, "1977: Qincheng jianyuli de 'Siren bang'" [1977: The "Gang of Four" in Qincheng Prison], *Tongzhou gongjin*, no. 1 (2010): 45.

37. Xiong Lei, "1976 nian, Hua Guofeng he Ye Jianying zenme lianshou de" [How Hua Guofeng and Ye Jianying United in 1976], *Yanhuang chunqiu*, no. 10 (2008): 3.

38. Tong Dexian, *Shifei changye: Ye Jianying zai Zhongguo geming de feichang suiyue* [Ye Jianying in the Extreme Times of the Chinese Revolution] (Bei-jing: Beijing shidai nongchao wenhua fazhan gongsi, 2012), 268.

39. Ye Yonglie, *Ye Yonglie caifang shouji* [Ye Yonglie's Personal Interview Notes] (Shanghai: Shanghai shehui kexueyuan chubanshe, 1993), 80. "Three drops of water" is a reference to the Chinese character 江 in Jiang Qing's last name: three strokes on the left side mean "water."

40. Xu Jingxian, *Shinian yi meng: Qian Shanghai shiwei shuji Xu Jingxian wenge huiyilu* [Ten Years a Dream: Reminiscences of Xu Jingxian, Former Party Secretary of Shanghai], 2nd ed. (Hong Kong: Shidai guoji chuban youxian gongsi, 2005), 214–15.

41. Li Xun, "Zhang Chunqiao he 'you gan'" [Zhang Chunqiao and "Feeling"], *Jiyi*, no. 144 (November 30, 2015): 21.

42. Li Haiwen, "Zhou Enlai shishi hou, Mao Zedong weihe zhiding Hua Guofeng wei dai zongli, xia" [After Zhou Enlai's Death, Why Did Mao Zedong Name Hua Guofeng as Acting Premier? Part 2], *Jianghuai wenshi*, no. 2 (2016): 26.

43. Sun and Teiwes, *End of the Maoist Era*, 72–73.

44. Jiang Qing, "Jiang Qing zai da zhaohuhui qijian shanzi zhaokai de shiersheng qu huiyi shang de jianghua" [Jiang Qing's Talk at an Unauthorized Meeting of Twelve Provinces Held during a Heads-Up Meeting], March 2, 1976, History of Contemporary Chinese Political Movements.

45. Gao Yuan, *Hu Yaobang zai Zhongguo zhengtan de zuihou shinian* [Hu Yaobang's Last Ten Years in China's Political World] (Beijing: Zhongguo wenshi chubanshe, 1989), 143.

46. Xu, *Shinian yi meng*, 349.

47. Wang Fan and Dong Ping, *Hongqiang jiyi, er: Da shijian xiao xijie* [Memory of the Red Walls, 2: Small Details on Big Events] (Beijing: Dangdai Zhongguo chubanshe, 2010), 247.

48. Sun and Teiwes, *End of the Maoist Era*, 212–16.

49. Li and Wang, *"Siren bang" zai Shanghai yudang fumie ji*, 87–89.

50. Gao, *Wannian Zhou Enlai*, 561.

51. Zhu Yongjia and Zhu Shaojun, *Wannian Mao Zedong chongdu guwen neimu* [The Inside Story of Mao Zedong's Rereading of Ancient Texts in His Later Years] (Hong Kong: Xingke'er chuban youxian gongsi, 2012), 122–23.

52. Zhang Chunqiao, "Zhang Chunqiao zai quanjun ge da danwei zhengzhi bu zhuren zuotan hui shang de tanhua" [Zhang Chunqiao's Talk at the Military-Wide General Political Department Head of Every Major Danwei Discussion Meeting], March 1, 1975, History of Contemporary Chinese Political Movements.

53. Sun and Teiwes, *End of the Maoist Era*, 310.

54. Gao, *Wannian Zhou Enlai*, 576.

55. Suoliweng and Ouyang, *Xin faxian de Zhou Enlai, xia*, 788.

56. Li Xiannian bianxiezu, *Li Xiannian zhuan: 1949–1992, xia* [Biography of Li Xiannian: 1949–1992, Volume 2] (Beijing: Zhongyang wenxian chubanshe, 2009), 882.

57. Xu, *Shinian yi meng*, 376.

58. Pang and Feng, *Mao Zedong nianpu 1949–1976, diliujuan*, 614–15; and interview with a senior party historian.

59. Wu Si, *Chen Yonggui: Mao Zedong de nongmin* [Chen Yonggui: Mao Zedong's Peasant] (Hong Kong: Shidai guoji chuban youxian gongsi, 2009), 209.

60. Jiang Qing, "Jiang Qing zai Dazhai dui luyinzu tongzhi de jianghua" [Jiang Qing's Talk with Comrades from the Recording Group], September 17, 1975, History of Contemporary Chinese Political Movements.

61. Jiang Qing, "Jiang Qing zai Qinghua daxue gongcheng wulixi de jianghua" [Jiang Qing's Speech to Tsinghua University's Department of Engineering and Physics], September 29, 1976, History of Contemporary Chinese Political Movements.

62. Tong, *Shifei changye*, 244.

63. Yao Wenyuan, "Yao Wenyuan dui 'Hongqi' zazhi bianjizu zhaojiren de tanhua" [Yao Wenyuan's Talk with the Editorial Group of "Red Flag" Magazine], November 17, 1975, History of Contemporary Chinese Political Movements.

64. Yang Zhengquan, *Xinwen shijian de taiqian muhou: Wode qinli shilu* [Behind the Scenes of News Incidents: My Personal Experiences] (Beijing: Waiwen chubanshe, 2015), 76.

65. Ding, *Luonan yingxiong*, 236.

66. Jiang, "Jiang Qing zai da zhaohuhui qijian shanzi zhaokai de shiersheng qu huiyi shang de jianghua."

67. Zheng Zhong, *Mao Zedong yu "Wenhui bao"* [Mao Zedong and "Wenhuibao"] (Hong Kong: Zhongwen daxue chubanshe, 2010), 624–25.

68. Jiang Qing, "Jiang Qing zai Qinghua daxue de jianghua (jielu)" [Excerpt from Jiang Qing's Talk at Tsinghua University], October 1, 1976, History of Contemporary Chinese Political Movements.

69. Jiang Qing, "Jiang Qing zai Qinghua daxue nongcun fenxiao de jianghua" [Jiang Qing's Talk at Tsinghua University's Agriculture Satellite Campus], October 1, 1976, History of Contemporary Chinese Political Movements.

70. Zhang Gensheng, "Hua Guofeng tan fensui 'Siren bang'" [Hua Guofeng Discusses Smashing the "Gang of Four"], *Yanhuang chunqiu*, no. 7 (2004): 2.

71. Li Haiwen, "'Lishi zhuanzhe zhong de Hua Guofeng' xiezuo shimo" [A History of Writing "Hua Guofeng at the Historical Turning Point"], *Jianghuai wenshi*, no. 5 (2015): 22.

72. Gu Mu, *Gu Mu huiyilu* [Memoirs of Gu Mu] (Beijing: Zhongyang wenxian chubanshe, 2014), 288–89.

73. Ji Xichen, "Hongqiang nei de shengsi juedou" [The Life and Death Struggle inside the Red Walls], *Juece yu xinxi* 242–43 (February 2005): 107.

74. Xiao Mu, "Wang Hongwen mishu Xiao Mu gei Shanghai shiwei de xin" [Letter to the Shanghai Party Committee from Xiao Mu, Secretary to Wang Hongwen], September 18, 1976, History of Contemporary Chinese Political Movements.

75. Yao wanted equal coverage for the four members of the PSC and Jiang Qing, who was not a PSC member. However, she was Mao's widow, and it was the Chairman's funeral. Qing Ye and Fang Lei, *Deng Xiaoping zai 1976, xia* [Deng Xiaoping in 1976, Volume 2] (Shenyang: Chunfeng wenyi chubanshe, 1993), 122.

76. Xu Jingxian, "Xu Jingxian de chubu jiefa jiaodai" [Xu Jingxian's First Exposure], November 5, 1976, History of Contemporary Chinese Political Movements.

77. Li, "Zhang Chunqiao he 'you gan.'"

78. Zheng, *Zhang Chunqiao*, 720 (emphasis added).

79. Li and Wang, *"Siren bang" zai Shanghai yudang fumie ji*, 69; and Xu Zhigao, *Shanghai wenge jiceng shilu: 1969–1977 nian xingao gongzuo biji* [True Record of the Shanghai Cultural Revolution at the Grassroots: 1969–1977 New Draft Work Notes] (Hong Kong: Siji chuban youxian gongsi, 2018), 234.

80. Tong, *Shifei changye*, 251.

81. Ye Xuanji, "Ye Shuai yu fensui 'Siren bang'" [Marshal Ye and the Smashing of the "Gang of Four"], *Nanfang zhoumo*, October 1, 2011, http://www .infzm.com/content/63693.

82. Li and Wang, *"Siren bang" zai Shanghai yudang fumie ji*, 59.

83. Ibid., 63.

84. Qing and Fang, *Deng Xiaoping zai 1976, xia*, 227.

85. Jiang, "Jiang Qing zai Qinghua daxue nongcun fenxiao de jianghua."

86. Bu Weihua, *"Zalan jiu shijie": Wenhua da geming de dongluan yu haojie 1966–1968* ["Smash the Old World": The Chaos and Disaster of the Cultural Revolution, 1966–1968] (Hong Kong: Zhongwen daxue dangdai Zhongguo wenhua yanjiu zhongxin, 2009), 793–94.

87. Wang Nianyi, "Wang Nianyi shuxin xuanji" [Selection of Wang Nianyi's Books and Letters], *Jiyi*, no. 1 (September 13, 2008): 29.

88. Alexander C. Cook, *The Cultural Revolution on Trial: Mao and the Gang of Four* (Cambridge: Cambridge University Press, 2016), 181.

89. Suoliweng and Ouyang Longmen, *Xin faxian de Zhou Enlai, shang* [The Newly Discovered Zhou Enlai, Volume 1] (Hong Kong: Mingjing chubanshe, 2009); and Suoliweng, *Zhou Enlai yu Lin Biao, xia* [Zhou Enlai and Lin Biao, Volume 2] (Deer Park, NY: Mingjing chubanshe, 2012), 403–60.

90. Ma Kechang, *Tebie bianhu: Wei Lin Biao, Jiang Qing fangeming jituan anzhu fan bianhu jishi* [Special Defense: Record of the Defense of Lin Biao and Jiang Qing, the Principal Criminals of the Counterrevolutionary Clique] (Beijing: Zhongguo chang'an chubanshe, 2007), 70.

91. Qing and Fang, *Deng Xiaoping zai 1976, xia*, 323.

92. Xiao Donglian, *Zhonghua renmin gongheguo shi, di 10 juan. Lishi de zhuanzhe: Cong boluan fanzheng dao gaige kaifang* [History of the People's Republic of China, Volume 10. Historical Change: From Setting Things Right to Reform and Opening] (Hong Kong: Zhongwen daxue dangdai Zhongguo wenhua yanjiu zhongxin, 2008), 304–7.

93. Gao, *Wannian Zhou Enlai*, 480.

94. Shi Yun, *Zhang Chunqiao Yao Wenyuan shizhuan: Zizhuan, riji, gongci* [True Story of Zhang Chunqiao and Yao Wenyuan: Autobiography, Diary, Confession] (Hong Kong: Sanlian shudian youxian gongsi, 2012), 390–91.

95. Ibid., 397.

96. Patricia M. Thornton, "The Cultural Revolution as a Crisis of Representation," *China Quarterly*, no. 227 (September 2016): 713; Li Xun, *Geming*

zaofan niandai: Shanghai wenge yundong shigao, I [Age of Revolution and Rebellion: History of the Cultural Revolution Movement in Shanghai, Volume 1] (Hong Kong: Oxford University Press, 2015), 21; and Joel Andreas, *Disenfranchised: The Rise and Fall of Industrial Citizenship in China* (New York: Oxford University Press, 2019), 125–27.

97. Yin Hongbiao, *Shizongzhe de zuji: Wenhua da geming qijian de qingnian sichao* [Footprints of the Disappeared: Thinking of Youth during the Cultural Revolution] (Hong Kong: Zhongwen daxue chubanshe, 2009).

98. Andrew Walder, *China under Mao: A Revolution Derailed* (Cambridge, MA: Harvard University Press, 2015), 285.

99. Li, *Geming zaofan niandai*, 1:259.

100. Wu Yiching, *The Cultural Revolution at the Margins: Chinese Socialism in Crisis* (Cambridge, MA: Harvard University Press, 2014), 106.

101. Xu Youyu, *Xingxing sese de zaofan: Hongweibing jingshen suzhi de xingcheng ji yanbian* [Rebels of All Stripes: A Study of Red Guard Mentalities] (Hong Kong: Zhongwen daxue chubanshe, 1999), 173.

102. Li Xun, *Geming zaofan niandai: Shanghai wenge yundong shigao, II* [Age of Revolution and Rebellion: History of the Cultural Revolution Movement in Shanghai, Volume 2] (Hong Kong: Oxford University Press, 2015), 1097.

103. Ibid., 1428.

104. Yin, *Shizongzhe de zuji*, 66, 85.

105. Jin Dalu, "Zhang Chunqiao weishenme cuizhe Zhou Xinfang" [Why Zhang Chunqiao Snapped Zhou Xinfang], *Yanhuang chunqiu*, no. 12 (2015): 55.

106. Chen Yun, *Chen Yun wenxuan: 1956–1985* [Selected Works of Chen Yun: 1956–1985] (Beijing: Renmin chubanshe, 1986), 274.

107. Xu, *Xingxing sese de zaofan*, 59.

108. Zheng, *Zhang Chunqiao*, 386–87.

109. Yin, *Shizongzhe de zuji*, 432.

110. Shi Yun and Li Danhui, *Zhonghua renmin gonghe guo, di 8 juan. Nanyi jixu de "jixu geming": Cong pi Lin dao pi Deng, 1972–1976* [The People's Republic of China, Volume 8. The "Continuous Revolution" That Was Difficult to Continue: From Criticizing Lin to Criticizing Deng, 1972–1976] (Hong Kong: Zhongwen daxue dangdai Zhongguo wenhua yanjiu zhongxin, 2008), 618.

111. Elizabeth J. Perry and Xun Li, *Proletarian Power: Shanghai in the Cultural Revolution* (Boulder, CO: Westview, 1997), 29.

112. Shi and Li, *Zhonghua renmin gonghe guo, di 8 juan*, 3, 62.

113. Deng Liqun, *Deng Liqun guoshi jiangtanlu*, 7 [Record of Deng Liqun's Lectures on National History, Volume 7] (Beijing: "Zhonghua renmin gongheguo shigao" bianweihui, 2000), 163.

114. Li, *Geming zaofan niandai*, 1:597.

115. Ibid., 716.

116. Yin, *Shizongzhe de zuji*, 72.

117. Andrew Walder, *Chang Ch'un-Ch'iao and Shanghai's January Revolution* (Ann Arbor: Center for Chinese Studies, University of Michigan, 1978); and Wu, *Cultural Revolution at the Margins*, 124–30.

118. Xu Jingxian, *Wenge mingren Xu Jingxian zuihou huiyi* [Cultural Revolution Celebrity Xu Jingxian's Last Reminiscences] (Hong Kong: Xingke'er chuban youxian gongsi, 2013), 132–45.

119. Zheng, *Zhang Chunqiao*, 591–92.

120. Zhang Chunqiao, "Zhang Chunqiao guanyu 'Pi Deng fanyou' yundong de jianghua" [Zhang Chunqiao's Speech on the Campaign to "Criticize Deng and Oppose Rightism"], June 28, 1976, History of Contemporary Chinese Political Movements.

121. Jiang, "Jiang Qing zai Qinghua daxue nongcun fenxiao de jianghua."

122. AVP RF, fond 0100, opis 63, papka 552, delo 6, list 230.

123. Pang and Feng, *Mao Zedong nianpu 1949–1976, diliujuan*, 553.

124. Ibid., 572.

125. Yao Wenyuan, "Yao Wenyuan dui 'Hongqi' zazhi bianjizu zhaojiren de tanhua" [Yao Wenyuan's Talk with the "Red Flag" Magazine Editors' Group], February 5, 1975, History of Contemporary Chinese Political Movements.

126. Qi, *Qi Benyu huiyilu, xia*, 375–76.

127. Jiang Qing, "Jiang Qing jiejian Dazhai dadui ganbu he sheyuan shi de jianghua" [Jiang Qing's Speech When Meeting Dazhai Cadres and Commune Members], September 12, 1975, History of Contemporary Chinese Political Movements.

128. Yao Wenyuan, "Yao Wenyuan dui 'Hongqi' zazhi bianjizu zhaojiren chuanda Mao zhuxi zhishi" [Yao Wenyuan's Dissemination of Chairman Mao's Directive with the "Red Flag" Magazine Editors' Group], June 23, 1975, History of Contemporary Chinese Political Movements.

129. Lowell Dittmer, "The Radical Critique of Political Interest, 1966–1978," *Modern China* 6, no. 4 (October 1980): 375.

130. Li, *Geming zaofan niandai*, 2:1272–73.

131. Jeremy Brown, *City versus Countryside in Mao's China: Negotiating the Divide* (Cambridge: Cambridge University Press, 2014), 218, 223.

132. Sun and Teiwes, *End of the Maoist Era*, 352.

133. Zhang, "Zhang Hanzhi tongzhi jianghua."

134. Hua, "Hua Guofeng he zhongyang lingdao tingqu caizhengbu huibao shi de zhishi" [Directives of Hua Guofeng and Central Party Leaders While Listening to a Report from the Ministry of Finance], November 5, 1976, History of Contemporary Chinese Political Movements.

135. Yang, *Xinwen shijian de taiqian muhou*, 66–67.

136. Luo Pinghan, Lu Yi, and Zhao Peng, *Zhonggong dangshi zhongda zhengyi wenti yanjiu* [Research on Controversial Major Issues in Party History] (Beijing: Renmin chubanshe, 2013), 358–59.

137. Wu Zhong, "Wu Zhong tan zhua 'Siren bang'" [Wu Zhong Discusses Grabbing the "Gang of Four"], *Yanhuang chunqiu*, no. 5 (2012): 31.

138. Deng Xiaoping, *Youguan Deng Xiaoping fuchu de wenjian* [Documents on Deng Xiaoping's Return to Work] [1977]. Available in the Fairbank Center Collection.

139. Julian B. Gewirtz, *Unlikely Partners: Chinese Reformers, Western Economists, and the Making of Global China* (Cambridge, MA: Harvard University Press, 2017), 42.

140. Odd Arne Westad, "The Great Transformation: China in the Long 1970s," in *The Shock of the Global: The 1970s in Perspective*, ed. Niall Ferguson, Charles S. Maier, Erez Manela, and Daniel J. Sargent (Cambridge, MA: Harvard University Press, 2010), 67.

141. Fang Mao, "Hua Guofeng yu duiwai kaifang" [Hua Guofeng and the Opening-Up], *Yanhuang chunqiu*, no. 5 (2016): 9–15; Peter E. Hamilton, "Rethinking the Origins of China's Reform Era: Hong Kong and the 1970s Revival of Sino-US Trade," *Twentieth-Century China* 43, no. 1 (January 2018): 67–88; and Federico Pachetti, "The Roots of a Globalized Relationship: Western Knowledge of the Chinese Economy and US-China Relations in the Long 1970s," in *China, Hong Kong, and the Long 1970s: Global Perspectives*, ed. Odd Arne Westad and Priscilla Roberts (Cham, Switzerland: Palgrave Macmillan, 2017), 181–203.

142. Christian Talley, *Forgotten Vanguard: Informal Diplomacy and the Rise of United States–China Trade, 1972–1980* (Notre Dame, IN: University of Notre Dame Press, 2018), 8.

143. Shi, *Zhang Chunqiao Yao Wenyuan shizhuan*.

144. Zheng, *Zhang Chunqiao*, 194–95.

145. Ibid., 286–87.

146. Ibid., 630–31.

147. Zhang Xianyang, "Zai lilun gongzuo wuxu hui shang de ji ci fayan" [A Few Speeches at the Theory Work Meeting], *Yanhuang chunqiu*, no. 7 (2016): 18.

148. Yan Changgui, "Jiang Qing jiujing shi zenyang yi ge ren" [Who Was Jiang Qing as a Person Exactly?], *Jiyi*, no. 135 (July 15, 2015), online.

149. Zhang Chunqiao, *Zhang Chunqiao yuzhong jiashu, shang* [Zhang Chunqiao's Prison Correspondence with His Family, Volume 1] (Hong Kong: Zhongwen daxue chubanshe, 2015), 229.

150. Sun and Teiwes, *End of the Maoist Era*, 18.

151. Qiu Huizuo, *Qiu Huizuo huiyilu, xia* [Memoirs of Qiu Huizuo, Volume 2] (Hong Kong: Xin shiji chuban ji chuanmei youxian gongsi, 2011), 930.

152. Yang, *Tingyuan shenshen Diaoyutai*, 282–89.

153. Mao Zedong, "Tong Deng Xiaoping guanyu piping 'Siren bang' de yici tanhua (jielu)" [A Talk with Deng Xiaoping on Criticizing the "Gang of Four" (excerpt)], June 1975, History of Contemporary Chinese Political Movements.

154. Zhang, "Zhang Hanzhi tongzhi jianghua."

155. Sun and Teiwes, *End of the Maoist Era*, 18.

156. Andreas, *Disenfranchised*, 155.

157. Chen Yinan, *Qingchun wuhen: Yige zaofanpai gongren de shi nian wenge* [No Hate When Young: A Leftist Rebel Worker's Ten Years of Cultural Revolution] (Hong Kong: Chinese University Press, 2006), 443–45.

158. Jiang, "Jiang Qing zai Dazhai dui luyinzu tongzhi de jianghua."

159. Xu, "Xu Jingxian de chubu jiefa jiaodai."

160. Fan Daren, "'Liangxiao' ji pian zhongdian wenzhang de xiezuo jingguo" [The Process of "Liangxiao" Writing Several Important Articles], *Yanhuang chunqiu*, no. 3 (2014): 16–24.

161. Andreas, *Disenfranchised*, 147–49, 157.

162. Zheng, *Zhang Chunqiao*, 702.

163. Keith Forster, *Rebellion and Factionalism in a Chinese Province: Zhejiang, 1966–1976* (Armonk, NY: M. E. Sharpe, 1990), 180.

164. Liu Yan, "Wo zai 'zhongyang dushu ban' de jianwen, shang" [What I Saw at the "Central Study Group," Part 1], *Dangshi bolan*, no. 1 (2009): 12–14.

165. Xiong, "1976 nian, Hua Guofeng he Ye Jianying zenme lianshou de," 4.

166. Ibid.

167. Wang Dongxing, "Wang Dongxing zai quanguo xuanchuan gongzuo huiyi shang de jianghua" [Wang Dongxing's Speech at the National Propaganda Work Conference], November 18, 1976, History of Contemporary Chinese Political Movements.

168. Witke, *Comrade Chiang Ch'ing*, 15.

169. Yu Feng, *Bali du andan le* [The City of Paris Went Dark] (Wuhan: Hubei renmin chubanshe, 2004), 83–85.

170. Lu Hsun, *Selected Works of Lu Hsun*, ed. Hsien-yi Yang and Gladys Yang, vol. 4 (Beijing: Foreign Languages Press, 1960).

171. Witke, *Comrade Chiang Ch'ing*, 138.

172. Wang Fang, *Wang Fang huiyilu* [Memoirs of Wang Fang] (Hangzhou: Zhejiang renmin chubanshe, 2006), 201.

173. "Wang Hongwen, Zhang Chunqiao, Jiang Qing, Yao Wenyuan fandang jituan zuizheng cailiao zhi er" [Wang Hongwen, Zhang Chunqiao, Jiang Qing, and Yao Wenyuan Anti-Party Clique Crime Material, Volume 2], March 1977, 45–52, Stanford East Asia Library, Stanford, CA; and Wang, *Cong "Tong Huaizhou" dao shen Jiang Qing*, 70–71.

174. Shen Guofan, "Jiang Qing dangguo pantu ma?" [Was Jiang Qing a Traitor?], *Bainianchao*, no. 4 (2008): 65–67; Xu Renjun, "Xu Mingqing yu 'baobi Jiang Qing' wenti" [Xu Mingqing and the Question of "Covering Up for Jiang Qing"], *Bainianchao*, no. 8 (2003): 38–45; and Chen Chusan, *Renjian zhong wan qing: Yige suowei "hong er dai" de rensheng guiji* [The World Values Late Clarity: The Life Path of the So-Called "Red Second Generation"] (Deer Park, NY: Mingjing chubanshe, 2017), 396–97.

175. Geng Geng, "Le Yuhong de kanke yi sheng" [Le Yuhong's Bumpy Life], *Dangshi bolan*, no. 1 (2008): 10–15.

176. Mao Zedong, "Tong zai Jing zhongyang zhengzhiju weiyuan de tanhua" [Conversation with Politburo Members in Beijing], May 3, 1975, History of Contemporary Chinese Political Movements.

177. Zheng Wang, *Finding Women in the State: A Socialist Feminist Revolution in the People's Republic of China, 1949–1964* (Oakland: University of California Press, 2017), 9–10; and Yan, "Jiang Qing jiujing shi zenyang yi ge ren."

178. Li Haiwen, "Guanyu Jiang Qing de liangjian shi" [Two Matters about Jiang Qing], *Shiji*, no. 1 (2017): 60–61.

179. Wang, *Wang Fang huiyilu*, 202.

180. Yan Changgui, "Mao Zedong Jiang Qing jiehun, zhongyang you wu 'yue fa san zhang'" [Did the Party Have a "Three Point Decree" When Mao Zedong and Jiang Qing Married?], *Tongzhou gongjin*, no. 8 (2008): 42–46; and Jin Chunming, "Yi dian buchong he sikao" [A Little Supplement and Consideration], *Tongzhou gongjin*, no. 12 (2008): 39–40.

181. Wu Faxian, *Wu Faxian huiyilu* [Memoirs of Wu Faxian] (Hong Kong: Xianggang beixing chubanshe, 2006), 706–8.

182. Shi and Li, *Zhonghua renmin gonghe guo, di 8 juan*, 197.

183. Suoliweng, *Zhou Enlai yu Lin Biao, shang* [Zhou Enlai and Lin Biao, Volume 1] (Deer Park, NY: Mingjing chubanshe, 2012), 353–54.

184. Yan, "Mao Zedong Jiang Qing jiehun, zhongyang you wu 'yue fa san zhang.'"

185. Keith McMahon, *Women Shall Not Rule: Imperial Wives and Concubines in China from Han to Liao* (Lanham, MD: Rowman and Littlefield, 2013); and Keith McMahon, *Celestial Women: Imperial Wives and Concubines in China from Song to Qing* (Lanham, MD: Rowman and Littlefield, 2016).

186. Chen Dabin, "Jiang Qing zai Xiaojinzhuang de naoju" [Jiang Qing's Farce at Xiaojinzhuang], in *Xin Zhongguo koushu shi, 1949–1978* [Oral History of New China, 1949–1978], ed. Qu Qingshan and Gao Yongzhong (Beijing: Zhongguo renmin daxue chubanshe, 2015), 509.

187. Qiu, *Qiu Huizuo huiyilu, xia*, 578.

188. Hua Guofeng, "Hua Guofeng he zhongyang lingdao tingqu caizhengbu huibao shi de zhishi."

189. Wang, "Wang Dongxing zai quanguo xuanchuan gongzuo huiyi shang de jianghua."

190. Wu Guixian, "Wu Guixian: Bolan rensheng hou de zhizhuo yu danding" [Wu Guixian: Perseverance and Composure after a Life of Big Waves], *Hongyan chunqiu*, no. 4 (2010): 70.

191. Witke, *Comrade Chiang Ch'ing*, 6.

192. Wang and Dong, *Hongqiang jiyi, er*, 249.

193. Yan Changgui, ed., *Huanyuan yige zhenshi de Jiang Qing: Jiang Qing shenbian gongzuo renyuan fangtan jishi* [Restoring the True Jiang Qing: Record

of Conversations with Jiang Qing's Assistants] (Hong Kong: Chuban gongfang youxian gongsi, 2018), 288.

194. Ibid., 178.

195. Pang and Feng, *Mao Zedong nianpu 1949–1976, diliujuan*, 556.

196. Yan and Wang, *Diaoyutai yi wang*, 295.

197. Gao, *Wannian Zhou Enlai*, 579.

198. Shi, *Zhang Chunqiao Yao Wenyuan shizhuan*, 65–72.

199. Zheng, *Zhang Chunqiao*, ix.

200. Shi, *Zhang Chunqiao Yao Wenyuan shizhuan*, 90–100.

201. Xu, *Shinian yi meng*, 395–97.

202. Qiu, *Qiu Huizuo huiyilu, xia*, 635.

203. Shi and Li, *Zhonghua renmin gonghe guo, di 8 juan*, 188.

204. Li, *Geming zaofan niandai*, 2:914.

205. Li Haiwen, "Zhang Chunqiao qi ren" [The Person Zhang Chunqiao], *Yanhuang chunqiu*, no. 1 (2016): 76–77.

206. Li, *Geming zaofan niandai*, 1:32.

207. Yan and Wang, *Diaoyutai yi wang*, 478.

208. Zhu and Zhu, *Wannian Mao Zedong chongdu guwen neimu*, 169.

209. Shi and Li, *Zhonghua renmin gonghe guo, di 8 juan*, 190.

210. Xu, *Shinian yi meng*, 279.

211. Ibid., 287.

212. Li, *Geming zaofan niandai*, 1:203.

213. Wu Jicheng and Wang Fan, *Hongse jingwei: Zhongyang jingweiju yuan fu juzhang Wu Jicheng huiyilu* [Red Bodyguard: Memoirs of Wu Jicheng, Former Vice Commander of the Central Guards Bureau] (Beijing: Dangdai Zhongguo chubanshe, 2003), 404.

214. Zhu and Zhu, *Wannian Mao Zedong chongdu guwen neimu*, 26.

215. Xu Jingxian, "Xu Jingxian gei Zhang Chunqiao Yao Wenyuan de xin" [The Letter Xu Jingxian Wrote to Zhang Chunqiao and Yao Wenyuan], March 10, 1975, History of Contemporary Chinese Political Movements.

216. Li, "Zhang Chunqiao he 'you gan.'"

217. Xie Piao, "Baocun Mao Zedong yiti de riri yeye" [The Days and Nights of Protecting Mao Zedong's Remains], *Yanhuang chunqiu*, no. 7 (2016): 27.

218. Li Haiwen, "You liangzhi de ren bu ying chenmo" [Those with a Conscience Should Not Be Silent], *Beijing chenbao*, August 9, 2015.

219. Sun and Teiwes, *End of the Maoist Era*, 493.

220. Wang, "Wang Dongxing zai quanguo xuanchuan gongzuo huiyi shang de jianghua."

221. Xu, *Shinian yi meng*, 289.

222. Zhang Yufeng, "Huiyi Mao zhuxi qushi qian de yixie qingkuang" [Remembering a Few Situations before Chairman Mao Died], 1977 [?]. Available in the Fairbank Center Collection, H. C. Fung Library, Harvard University, Cambridge, MA.

223. Mao, "Tong zai Jing zhongyang zhengzhiju weiyuan de tanhua."

224. Suoliweng and Ouyang, *Xin faxian de Zhou Enlai, xia*, 758.

225. Yan Changgui, *Zhongnanhai wenge neimu: Jiang Qing shouren mishu qinli shilu* [Inside the Zhongnanhai Cultural Revolution: The Personal Record of Jiang Qing's First Secretary] (Hong Kong: Dashan wenhua youxian gongsi, 2014), 210.

226. Wang Fan and Dong Ping, *Hongqiang yisheng: Wo qinli de Zhongnanhai wangshi* [Doctor in the Red Walls: Events I Personally Experienced in Zhongnanhai] (Beijing: Zuojia chubanshe, 2006), 331.

227. Yan, "Jiang Qing jiujing shi zenyang yi ge ren."

228. Chen Boda, *Chen Boda yigao: Yuzhong zishu ji qita* [Chen Boda's Posthumous Manuscript: Prison Diaries and Other Materials] (Hong Kong: Tiandi tushu youxian gongsi, 1998), 89–90.

229. Wu, *Wu Faxian huiyilu*, 755.

230. Pang and Feng, *Mao Zedong nianpu 1949–1976, diliujuan*, 569.

231. Qing and Fang, *Deng Xiaoping zai 1976, xia*, 84.

232. Shi and Li, *Zhonghua renmin gonghe guo, di 8 juan*, 701–4.

233. Qiu, *Qiu Huizuo huiyilu, xia*, 639.

234. Jiang, "Jiang Qing zai da zhaohuhui qijian shanzi zhaokai de shiersheng qu huiyi shang de jianghua."

235. Pang and Feng, *Mao Zedong nianpu 1949–1976, diliujuan*, 562.

236. Li, *Geming zaofan niandai*, 1:16.

237. Perry and Li, *Proletarian Power*, 38–39.

238. Qiu, *Qiu Huizuo huiyilu, xia*, 626.

239. Pang and Feng, *Mao Zedong nianpu 1949–1976, diliujuan*, 641.

240. Lowell Dittmer, "Bases of Power in Chinese Politics: A Theory and an Analysis of the Fall of the 'Gang of Four,'" *World Politics* 31, no. 1 (October 1978): 48.

241. Li Haiwen, "Hua Guofeng: Mao Zhou dou Lin Biao ling wo shouyi feiqian" [Hua Guofeng: I Benefited from Mao and Zhou's Fight against Lin Biao], *Duowei*, November 12, 2016, http://history.dwnews.com/news/2016-11-12/59781580.html.

242. Shi and Li, *Zhonghua renmin gonghe guo, di 8 juan*, 627–79; and Li Haiwen, "Hua Guofeng zai fensui 'Siren bang' qianhou" [Hua Guofeng before and after Destroying the "Gang of Four"], *Nanfang zhoumo*, October 8, 2011.

243. Zhou Qicai, "Zhongyang zhengzhiju Yuquanshan jinji huiyi" [Emergency Politburo Session at Yuquanshan], *Shiji*, no. 3 (2006): 21.

244. Li and Wang, "*Siren bang*" *zai Shanghai yudang fumie ji*, 278.

245. Pang and Feng, *Mao Zedong nianpu 1949–1976, diliujuan*, 583.

246. Shi and Li, *Zhonghua renmin gonghe guo, di 8 juan*, 686.

247. Ibid., 686; and Sun and Teiwes, *End of the Maoist Era*, 526.

248. Li and Wang, "*Siren bang*" *zai Shanghai yudang fumie ji*, 55.

249. Ibid., 43.

250. Ibid., 77.

251. Zheng Shenxia, *Ye Jianying nianpu, 1897–1986, xia* [Chronology of Ye Jianying, 1897–1986, Volume 2] (Beijing: Zhongyang wenxian chubanshe, 2007), 1107–8.

252. Wu, *Wu De koushu*, 237; Zhang, "Hua Guofeng tan fensui 'Siren bang,'" 3; Cheng Min and Jian Jun, "Jinian fensui 'Siren bang' 35 zhou nian zuotan zongshu" [Summary of the Discussion Meeting on the Thirty-Fifth Anniversary of the Smashing of the "Gang of Four"], *Yan-huang chunqiu*, no. 11 (2011): 2; and Li, "Hua Guofeng zai fensui 'Siren bang' qianhou."

253. Yao Yilin and Yao Jin, *Yao Yilin bai xitan* [One Hundred Night Conversations with Yao Yilin] (Beijing: Zhonggong dangshi chubanshe, 2008), 256–57; and Xuezhi Guo, *The Politics of the Core Leader in China: Culture, Institution, Legitimacy, and Power* (Cambridge: Cambridge University Press, 2019), 353.

254. Xiong, "1976 nian, Hua Guofeng he Ye Jianying zenme lianshou de," 7.

255. Li Haiwen, "Hua Guofeng heshi yuejian Li Xin" [When Did Hua Guofeng Meet Li Xin?], *Bainianchao*, no. 2 (2013): 35.

256. Li, "Hua Guofeng zai fensui 'Siren bang' qianhou."

257. Ibid.

258. Cheng and Jian, "Jinian fensui 'Siren bang' 35 zhou nian zuotan zongshu," 1.

259. Wu, *Wu De koushu*, 238.

260. Ye Yonglie, *"Siren bang" xingwang, xia juan* [The Rise and Fall of the "Gang of Four," Volume 3] (Beijing: Renmin ribao chubanshe, 2009), 13.

261. Shi and Li, *Zhonghua renmin gonghe guo, di 8 juan*, 678–79.

262. Zhongguo geming bowuguan, *Zhongguo gongchandang dangzhang huibian* [Collection of CCP Party Charters] (Beijing: Renmin chubanshe, 1979), 215–16.

263. Wu Jianhua, "Xiangyi fensui 'Siren bang' de qianqian houhou" [Remembering in Detail before and after Smashing of the "Gang of Four"], in *Zhongguo gongchandang koushu shiliao congshu diyijuan* [CCP Collection of Oral Historical Materials, Part 1], ed. Ouyang Song, Gao Yongzhong, Chen Xi, and Liu Ronggang (Beijing: Zhonggong dangshi chubanshe, 2013), 369.

264. Chen Donglin, "Xishuo fensui 'Siren bang,' shang" [The Smashing of the "Gang of Four" in Detail, Part 1], *Dangshi bolan*, no. 1 (2010): 33.

265. Jin Chongji and Pang Xianzhi, *Mao Zedong zhuan, 1949–1976, xia* [Biography of Mao Zedong, 1949–1976, Volume 2] (Beijing: Zhongyang wenxian chubanshe, 2003), 1557–58.

266. Wu, *Wu Faxian huiyilu*, 782, 807.

267. Yan, *Huanyuan yige zhenshi de Jiang Qing*, 258.

268. Yang, *Tingyuan shenshen Diaoyutai*, 189.

269. Yan, "Jiang Qing jiujing shi zenyang yi ge ren."

270. Yang, *Tingyuan shenshen Diaoyutai*, 108–9.

271. Li, "You liangzhi de ren bu ying chenmo."

272. Witke, *Comrade Chiang Ch'ing*, 193.

273. Chi Houze, "Pu Zhanya shangxia 'zeichuan' ji" [Record of Pu Zhanya Getting on and off the "Pirate Ship"], *Wangshi*, no. 25 (November 4, 2005), online.

274. Li, *Geming zaofan niandai*, 2:920.

275. Xu, *Shinian yi meng*, 373.

276. Zhang, *Zhang Chunqiao yuzhong jiashu, shang*, 275.

277. Schoenhals and MacFarquhar, *Mao's Last Revolution*, 438.

278. Xu, *Shinian yi meng*, 94.

279. Pang and Feng, *Mao Zedong nianpu 1949–1976, diliujuan*, 511–15.

280. Li and Wang, *"Siren bang" zai Shanghai yudang fumie ji*, 180.

281. Qing Ye and Fang Lei, *Deng Xiaoping zai 1976, shang* [Deng Xiaoping in 1976, Volume 1] (Shenyang: Chunfeng wenyi chubanshe, 1993), 155.

282. "Nanjing junqu dangwei guanyu xuexi Jiang Qing tongzhi gei ershijun fanghua lian de xin de bao gao" [Nanjing Military Region Party Committee Report on Comrade Jiang Qing's Letter to the Twentieth Army's Chemical Warfare Defense Company] (Red Guard Publications Supplement 2, Volume 6, Center for Chinese Research Materials, Oakton, VA, January 17, 1974).

283. Elizabeth J. Perry, *Patrolling the Revolution: Worker Militias, Citizenship, and the Modern Chinese State* (Lanham, MD: Rowman and Littlefield, 2005), chap. 5.

284. Li, *Geming zaofan niandai*, 2:1545.

285. Ibid., 1554–55.

286. Qiu, *Qiu Huizuo huiyilu, xia*.

287. Chen, "Xishuo fensui 'Siren bang,' shang."

288. Zheng, *Ye Jianying nianpu, 1897–1986, xia*, 1090.

289. Yang Chengwu nianpu bianxiezu, ed., *Yang Chengwu nianpu 1914 nian–2004 nian* [Yang Chengwu Chronology 1914–2004] (Beijing: Jiefangjun chubanshe, 2014), 498.

290. Zhu Ying and Wen Jinghu, *Su Yu nianpu* [Chronology of Su Yu] (Beijing: Dangdai Zhongguo chubanshe, 2006), 452–59.

291. Ye, "Ye Shuai yu fensui 'Siren bang.'"

292. Li, "Hua Guofeng heshi yuejian Li Xin," 35.

293. Ye, "Ye Shuai yu fensui 'Siren bang.'"

294. Ibid.

295. Yang Chengwu nianpu bianxiezu, *Yang Chengwu nianpu 1914 nian–2004 nian*, 516.

296. Zhang, "Hua Guofeng tan fensui 'Siren bang,'" 2.

297. Wu, "Xiangyi fensui 'Siren bang' de qianqian houhou."

298. Tong, *Shifei changye*, 285.

299. Xiong, "1976 nian, Hua Guofeng he Ye Jianying zenme lianshou de," 4.

300. Shi and Li, *Zhonghua renmin gonghe guo, di 8 juan*, 672.

301. Cheng and Jian, "Jinian fensui 'Siren bang' 35 zhou nian zuotan zongshu," 2.

302. Yang Chengwu nianpu bianxiezu, *Yang Chengwu nianpu 1914 nian–2004 nian*, 516–17.

303. "Chi Haotian zhuan" xiezuozu, ed., *Chi Haotian zhuan* [Biography of Chi Haotian] (Beijing: Jiefangjun chubanshe, 2009), 191–206.

304. Li and Wang, *"Siren bang" zai Shanghai yudang fumie ji*, 73.

305. Li, *Geming zaofan niandai*, 1:1592.

306. Li and Wang, *"Siren bang" zai Shanghai yudang fumie ji*, 30.

307. Ibid., 32.

308. Wu and Wang, *Hongse jingwei*, 408–9.

309. Cook, *Cultural Revolution on Trial*, 7.

310. Xiao, *Zhonghua renmin gongheguo shi, di 10 juan*, 296–317.

311. Keith Forster, "China's Coup of October 1976," *Modern China* 18, no. 3 (July 1992): 263–303; and Andrew Scobell, "Military Coups in the People's Republic of China: Failure, Fabrication, or Fancy?," *Journal of Northeast Asian Studies* 14 (1995): 25–46.

312. Sun and Teiwes, *End of the Maoist Era*, 550.

313. Wu, "Xiangyi fensui 'Siren bang' de qianqian houhou," 376.

314. Li, "Hua Guofeng heshi yuejian Li Xin," 35.

315. Li Haiwen, "Tiananmen shijian de qianqian houhou, xia" [Before and after the Tiananmen Incident, Part 3], *Jianghuai wenshi*, no. 5 (2016): 45.

316. Pang Xianzhi and Feng Hui, eds., *Mao Zedong nianpu 1949–1976, diwujuan* [Chronology of Mao Zedong 1949–1976, Volume 5] (Beijing: Zhongyang wenxian chubanshe, 2013), 534.

317. Andrew G. Walder, "Bending the Arc of Chinese History: The Cultural Revolution's Paradoxical Legacy," *China Quarterly*, no. 227 (September 2016): 613–31.

318. Li and Wang, *"Siren bang" zai Shanghai yudang fumie ji*, 54.

319. Fang Weizhong, ed., *Zai fenglang zhong qianjin: Zhongguo fazhan yu gaige biannian jishi, 1977–1989, diyi fence, 1977–1978 nianjuan* [Moving Forward among the Stormy Waves: Chronological Record of China's Development and Reforms, 1977–1989, Volume 1, 1977–1978] (2004), 60. Available in the Fairbank Center Collection.

320. Ibid., 36.

321. Li, "Zhonggong shida hou xingcheng de 'Siren bang' yu zhengzhiju duoshu de duili," 41.

322. Qiu, *Qiu Huizuo huiyilu, xia*, 639.

323. Li, "Hua Guofeng zai fensui 'Siren bang' qianhou."

324. Sun and Teiwes, *End of the Maoist Era*, 588.

Chapter 5. The Fall of Hua Guofeng

1. Cheng Guanjun, "Ye Xuanji jiangshu fensui 'Siren bang' yu Deng Xiaoping fuchu" [Ye Xuanji Discusses the Smashing of the "Gang of Four" and the Return of Deng Xiaoping], *Tongzhou gongjin*, no. 2 (2012): 22–25; and

Deng Rong, *Deng Xiaoping and the Cultural Revolution: A Daughter Recalls the Critical Years* (Beijing: Foreign Languages Press, 2002), 440–41.

2. Frederick C. Teiwes, "The Paradoxical Post-Mao Transition: From Obeying the Leader to 'Normal Politics,'" *China Journal*, no. 34 (July 1995): 55–94.

3. Xuezhi Guo, *The Politics of the Core Leader in China: Culture, Institution, Legitimacy, and Power* (Cambridge: Cambridge University Press, 2019), 296–97; Lowell Dittmer, "Mao's Forgotten Successor: The Political Career of Hua Guofeng," *China Quarterly*, no. 205 (March 2011): 174–76; and Robert Weatherley, *Mao's Forgotten Successor: The Political Career of Hua Guofeng* (Basingstoke, UK: Palgrave Macmillan, 2010).

4. Pang Xianzhi and Feng Hui, eds., *Mao Zedong nianpu 1949–1976, diliujuan* [Chronology of Mao Zedong 1949–1976, Volume 6] (Beijing: Zhongyang wenxian chubanshe, 2013), 512.

5. Xiong Lei, "Ye Jianying lianshou Hua Guofeng ye dou bu gou Deng Xiaoping" [Ye Jianying with Hua Guofeng Together Could Not Defeat Deng Xiaoping], *Aboluowang*, May 19, 2017, https://www.aboluowang.com/2017/0519/931799.html. In the version of this article published in *Yanhuang Chunqiu*, this line was cut. However, its veracity was confirmed during interviews.

6. Dong Daling, *Deng Xiaoping bu ke gaoren de mimi* [Untold Secret of Deng Xiaoping] (Deer Park, NY: Mingjing chubanshe, 2013), 31.

7. Carter Library, National Security Affairs, Staff Material, Far East, Oksenberg Subject File, Box 56, Policy Process: 5/16–31/78, Secret; Sensitive.

8. Li Haiwen, "Hua Guofeng tan shi zhuan xiezuo" [Hua Guofeng Discusses the Writing of History], *Yanhuang chunqiu*, no. 4 (2015): 10.

9. Deng Liqun, *Deng Liqun guoshi jiangtanlu 3* [Record of Deng Liqun's Lectures on National History, Volume 3] (Beijing: "Zhonghua renmin gongheguo shigao" bianweihui, 2000), 359.

10. Xiao Donglian, *Zhonghua renmin gongheguo shi, di 10 juan. Lishi de zhuanzhe: Cong boluan fanzheng dao gaige kaifang* [History of the People's Republic of China, Volume 10. Historical Change: From Setting Things Right to Reform and Opening] (Hong Kong: Zhongwen daxue dangdai Zhongguo wenhua yanjiu zhongxin, 2008), 343.

11. Yang Zhengquan, *Xinwen shijian de taiqian muhou: Wode qinli shilu* [Behind the Scenes of News Incidents: My Personal Experiences] (Beijing: Waiwen chubanshe, 2015), 196–97.

12. Wu Zhong, "Wu Zhong tan zhua 'Siren bang'" [Wu Zhong Discusses Seizing the "Gang of Four"], *Yanhuang chunqiu*, no. 5 (2012): 29–31.

13. Zhu Huaxin, *Zhengzhi woxuan zhong de "Renmin ribao"* [*People's Daily* in the Political Winds] (Hong Kong: Tiandi tushu youxian gongsi, 2011), 214.

14. Li, "Hua Guofeng tan shi zhuan xiezuo," 8.

15. Hu Jiwei, *Cong Hua Guofeng xiatai dao Hu Yaobang xiatai* [From the Fall of Hua Guofeng to the Fall of Hu Yaobang] (Brampton, ON: Mingjing chubanshe, 1997), 85.

16. Han Gang, "Guanyu Hua Guofeng de ruogan shishi (xu)" [Some Historical Facts Regarding Hua Guofeng (Part 2)], *Yanhuang chunqiu*, no. 3 (2011): 9.
17. Li, "Hua Guofeng tan shi zhuan xiezuo," 7.
18. If not for the extremely high credibility of these two sources, I would not have included this information. However, extraordinary claims require extraordinary evidence, so this possibility should still be treated only as a hypothesis.
19. Hu, *Cong Hua Guofeng xiatai dao Hu Yaobang xiatai*, 84–85.
20. Ezra F. Vogel, *Deng Xiaoping and the Transformation of China* (Cambridge, MA: Harvard University Press, 2011), 185.
21. Harry Harding, *China's Second Revolution: Reform after Mao* (Washington, DC: Brookings Institution, 1987), 56.
22. Han Gang, "Guanyu Hua Guofeng de ruogan shishi" [Some Historical Facts Regarding Hua Guofeng], *Yanhuang chunqiu*, no. 2 (2011): 16.
23. Ye Xuanji, "Ye shuai zai shiyijie sanzhong quanhui qianhou" [Marshal Ye before and after the Third Plenum of the Eleventh Party Congress], *Nanfang zhoumo*, October 30, 2008, https://view.news.qq.com/a/20140811/016185.htm.
24. Wu Jianhua, "Ye Jianying Wang Dongxing mitan chuzhi 'Siren bang'" [Ye Jianying and Wang Dongxing Secretly Discuss Defeating the "Gang of Four"], *Yanhuang chunqiu*, no. 2 (2013): 16.
25. "Zhongyang changwei zai liuzhong quanhui yubei hui ge xiaozu zhaoji ren pengtou hui shang de jianghua" [Speeches by the Members of the Standing Committee at the Meeting of Group Conveners During the Sixth Plenary Session of the Eleventh Party Congress], June 22, 1981, History of Contemporary Chinese Political Movements, Chinese University Press.
26. Ibid.
27. Chung Yen-lin, "The Ousting of General Secretary Hu Yaobang: The Roles Played by Peng Zhen and Other Party Elders," *China Review* 19, no. 1 (February 2019): 89–122.
28. "Zhonggong zhongyang zhuanfa de zhongyang changwei zai shiyijie liuzhong quanhui qijian zhaokai gezu zhaojiren huiyi shang de jianghua" [Speeches by the Members of the Standing Committee at the Meeting of Group Conveners During the Sixth Plenary Session of the Eleventh Party Congress Distributed by the Party Center], June 23, 1981, History of Contemporary Chinese Political Movements; and Frederick C. Teiwes and Warren Sun, "Hua Guofeng, Deng Xiaoping, and Reversing the Verdict on the 1976 'Tiananmen Incident,'" *China Review* 19, no. 4 (November 2019): 87.
29. Richard Baum, *Burying Mao: Chinese Politics in the Age of Deng Xiaoping* (Princeton, NJ: Princeton University Press, 1994), 42.
30. Li Haiwen and Wang Shoujia, *"Siren bang" zai Shanghai yudang fumie ji: 1976.10–1979.10* [Record of the Destruction of the Remaining Cohorts

of the "Gang of Four": October 1976–October 1979] (Beijing: Zhongguo qingnian chubanshe, 2015), 129.

31. Deng, *Deng Xiaoping and the Cultural Revolution*, 445–47.
32. Leng Rong and Wang Zuoling, *Deng Xiaoping nianpu (1975–1997)* [Chronology of Deng Xiaoping (1975–1997)], 2 vols. (Beijing: Zhongyang wenxian chubanshe, 2004), 1:153–55.
33. Han, "Guanyu Hua Guofeng de ruogan shishi," 11–12.
34. Hua Guofeng, "Hua Guofeng zai zhongyang zhengzhiju huiyi shang de jianghua" [Hua Guofeng's Talk at the Politburo Meeting], January 6, 1977, History of Contemporary Chinese Political Movements.
35. Interview with a party historian.
36. Deng, *Deng Liqun guoshi jiangtanlu*, 3:348.
37. Xiong Lei, "1976 nian, Hua Guofeng he Ye Jianying zenme lianshou de" [How Hua Guofeng and Ye Jianying United in 1976], *Yanhuang chunqiu*, no. 10 (2008): 8.
38. Deng, *Deng Liqun guoshi jiangtanlu*, 3:356.
39. Teiwes and Sun, "Hua Guofeng, Deng Xiaoping, and Reversing the Verdict."
40. For the two best English-language accounts of the incident, see Frederick C. Teiwes and Warren Sun, *The End of the Maoist Era: Chinese Politics during the Twilight of the Cultural Revolution, 1972–1976* (Armonk, NY: M. E. Sharpe, 2007), 466–96; and Roderick MacFarquhar and Michael Schoenhals, *Mao's Last Revolution* (Cambridge, MA: Harvard University Press, 2006), 422–30.
41. Han, "Guanyu Hua Guofeng de ruogan shishi," 13–14.
42. Xu Qingquan, *Wentan boluan fanzheng shilu* [The True Story of Setting Things Right in the Cultural Sphere] (Hangzhou: Zhejiang renmin chubanshe, 2004), 19–54.
43. Han, "Guanyu Hua Guofeng de ruogan shishi," 17.
44. Interview with a senior party historian.
45. Baum, *Burying Mao*, 4.
46. Harding, *China's Second Revolution*, 54–58.
47. Alexander Pantsov, with Steven I. Levine, *Deng Xiaoping: A Revolutionary Life* (New York: Oxford University Press, 2015), 336.
48. Frederick C. Teiwes and Warren Sun, "China's New Economic Policy under Hua Guofeng: Party Consensus and Party Myths," *China Journal*, no. 66 (July 2011): 2.
49. Frederick C. Teiwes and Warren Sun, *Paradoxes of Post-Mao Rural Reform: Initial Steps toward a New Chinese Countryside, 1976–1981* (New York: Routledge, 2016).
50. Joseph Torigian, "The Party's Interests Come First: The Life of Xi Zhongxun, Father of Xi Jinping" (unpublished manuscript, March 1, 2021).
51. Cheng Zhongyuan, "1977–1978: Jingji lingyu de sixiang jiefang yu gaige kaifang de qibu" [1977–1978: Thought Liberation in the Economic Field

and the Start of Reform and Opening], *Jinyang xuekan*, no. 3 (2010): 49–59.

52. Yuan Zhendong, "1978 nian quanguo kexue dahui: Zhongguo dangdai keji shishang de lichengbei" [The 1978 Nationwide Scientific Conference: A Landmark in China's Modern Science and Technology History], *Kexue wenhua pinglun* 5, no. 2 (February 2008): 37–57.

53. Li Zhenghua, "A Study of the 1978 State Council Conference to Discuss Principles," in *Selected Essays on the History of Contemporary China*, ed. Zhang Xingxing (Boston: Brill, 2015), 30–53.

54. Hu Shao'an, *Jingwei renmin: Xiang Nan zhuan (shang)* [Respect the People: Biography of Xiang Nan (Part 1)] (Hong Kong: Tiandi tushu youxian gongsi, 2004), 198–99.

55. Interviews with two senior party historians.

56. Han, "Guanyu Hua Guofeng de ruogan shishi," 14. This is the most famous formulation of the "two whatevers," but there are three other versions. First, Hua made a similar sounding remark soon after the Gang of Four were arrested, but he was referring narrowly to how criticism of the Gang of Four should proceed. Second, Wu De, mayor of Beijing, used close language around the same time, but it was hardly a statement of a political platform. Third, Hua made the last "two whatever"–ish comment at the March 1977 meeting, but this was the same meeting at which it was more broadly announced that Deng would return to work, and it was less extreme sounding than the February version.

57. Vogel, *Deng Xiaoping and the Transformation of China*, 188.

58. Li Zhuang, *"Renmin ribao" fengyu sishinian* [Forty Years of Wind and Rain at *People's Daily*] (Beijing: Renmin ribao chubanshe, 1993), 322.

59. Deng Liqun, *Deng Liqun zishu: Shierge chunqiu (1975–1987)* [Deng Liqun's Self-Statement: Twelve Springs and Autumns, 1975–1987] (Hong Kong: Dafeng chubanshe, 2006), 84.

60. Han Gang, "'Liangge fanshi' de youlai jiqi zhongjie" [Origins of the "Two Whatevers" and Their End], *Zhonggong dangshi yanjiu*, no. 11 (2009): 57.

61. Han Gang, "'Liangge fanshi' de yiduan gong'an" [The Case of the "Two Whatevers"], *Yanhuang chunqiu*, no. 2 (February 2016): 1–9.

62. Hubei Provincial Archives, SZ-1-4-501-(19–21).

63. Pantsov, with Levine, *Deng Xiaoping*, 326–27.

64. Ye might have been making an implicit warning to Deng not to overstep his bounds. Hubei Provincial Archives, SZ-1-4-501-(11–13).

65. Cheng Zhongyuan, Wang Yuxiang, and Li Zhenghua, *Zhuanzhe niandai: 1976–1981 de Zhongguo* [Era of Change: China in 1976–1981] (Beijing: Zhongyang wenxian chubanshe, 2008), 40.

66. Feng Lanrui, *Bie you ren jian xing lu nan: 1980 niandai qianhou Zhongguo sixiang lilun fengyun ji qita* [Don't Make It Difficult for People to Travel: Chinese Thought and Theory in the 1980s and Others] (Hong Kong: Shidai guoji, 2005), 88–89.

67. Leng and Wang, *Deng Xiaoping nianpu (1975–1997)*, 1:159–60.

68. Han, "'Liangge fanshi' de yiduan gong'an," 9.

69. Hubei Provincial Archives, SZ-1-4-791.

70. Han Gang, "Quanli de zhuanyi: Guanyu shiyijie sanzhong quanhui" [A Shift in Power: About the Third Plenum of the Eleventh Party Congress], *Lingdaozhe*, no. 1 (2009): 126–27.

71. Shen Baoxiang, "Hu Yaobang de yici fayan" [A Speech Given by Hu Yaobang], *Tongzhou gongjin*, no. 11 (2012): 61–62.

72. Ma Peiwen, "Bi de cheng qing de yi zhuang zhong da shishi" [A Very Important Historical Fact That Must Be Clarified], *Yanhuang chunqiu*, no. 1 (2015): 22–23.

73. Wang Qianghua, "Zai xin de lishi qidian shang jixu jiefang sixiang: Jinian 1978 nian zhenli biaozhun taolun 30 zhou nian" [Continue to Liberate Thinking at the New Historical Turning Point: Commemorating the Thirtieth Anniversary of the 1978 Discussion of the Truth Criterion], *Bolan qunshu* 4 (April 2008): 4–12.

74. Shen Baoxiang, *Zhenli biaozhun wenti taolun shimo* [The Debate on the Criterion of Truth Issue from Beginning to End] (Beijing: Zhongguo qingnian chubanshe, 1997), 108–9.

75. Cheng, Wang, and Li, *Zhuanzhe niandai*, 93.

76. Shen, *Zhenli biaozhun wenti taolun shimo*, 114.

77. Ibid., 71–72.

78. Long Pingping, "Deng Xiaoping shi zhenli biaozhun wenti da taolun de fadongzhe yu lingdaozhe" [Deng Xiaoping Was the Initiator and Leader of the Discussion on the Criterion of Truth], *Beijing dangshi*, no. 3 (2008): 11–13.

79. Shen Baoxiang, "Hu Yaobang yu Hua Guofeng: Wo suo zhidao de ruogan qingkuang (xia)" [Hu Yaobang and Hua Guofeng: A Few Situations I Know (Part 2)], *Tongzhou gongjin*, no. 12 (2009): 46.

80. Hu Deping, "Yaobang tongzhi zai 'zhenli biaozhun' da taolun de qianqian houhou zhong pian" [Comrade Yaobang before and after the Big "Truth Criterion" Debate Part 2], *Caijing* 213, no. 8 (June 9, 2008): 147.

81. Sun Xingsheng, "'Zhongguo qingnian' fukan fengpo" [The Turbulence about "China Youth" Resuming Publication], *Bainianchao*, no. 10 (2008): 53.

82. Chen Liming, "Da dao zhongyang zui gao lingdao ceng de yichang 'bimo guansi': Tan Zhenlin guanyu zhenli biaozhun wenzhang fabiao de qianqian houhou" [The "War of Words" That Reached the Highest Leadership Level: The Ins and Outs on the Publication of Tan Zhenlin's Article on the Truth Criterion], *Xiangchao*, no. 4 (2004): 43–45.

83. Hubei Provincial Archives, SZ-1-4-791-(4–6).

84. Li Rui, "Yaobang qushi qian de tanhua" [Yaobang's Conversation before Death], in *Huainian Yaobang di si juan* [Remembering Yaobang, Volume 4], ed. Zhang Liqun, Zhang Ding, Yan Ruping, and Li Gongtian (Hong Kong: Yatai guoji chuban youxian gongsi, 2001), 296.

85. Han, "Guanyu Hua Guofeng de ruogan shishi (xu)," 9.

86. Cheng, Wang, and Li, *Zhuanzhe niandai*, 23.

87. Ibid., 21.

88. I thank Warren Sun for clarifying this point.

89. Han, "Guanyu Hua Guofeng de ruogan shishi," 18.

90. Leng and Wang, *Deng Xiaoping nianpu (1975–1997)*, 1:394.

91. Han, "Guanyu Hua Guofeng de ruogan shishi," 18.

92. Ibid.

93. Hu, "Yaobang tongzhi zai 'zhenli biaozhun' da taolun de qianqian houhou zhong pian," 148.

94. Man Mei, *Huiyi fuqin Hu Yaobang, xia* [Remembering My Father Hu Yaobang, Part 2] (Hong Kong: Tiandi tushu youxian gongsi, 2016), 491–92.

95. Hu, *Cong Hua Guofeng xiatai dao Hu Yaobang xiatai*, 88.

96. Su Shaozhi, *Shinian fengyu: Wenge hou de dalu lilun jie* [Ten Years of Wind and Rain: The Theoretical World in the Mainland after the Cultural Revolution] (Taipei: Shibao wenhua chuban qiye youxian gongsi, 1996), 105–7.

97. Han, "Quanli de zhuanyi," 128.

98. Roderick MacFarquhar, "The Succession to Mao and the End of Maoism, 1969–1982," in *The Politics of China*, 3rd ed. (New York: Cambridge University Press, 2011), 246–336; Harding, *China's Second Revolution*; and Baum, *Burying Mao*.

99. Zhao Shukai, "Yi duan pushuo mili de lishi" [A Bewildering Period of History], *Zhongguo fazhan guancha*, October 26, 2015.

100. Tong Dexian, *Shifei changye: Ye Jianying zai Zhongguo geming de feichang suiyue* [The World Is Not a Long Night: Ye Jianying in the Extreme Times of the Chinese Revolution] (Beijing: Beijing shidai nongchao wenhua fazhan gongsi, 2012), 251.

101. Vogel, *Deng Xiaoping and the Transformation of China*, 185.

102. Frederick C. Teiwes, "The Study of Elite Political Conflict in the PRC: Politics inside the 'Black Box,'" in *Handbook of the Politics of China*, ed. David S. G. Goodman (Northampton, MA: Edward Elgar, 2015), 32.

103. "Wang Dongxing yu Hu Yaobang Chen Yeping de tanhua" [A Conversation between Wang Dongxing and Hu Yaobang and Chen Yeping], June 9, 1978, History of Contemporary Chinese Political Movements.

104. Hubei Provincial Archives, SZ-1-4-791.

105. Zhu Jiamu, *Wo suo zhidao de shiyijie sanzhong quanhui* [What I Know about the Third Plenum of the Eleventh Central Committee] (Beijing: Zhongyang wenxian chubanshe, 1998), 51.

106. Li, "Hua Guofeng tan shi zhuan xiezuo," 9.

107. Xiao, *Zhonghua renmin gongheguo shi, di 10 juan*, 343.

108. Hu, *Cong Hua Guofeng xiatai dao Hu Yaobang xiatai*, 73–83.

109. Xiao, *Zhonghua renmin gongheguo shi, di 10 juan*, 393.

110. "Zhongyang changwei zai liuzhong quanhui yubei hui ge xiaozu zhaoji ren pengtou hui shang de jianghua."

111. Feng Wenbin, "Feng Wenbin tongzhi chuanda Liu Zhong quanhui jingshen de baogao" [Report on Comrade Feng Wenbin's Communication of the Spirit of the Sixth Plenum], July 4, 1981, in author's personal collection.

112. Alice L. Miller, "Projecting the Next Politburo Standing Committee," *China Leadership Monitor*, no. 49 (Winter 2016): 49.

113. Deng Xiaoping, *Deng Xiaoping wenxuan* [Selected Works of Deng Xiaoping], vol. 2 (Beijing: Renmin chubanshe, 2006), 347.

114. Deng, *Deng Liqun zishu*, 183.

115. Li Lun, *Zhuanfang Zhao Ziyang: 1992–2004 yu youren de tanhua* [Special Interviews with Zhao Ziyang: Conversations with Friends 1992–2004] (Hong Kong: Jingcheng wenhua shiye gongsi, 2006), 44.

116. Interviews with senior party historians.

117. Nie Li, *Shan gao shui chang: Huiyi fuqin Nie Rongzhen* [High Mountains and Long Water: Remembering My Father, Nie Rongzhen] (Shanghai: Shanghai wenyi chubanshe, 2006), 368.

118. Zheng Shenxia, *Ye Jianying nianpu, 1897–1986, xia* [Chronology of Ye Jianying, 1897–1986, Volume 2] (Beijing: Zhongyang wenxian chubanshe, 2007), 1173.

119. Xu Xiangqian nianpu bianxiezu, *Xu Xiangqian nianpu, 1977 nian–1990 nian* [Chronology of Xu Xiangqian, 1977–1990] (preofficial publication version of *Xu Xiangqian nianpu*, 2012), 1010–11.

120. Ibid., 1021.

121. Ibid., 1021–24.

122. "Quarterly Chronicle and Documentation (January–March 1980)," *China Quarterly*, no. 82 (June 1980): 381–82.

123. Zheng, *Ye Jianying nianpu, 1897–1986, xia*, 1173.

124. Interview with a senior party historian.

125. Xiao, *Zhonghua renmin gongheguo shi, di 10 juan*, 195.

126. Ibid.

127. Ibid., 15.

128. Ibid., 386.

129. Deng Liqun, "'Guanyu jianguo yilai dangde ruogan lishi wenti de jueyi' qicao guocheng he zhuyao neirong de jieshao: Zai zhu Jing budui yishang ganbu huiyi shang de jianghua" [Introduction to the Writing Process and Main Content of the "Resolution on Certain Questions in the History of Our Party since the Founding of the People's Republic of China": Speech at the Meeting of Cadres at the Division Level and Above in the Troops Stationed in Beijing], *Xuanchuan jianbao, zengkan*, July 1981, 89. Available in the Fairbank Center Collection, H. C. Fung Library, Harvard University, Cambridge, MA.

130. Interview with a party historian.

131. Wu, "Ye Jianying Wang Dongxing mitan chuzhi 'Siren bang.'"

132. "Zhongyang changwei zai liuzhong quanhui yubei hui ge xiaozu zhaoji ren pengtou hui shang de jianghua."

133. Deng Liqun, "Guanyu jianguo yilai ruogan lishi wenti de jueyi de qicao guocheng" [Regarding the Writing Process of the Decision on History since the Founding of the Party], July 1981, 116. Available in the Fairbank Center Collection.

134. Guofang daxue "Xu Xiangqian nianpu" bianweihui, ed., *Xu Xiangqian nianpu, xia* [Chronology of Xu Xiangqian, Part 2] (Beijing: Jiefangjun chubanshe, 2016), 429.

135. Hu Deping, "Weihe 'Yaobang bu yuan dong Hua Guofeng'?" [Why Was It That "Yaobang Was Not Willing to Move Hua Guofeng"?], *Yanhuang chunqiu*, no. 8 (2010): 53–55.

136. Man Mei, *Sinian yiran wujin: Huiyi fuqin Hu Yaobang* [Longing Still Never Ends: Remembering My Father, Hu Yaobang] (Beijing: Beijing chubanshe, 2005), 374.

137. Xiao, *Zhonghua renmin gongheguo shi, di 10 juan*, 390.

138. Hu, "Weihe 'Yaobang bu yuan dong Hua Guofeng'?," 54.

139. Zhang Wanshu, *Gaige de niandai: 1977–1989 nian hongse de dalu* [The Era of Reform: The Red Mainland 1977–1989] (Hong Kong: Tiandi tushu youxian gongsi, 2013), 258.

140. Han, "Quanli de zhuanyi," 133.

141. Xiao, *Zhonghua renmin gongheguo shi, di 10 juan*, 343.

142. Han, "Quanli de zhuanyi,"136.

143. Hu Jiwei, *Hu Zhao xinzheng qishilu: Bingdui "xin minzhu zhuyi" jinxing poxi* [The Beginnings of Reform under Hu Yaobang and Zhao Ziyang (*sic*)] (Hong Kong: Xin shiji chubanshe, 2012), 157–58.

144. Cheng, Wang, and Li, *Zhuanzhe niandai*, 437.

145. Deng, *Deng Liqun zishu*, 168–70.

146. Xiao, *Zhonghua renmin gongheguo shi, di 10 juan*, 384.

147. Ibid., 385.

148. Han, "Quanli de zhuanyi," 133.

149. Hu, *Cong Hua Guofeng xiatai dao Hu Yaobang xiatai*, 80–83.

150. Zhang, *Gaige de niandai*, 234.

151. Deng, *Deng Liqun zishu*, 171.

152. Zhang Sheng, *Cong zhanzheng zoulai: Liang dai junren de duihua* [Returning from War: A Conversation between Two Generations of Military Men] (Beijing: Zhongguo qingnian chubanshe, 2008), 381.

153. June Teufel Dreyer, "Deng Xiaoping: The Soldier," *China Quarterly*, no. 135 (September 1993): 536–50; and David S. G. Goodman, *Deng Xiaoping and the Chinese Revolution: A Political Biography* (New York: Routledge, 1994).

154. Zhonggong zhongyang wenxian yanjiushi, *Deng Xiaoping zhuan (1904–1974)* [Biography of Deng Xiaoping (1904–1974)], vol. 1 (Beijing: Zhongyang wenxian chubanshe, 2014), 236.

155. David S. G. Goodman, *Social and Political Change in Revolutionary China: The Taihang Base Area in the War of Resistance to Japan, 1937–1945* (Lanham, MD: Rowman and Littlefield, 2000).

156. Gary J. Bjorge, *Moving the Enemy: Operational Art in the Chinese PLA's Huai Hai Campaign*, Leavenworth Papers 22 (Fort Leavenworth, KS: Combat Studies Institute Press, 2004).

157. Zhonggong zhongyang wenxian yanjiushi, *Deng Xiaoping zhuan (1904–1974)* [Biography of Deng Xiaoping (1904–1974)], vol. 2 (Beijing: Zhongyang wenxian chubanshe, 2014), 747.

158. Xi Qixin, *Zhu Guangya zhuan* [Biography of Zhu Guangya] (Beijing: Zhongguo qingnian chubanshe, 2017), 481–82, 487.

159. Zheng, *Ye Jianying nianpu, 1897–1986, xia*, 1130.

160. Jin Chongji, Chen Qun, and Cao Yingwang, *Chen Yun zhuan, xia* [Biography of Chen Yun, Part 2] (Beijing: Zhonggong zhongyang wenxian chubanshe, 2005), 1495.

161. Han Gang, "Cong Hua Guofeng zhuzheng dao Deng Xiaoping hexin quanli shijiao de jiedu" [Interpretation from the Perspective of the Leadership of Hua Guofeng to Deng Xiaoping as the Core Authority], YouTube, November 29, 2017, https://www.youtube.com/watch?v=Np5ldobfHjc &ab_channel=%E5%BC%80%E5%BF%83%E5%B1%E5%A5 %BD.

162. Ibid.

163. Vogel mentions this incident but provides no footnotes and does not identify it as an important mechanism for the fallout between Deng and Hua. Vogel, *Deng Xiaoping and the Transformation of China*, 229.

164. Haijun zhengzhibu bianyanshi, ed., *Haijun zhengzhi gongzuo dashiji 1949.4–1989.4* [Chronicle of Major Developments in Navy Political Work: April 1949–April 1989] (Beijing: Guofang daxue chubanshe, 1993), 386.

165. Huang Yao and Zhang Mingzhe, *Luo Ruiqing zhuan* [Biography of Luo Ruiqing] (Beijing: Dangdai Zhongguo chubanshe, 1996), 608.

166. "Liuzhong quanhui chuanda tigang fulu: Hua Guofeng tongzhi de zhuyao cuowu" [Addendum to the Distributed Outline of the Third Plenum: The Major Mistakes of Comrade Hua Guofeng], July 7, 1981, History of Contemporary Chinese Political Movements.

167. Qiao Ya, "Luetan Xiao Jingguang, Su Zhenhua zhijian de shifei enyuan" [A Brief Discussion of the Rights and Wrongs between Xiao Jingguang and Su Zhenhua] (Jinian kaiguo shangjiang Su Zhenhua danchen 100 zhounian huodong, n.d.), in author's personal collection.

168. Yang Zhaolin, Chou Yunzhou, and Qiao Ya, *Cong gaoshan dao dahai: Gongheguo shangjiang Su Zhenhua* [From the High Mountains to the Great Seas: General of the Republic Su Zhenhua] (Beijing: Jiefangjun chubanshe, 2001), 434–35.

169. Yu Ruxin, "Junwei zhuxi weishenme bu neng jianyue haijun?" [Why Can't the Chairman of the CMC Inspect the Navy?], *Fenghuayuan* 429 (2003), online.

170. Yang Jisheng, *Zhongguo gaige niandai de zhengzhi douzheng* [Political Struggle in China during the Era of Reform] (Hong Kong: Excellent Culture Press, 2004), 94.

171. Shen, *Zhenli biaozhun wenti taolun shimo*, 121.

172. Lu Zengyan, "Wei Guoqing zai dang de shiyijie sanzhong quanhui qianhou" [Wei Guoqing before and after the Third Plenum of the Eleventh Party Congress], *Bainianchao*, no. 12 (December 2015): 4–12.

173. Ibid.; and Zhang Guanghua, *Zhenshi de huiyi 1961 zhi 1981* [True Memory 1961 to 1981] (Beijing: Beijing shidai nongchao wenhua fazhan gongsi, 2009), 478.

174. Zhang, *Zhenshi de huiyi 1961 zhi 1981*, 478; and Shen, *Zhenli biaozhun wenti taolun shimo*, 121.

175. Lu, "Wei Guoqing zai dang de shiyijie sanzhong quanhui qianhou"; and Zhang, *Zhenshi de huiyi 1961 zhi 1981*, 478.

176. Leng and Wang, *Deng Xiaoping nianpu (1975–1997)*, 1:319.

177. Deng Xiaoping, "Speech at the All-Army Conference on Political Work," June 2, 1978, in *Selected Works of Deng Xiaoping*, vol. 2, *1975–1982* (Beijing: Foreign Languages Press, 1984), 128.

178. Hubei Provincial Archives, SZ-1-4-501-19.

179. Shen, *Zhenli biaozhun wenti taolun shimo*, 116–17.

180. Ibid., 138.

181. Ibid., 180.

182. Wu Jiang, *Shinian de lu: He Hu Yaobang xiangchu de rizi* [Ten-Year Road: The Days I Associated with Hu Yaobang] (Hong Kong: Jingbao wenhua qiye youxian gongsi, 1995), 40.

183. Chen Heqiao, *Chen Heqiao huiyi wenji* [Collection of Chen Heqiao's Memories] (Beijing: Guofang gongye chubanshe, 2000), 604.

184. Zhang, *Zhenshi de huiyi 1961 zhi 1981*, 470.

185. Jiang Siyi, ed., *Zhongguo gongchandang jundui zhengzhi gongzuo qishi nian shi: Zai "wenhua dageming" zhong shou sunhai, zai gaige kaifang zhong chuangzao xin jumian* [Seventy-Year History of the Communist Party's Military Political Work: Suffering Damage during the "Cultural Revolution," Creating a New Situation in the Reform and Opening Up], vol. 6 (Beijing: Jiefangjun chubanshe, 1991), 51.

186. Liao Hansheng, *Liao Hansheng huiyilu* [Memoirs of Liao Hansheng] (Beijing: Jiefangjun chubanshe, 2012), 587–88.

187. Zhang, *Zhenshi de huiyi 1961 zhi 1981*, 470–71.

188. Xiao Ke, *Xiao Ke huiyilu* [Memoirs of Xiao Ke] (Beijing: Jiefangjun chubanshe, 1997), 537.

189. Leng and Wang, *Deng Xiaoping nianpu (1975–1997)*, 1:534.

190. Deng Xiaoping, "Deng Xiaoping yu Hu Qiaomu Deng Liqun tanhua yaodian" [Key Points from Deng Xiaoping's Discussion with Hu Qiaomu and Deng Liqun], September 12, 1979, History of Contemporary Chinese Political Movements.

191. Interview with two senior party historians.

192. Zhang Guanghua, *Zhenshi de huiyi (xuji)* [True Memory (Part 2)] (Beijing: Beijing shidai nongchao wenhua fazhan gongsi, 2010), 222–23.

193. Jiang, *Zhongguo gongchandang jundui zhengzhi gongzuo qishi nian shi*, 6:52.

194. Ibid., 6:52.

195. This section was cut from Deng's official *Selected Works*. Wu, *Shinian de lu*, 90–91.

196. Leng and Wang, *Deng Xiaoping nianpu (1975–1997)*, 1:541.

197. Xiao, *Zhonghua renmin gongheguo shi, di 10 juan*, 201–2.

198. Ibid., 199 (emphasis added).

199. Ibid., 358.

200. MacFarquhar, "Succession to Mao and the End of Maoism," 323.

201. CIA, "Leadership Politics in Post-Mao China: The Fall of Hua Guofeng," August 1982, CIA Crest Database, College Park, MD.

202. Ruan Ming, *Deng Xiaoping: Chronicle of an Empire* (Boulder, CO: Westview, 1994), 76.

203. Interview with two party historians.

204. Deng, *Deng Liqun zishu*, 181.

205. Ruan, *Deng Xiaoping*, 79. This section was cut from the official *Selected Works*.

206. Cheng, Wang, and Li, *Zhuanzhe niandai*, 449.

207. Xiao, *Zhonghua renmin gongheguo shi, di 10 juan*, 374. In both the Chinese and English versions of Deng's *Selected Works*, Deng does not refer to the PLA but to "certain localities," and he does not mention that the documents were written by the GPD: "前些时候有的地方为了进行革命思想的教育，重提 '兴无灭资' 的口号. 有关文件我是看过的." Although Xiao Donglian footnotes Deng's speech in the *Selected Works*, his version of the quote refers to both the PLA and the GPD: "前些时候解放军为了进行革命思想的教育，重提 '兴无灭资' 的口号，总政治部文件我是看过的." Because Xiao is an exceptionally well-placed historian at the National Defense University, I have used his version.

208. Jiang, *Zhongguo gongchandang jundui zhengzhi gongzuo qishi nian shi*, 6:462–63; Leng and Wang, *Deng Xiaoping nianpu (1975–1997)*, 2:707–8; and Xiao, *Zhonghua renmin gongheguo shi, di 10 juan*, 393–494.

209. Leng and Wang, *Deng Xiaoping nianpu (1975–1997)*, 2:707–8.

210. Ibid., 2:717–18.

211. Two slightly different versions of this conversation are available in the History of Contemporary Chinese Political Movements database. One is meant for distribution; the other is not. I have used the version that is not for distribution, but my understanding of some statements is shaped by the clearer distributed version.

212. Deng, "Guanyu jianguo yilai ruogan lishi wenti de jueyi de qicao guocheng."

213. Nie Rongzhen, "Nie Rongzhen gei Deng Xiaoping Hu Yaobang Chen Yun de xin" [A Letter from Nie Rongzhen to Deng Xiaoping, Hu Yaobang,

and Chen Yun], June 30, 1980, History of Contemporary Chinese Political Movements.

214. Leng and Wang, *Deng Xiaoping nianpu (1975–1997)*, 2:753.

215. Ji Pomin, "Ting fuqin Ji Dengkui tan wangshi" [Listening to My Father, Ji Dengkui, Talk about the Past], *Nanfang zhoumo*, November 6, 2003, https://www.16lo.com/article/88324.

216. Shen, *Zhenli biaozhun wenti taolun shimo*, 136.

217. Yang Jisheng, *Zhongguo dangdai mingren zhengyao fang shuping ji* [Collection of Interviews and Commentaries on China's Modern Famous Individuals and Important Politicians], 2nd ed. (Hong Kong: Tiandi tushu youxian gongsi, 2014), 304.

218. Man, *Sinian yiran wujin*, 294.

219. Shen, *Zhenli biaozhun wenti taolun shimo*, 141.

220. Interviews with senior party historians.

221. Teiwes, "Study of Elite Political Conflict in the PRC," 32.

222. Deng, *Deng Liqun guoshi jiangtanlu*, 3:354.

223. Zhu Jiamu and Liu Shukai, *Chen Yun nianpu 1905–1995, xia juan* [Chronology of Chen Yun 1905–1995, Last Volume] (Beijing: Zhongyang wenxian chubanshe, 2000), 236.

224. Wang Jie and Li Lilin, "Suowei 'Chen Yun yiguan youqing' kaobian: Cong dizhi he jiaozheng 'suo qing' cuowu jiaodu qieru" [An Investigation into the So-Called "Chen Yun Always Was a Rightist": From the Perspective of Resisting and Correcting the "Left" Error], *Dang de wenxian*, no. 3 (2015): 81–86.

225. Zhang Jincai, "Chen Yun danren guo de lingdao zhiwu" [The Leadership Positions Held by Chen Yun], *Dangshi bolan*, no. 6 (2015): 16–19; and Tang Zhuo and Gao Yang, *Chen Yun shengping yanjiu ziliao* [Research Material on the Life of Chen Yun] (Beijing: Zhongyang wenxian chubanshe, 2013), 3–38.

226. Frederick C. Teiwes and Warren Sun, "China's Economic Reorientation after the Third Plenum: Conflict Surrounding 'Chen Yun's' Readjustment Program, 1979–80," *China Journal*, no. 70 (July 2013): 163–87.

227. Deng Xiaoping, "Deng Xiaoping zai Zhong Yue bianjing zuozhan qingkuang baogao hui shang de jianghua" [Deng Xiaoping's Speech at a Report Meeting on the Border War between China and Vietnam], January 6, 1977, History of Contemporary Chinese Political Movements.

228. Zheng, *Ye Jianying nianpu, 1897–1986, xia*, 1127.

229. Xiaoming Zhang, *Deng Xiaoping's Long War: The Military Conflict between China and Vietnam, 1979–1991* (Chapel Hill: University of North Carolina Press, 2015), 53–54.

230. Wang Fan, *Muji lishi: Guanyu dangdai Zhongguo dashi weiren de koushu shilu* [Witnessing History: Oral Record on Contemporary China's Main Events and Great People] (Changsha: Hunan wenyi chubanshe, 1998), 214.

231. Warren Sun, interview notes, in possession of the author.

232. Zhong Yanlin, *Wenge qian de Deng Xiaoping: Mao Zedong de "fu shuai,"* *1956–1966* [Deng Xiaoping before the Cultural Revolution: Mao Zedong's "Vice Commander," 1956–1966] (Hong Kong: Zhongwen daxue chubanshe, 2013), 163.

233. "Zhonggong zhongyang guanyu shiyijie liuzhong quanhui de juemi chuanda wenjian" [CC Confidential Document on the Sixth Party Plenum of the Eleventh Party Congress], July 4, 1981, Internal Report 1981.07.04, Box 1, Zhongguo gong chan dang, Hoover Institution Archives, Stanford University, Stanford, CA, 65.

234. Zhou Deli, *Yige gaoji canmouzhang de zishu* [Self-Account by a High-Ranking Staff Officer] (Nanjing: Nanjing chubanshe, 1992), 245.

235. Pantsov, with Levine, *Deng Xiaoping*, 350.

236. David M. Lampton, *Following the Leader: Ruling China, from Deng Xiaoping to Xi Jinping* (Berkeley: University of California Press, 2013), 185.

237. Zhang, *Gaige de niandai*, 231.

238. Vogel, *Deng Xiaoping and the Transformation of China*, 248.

239. Man, *Sinian yiran wujin*, 373–74.

240. Warren Sun, personal communication with author, March 23, 2016.

241. Hu, *Hu Zhao xinzheng qishilu*, 140.

242. Hu Yaobang, *Hu Yaobang wenxuan* [Selected Works of Hu Yaobang] (Beijing: Renmin chubanshe, 2015), 261–63.

243. Xiao, *Zhonghua renmin gongheguo shi, di 10 juan*, 396–97.

244. Teiwes, "Study of Elite Political Conflict in the PRC," 33.

Chapter 6. Conclusion

1. William Taubman, *Khrushchev: The Man and His Era* (New York: Norton, 2003), 578–619.

2. "Pis'mo V. M. Molotova v TsK KPSS (1964 g.)" [V. M. Molotov's Letter to the CC CPSU], *Voprosy istorii*, no. 3 (2012): 94.

3. William J. Tompson, "The Fall of Nikita Khrushchev," *Soviet Studies* 43, no. 6 (1991): 1101–21; Joseph Torigian, "'You Don't Know Khrushchev Well': The Fall of Khrushchev as a Challenge to 'Exchange' and 'Institutionalist' Explanations of Authoritarian Politics," *Journal of Cold War Studies*, 24, no. 1 (Winter 2022).

4. "Nepravlenaia stenogramma zasedaniia Prezidiuma TsK KPSS po voprosam, voznikshim vo vremia poezdki N. S. Khrushcheva po sel'skokhoziaistvennym regionam SSSR. 19 avgusta 1964 g." [Uncorrected Transcript of Meeting of the CC CPSU Presidium on the Issues during N. S. Khrushchev's Trip across the USSR Agricultural Regions. August 19, 1964], in *Nikita Khrushchev. 1964. Stenogrammy plenumov TsK KPSS i drugie dokumenty* [Nikita Khrushchev. 1964. Transcripts of the CC CPSU Plenums and Other Documents], comp. A. N. Artizov, V. P. Naumov, M. Iu.

Prozumenshchikov, Iu. V. Sigachev, N. G. Tomilina, and I. N. Shevchuk (Moscow: MFD, 2007), 95.

5. Aleksandr Maisurian, *Drugoi Brezhnev* [Another Brezhnev] (Moscow: Vagrius, 2004), 130.

6. P. E. Shelest, . . . *Da ne sudimy budete: Dnevnikovye zapisi, vospominaniia chlena Politbiuro TsK KPSS* [. . . So That You Won't Be Judged: Diary Notes, Memoirs by a Member of the Politburo of the CC CPSU] (Moscow: edition q, 1995), 203.

7. N. A. Barsukov, "Beseda s Egorychevym N. G. 19 sentiabria 1990 g." [Conversation with N. G. Egorychev. September 19, 1990], in *Neizvestnaia Rossiia. XX vek* [The Unknown Russia. Twentieth Century], ed. V. A. Kozlov, vol. 1 (Moscow: Istoricheskoe nasledie, 1992), 291; Taubman, *Khrushchev*, 7; and Ian D. Thatcher, "Brezhnev as Leader," in *Brezhnev Reconsidered*, ed. Edwin Bacon and Mark Sandle (New York: Palgrave Macmillan, 2002), 25.

8. Valerii Alekseev, "Kak snimali Khrushcheva: Beseda s uchastnikom tekh sobytii" [How Khrushchev Was Removed: A Conversation with a Participant in Those Events], *Dialog*, no. 7 (1993): 52.

9. Vladislav Zubok, Steven Casey, and Jonathan Wright, "'Do Not Think I Am Soft . . .': Leonid Brezhnev," in *Mental Maps in the Era of Détente and the End of the Cold War 1968–91*, ed. Steven Casey and Jonathan Wright (London: Palgrave Macmillan, 2015), 9.

10. Artemy M. Kalinovsky, *A Long Goodbye: The Soviet Withdrawal from Afghanistan* (Cambridge, MA: Harvard University Press, 2011), 23–24.

11. William Taubman, *Gorbachev: His Life and Times* (New York: Norton, 2017), 175.

12. Benjamin Yang, *Deng: A Political Biography* (Armonk, NY: M. E. Sharpe, 1998), 238–39; Ezra F. Vogel, "Chen Yun: His Life," *Journal of Contemporary China* 14, no. 45 (November 2005): 742; and Victor C. Shih, "Contentious Elites in China: New Evidence and Approaches," *Journal of East Asian Studies* 16, no. 1 (March 2016): 1–15.

13. Jonathan R. Stromseth, Edmund J. Malesky, and Dimitar D. Gueorguiev, *China's Governance Puzzle: Enabling Transparency and Participation in a Single-Party State* (Cambridge: Cambridge University Press, 2017), 8–9.

14. Chun Han Wong, "Revising History: A Museum Facelift Boosts China's Xi," *Wall Street Journal*, August 20, 2018, https://www.wsj.com/articles/revising-history-a-museum-facelift-boosts-chinas-xi-1534766401.

15. Xuezhi Guo, *The Politics of the Core Leader in China: Culture, Institution, Legitimacy, and Power* (Cambridge: Cambridge University Press, 2019), 305.

16. Lu Zhichao, *Haibian yiwang: Weirao Zhongnanhai de huiyi yu sikao* [Remembering the Past by the Sea: Memoirs and Thoughts Surrounding Zhongnanhai] (unpublished manuscript, 2008), 198.

17. Wang Xiaozhong, *Zhongguwei gongzuo jishi 1982–1987* [Record of Central Advisory Commission Work 1982–1987] (Hong Kong: Cosmos Books, 2013), 237.

18. Yang Jisheng, *Zhongguo gaige niandai de zhengzhi douzheng* [Political Struggle during the Reform Years] (Hong Kong: Tiandi tushu youxian gongsi, 2010), 287.

19. Dorothy J. Solinger, *Chinese Business under Socialism: The Politics of Domestic Commerce, 1949–1980* (Berkeley: University of California Press, 1984), 79.

20. Li Rui, *Li Rui koushu wangshi* [Li Rui Describes the Past] (Hong Kong: Dashan wenhua chubanshe youxian gongsi, 2013), 418.

21. Deng Liqun, *Deng Liqun guoshi jiangtanlu 3* [Record of Deng Liqun's Lectures on National History, Volume 3] (Beijing: "Zhonghua renmin gongheguo shigao" bianweihui, 2000), 410.

22. Xu Yongyue, "Wannian Chen Yun yu Deng Xiaoping: Xinxing xiangtong—Fang guojia anquanbu buzhang yuan Chen Yun tongzhi mishu Xu Yongyue" [Chen Yun and Deng Xiaoping in His Later Years: A Heart-to-Heart Interview with Xu Yongyue, Minister of Public Security and Former Secretary to Comrade Chen Yun], *Bainianchao*, no. 3 (March 2006): 13–17.

23. Guo, *Politics of the Core Leader in China.*

24. Joseph Torigian, "The Shadow of Deng Xiaoping on Chinese Elite Politics," *War on the Rocks* (blog), January 30, 2017, https://warontherocks.com/2017/01/the-shadow-of-deng-xiaoping-on-chinese-elite-politics/.

25. Joseph Torigian, "Elite Politics and Foreign Policy in China from Mao to Xi," Brookings Institution, January 22, 2019, https://www.brookings.edu/articles/elite-politics-and-foreign-policy-in-china-from-mao-to-xi/.

26. Wu Wei, *Zhongguo 80 niandai zhengzhi gaige de taiqian muhou* [On Stage and Backstage: China's Political Reform in the 1980s] (Hong Kong: Xin shiji chuban ji chuanmei youxian gongsi, 2013), 370–75.

27. Torigian, "Shadow of Deng Xiaoping on Chinese Elite Politics."

28. Lu Chaoqi, *Liusi neibu riji* [Internal Diary of June Fourth] (Hong Kong: Zhuoyue wenhua chubanshe, 2006); and Zhang Wanshu, *Lishi de da baozha: "Liu si" shijian quanjing shilu* [The Big Historical Explosion: The Entire Record of the "June Fourth" Incident] (Hong Kong: Tiandi tushu youxian gongsi, 2009).

29. Lu, *Haibian yiwang,* 159.

30. Guan Shan, "Ren Zhongyi tan Deng Xiaoping yu Guangdong de gaige kaifang" [Ren Zhongyi Discusses Deng Xiaoping and Reform and Opening in Guangdong], *Yanhuang chunqiu*, no. 8 (August 2008): 12.

31. Wang Yongzhi, "Benbao dujia zhuanfang Mao Zedong qian mishu Li Rui: 'Wo de jianyi, lao zhong qing san dai pubian zancheng'" [Exclusive Interview with Mao Zedong's Former Secretary Li Rui: "My Suggestions Are

Commonly Accepted by the Old, Middle, and Young Generations"], *21 shiji huanqiu baodao*, March 3, 2003.

32. O. G. Nazarov, *Stalin i bor'ba za liderstvo v bol'shevistskoi partii v usloviiakh NEPa* [Stalin and the Struggle for Leadership in the Bolshevik Party in the Conditions of the NEP] (Moscow: IVI RAN, 2002), 48–49.

33. J. Arch Getty, *Practicing Stalinism: Bolsheviks, Boyars, and the Persistence of Tradition* (New Haven, CT: Yale University Press, 2013), 153–63.

34. Ibid., 155.

35. Oleg Khlevniuk, *Stalin: New Biography of a Dictator* (New Haven, CT: Yale University Press, 2015), 82.

36. Stephen Kotkin, *Stalin*, vol. 1, *Paradoxes of Power, 1878–1928* (New York: Penguin, 2014), 419–20.

37. Khlevniuk, *Stalin*, 87.

38. Getty, *Practicing Stalinism*, 156.

39. Nazarov, *Stalin*, 128.

40. Hiroaki Kuromiya, *Stalin: Profiles in Power* (Harlow, UK: Pearson/Longman, 2005), 66.

41. Kotkin, *Stalin*, 1:519.

42. Nazarov, *Stalin*, 8.

43. Alexander Vatlin, "'Class Brothers Unite!': The British General Strike and the Formation of the 'United Opposition,'" in *The Lost Politburo Transcripts: From Collective Rule to Stalin's Dictatorship*, ed. Paul R. Gregory and Norman Naimark (New Haven, CT: Yale University Press, 2008), 57–77.

44. Kuromiya, *Stalin*, 68.

45. V. A. Sakharov, *"Politicheskoe zaveshchanie" Lenina: real'nost' istorii i mify politiki* [Lenin's "Political Testament": The Truth of History and the Myths of Politics] (Moscow: Izdatel'stvo Moskovskogo universiteta, 2003), 493–94.

46. Sheila Fitzpatrick, *On Stalin's Team: The Years of Living Dangerously in Soviet Politics* (Princeton, NJ: Princeton University Press, 2015), 17.

47. Kuromiya, *Stalin*, 64.

48. Kotkin, *Stalin*, 1:500, 531.

49. Sakharov, *"Politicheskoe zaveshchanie" Lenina*, 132–42.

50. Getty, *Practicing Stalinism*, 157; and Kuromiya, *Stalin*, 63.

51. Hiroaki Kuromiya, "Stalin in the Light of the Politburo Transcripts," in *The Lost Politburo Transcripts: From Collective Rule to Stalin's Dictatorship*, ed. Paul R. Gregory and Norman Naimark (New Haven, CT: Yale University Press, 2008), 45.

52. E. A. Rees, "Stalin as Leader 1924–1937: From Oligarch to Dictator," in *The Nature of Stalin's Dictatorship: The Politburo, 1924–1953*, ed. E. A. Rees (Basingstoke, UK: Palgrave Macmillan, 2004), 24.

53. Nazarov, *Stalin*, 92.

54. Vatlin, "Class Brothers Unite!," 72.

55. Kotkin, *Stalin*, 1:522–25.

56. Kuromiya, *Stalin*, 67.

57. Khlevniuk, *Stalin*, 78.

58. Kotkin, *Stalin*, 1:436–37.

59. Khlevniuk, *Stalin*, 83.

60. For an extensive investigation into the partisan role in North Korean politics, see Haruki Wada, *Kin Nichisei to Manshū kōnichi sensō* [Kim Il-sung and the Anti-Japanese War in Manchuria] (Tokyo: Heibonsha, 1992).

61. Kong Dan Oh, *Leadership Change in North Korean Politics: The Succession to Kim Il Sung* (Santa Monica, CA: RAND, 1988), 8.

62. Jae-Cheon Lim, *Kim Jong Il's Leadership of North Korea* (New York: Routledge, 2009), 54.

63. Kim Hakjoon, *Dynasty: The Hereditary Succession Politics of North Korea* (Stanford, CA: Walter H. Shorenstein Asia-Pacific Research Center Books, 2015), 79.

64. CIA, "The North Korean Succession," October 1, 1978, CREST, CIA-RDP81B00401R002100110012-7; and Oh, *Leadership Change in North Korean Politics*, 7.

65. Joseph Torigian, "Prestige, Manipulation, and Coercion: Elite Power Struggles and the Fate of Three Revolutions" (PhD diss., MIT, 2016).

66. CIA, "North Korean Succession."

67. Interview with a senior party historian.

68. CIA, "North Korea: The Party Elite and the Succession Issue," September 1, 1983, CREST, CIA-RDP84S00928R000100120003-7.

69. Jei Guk Jeon, "The Politics of Mourning Ritual in North Korea (1994–97)," *World Affairs* 162, no. 3 (January 2000): 126–36.

70. Heonik Kwon and Byung-Ho Chung, *North Korea: Beyond Charismatic Politics* (Lanham, MD: Rowman and Littlefield, 2012).

71. Shi Yun and Li Danhui, *Zhonghua renmin gonghe guo, di 8 juan. Nanyi jixu de "jixu geming": Cong pi Lin dao pi Deng, 1972–1976* [The People's Republic of China, Volume 8. The "Continuous Revolution" That Was Difficult to Continue: From Criticizing Lin to Criticizing Deng, 1972–1976] (Hong Kong: Zhongwen daxue dangdai Zhongguo wenhua yanjiu zhongxin, 2008), 598–99, 658.

72. Yoji Gomi, *Fuqin Jin Zhengri yu wo: Jin Zhengnan du jia gao bai* [My Father, Kim Jong-il, and I: Exclusive Interviews with Kim Jong-nam] (Hong Kong: Xin shiji chuban jichuanmei youxian gongsi, 2012), 83–84.

73. Jessica L. P. Weeks, *Dictators at War and Peace* (Ithaca, NY: Cornell University Press, 2014).

74. For example, Ken E. Gause identifies the sinking of the *Cheonan* as "critical to the succession" and the shelling of Yeonpyeong Island as "designed to bolster Kim Jong-un's credentials as a military leader." Gause, *North Korean House of Cards: Leadership Dynamics under Kim Jong-un* (Washington, DC: Committee for Human Rights in North Korea, 2015), 32. See also International Crisis Group, "North Korean Succession and the Risks of Instability" (Asia Report No. 230, International Crisis Group, 2012),

https://www.crisisgroup.org/asia/north-east-asia/korean-peninsula/north-korean-succession-and-risks-instability.

75. Frederick C. Teiwes, "The Study of Elite Political Conflict in the PRC: Politics inside the 'Black Box,'" in *Handbook of the Politics of China*, ed. David S. G. Goodman (Northampton, MA: Edward Elgar, 2015), 21–41.

76. Giovanni Capoccia and R. Daniel Kelemen, "The Study of Critical Junctures: Theory, Narrative, and Counterfactuals in Historical Institutionalism," *World Politics* 59, no. 3 (April 2007): 341–69.

77. Joseph Fewsmith, *Rethinking Chinese Politics* (Cambridge: Cambridge University Press, 2021), 7.

78. Si Wu and George Yin, "China's Political Economy after 40 Years of Reform," *National Interest*, December 10, 2018, https://nationalinterest.org/feature/china%E2%80%99s-political-economy-after-40-years-reform-38377.

Index

agriculture and agricultural policies, 47, 49, 108, 146

Andreas, Joel, 111–12

Andropov, Iurii, 195

anti-party group: collective leadership and, 50; compromising material against, 72–76; deliberations against, 17, 76–78, 82–83; de-Stalinization and, 61, 68; Gang of Four compared to, 125, 127; move against Khrushchev by, 50–51, 76–78; power ministries and, 79–81; prestige of, 17, 69–73; Zhukov and, 17, 45–46, 76–81, 248n207

Aristov, Averkii, 73

Artem'ev, Pavel, 40

atomic programs. *See* nuclear weapons

audience costs (domestic pressures), 206–7

Austria, Soviet foreign policy on, 54, 55, 239n62

authority model: anti-party group deliberations and, 45–46, 81; case study selection and, 12; Deng Xiaoping and, 18; Gang of Four and, 52, 56, 84–87; Hua Guofeng's fall and, 17–18, 137–38; Kim Jong-il and, 204–6; methodological approach to, 12–15; Stalin's rise and, 200–202;

theory of, 4, 6–8. *See also* coercion; compromising material; prestige; rules and boundaries

Barbalet, J. M., 4–5

Baum, Richard, 142, 145

Belorussian resistance, 28–29

Beria, Lavrentii, 16–17; arrest of, 33–36, 40; Bulganin and, 25, 27, 29–30, 32, 33, 38; decision-making bodies on, 33–34; deliberations against, 31–33; de-Stalinization and, 24, 61, 65; forged diaries of, 21; historical legacies and compromising material on, 21, 26–31, 42; institutionalization and, 37–38, 41; Kaganovich and, 22, 24, 31, 33; legitimacy of actions against, 35–37; Malenkov nominated by, 20; Molotov and, 22–27, 29, 32, 33, 35, 36, 40, 243n112; nuclear program and, 26–28, 38–39, 42, 233n110; Pervukhin and, 27, 33; policies of, 24–26, 42–43; political style of, 22–24; power ministries and, 21–22, 37–40, 42–43; Presidium appointment of, 19; Shepilov on, 24, 31; Stalin and, 24, 27; threat of coercion and, 17, 39–40; Voroshilov and, 22–23, 27,

Index